The Post' ... Child

The Posthuman Child combats institutionalised ageist practices in primary, early childhood and teacher education. Grounded in a critical posthumanist perspective on the purpose of education, it provides a genealogy of psychology, sociology and philosophy of childhood in which dominant figurations of child and childhood are exposed as positioning child as epistemically and ontologically inferior. Entangled throughout this book are practical and theorised examples of philosophical work with student teachers, teachers, other practitioners and children (aged 3–11) from South Africa and Great Britain. These engage arguments about how children are routinely marginalised, discriminated against and denied, especially when the child is also female, black, lives in poverty and whose home language is not English. The book makes a distinctive contribution to the decolonisation of childhood discourses.

Underpinned by good-quality picturebooks and other striking images, the book's radical proposal for transformation is to reconfigure the child as rich, resourceful and resilient through relationships with (non-)human others, and it explores the implications for literary and literacy education, teacher education, curriculum construction, implementation and assessment. It is essential reading for all who research, work and live with children.

Karin Murris is Associate Professor at the School of Education, University of Cape Town, South Africa.

Series Title: Contesting Early Childhood
Series Editors: Gunilla Dahlberg and Peter Moss

This groundbreaking series questions the current dominant discourses surrounding early childhood, and offers instead alternative narratives of an area that is now made up of a multitude of perspectives and debates.

The series examines the possibilities and risks arising from the accelerated development of early childhood services and policies, and illustrates how it has become increasingly steeped in regulation and control. Insightfully, this collection of books shows how early childhood services can in fact contribute to ethical and democratic practices. The authors explore new ideas taken from alternative working practices in both the Western and developing world, and from other academic disciplines such as developmental psychology. Current theories and best practice are placed in relation to the major processes of political, social, economic, cultural and technological change occurring in the world today.

Titles in the *Contesting Early Childhood* series include:

Murris (2016) *The Posthuman Child*

Cagliari, Castagnetti, Giudici, Rinaldi, Vecchi and Moss (2016) *Loris Malaguzzi and the Schools of Reggio Emilia*

Davies (2014) *Listening to Children*

Moss (2014) *Transformative Change and Real Utopias in Early Childhood Education*

Sellers (2013) *Young Children becoming Curriculum*

Taylor (2013) *Reconfiguring the Natures of Childhood*

Moss (2013) *Early Childhood and Compulsory Education*

Vecchi (2010) *Art and Creativity in Reggio Emilia*

Taguchi (2009) *Going Beyond the Theory/Practice Divide*

Olsson (2009) *Movement and Experimentation in Young Children's Learning*

Edmiston (2007) *Forming Ethical Identities in Early Childhood Play*

Rinaldi (2005) *In Dialogue with Reggio Emilia*

MacNaughton (2005) *Doing Foucault in Early Childhood Studies*

Penn (2005) *Unequal Childhoods*

Dahlberg and Moss (2005) *Ethics and Politics in Early Childhood*

The Posthuman Child

Educational transformation
through philosophy with
picturebooks

Karin Murris

Routledge
Taylor & Francis Group
LONDON AND NEW YORK

First published 2016
by Routledge
2 Park Square, Milton Park, Abingdon, Oxon OX14 4RN

and by Routledge
711 Third Avenue, New York, NY 10017

Routledge is an imprint of the Taylor & Francis Group, an informa business

© 2016 K. Murris

British Library Cataloguing in Publication Data
A catalogue record for this book is available from the British Library

Library of Congress Cataloging in Publication Data
A catalog record for this book has been requested

ISBN: 978-1-138-85843-5 (hbk)
ISBN: 978-1-138-85844-2 (pbk)
ISBN: 978-1-315-71800-2 (ebk)

Typeset in Bembo and Gill Sans
by Florence Production Ltd, Stoodleigh, Devon, UK
Printed and bound by CPI Group (UK) Ltd, Croydon, CR0 4YY

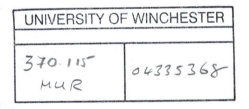

For my children, my grandchildren and all children
still to (be)come

Contents

Figures and tables

Figures

Tables

Introduction

Peter Moss, Series Editor

The aims of Karin Murris in this new book in the *Contesting Early Childhood* series are ambitious, important and very urgent: to offer a posthuman reconfiguration of the child; to propose educational practices that are ethical and just; and to argue for a 'relational material subjectification' as one of the main purposes of education.

For those readers unfamiliar with posthumanism, Murris provides an accessible introduction to this paradigmatic position. From this perspective,

> all earth dwellers [are] mutually entangled and always becoming, always intra-acting with everything else (Barad, 2007). Posthuman child *is* relational. There is no prior existence of individuals with properties, competencies, a voice, agency, etc. Individuals materialise and come into being through relationships; and so does meaning. There is ontological, as well as epistemological equality between species and between different members of each species.

The focus is on connectivity and interdependency between all 'earth dwellers', including human animals, other animals and nonhumans (e.g. machines), with 'a relational ethic of collective responsibility for the shared intra-connected natureculture world'. In such a relationship, nature cannot be reduced to a mere object for human study, it is not something 'out there' awaiting discovery by humans, who are instead an inextricable part of nature itself. Posthumanism is not only critical of human-centredness, but of child-centredness, turning away from the idea of the child as autonomous agent and turning towards the idea of the child enmeshed in an immense web of material and discursive forces, 'always intra-acting with everything else'. But it is also critical of humanism's view of the child, consigned with many other 'earth dwellers' to an inferior position as lesser beings, outside the charmed circle of fully developed adult person, the apogee of existence.

From this starting point, Karin argues that education today suffers ontoepistemic injustice, an ageist prejudice in which adults claim to know what is true knowledge and therefore educationally worthwhile – leaving children not listened to because being child gives them no claim to knowledge, any knowledge that they offer being not listened to. Instead children must wait for knowledge, either to be supplied by adults or through innate biological processes of development, both ending in the goal of adult maturity. The book sets out to help transform education and schools by ending this injustice, offering a variety of educational practices that can work towards this transformation: philosophy with children in a community of enquiry; working democratically; reciprocal and responsive listening (in which the educator does not know the answers to the questions posed); and a variety of tools including picturebooks, bodymind maps and diffractive journals (all richly illustrated in the photographs, figures and tables that interweave with the text).

Central to this transformed education is for 'children and students to bring something new to the world' and to speak with their own voice, which brings us to the educational aim of 'subjectification'. Karin draws here on the work of educational philosopher Gert Biesta, but also extends it by using a diffractive methodology, reading Biesta together with Karen Barad diffractively through one another. Biesta argues that education works in three domains and has three concurrent, overlapping purposes or aims, and that the art of teaching is to find the right balance between these three aims: schooling or *qualification*; *socialisation*; and '*subjectification*'. Qualification involves equipping students with the right kind of knowledge, skills and dispositions for future life, including employment (for example, as teachers); socialisation involves enabling students to *become part of an existing order* and the creation of an identity through identification with that order (for example, the teaching profession). But subjectification, as Biesta writes,

> might perhaps be best understood as the opposite of the socialisation function. It is precisely not about the insertion of 'newcomers' into existing orders, but about ways of being that hint at independence from such orders, ways of being in which the individual is not merely a 'specimen' of a more encompassing order.
>
> (2010, p. 21)

Subjectification as educational purpose takes us away from a view of education as imparting knowledge that is held to be an accurate representation of a pre-existing reality, what Charles Taylor calls 'modern representational epistemology' (1995, p. 5). It turns us instead towards what Biesta and his colleague Deborah Osberg term an 'emergentist' epistemology and defined as the creation of new properties.

> [C]ontemporary understandings of emergence have retained the idea that emergence introduces properties that are novel and sometimes even inconceivable or unimaginable . . . Strong emergence therefore presents a direct challenge to determinism (the idea that given one set of circumstances

there is only one logical outcome) ... [If] we think of knowledge (or knowing) not as *determined* by our engagement with the present, but as *emerging* from our engagement with the present ... each knowledge event – which is to say each taking place of knowledge (knowing) – is necessarily *also radically new*.

Osberg and Biesta, 2007, pp. 33, 34, 40: original emphasis

Adding the material to what Biesta proposes, Karin argues that important conditions for subjectification in an emergent epistemology and pedagogy are plurality and difference, and interdependent, posthuman relationships with all 'earth dwellers'. Processes of meaning-making, of creating new knowledge, involve not just human beings, but intra-actions with other animals and matter.

In her exploration of the meaning and potentiality of the posthuman child, Karin works with theorists and experiences that have figured in previous books in the series: the Dutch 17th-century philosopher Baruch Spinoza, who 'continues to be an inspiration for many contemporary posthumanists' with his 'idea that not only human bodies, but also their minds are *part* of nature, not in control of it, or in command of it'; French philosophers Gilles Deleuze and Felix Guattari, who help to show how the concept of 'knowledge as a rhizome works, and how we should think of 'learning' with a focus on *difference*, rather than *sameness*'; feminist theorist Karen Barad, with a deep interest in physics, who contends that '"matter" (the material) and "meaning" (the discursive) are always entangled like waves interfering with one another diffractively creating a new pattern without clear identity-producing boundaries'; and the municipal schools of Reggio Emilia, whose pedagogical philosophy 'is able to offer a rhizomatic curriculum that fits the posthuman child' and 'puts a stop to current discriminatory ageist practices'.

But Karin adds additional themes, new to the series, to her assemblage of ideas and practices. Her deep interest in and commitment to philosophy with children undertaken in a community of enquiry, 'to learn to "think-for-yourself-through-thinking-with-others"', has already been mentioned. Though she acknowledges that there are widely differing interpretations of what this means in concept and practice: '[d]ifferences in practice depend to a large degree on one's philosophy of education (e.g. humanist or posthumanist, and the implications for a particular subjectivity), one's interpretation of both "community" and "enquiry" and the particular balance of the two'. But from her understanding and enactment, a philosophy with children is

a rhizomatic intra-active pedagogy bring[ing] about an epistemological change, a shift in power, and requires an unlearning of didactic teaching practices. It disrupts how children are routinely listened to, challenges what counts as knowledge and disturbs the authority of the teacher as the person who asks the questions that matter. Finally, it assumes child as rich, resilient and resourceful (e)merging in unbounded materialdiscursive [sic] relationships.

She also foregrounds the potential of childhood studies, using it in her teacher education curriculum to enable emerging teachers 'to become more aware of the figurations of child and childhood we all bring to our educational practices and observations' and of 'how figurations of child [can] wrongfully position children as lesser beings ontologically – the reason why they have been, and still are, excluded from practices and many decision-making processes in education'. Once again, she questions common understandings of childhood studies, observing how '[b]roadly speaking there has been a shift in childhood studies from psychology of childhood, to sociology of childhood, to philosophy of childhood, although psychology is still the dominant discipline in early childhood education policies, practices and curriculum design globally'.

Last, but not least, Karin brings a new African perspective to this book series, living in South Africa and working with students in that country being educated to become teachers. (Although some of the examples she draws on come from elsewhere, notably England and Wales, where she has also lived and worked.)

While being a persuasive advocate for posthuman and related perspectives, Karin is critical of some other perspectives that are widespread in early childhood education today. The Cartesian dualist epistemology and search for certainty ('still written in our bones'); developmentalism, with its 'lack of methodological validity, a normative process, complexity reduction, preparation for a capitalist economical workforce, evolutionary bias, and otherising child'; and various common images or figurations of the child, which serve to perpetuate what she terms ontoepistemic injustice, the result of reading Barad and Fricker diffractively. But her critiques are not limited to the products of modernity. Social constructionism and poststructuralism are both problematic, from a posthumanist perspective, with their unremitting focus on the social and discursive at the expense of recognising the material.

For me, one of the great strengths of the *Contesting Early Childhood* series has been the way it has connected new theoretical perspectives with actual pedagogical practice, whether that is with young children in the classroom or teacher students in the university. Our books do not just explore ideas, understandings and concepts that are often new to early childhood education; they show they can be put to work, the possibility of 'doing Foucault in early childhood studies' as one of the earlier books in the series was titled (MacNaughton, 2005). I suspect that such application in early childhood of new theoretical perspectives is rather unusual across the field of education: educationalists from compulsory school or university sectors may be writing about Foucault or Deleuze or Barad, but how many are 'doing' them? So though working with new perspectives, with 'alternative narratives' that question the current dominant discourses surrounding early childhood, may not be easy, this series shows it is perfectly possible, and could be more widely extended, if only a fraction of the resources devoted to enacting dominant discourses was diverted to alternative narratives and the rich experimentation to which they can give rise.

Karin's book is yet another example of how to work with alternative narratives. Whether working directly with young children in primary school or with student teachers in university, Karin shows vividly what it means to apply a posthuman perspective and to do philosophy with children and philosophy-focused childhood studies with young people. Both children and young people seem to thrive, as we can hear and see in the text. And it is with the voice of one of Karin's students that I choose to end this foreword. Deeply engaged in Karin's curriculum of childhood studies, this future teacher sums up the situation we face today – the potentiality for alternatives, the desire for new thinking and doing, and the difficulty of breaking away from the status quo – and does so with a mix of hope and frustration:

> It's so tricky and at times awkward for me to get out of this humanist perspective, and I think that it's because we are just so accustomed to it, very much like we are to reflection. In this way I can see that posthumanism does work. However what is bugging me is how do we get the whole world to see life in this way? How can we transfer what we have learnt to the bigger and broader social setting outside of our classroom? Surely this idea needs legs and mouths and ears to spread it? Perhaps it started as a thought but how did it grow beyond that? Just want to see what you guys think.

Acknowledgements

Many people have intra-acted with the development and writing of this book, which has been a wonderful project and a real privilege. I am very grateful to Alison Foyle from Routledge and to editors Peter Moss and Gunilla Dahlberg, who agreed to have my work included in their prestigious, groundbreaking series. Many of the books included in it have informed my thinking and writing. Of course, my philosophical wonderings and pedagogical experimentation have also been made possible by the thousands of teacher educators, philosophers, teachers, students and learners I have had the privilege to work with for over the past twenty-five years. In particular, my long-standing friendship and collaboration with Joanna Haynes stands out as unique and precious.

For this book in particular I am very grateful to Vivienne Bozalek, who reintroduced me to Rosi Braidotti and her ideas through a posthumanism research project funded by the South African National Research Foundation. Since then she has helped me run a posthumanism reading group, and our weekly diffractions are the highlights of my current work. My thinking and being (e)merge through these encounters and I therefore cannot sufficiently acknowledge individual contributions. I can only say that without the members of this group's commitment, enthusiasm, deep insights and friendship this book would not have been possible. My heartfelt thanks in particular go to: Vivienne Bozalek, Veronica Mitchell, Carmen Blyth, Siddique Motala, Brenda Leibowitz, Theresa Giorza, Rouxnette Meiring, Judy Crowther, Kristy Stone, Robyn Thompson, Jakob Pedersen, Sumaya Babamia, Daniela Gachago, Susan Newton-King, Allison Fullard and Chantelle Gray.

I am especially grateful to Nabeela Kidy for her breathtakingly beautiful drawings 'Ceci n'est pas une enfante' and 'Knowledge as an entanglement of spaghetti'. The agency of these powerful images is felt throughout the book and supports the key arguments I am making. Conor Ralphs' graphic design in two images clearly expresses some key distinctions in Western metaphysics.

Much thanks also to my postgraduate student teachers at the University of Cape Town for giving me permission to use written and visual examples from their work, and in particular Hlengiwe Mkhize and Tarryn Welsh for kindly sharing their bodymind maps. Special mention also for Des Hugo and Tessa

Browne for welcoming me into the Africa Reggio Emilia Alliance and for their ideas and support. The Reggio Emilia reading group we have set up at the University of Cape Town also provides a much-needed platform to rethink childhood education. For the practical application of my pedagogical ideas, the work of Sara Stanley in the Cape Flats and our many conversations and time spent together have been inspirational.

Thanks also to my son Liam Geschwindt for letting me use his photos and a photo of him; Di and John Donaldson for the use of the photo of the labyrinth brooch and Jill Joubert for all her wonderful ideas about labyrinths and art education. Thanks also to Clare Verbeek for her permission to use part of an article we wrote together, and for her friendship and support in the workplace and beyond. Permission for using some data of co-written articles has also kindly been granted by co-authors Vursha Ranchod and Joanna Haynes. I am also grateful to Robyn Thompson and her foundation phase learners who have shared their work so generously with me in the past, and their rich ideas are included again in the final chapter.

I am grateful to the Faculty of Humanities at the University of Cape Town for supporting my work on this manuscript. Special thanks also to Jacqui Dornbrack, who took over from me as Chair of the Western Cape Reading Association of South Africa committee during the first six weeks of this period, and Janet Condy for always being there when I needed her. With a large national and international pan-African literacy conference looming, this generous support from her and all the other committee members was invaluable.

My very special thanks to Simon Geschwindt, who edited this book and provided critical and creative comments not only to the manuscript, but diffracted regularly with my philosophical wonderings and musings in our life together. Warmth and deep appreciation goes to my wonderfully supportive family, including our cat and dogs, who have stood by me and actively supported me in writing this book. The environment that has had agency in the production of this book includes our cosy home, the pool, the sea and the beautiful Western Cape climate. My regular intra-actions with the waves in Muizenberg and the dog-walks at Noordhoek beach (e)merge in this book.

My thanks go to the following publishers for their permission to reproduce the respective illustrations: Andersen Press for the three images from David Tusk Tusk, copyright © 1978 David McKee, and Random House for one image from Anthony Browne's Voices in the Park (Artwork © Anthony Browne), which was reproduced by permission of Random House Children's Publishers, a division of The Random House Group. Illustrations © 2008 Brun Limited. From Little Beauty by Anthony Browne. Reproduced by permission of Walker Books, London SE1 1 5HJ, www.walker.co.uk.

The book has benefited from sections of articles that I have published before but reanalysed using a posthumanist orientation. Some key ideas about the aims of education in Chapter 2 are from Murris and Verbeek (2014). Part of Chapter 6 is a rewritten version of parts of Murris (2013b). Data in Chapters

8 and 10 are a modified version of Murris (2014a). Chapter 10 includes a response to Pat Enciso's commentary on my case-study. The *Tusk Tusk* example has also been used for Haynes and Murris (2013). However, in both cases, although the same data, in this book they have been used for a posthumanist analysis. Some arguments about literacy education in Chapters 8 and 9 were taken from Murris (2014c). Much of Chapter 9 was published in Murris (2015c). However, the posthuman analysis has been strengthened and integrated with some data from Murris and Ranchod (2015). Finally, in various chapters of the book, short sections have been used of Murris (2008).

Chapter 1

Laika

Though a mere speck, a blip on the radar screen of all that is, Man is the center around which the world turns. Man is the sun, the nucleus, the fulcrum, the unifying force, the glue that holds it all together. Man is an individual part from all the rest. And it is this very distinction that bestows on him the inheritance of distance, a place from which to reflect – on the world, his fellow man, and himself. A distinct individual, the unit of all measure, finitude made flesh, his separateness is the key.

Barad, 2007, p. 134

Slow minds

More than 25 years ago, a conversation between two teachers in a staffroom set in motion what for me became a radical process of educational transformation. The doctoral research it inspired profoundly changed my understandings of childhood, adulthood, and, indeed of academic philosophy. The teachers were talking about a nine-year-old girl in my class called Laika.[1] One of them said, 'Laika is a slow thinker'. It puzzled and deeply troubled me. Does thinking indeed go slow or fast like an *object*? Picking up the teachers' sense of frustration with Laika, the use of the metaphor[2] 'slow thinker' affected me because[3] of the injustice done to her – an ontological *and* epistemic injustice. The metaphor expressed a clear intellectual deficit, assuming that if Laika's thinking had been *faster*, she would have been a *better* thinker. Evaluative judgements were made not only about her intellectual capacity, but also about her *being* ('onto').

I felt sorry for Laika, who was only nine years old, and much of her academic future and well-being seemed to be in the hands of these foundation phase[4] teachers whose thinking and actions were structured by their use of a particular metaphorical language. I wondered how it was possible to think and talk about minds in this way – comparing them to objects in the world going *fast* or *slow*, being more or less *mature* (like a piece of cheese). There seemed so little scope for teachers to change the speed of Laika's mind – this was how she *is*.

The metaphors we think with are profoundly moral and political. They have *agency* and are the 'legs of language' that 'keep us moving in a certain direction' (Kirby and Kuykendall, 1991, p. 11). They are a salient influence on how we perceive the world and relate to other people as well as our own 'selves' (Lakoff and Johnson, 1980, p. 3). I theorised the educational implications of these engrained habits of thought about how Laika was treated by her teachers in class, and by her parents, her classmates, and the educational system (through, for example, setting limited time for tests and exams) (Murris,1997). Metaphorical language makes it possible to evaluate Laika's thinking as 'quick' or 'slow', with a mind that *is* 'open', 'broad' or 'narrow' and 'occupied' with problems, which she can get 'off her mind', or 'put out of her mind' by talking about them. In class, a teacher can start off by trying 'to find a common ground' in order to know 'where the child is', so that she can 'point things out' or 'give her new ideas'. Philosopher George Lakoff and linguist Mark Johnson analyse how such *orientational* metaphors shape how we think and talk about 'the' mind, and emphasise that such metaphors are culturally and historically relative, and that they organise a whole system of concepts with respect to one another (Lakoff and Johnson, 1980, pp. 15–16; 1999). This has produced a spatial orientation of 'a' mind that can be up/down, in/out, front/back, on/off, deep/shallow, central/peripheral. They explain the physical and cultural basis of these metaphors:

> In our culture people view themselves as being in control over animals, plants, and their physical environment, and it is their unique ability to reason that places human beings above other animals and gives them control. CONTROL IS UP thus provides a basis for MAN IS UP and therefore for RATIONAL IS UP.
>
> Lakoff and Johnson, 1980, p. 17

My research at the time (Murris, 1997) involved analysing how these concepts shape fundamental educational values, for example, how the metaphorical structuring 'More is up' underlies our values of 'progress' and 'knowledge increase' and how these metaphors are so integrated in our everyday language that for many, expressions such as 'she is fragile' or 'she is disturbed' are taken as direct, literal descriptions of mental phenomena, being either true or false. Common knowledge claims are directly related to understanding the mind as an object, especially 'mind-as-an-eye' – what we know best about the world is what we can *perceive*. The Western tradition in philosophy has understood our primary relation to objects as one of knowledge – with human *optics* as its paradigm: one 'stares at' (*begafft*) the world rather than 'doing' something with it (*hantieren*) (Heidegger, 1927/1979, paras. 12, 13). As a result, the language we use to describe children's thinking is predominantly visual: some children are *brilliant* or *bright*; their thinking can be *clear-headed*, for example, when they *see* solutions to problems. Children can also get the whole *picture*, for example, when teachers ask them to *look* at it from a different *point* of view and to put forward a *clear* or *transparent* argument (Lakoff and Johnson, 1980, p. 51).

The *heart* or the *core* of my argument in this section (hopefully an *eye*-opener) is that the abstract concept actually created[5] in the mind-as-an-eye metaphor is 'mind-space', that is, the singular space in which the 'seeing' is going on. This makes it possible to talk about mind-space as if it were an actual physical space. Conceptualising mind as a space independent from the body has had profound implications for educational theories and practices since the Enlightenment. Thinking is seen as *static*. Thoughts happen in the 'inner' spheres of the mind before or after interaction with the 'outside' world. Philosopher Richard Rorty argues that the metaphor of the mind as a mirror 'containing' various more or less accurate representations of nature is responsible for this view of thinking, and of knowledge in general (Rorty, 1980). Much of modern science has retained this humanist, Cartesian conception of the mind as a 'thinking thing' with a separate existence from the body (see Chapter 3 in particular). Gilles Deleuze and Felix Guattari, both highly critical of psychoanalysis, reject the idea of mind-spaces, such as the unconscious as singular ('one Wolf'), a unity:

> How stupid, you can't be one Wolf, you're always eight or nine, six or seven. Not six or seven wolves all by yourself all at once, but one wolf among others, with five or six others . . . Freud tried to approach crowd phenomena from the point of view of the unconscious, but he did not see clearly, he did not see that the unconscious itself is fundamentally a crowd.
>
> Deleuze and Guattari, 1987/2013, pp. 32–3

The unconscious is a 'crowd'; it is multiple, not singular. You can't say '*I am this, I am that*' (Deleuze and Guattari, 1987/2013, p. 33). Hillevi Lenz Taguchi (2013, pp. 708–9) explains that for Deleuze, thinking is an *act*, not something an 'I' does. Similarly, about their co-authoring Deleuze and Guattari (1987/2013, p. 3) write: 'Since each of us was several, there was already quite a crowd'. 'Mind', 'consciousness', 'the unconscious', 'thinking', they are all concepts that are assumed in psychology and psychoanalysis to be a space that is One, and assume 'deep dualism'[6] (Leal and Shipley, 1992, p. 34). This philosophical position has practical (and possibly harmful) consequences for how we act and treat people and for how we regard knowledge.

Descartes' famous dictum, 'I think, therefore I am' (*cogito ergo sum*) constructed a particular subjectivity in Western thought: 'a subject that constitutes and defines itself through its own constructive activity' (Dahlberg, 2003, p. 264). Inspired by Taylor, Dahlberg argues that 'in modernity the autonomous and self-conscious subject has been the locus of certainty and truth and the first principle from which everything arises and to which all must be returned'

(Dahlberg, 2003, p. 264). The Cartesian quest for certainty and the search for a foundation of knowledge assume that there is '. . . an essentially transcultural, historical, indubitable fixed point, or bedrock, from which a more or less foolproof method will trace those appropriately related beliefs that can then be embraced with as much certainty as is the foundation' (Benjamin and Echeverria, 1992, pp. 65–6).

Poor Alice

According to this Cartesian view – as British philosopher John Locke argued – knowledge is possible by *representing* 'outer space' (the 'external' world) in 'inner space' (the Cartesian mind). This dualist epistemology is powerfully expressed by Lewis Carroll (1865/2013, p. 58) when he lets child prodigy Alice utter the words 'Really, now you ask me . . . I don't think –', to which the Mad Hatter replies: 'Then you shouldn't talk'. Poor Alice is reminded to think *before* she speaks. For the Mad Hatter the thoughts are already 'there' in mind-space, and just need to be expressed. The assumption is that pair or group work would not help Alice construct new thoughts of any value. There is no point in Alice having tea-time conversations with the White Rabbit (if he had not been in such a terrible rush, of course), other than to communicate the thoughts already in her head. Teachers commonly believe it is their job to 'fill' children's 'empty' singular minds with knowledge, and that knowledge comprises beliefs that accurately represent or mirror the world as it is (Benjamin and Echeverria, 1992, p. 64). As a result, the teacher's role is much more active than that of the learners. Learners' more passive role is restricted to the taking of notes, the memorising of 'facts', listening to and answering teachers' questions, and their 'knowledge' is evaluated individually, usually by written tests. Educating Alice with her enquiring (multiple) mind(s) would be a frustrating business for any teacher working within a dualist philosophy of education. Educational theorists and practitioners Martin Benjamin and Eugenio Echeverria sum up the implications for what knowledge means to a Cartesian dualist:

> Knowledge, in this view, is acquired passively rather than actively, is more the product of careful observation than of pragmatic exploration. It is also largely individualistic; any singular knower with a properly receptive mind is, in principle, capable of acquiring knowledge of the world by him or herself.
>
> Benjamin and Echeverria, 1992, p. 65

From a dualist perspective it is difficult to see the educational value of thinking *with* and *alongside* children, of 'allowing' children to ask their own (philosophical) questions, of learning in pairs, small groups and as a 'community of enquiry' (the pedagogy of an approach to teaching and learning called *philosophy with children*). In order to explore such possibilities for educational transformation in depth (see Part II), the philosophical justifications for such a necessary shift in orientation are offered first in Part I of this book.

Territoriality

The mind/body dualism is the core dichotomy that this book aims to disrupt, and with it the engrained belief that humans' 'unique ability to reason' places them 'above' and 'gives them control' over animals, plants, and their physical environment (see the quote at the beginning). Leal and Shipley offer a psychoanalytical explanation for the tendency in human beings to embrace a dualist philosophy and to create 'an unbreachable gap between themselves and everything else, particularly other people; . . . a split between self and not self' (Leal and Shipley, 1992, p. 34). Lakoff and Johnson explain the need for such an ontological split by referring to what they describe as one of human beings' basis instincts, *territoriality*:

> We are physical beings, bounded and set off from the rest of the world by the surface of our skins, and we experience the rest of the world as outside us. Each of us is a container with a bounding surface, an in-out orientation. We project our own in-out orientation onto other physical objects . . . [but we also] . . . impose this orientation on our natural environment.
>
> Lakoff and Johnson, 1980, p. 29

The dualist structure of our everyday, scientific and philosophical languages and discourses has had, and still has, a profound influence on people's claims to truth, not just about children like Laika or Alice, but about *all* children. Discourses are not the same as languages. They are more than what is, or is not, said; they determine what counts as meaningful, and what can or cannot be said in a particular time, culture, context or group of people (Barad, 2007, p. 146; Lenz Taguchi, 2010, p. 53).

Published in 1980, Lakoff and Johnson's book *Metaphors We Live By* was groundbreaking. It convincingly argued how our conceptual system is grounded in a constant interaction with the physical and cultural environment, and therefore that thoughts, actions and values are not 'disembodied'; they are always already related to the fact that we 'have' (non-dualistic language: *are*) bodies. I included their ideas when arguing for a *postmodern* (post-dualist) education. I also pointed out the highly resilient conceptual confusion in contemporary education – that the mind is understood as if it were a physical body that grows 'naturally' and 'matures' in stages (Murris, 1997; see also Egan 2002, pp. 79–82). I theorised that thoughts are not created 'in' mind-space, but are created in the *relational* and *dynamic* process of interaction itself, thereby offering a philosophical justification for interactive, dialogical and democratic pedagogies (Murris, 1997).

However, this book is quite a radical break from my original philosophical orientation. It embraces a non-hierarchical *monist* philosophy of education that is critical of the *anthropocentric gaze* – 'a gaze that puts humans above other matter in reality' and the idea that language constructs reality as it 'reduces our world to a social world, consisting only of humans and neglecting all other non-human forces that are at play' (Hultman and Lenz-Taguchi, 2010, p. 526). This posthumanist thinking has profound implications for how children are regarded and for research in early childhood education. Apart from drawing on insights in philosophy of language and a focus on the discursive, I argue that the ontological inclusion of the *material* and the *materiality* of bodies (including nonhuman bodies) requires a philosophy of education that disrupts the mind/body thesis, and therefore, the Nature/Culture dichotomy that depends on it. In a sense the latter is still assumed in poststructuralism, social constructionism, social constructivism and even postmodernism[7] – limited as they are to human social practices (Barad, 2007, p. 145). Denaturalising childhood is linked to the 'linguistic turn' in the history of ideas (Taylor, 2013, p. xvi). This is the idea that language and discourses shape how we understand the world. A further shift in theorising child and childhood is the contemporary 'material turn' that attributes agency (also) to the material world and that problematises the idea that learning takes place 'in' the child. But, as I shall argue, it is always 'in' the space 'between' the person as embodied organism and the material world (e.g. the furniture in the room, the clay in her hand, the picturebook on the table), taking into account the situated time–space relations between all material organisms that act upon each other (Lenz Taguchi, 2010, p. 36).

The Posthuman Child distances itself from a language that presupposes that people can be 'carved up' into those separate entities 'body' and 'mind'; it assumes 'new beginnings and becomings' through a deterritorialisation of thinking (Deleuze and Guattari, 1987/2013) – a thinking without representationalism. Plato introduced the idea in Western thinking that the verb 'to be' has a static meaning. He applied the notion of identity only to the intelligible world (the realm of reason and rationality) and not to the world of the senses. For Plato, the realm of reason is 'being', not 'becoming', and in that world everything is what it *is*. Philosopher Trevor Curnow (1995, p. 25) points out how Plato's dualism 'erected the structure of a logic which operates in terms of a strict either/or. Such a logic is possible precisely because identity is not problematic'. As a result, in Western thinking to *be* a slow thinker, intelligent, artistic, etc., suggests the impossibility, or, at least, unlikelihood of *change*. Laika simply thinks slowly; there is not much a teacher can do about it. This takes no account of the fact that living organisms constantly and visibly change.

Subjectivity-as-breathing

Psychologist Julian Jaynes argues that the verb 'to be' is not *literal* language, but that the concept is generated from a metaphor about breathing and growing. He maintains that the verb 'to be' comes from the Sanskrit verb 'bhu', which means 'to grow', or 'make grow', while 'am' and 'is' have evolved from the same root as the Sanskrit 'asmi' which means 'to breathe' (Jaynes, 1990, p. 51). A relational materialist or posthumanist conception of subjectivity-as-breathing offers imaginative possibilities for a way of being with others that queers[8] an either/or logic. Laika's breath not only goes through her lungs, but also make her cells breathe and her breath goes beyond the boundaries of her skin when 'it' leaves 'her' body and intra-acts with 'other' bodies[9]. A posthuman subjectivity that goes beyond the boundaries of atomistic individual selves makes us think differently about teaching (Chapter 7) and teachers (Chapter 8), as expressed through a new figuration – that of the pregnant stingray.

This book aims to disrupt various dualist metaphors that shape ageist[10] pedagogical practices and curricula, not only though theorising, but also through real 'materialdiscursive' encounters with children and (student) teachers *doing* philosophy and through structured engagement with activities and examples. I have not hyphenated the use 'materialdiscursive'; this is to indicate that both 'material' and 'discursive' are *simultaneously* produced.[11] For the same reason, I use the unhyphenated term 'bodymind'.[12] The book proposes that thinking is embodied and transcorporal – a subjectivity that is not singular, independent, gendered or racialised (Lenz Taguchi, 2013), nor essentialised through ageist prejudice.

Moreover, how we think about Laika's thinking (or her '*essence*') depends not only on the *existence* of bodily interaction and communicative relationships with other human animals, but also on other material conditions – 'the non-human in the data' (Larson and Phillips, 2013, p. 20).

Laika's school was situated in a very affluent town in southern England, but its catchment area served mainly a large council housing estate. Around two-thirds of the children were from low-income families qualifying for free school meals. The new headteacher's strong political vision and commitment turned this small school into a sanctuary for children who had 'nowhere else to go' – a reputation that spread and attracted more 'troublesome' children, some of whom had been expelled from other schools as often as three or four times. The modern school's layout on a slope was unusual. It was an 'open school' with many spaces for teaching, but few walls and doors to separate them. Another challenge to staff were the school's many outside doors, as well as odd corners where children could hide, hindering adequate supervision (*surveillance*[13] of children's movements and actions). One room at the lowest part of the building was reserved for reading and books. This space became very special for me for a couple of years (and materialised itself, and still does, in the theories I currently practice).

'Plato's Cave'

The room allocated to my teaching was circular, with only one entrance – perfect for sessions in philosophy with picturebooks. After I started working there as a philosopher-in-residence with all the children aged between four and eleven years old, the room was soon nicknamed 'Plato's Cave'. I valued the space as a sanctuary for children's academic freedom, although it would be naïve to suggest that they felt completely 'safe' to express their thoughts. Passive power operates in subtle ways. I might not have been their regular teacher, but the mere fact that I was older and seemed to 'own' the space and could hand out punishments or talk to their teachers or parents influenced and regulated their behaviour (Fricker, 2007, pp. 9–10). But at least they were sufficiently uninhibited to talk about death and other topics that mattered to them, such as children's rights, the treatment of animals, time travel or imaginary friends. As a philosopher-in-residence I was positioned as a different kind of grown-up from the teachers in the school, which enabled us to construct a different kind of relationship and therefore knowledge together (Petersen, 2014, p. 37). There were occasions when their philosophical ideas provoked censorial responses from their regular teachers (Haynes and Murris, 2012). In Chapter 10, I explore in depth how working philosophically with children from a posthumanist perspective demands different responses to 'taboo subjects' for reasons of social *and* ontoepistemic justice (Chapter 6).

The *archi-text-ure* of Laika's philosophy 'classroom' definitely contributed to building 'communities of enquiry', the pedagogy of philosophy with children. In some classes there were more than 30 children, and squeezing them all into the circular room meant that their bodies touched each other and most could see each other's faces and hear each other speak[14] more easily than in more conventional seating arrangements. The room had windows that let in a lot of light (also sun in the early afternoon). In the middle there was an omnidirectional microphone on a large stand – the only recording system in the early 1990s that made it possible to hear everybody. I used it to audiotape all my philosophical enquiries.

Such a microphone is an 'apparatus'; it is 'a doing, not a thing' (Barad, 2007, p. 183). Posthumanist Karen Barad (2007, p. 3) explains that 'matter' (the material) and 'meaning' (the discursive) are always entangled like waves interfering with one another *diffractively*, creating a new pattern without clear identity-producing boundaries.[15] The physical and conceptual come together in the apparatus and form a 'non-dualistic whole'. The meaning of the philosophical concepts the children were examining materialised 'in relation to the particular apparatus used' (Barad, 2007, p. 120).

In our philosopher's cave the recording apparatus also 'interfered' with knowledge production, but not in the sense that it 'distorted' the 'truth'. Looking back, it was not an objective instrument for *re-presenting* what the children had said, or not said, in class, despite the fact that at the time I used it with exactly that in mind. Many factors influence what children and teacher as-a-matter-of-fact say, or do, in class; this book explores these from a posthumanist perspective, also known as 'relational materialism', 'critical posthumanism', 'feminist posthumanism' or 'new materialism'.

For Barad, 'power relations materialise in the intra-action between/with the material and the discursive'[16] (Jackson and Mazzei, 2012, p. 265). A focus on materiality draws the attention away from the human animals in my class. It opens up possibilities to 'ac-knowledge' how the space helped our philosophical practice to materialise. The circular room was a material force that helped to produce an intimate space of belonging where for a brief moment each week the children could ask and explore their own open-ended philosophical questions about picturebooks.[17] The space was an entangled state of both 'social' and 'natural', 'material' and 'discursive' (Jackson and Mazzei, 2012, p. 269). The children were aware that I was doing research and that their ideas mattered to me and some of the other adults in the school. They were not used to be listened to philosophically by their regular teachers,[18] but the children knew that it was valued, especially by the headteacher.

He had spotted an article in *The Guardian* newspaper (Bates, 1990) of my work with children. To employ a philosopher in a primary school was extremely unusual, but, being familiar with academic philosophy himself, he speculated that philosophy with children could help the many children in his school who had behavioural problems and learning difficulties. Sometimes he and some of the regular teachers joined in the sessions, mainly observing, but sometimes they were unable to resist the temptation to share their own ideas. Their inclusion (or exclusion) also mattered to the discursive meanings that materialised.

Like an earthworm

For the purpose of this book I select one incident out of many from memory. Barad (2007, p. ix) is correct when claiming that memory is not 'a record of a fixed past that can *ever* be fully or simply erased, written over, or recovered (that is, taken away or taken back into one's possession, as if it were a thing that can be owned)'. It is true that 'the past is never finished' and that remembering is not linear,[19] but always 'a reconfiguring of past and future that is larger than any individual' (Barad, 2007, p. ix). I cannot step out of my past and reflect on it from a distance, bury it or shake it off as it were. By implication it would be wrong to say that the voice in this book is 'my' voice, that is, a voice emanated 'from a singular subject' (Jackson and Mazzei, 2012, p. 3).[20] By 're-turning' in my bodymind to my philosopher's cave, I do not go 'back to a past that was' (Barad, 2014, p. 168), as if past moments were like 'beads on a string' (Barad, 2007, p. 394), but like 'an earthworm' making compost, I turn 'the soil over and over – ingesting and excreting it, tunnelling through it, burrowing, all means of aerating the soil, allowing oxygen in, opening it up and breathing new life into it' (Barad, 2014, p. 168). In view of this, I now bring a very different philosophical perspective to 'my' memories.

Peter (aged nine at the time), later described by his regular teacher to me as the 'ringleader' of 'trouble' in that class, burst into tears when his class discussed a question they had raised and chosen for further philosophical enquiry: 'Do ghosts exist?'. As a baby, Peter had survived a car crash, but his young mother had not been so lucky. Without a seat belt she had been catapulted out of the car and killed instantly. From an early age Peter had talked to his mother – a ghost, he explained, who travelled with him wherever he went, day and night. Of course, the outcome of the children's philosophical enquiry (the answer to the question whether ghosts exist or not) deeply mattered to Peter; the material possibility of communicating with his mum depended upon it. The class was visibly moved when Peter told, almost shouted, his story. I kept quiet. Frankly, I was not sure what would be best to say, or do. Interestingly, Laika, who had been sitting next to Peter when he started to cry, took the initiative. She cut through the awkward silence and talked (I vaguely recall people telling me later) about random things. I was not listening. I simply could not. My attention was elsewhere 'in' my bodymind. I noticed tears welling up in my eyes, my throat getting very dry and feelings of sadness, but also excitement about what was happening. The responsibility weighed heavily on me, and I thought frantically what would be the best intervention. Not knowing for sure, I simply did nothing. My silence helped materialise Laika's agency – 'we' were mutually entangled (as well as with all other phenomena, such as Peter, the other children and nonhuman others).

Her talking about 'nothing' in particular gave others the opportunity to feel and think about Peter's story; her insight into what was required there and then was remarkable. The class felt heavy and full of care. The materialdiscursive incident left its marks on the bodyminds in the room. It proved to be significant how they thought and behaved after that incident, not only in the cave, but also after returning to their other classes (so the other teachers told me).

Philosophy matters

Philosophy with children is more than 'just talk' or 'playing with ideas', as sceptics have suggested (Murris, 2000). There is a seriousness to the pursuit, like the tense alertness of 'our' Labrador when she is fetching her ball, or a child fully immersed and lost in play that 'demands concentration and is marked by absorption and pleasure' (Griffiths, 2014, p. 124). What happens *matters*. It leaves its mark on the world and on our bodyminds that are *part* of this world. It changes what we think, what we feel, what we do. It makes a *difference*. Peter's usual cool façade had been pierced when the class decided that there was not enough evidence to claim that ghosts exist. If ghosts do not exist, he logically deducted, then his mum's voice cannot be real. This conclusion was of course devastating for him, and his outburst had become a significant moment in building a *community* with that class – a 'daily *doing* of community, a doing that is emergent in ongoing encounters, a doing that cannot be mandated through moralism, or through regulations' (Davies, 2014, p. 6).

Through the encounter, the other children found out about Peter's 'ghost-mother'. The concrete material conditions of her death created vivid images 'in' my bodymind. His personal narrative became *entangled* with the conceptual ('Do ghosts exist?') and gave the philosophical work a sense of surprise and urgency. Drawing on Deleuze and Parnet, Bronwyn Davies (2014, p. 6) describes such an encounter as 'an intensity. A becoming that takes you outside the habitual practices of the already known'. Maggie MacLure (2013, p. 661) talks about data that 'glow', invoking, what she describes as 'something abstract or intangible that exceeds propositional meaning ... decidedly embodied [and] material-linguistic'. What happened could not have been predicted in my planning. All of us learned (made new connections) about the concept 'ghost', and at the same time we changed how we understood and related to Peter. We did not get to know Peter better *psychologically*, or learn something new in the *abstract* about ghosts, but the experience was profoundly *existential*.[21] Peter's testimony about what 'ghosts' mean as a *lived experience* entangled with the children's (as well as my own and other educators') responses had brought something new into existence.

The cave's 'wallpaper'

All four classes in the school had their one-hour turn in 'Plato's Cave' each week. I used the same picturebook with each age group. Often they were allowed or encouraged to make follow-up drawings by their regular teachers and do other activities (such as drama or role-play) after their return to their classrooms. The drawings (sometimes cartoons) were hung up in the cave. Over time, these drawings became the cave's 'wall paper' which acted as what physicistphilosopher[22] Barad calls a 'performative agent' (Barad, 2003, 2007). Posthumanism theorises the idea that *things* (matter) are dynamic and have *agency* (Bennett, 2010, Coole and Frost, 2010; Hekman, 2010; Jackson and Mazzei, 2012; Braidotti, 2013). This is not something or someone *has*, but an enactment (Barad, 2007, p. 235). Matter is an 'active participant in the worlds' becoming' (Barad, 2007, p. 136). The 'wall paper' can 'perform', because it is (for example) made up of dynamic atoms, a characteristic walls share with human animals and nonhuman animals. It has 'force and power to transform our thinking and being' (Lenz Taguchi, 2010, p. 4).[23] Quantum physics provides 'multiple and robust' empirical evidence that atoms are not as 'simple' as they were once thought to be (Barad, 2007, p. 353). They are *real* in the sense that they are bits of matter that can be 'seen', picked up, one at a time, and moved (Barad, 2007, p. 354). They can be further divided into subatomic particles such as, for example, quarks and electrons, but importantly they do not take up determinate positions *'in' space and time* (Barad, 2007, p. 354). They cannot be *located*, as their being extends ontologically across different spaces and times (Barad, 2007, p. 383). In Chapter 3 I explore in more detail how relational materialism disrupts Western metaphysics, including its basic ontological assumption that the epistemological 'line' that separates subject from object is fixed (the thinking subject that thinks *about* the world). In a posthuman ontology the line 'between' object and subject does not pre-exist 'particular practices of their engagement, but neither is it arbitrary'. The specific nature of the material practices that are enacted configure object and subject (Barad, 2007, p. 359).

Intra-action

The children's drawings and writing were not only an expression of ideas, but also literally made up of dynamic atoms. Therefore, in a very *real* sense, the *materiality* of their (also) discursive production generated (potentially infinite) new ideas. The children were 'intra-acting' with it and each other, and so was I. As opposed to the more familiar 'inter-action', *intra-action* (Barad, 2007; 2013, p. 815) does not presuppose individualised existence – not only of subjects, but also of objects 'in' the world – and like other critical posthumanists such as Rosi Braidotti, Barad emphasises mutual relationality: things 'are' because they are in relation to and influencing each other. Intra-action is different from 'interaction' in that 'nature' and 'culture' are never 'pure', are never unaffected by each other, but are always in relation. The entanglement of all human and nonhuman phenomena intra-acting with one another means that it is im-possible to say where the boundaries *are* of each child, or the teacher, or the furniture, or the drawings, and so forth (not only from an *epistemological*, but also from an *ontological* point of view). They do not stand in 'a relationship of externality to each other' (Barad, 2007, p. 152). Therefore, 'agency no longer belongs to the human alone who acts upon the non-human' (Larson and Phillips, 2013, p. 21). The implications for teaching, learning and research are profound. Now, at this moment 'in' spacetime, thinking back about past practices (which are never left behind), I re-cognise how, as a teacher and researcher, I was not distanced 'outside' or 'external' to the intra-actions. Similarly, neither am I now distanced from the act of re-membering these incidents 'in' the past. I am and was fully implicated; and that is part of the materialdiscursive practice.

The children spotted new work hung on the wall, or noticed old work already there, often during the lessons, making new *rhizomatic* connections[24] (Deleuze and Guattari, 1987/2013), and generating 'fresh' questions for the class to consider. Introduced by Deleuze and Guattari, the 'rhizome' is knowledge constructed as non-hierarchical, without a root, trunk and branches (like the tree metaphor of knowledge), but as something that 'shoots in all directions with no beginning and end, but always *in between*, and with openings toward other directions and places' (Dahlberg, 2003, p. 280). The wallpaper was both material *and* discursive and had the power to affect and be affected. Without the force enacted by the wallpaper, some of our conversations would not have taken place. Sometimes whole lessons emerged out of spontaneous intra-actions, causing us to abandon what I had planned as a starting point for our philosophical enquiries.

Thinking about human intra-actions in this 'new' way has implications for how we view Laika's thinking as 'slow' or 'fast'. It is only when we separate 'I' from 'matter' that as educators we focus on what 'the subject of learning is capable of – what s/he understands, how developed and mature s/he is, and what s/he is able to conceptualise or perform' (Lenz Taguchi, 2010, p. 57). In contrast, when learning is not positioned 'within' a subject, but is conceptualised as a dynamic, relational process of intra-action, Laika's thinking is always intra-acting with other bodyminds and the material environment that is also discursive. Thinking is not 'in' the mind as a mental activity, but always entangled and 'transcorporeal . . . involving other faculties than the mind . . . [making] matter intelligible in new ways' (Lenz Taguchi, 2012, p. 267). The girl Laika 'does not exist *unaltered* over time or *outside the connections*' with non-human others (Hultman and Lenz Taguchi, 2010, p. 531; my emphasis). At the same time, thinking and conceptualising minds are also *material*: there is 'a flow of information between cells, fluids and synapses of thought' (Lenz Taguchi, 2010, p. 47).

Picturebooks in the cave

Although the starting point for these lessons emerged sometimes organically, these sessions were not chaotic or without structure. They were structured according to a more or less set pattern characteristic of the pedagogy of philosophy with children.[25] Children questioned a text philosophically – usually a picturebook.

With my background in children's literature as a qualified youth librarian (before taking up academic philosophy for further study), the first good-quality picturebooks had just been published. Their potential for philosophising, and their superiority over other texts, made them an obvious choice (Murris, 1992, 2015b). The writings of Canadian educationalist Kieran Egan (1988, 1992, 1995) also deeply affected how I theorised my choice of picturebooks (Murris, 1993, 1994, 1997) and the role of the imagination in teaching (see Chapters 7 and 9).

The idea of using picturebooks for philosophy with children quite quickly became popular in the field, especially for practical reasons. But it has also caused profound disagreements and controversies. Philosophy with picturebooks does not only query the assumption of the established 'Philosophy for Children' (P4C) curriculum that a good text should *model* the community of enquiry pedagogy (Murris, 2015b), but it has also provoked strong reactions in literacy education (e.g. comprehension, readers' response), literary studies and literary criticism (Arizpe, 2012; Haynes and Murris, 2012). The democratic nature of philosophy with picturebooks as an intra-active pedagogy also causes resistance (Haynes and Murris, 2012; and see Chapter 10 in particular). In communities of philosophical enquiry, children create an *emergent* curriculum rather than a curriculum that is 'done to' them, with all the profoundly problematic ethical and political dimensions that entails (Dahlberg and Moss, 2005). Darren Chetty (2014) has theorised a useful critique of my use of particular picturebooks (e.g. by David McKee) for their suitability in a community of philosophical enquiry in the context of post-colonial education. Chapter 10 includes a response to his and similar poststructuralist's critique (see also, Murris, 2008). Elsewhere (Murris, 2000), I have responded to critique by academic philosophers that philosophy with children is not 'real' philosophy. What is often misunderstood is the dynamic *entanglement* of a reconceptualisation of philosophy, the democratic practice of the community of enquiry pedagogy, the competent child as (implied) philosophical reader, teachers as philosophical readers of the text, and the epistemological ambiguity and aesthetic qualities of the picturebooks selected (Haynes and Murris, forthcoming).

Interwoven in this introduction are 'diffractions' (see below) of 'earlier' practices using a posthumanist philosophy. In *The Posthuman Child* I bring a fresh orientation to my use of picturebooks as starting points for philosophy with children and/or student teachers. I move beyond, and at the same time include, the more traditional semiotic framework when using picturebooks for literacy. I also show that philosophical engagement does not involve only two very different interdependent[26] sign systems (the images and the words) (Sipe, 1998, 2012; Nikolajeva and Scott, 2000, 2006); I also include the book's *materiality* (e.g. its graphic design, use of colours, the medium [paper, virtual etc.]). Like all learning, philosophy with picturebooks involves the imagination, emotions, lust and desire (Lenz Taguchi, 2010, p. 59). Moreover, picturebooks can be used as texts with children in class to disrupt discriminatory binaries (Chapter 9). Carefully selected picturebooks are a good choice for an intra-active posthuman pedagogy, although of course Plato himself would not have agreed. For him, 'the path out' of his cave was through reason (the intelligible realm), not the senses. His philosophy separated mind from body, reason from imagination, truth from opinion, mathematics from the arts, and his metaphysics still shapes what we value today in mainstream educational theories and practices, policies and curriculum design.

Throughout this book I show how philosophy with picturebooks creates more epistemically just educational relationships 'between' adults, children and nonhuman others by creating opportunities for educators[27] to *experience* for themselves the materialdiscursive force of young children's philosophical thinking, and how picturebooks can be used as texts in pre-service and in-service teacher education.

A diffractive methodology

I continue my 'journey' to past experiences in my philosopher's cave, not so much interpreting or reflecting,[28] but *diffracting*.[29] The diffractive methodology has been developed by Karen Barad (1995, 2007, 2014) building on Donna Haraway's notion of diffraction (Haraway, 1992) introduced as a metaphor[30] to help 'rethink difference/s beyond binary oppositions' (Kaiser and Thiele, 2014, p. 165). The salient implications of using a diffractive methodology for pedagogy and educational research have been explored only recently by Hillevi Lenz Taguchi (2010, 2012, 2013), Anna Palmer (2011), Karin Hultman (with Lenz Taguchi, 2010), Alecia Jackson and Lisa Mazzei (2012), and much of this book's diffractive rereading of my philosophical work with children, students and teachers has been inspired by their ideas. More than any other methodology, diffraction moves beyond mind/body binaries (Lenz Taguchi, 2013, p. 1103). Barad (2007, p. 74) uses the term 'diffraction' from physics to describe how 'simply stated, diffraction has to do with the way waves combine when they overlap (see Figure 1.1) and the apparent bending and spreading of waves that occurs when waves encounter an obstruction'.

Diffraction means 'to break apart in different directions' (Barad, 2014, p. 168). Diffraction patterns hold for water waves, as well as sound waves, or light waves (Barad, 2007, p. 74). She asks us to consider the familiar example of two stones thrown close together into a pond, which she describes as follows:

> the disturbances in the water caused by each stone propagate outward and overlap with each other, producing a pattern that results from the relative differences (in amplitude and phase) between the overlapping wave components . . . The waves are said to interfere with each other, and the pattern created is called an interference or diffraction pattern.
>
> Barad, 2007, pp. 76–7

Figure 1.1 Noordhoek beach in Cape Town.

It is where they interfere or overlap that the 'waves change in themselves in intra-action' (Lenz Taguchi, 2010, p. 44) and create a 'superposition' (Barad, 2007, p. 76). The diffraction as a force and movement is *part* of the difference made in the intra-action. The new water pattern is not separated or different from the identity of the person who threw the stones in the pond. For Barad, diffraction is not a metaphor as it was for Haraway, but it denotes phenomena of matter itself (Sehgal, 2014, p. 188). Waves are not bounded objects, but disturbances. With the help of Deleuze, Lenz Taguchi (2010, p. 58) explains what this means. She writes: 'Deleuze proposes a difference without a negation, a difference that is a difference *in itself* and not as an opposite or negative to something'. A wave differentiates from itself in every intra-action. The wave is forever becoming. What is meant here is 'difference *in* itself rather than different in comparison to something else (Lenz Taguchi, 2010, p. 58). The same holds for other organisms – a human animal such as myself – when diffracting 'my' memories of the philosopher's cave.

The routine and familiarity of the space and the 'apparatus' (Barad, 2007) of philosophy with children generated many new concepts and narratives. The young children's philosophising also stretched my bodymind to the limit. Unlike my own university education, I had to *be* philosophical as opposed to *use* the philosophical knowledge I *possessed* to teach the children a subject with a distinct content. At the time, my empiricist epistemology often hindered my *responsive* listening. I saw myself (a self I also still 'am', and also will be, as the past cannot be 'discarded') as a philosopher teacher and researcher, an indivi-dual with certain attributes, qualities and properties, interacting with indivi-dual children – paid to teach the five classes in 'Plato's Cave' one hour a week. My objective was to create community of enquiries about philosophical topics I knew more about myself through my philosophical education. I saw myself as ultimately being responsible for an educational process of *formation*; the onus had been put on me to show that philosophy with children could help these youngsters to behave more responsibly and be better learners and citizens. After all, that was what I was being paid for.

The idea here is not to reconstruct a narrative that describes how 'I' 'was', but 'to respond, to be responsible, to take responsibility for . . . the entangled relationalities of inheritance that ['I' 'am']' and to put myself (which is never one or self) at risk in 'moving towards in what is to-come' (Barad, 2014, p. 183). Diffraction helps materialise an important new insight. 'Back then', I assumed that knowledge acquisition is *mediated* by the more expert and knowledgeable other through schooling; a linear journey from child to the more 'fully-human' adult philosopher (to be achieved at some point in the future).[31] Barad diffractively reads the 'important insights from natural and social theories through one another' (Barad, 2007, p. 232). It opens up possibilities to regard children such as Laika as neither biologically determined, as Piagetian stage theories suggest, nor as having a socially constructed identity. The former position ignores the social and the latter the physical, the biological and the material. At the same time, both take the nature–social binary for granted (Taylor, 2013).[32]

Like all animals, human animals *are* bodyminds; children are no exception. Laika's thoughts are always materialdiscursively intra-acting with the world. Her thoughts do not *have* properties such as 'slow', 'fast', 'mature', 'immature', 'philosophical' or 'concrete'. Thinking is *part* of 'the' world; an intra-active engagement with specific configurations of the world. So it does not make sense to say that Laika's thinking *is* slow as if it were a separable individual thing 'in' the world. It is not an 'I' that does the thinking, but thinking simply 'hits us' as we engage with the world (Lenz Taguchi, 2013) (see Chapter 4 for this important shift in subjectivity).

As my doctoral research progressed I increasingly felt the weight of the responsibility of introducing children to philosophy. Was my role to encourage children *to think like adult philosophers*? – to create the ideal 'philosopher's child' (Murris, 2015b)? Concerned with social justice, I had focused mainly in my research on finding evidence that young children could indeed *think like adult philosophers*. Surely, I speculated, they were intelligent enough and capable of abstract thought?

Pertinent questions emerged for me. If it is true that literacy changes how people think (Egan,1988, 1992, 2002), then what might I be 'missing' as a researcher when interpreting young children's philosophical dialogues? Also stirred, provoked and supported by my friend and colleague Joanna Haynes, my thinking and practices started to shift slowly, but substantially.[33] From a passionate attempt to argue that the children in my 'cave' not only *could*, but also *should* think like adult philosophers, I started to question the normativity of my own practices and ended up focusing and valuing the *differences* between children's contributions and those of older children and adults. This shift is recorded elsewhere (Murris, 1997). Relational materialism has opened up new possibilities for theorising my materialdiscursive philosophical practices, and this book materialises some of these new ideas.

The objective of this book is not to provide evidence that young children (aged 3–11) are 'real' philosophers according to the criteria of analytic academic philosophy. I use the theorised practice of philosophy with children as a materialdiscursive lever to bring about change in how children's competencies as thinkers are judged *through* philosophical enquiries. *The Posthuman Child* is like a 'building site' (Braidotti,1991, p. 2) that involves '. . . selection of elements, the distribution of tasks, and the overall plan for the project are the key to what is called the "materiality" of ideas'. The craftsmanship involved is not that of building scaffolds with predetermined structures: the material and the shape are unpredictable, infinite and relational.

The idea of the book is to show educators how philosophical enquiries with children can bring about educational transformation. The childhood studies course that I have conceptualised at the university where I currently work uses the content of this book as its core, and I argue that it could be an essential part of the early-years and primary teacher education curriculum and also Honours and Masters courses. The course has a dual aim: to engage critically with educators' conceptions of children as thinkers; and secondly, to equip educators' with some ideas to conduct their own philosophical enquiries. With these aims in bodymind, the book is carefully structured like a labyrinth, which I describe in Chapter 2, and finishes with a short overview of each chapter. Part I very much focuses on the 'why' of my particular philosophical approach to teaching and learning and curriculum construction. This is followed[34] in Part II with more practical ideas of what childhood education from a posthumanist perspective looks like in the classroom. In the next chapter I offer a justification for the childhood studies course that inspired me to write this book. I do this by using the diffractive methodology as set out in this introduction on Barad's relational materialism and the aims of education as set out by philosopher of education Gert Biesta. I read them diffractively through one another.

Notes

1 As in the case of almost all children's names in this book, Laika is a pseudonym, in this case for a boy. Laika was the name of a stray dog launched on a one-way trip into space by the Russians in 1957. She died a painful death within a week, from overheating and panic (from: http://news.bbc.co.uk/2/hi/science/nature/2367681.stm, accessed 21 December 2014). I wrote about the same boy in my PhD thesis (Murris, 1997), but have changed the name and the gender.

2 By 'metaphor' I mean the use of one kind of entity or experience to describe another entity or experience, because of some similarity between them (an adaptation of the definitions given by Julian Jaynes (1990, p. 48) and Lakoff and Johnson (1980, p. 178). Jaynes (1990, pp. 48–49) mentions the useful distinction in every metaphor between a metaphrand, that is, the thing to be described (less known) and the metaphier, that is, the thing or relation used to elucidate it (known). We will see below the importance of the human eye as a common metaphier in how it has shaped educational theories and practices.

3 Important to note here that I did not *feel* the emotion first and *then* thought about the reasons why this might be. Emotion is here conceptualised as a *judgement* that is neither just cognitive, nor just affective, but both, and also materialdiscursive.

4 In South Africa the foundation phase stretches roughly speaking between ages four and nine.

5 It is important to note that these metaphors create ontological concepts.

6 Leal and Shipley call it *deep* dualism, first because it has such a 'profound grip on us', but also, they claim, because it underlies all other dualisms (Leal and Shipley, 1992, p. 35).

7 See in particular chapters 4, 5 and 10.

8 Inspired by poststructuralist feminist writers (e.g. Taylor, 2013, p. 64), I use the verb 'queer' as a 'reconstructive' impulse to disrupt the nature/culture binary.

9 With thanks to Veronica Mitchell, who made this imaginative connection.

10 Ageism, like sexism and racism, is 'prejudice or discrimination on the basis of a person's age' (from: www.oxforddictionaries.com/us/definition/american_english/ageism, accessed 1 December 2014).

11 This is a key shift in material feminist thought, expressed by Jackson and Mazzei (2012, p.110 fn1) with a double arrow: material '<->discursive'. I prefer the

ontological wholeness of 'materialdiscursive' and explain later in this chapter the reasons for the preference.

12 I have seen this concept first used by Lenz Taguchi (2012), who draws on Floyd Merrell. The word 'bodymind' expresses the insight that humans are non-dualistic 'wholes'. See the rest of this chapter and chapters 3 and 4 in particular for a philosophical explanation, as well as my proposal to use 'iii' instead of 'I' or 'ii' to express not just a holistic subjectivity, but 'bodymindmatter'.

13 Drawing on Deleuze, Dahlberg and Moss (2005, p. 50) argue how surveillance is 'designed into the flows of everyday existence, enabling the continuous monitoring of conduct'.

14 I deliberately avoid an indivi-dualised use of the concept 'voice'. See below and Chapter 6 in particular.

15 This is explained in more depth below in the section below entitled 'A diffractive methodology'.

16 Diffractive readings of data are not poststructuralist. The latter emphasise how *discourses* function to produce power relations (Jackson and Mazzei, 2013, p. 265) and ignore how discourses are also material.

17 Interestingly, using picturebooks that are usually meant for young children did not deter engaged participation by the older ones, even by the 9- and 10-year-olds who thought they were books 'for babies'. Turning their concerns into philosophical questions worthy of our collaborative consideration, e.g. by proposing to include the question 'When are books for babies? and when are they for older people?', was a discursive *and* material intervention of philosophical listening.

18 Of course I am not blaming individual teachers here, as it is the curriculum that does not value philosophical engagement with information and ideas (see Chapter 2 for the three aims of education I propose).

19 Barad (2014) argues how quantum physics shows empirically that time is never just 'here' or 'now', but a dis/continuous movement a di/chotomy and queers (that is, an undoing of identity) the distinction between continuity and discontinuity.

20 Inspired by Deleuze and Guattari, Jackson and Mazzei I use the idea of a 'Voice without Organs'; see Chapter 6 in particular.

21 The existential is often reduced to the psychological (see e.g. the imagery of the 'fragile child' in Chapter 5).

22 A hyphen would emphasise a false distinction between the two. She is both at the same time a physicist and a philosopher.

23 Lenz Taguchi (2010, p. 4) gives as an example the power coffee has when intra-acting with our bodies, heating them from within.

24 See Chapter 7 for two rhizomatic pedagogies, and Chapter 8 for knowledge as a rhizome and the implications for the role of the teacher in philosophy with children.

25 See Chapter 7 in particular.

26 Hence the spelling of 'picturebooks' instead of 'picture books'.

27 Throughout this book I use 'educators' to mean early-years practitioners, student teachers, teachers, teacher educators and more 'informal' educators such as parents.

28 *Reflection* is the currently popular method of the arts, humanities and social sciences. It assumes that there is a knowing subject who looks in a (metaphorical) mirror and either sees her/himself accurately in the mirror, or, mirrors the world accurately through the language s/he uses. Posthumanism is a response to this representationalism and posits a new materialism: the material world is present and does not need to be mediated in order to be known (Barad, 2007, p. 379).

29 The difference with reflection as the current dominant methodology in the social sciences is explored further in chapters 3 and 5.

30 For Barad, diffraction is not a metaphor, but describes the world as it is.

31 Of course, this educational philosophy is still dominant in curriculum construction and educational policies and practices. See e.g. File, Basler Wisneski and Mueller (2012).
32 This new ontoepistemology is explained in much detail in Chapter 3.
33 This shift in my work is reflected by the different reading of the very same dialogue with children 20 years later (see: Murris 1992, 1993, 2013a).
34 Without setting up a false theory/practice binary, because theorising is a material practice. (see: Barad, 2007, p. 55). Practical examples, activities and tasks have also been included in Part I.

A posthumanist philosophical orientation

Chapter 2

The labyrinth

Enacting all three aims of teacher education

Any educational programme needs to include a philosophical justification for its priorities in terms of content. What are the core subjects to be included and what are the aims of education[1] that underpin such a proposal? In this context the writings of contemporary philosopher of education, Gert Biesta, are inspiring. I have used his three aims of education previously (Murris and Verbeek, 2014) to conceptualise the subject childhood studies as a compulsory core subject in initial teacher education. In this chapter I build on my earlier work and read diffractively Karen Barad's relational materialism and Biesta's three aims of education 'through one another' (Barad, 2007). The new insights that emerge include how a relational materialist interpretation of Biesta's 'subjectification' informs the pedagogies I propose for a posthumanist early childhood education. This chapter serves as a justification for the particular childhood studies course I teach, as described and argued for in this book. After outlining the 'why' and the 'how' of my childhood studies course, I give an overview of the book and suggest how it could be used in teacher education. I then invite readers to enter the 'labyrinth'.

The aims of (teacher) education

Gert Biesta argues that education works in three domains and has three concurrent, overlapping purposes or aims[2] (Biesta, 2010, 2014). For Biesta, the art of teaching is to find the right balance between these three aims, which cannot be predicted or controlled, and which involve risk-taking (Biesta, 2014, p. 147). Education, he argues, should concern itself not only with schooling or *qualification*, but also with *socialisation* and what he calls 'subjectification'. So, what is the difference between the three aims he proposes as applied to *teacher* education?

Institutions that prepare teachers need to ensure that students are qualified, that they are equipped with the right kind of knowledge, skills and dispositions to teach children ('qualification'). They also need to ensure that 'newcomers' to the profession are familiarised with the values and traditions that enable student teachers to live and work within existing educational practices, and to learn how to behave in ways teachers are expected to do ('socialisation') (Biesta, 2014, p. 128). Educationalists differ in their opinions as to whether teacher education should include more than these two, but Biesta enriches this debate by offering an important third aim, 'subjectification', which relates to how education impacts on the person. Although each aim of education is legitimate, Biesta does prioritise them, and regards the third, 'subjectification' as fundamental for education. It is on this basis that questions about knowledge, skills and dispositions, competence and evidence can be asked. To appreciate this prioritisation, I unpack further what he means by 'subjectification' and examine the kind of subjectivity it assumes.

Subjectification

Education's aim of socialisation is different from that of subjectification, but is easily confused with it (Biesta, 2014, p. 129). The former is about *becoming part of an existing order* and the creation of an identity through identification with that order. Subjectification, on the other hand, is guided by freedom and is about existence 'outside' such orders (Biesta, 2012, p. 13). It is about the formation and transformation of students and teachers into 'subjects' (Biesta, 2010, p. 21), by which Biesta means that teachers, and ultimately the children they teach, are *coming into presence* as individuals, as independent agents actively shaping society.

However, this cannot be done in isolation; especially in his later work, Biesta (2014) extends his existential and relational take on subjectivity to include Hannah Arendt's notion of action. Each person's 'coming into presence' depends on how their beginnings are taken up by others, and, importantly, he adds: 'the ways in which others take up my beginnings are radically beyond my control' (Biesta, 1994, p. 143). As others have the freedom to take up a subject's beginnings as they wish, a subject's *coming into world* is always shaped by the actions of others. He explains the educational implication:

> . . . the responsibility of the educator can never only be directed towards individuals – individual children – and their 'coming into presence' but also needs to be directed to the maintenance of a space in which, as Arendt puts it, 'freedom can appear.' It is, therefore, a double responsibility: for the child *and* for the world.
>
> Biesta, 2014, p. 144

So, plurality and difference are necessary conditions for the *event* of subjectivity. Difference is not perceived by Biesta as comparing subjects with one another (which would be 'uniqueness-as-difference'). Inspired by philosopher Emmanuel Levinas, he proposes 'uniqueness-as-irreplaceability' (Biesta, 2014, p. 144). Importantly, 'uniqueness' for Biesta is not a property, essence or quality of an individual, but *manifests itself in the relationship with others*. Others are necessary for uniqueness to be articulated, for a subject to become singular in an ethical sense. Biesta makes no epistemological or ontological claims about what the subject *is* (Biesta, 2014, p. 145).

This subject also 'has' a voice of the 'stranger' (Biesta, 2006). Drawing on Bauman, he explains that the stranger is not a 'natural category', but is produced by 'a specific construction of what is own, proper, familiar, rational' (Biesta, 2006, p. 59). Children or teachers, for instance, acquire a voice, are able to speak, when they become a member of the rational community, and *what* they say is according to the rules and principles of the rational discourse of the community they represent, that is, 'what certain groups hold rational knowledge to be' (Biesta, 2006, p. 57). What this means is that what is said by *this* particular speaker in *this* particular voice is 'inessential' (Biesta drawing on Lingis, 2006, p. 58). People speak only with their *own* voice when they are *outside* the rational community (Biesta, 2010, p. 88). Importantly, Biesta is *not* saying that the voice of the excluded other should always be celebrated *because* it is other or strange, but simply the need to be aware that 'what counts as strange depends on what counts as familiar' (Biesta, 2006, p. 59).

For Biesta, the aim of education should not be a mere focusing on the acquisition of knowledge, or a process of socialisation into an existing order, but to speak with one's own voice and to bring something new into the world. He explains:

> membership of the rational community gives people a voice. It enables them to speak, but it is speech in the capacity of their membership of the rational community. This means that the voice by which they speak in this capacity is a *representative* voice. This means, however, that the thing that matters when they speak is *what* is said. But *how* it is said and, more importantly, *who* is saying it is immaterial as long as what is said (and done) 'makes sense'. This, in turn, means that when I speak in this capacity I do not speak with my own voice but with the common voice of the community I represent. When I speak in this capacity we are, therefore, *interchangeable*.
>
> Biesta, 2010, p. 87; my italics

The rational community, in other words, affords individuals a particular kind of communication, one that is depersonalised and representational; it does not matter *who* speaks. In contrast, 'subjectification' as an aim of teacher education is about speaking with one's 'own' unique-as-irreplaceable voice, and bringing something new into the world. Perhaps an example in academia would be that we often socialise students into speaking with a representative voice, with the 'common voice of the community', for example, by asking them to reflect back or 'internalise' developmental or social constructivist learning theories as truths, rather than as philosophies of education that can be critiqued. The same holds for certain poststructuralists' claims to knowledge about how race, gender and class construct subjectivities (forms of 'socialisation' in this framework, not subjectification; see Chapter 10). However, how helpful is it to make such a hard distinction between socialisation and subjectification as if one excludes the other? It is helpful though to explicitly address subjectification. How can a course in teacher education *also* bring about subjectification? I understand Biesta as saying that subjectification is not an outcome, or a thing to be produced, an essence or identity, but an *event*.

Educational action is not guided by what a student might become; as teacher educators we should show 'an interest in that which announces itself as a new beginning, as newness, as natality, to use Arendt's term' (Biesta, 2014, p. 143). Teaching is not a quality or something a person possesses; it emerges only in an encounter with the other, because a teacher can never control the 'impact' her/his activities have on her/his students (Biesta, 2014, pp. 54, 56).[3] Or, as we have seen above, he/she cannot control how others take up her beginnings. So what could this look like in practice?

Subjectification has to do with acting in a public space (Biesta 2006, p. 61), taking responsibility for our actions and making wise educational judgements. For Biesta, making such judgements is at the heart of what teachers in the classroom do – usually in the heat of the moment. How then does the student teacher transform towards making wise educational decisions? I first consider Biesta's propositions about this, and then read his ideas diffractively through Karen Barad's relational materialism.

Biesta (2013) argues that we can develop the ability to make wise (virtuous) educational decisions only by *doing* it. Teachers make *situated* judgements about what is educationally desirable in each of the three educational aims. This cannot be handed out in lectures as templates or prescribed through textbooks. The teacher's role, for Biesta,[4] is that of a *person* who *mediates* in any concrete moment between child and curriculum when making practical judgements.[5] It follows, therefore, that especially in the foundation phase and primary education, knowledge about the *child* is critical (for example, knowledge about what a child can be expected to achieve in terms of, for example, reasoning, morality, subject knowledge acquisition). But, as Biesta (2014, p. 142) insists, such childhood education should not be in terms of 'a truth about what the child is and what the child must become' (e.g. autonomous, rational).

As we will see in chapters 4 and 5, such claims to knowledge about child have been deconstructed (e.g. Burman, 2008a) and reconstructed (e.g. Lenz Taguchi, 2010) in the last two decades from a philosophical (Matthews, 1994; Kohan, 2002, 2015; Haynes and Murris, 2012; Kennedy, 2013), sociological (Dahlberg, Moss and Pence, 1999/2013), cultural-historical, postmodern, poststructuralist and feminist perspective (Nolan and Kilderry, 2010, p. 108). If we take such contestations seriously, we need to foreground pedagogy and knowledge of child and childhood in teacher education.[6]

Reading subjectification diffractively

The methodological shift from 'reflection' to 'diffraction' is inspired by Karen Barad's relational materialism.[7] When reading Biesta's notion of subjectification diffractively, new insights are produced that help to construct a curriculum that disrupts current discriminatory (ageist) practices. Biesta's relational subjectivity sketched above involves surrendering the idea that individual subjectivity is pre-social. As he explains, teaching and learning is not a:

> ... one-way process in which culture is transferred from one (already acculturated) organism to another (not yet acculturated) organism, but as a co-constructive process, a process in which *both participating organisms* play an active role and in which meaning is not transferred but produced.
>
> Biesta, 1994, pp. 311–12; my emphasis

In other words, meaning is the result of co-constructive processes between two or more organisms. Production of meaning is not a 'one-way process'. Both human subjects (adult *and* child) 'constitute the meaning of what is learned' (Biesta, 1994, p. 315) – a subject is an existential *event*, not an identity or essence (Biesta, 2014, p. 143). Therefore, education should not start from ideas about what children (or students) should become (according to the adult responsible for their education), but 'by articulating an interest in that which announces itself as a new beginning' (Biesta, 2014, p. 143). 'Coming into the world' cannot be done in isolation, and meaning can be co-produced only when child is treated as a subject (and not as an object as for example in nature realist scientific approaches to child study).[8]

Although Barad would probably be sympathetic towards Biesta's proposal of a relational subjectivity, she maintains that meaning and matter are always ontologically entangled and she therefore queers[9] an anthropocentric epistemology (the idea that meaning making is a process between humans only). She writes: 'Neither discursive practices nor material phenomena are ontologically prior or epistemologically prior ... matter and meaning are mutually articulated' (Barad, 2007, p. 152). Therefore teaching means 'transcorporeal engagements, involving other faculties than the mind ... [making] matter intelligible in new ways' (Lenz Taguchi, 2012, p. 267). For a posthumanist or relational materialist, human and nonhuman matter always exist in entangled intra-active relations. Barad's neologism 'intra-action' or 'intra-activity'[10] should not be confused with notions such as 'inter-subjectivity' or 'inter-activity', which assume pre-social independently existing *human* subjects (in relation with one another) – the kind of subjectivity assumed by psychological scientific discourses, for example. As Anna Palmer explains:

> Barad brings our attention to the agency of the environment, things, materials and places in the on-going interrelations and mutual processes

of transformation emerging *in-between human organisms and matter and in-between different matter irrespective of human intervention.*

Palmer, 2011, p. 6; my emphasis

Despite the transformational potential to think in terms of teaching as a relational encounter, in that sense Biesta's notion of 'subjectification' is still a *humanist* notion. Inspired by Levinas and Arendt, Biesta's ethics of subjectivity is not formulated in indivi-dual metaphysical terms such as 'being', 'essence' or 'nature' (Biesta, 2014, p. 19), but *agency* seems to be attributed to human subjects and the discursive only, and his philosophy does not take into account the agential performativity of *matter* (Barad, 2003, 2007).

A posthumanist articulation of teaching and learning disrupts how in education we traditionally see the subject (either the learner or the teacher) who learns and knows, and the materiality of teaching. With matter, Barad (2014) does not mean mere inactive stuff that is in need of something else to bring it alive. Matter is not a thing, 'in' time and space, but it materialises and unfolds different temporalities. At the same time, reading Biesta diffractively gives the insight that the aims of education can include knowledge and skills *and* socialisation *and* subjectification (and disrupts either/or logic). Often curriculum construction or educational policies choose one aim of education at the expense of others.[11]

Relational material subjectification

Biesta's distinction between the three aims of education constitutes an important 'agential cut' (Barad, 2007). An agential cut is a specific intra-action. It is not the case that there are no separations or differentiations, but they are always within relationships (Barad, 2012, p. 77). Reading Barad and Biesta diffractively creates the new idea that subjectification is not only discursive, but, importantly, also *material* – the materiality of the human and nonhuman bodies involved in producing the event. It even includes the idea that the letters (in books in ink, or on the computer screen) have *agency*. Reading about the three aims of education literally brings about new possibilities for pedagogical practices in the (university) classroom. In particular, Biesta's notion of subjectification adds to our pedagogical knowledge the idea of the voice of the 'stranger' in communities. The communal aspect is key to transformation and subjectification. As Davies (2014, p. 12) argues: 'Community is not so much a place, or a finite group of people, but a way of mattering, a way of engaging with the world, and of re-configuring that world as a place where self and other matter, and make a difference, to each other and with each other'. Participation in a community, she continues, is becoming part of an 'ongoing experimentation' (Davies, 2014, p. 12). Davies points out how adults can learn from children in how to engage in reciprocal listening: 'children open themselves up in multiple ways to new possibilities, and in doing so make the very basis of an ethical community possible' (Davies, 2014, p. 12).

This book is about reciprocal and responsive listening to the voice of others (including 'strangers') in a community of philosophical enquiry (Haynes, 2007), and how challenging this can be for adults' listening. In my collaborative work with Joanna Haynes, child as stranger (in Biesta's sense) is a recurring feature. One of our key arguments is that listening to child's voice *as* stranger is possible only if we constantly question the pigeon-holing of child thinking: as naïve, as other, or as mere indicator of a predetermined developmental phase (Haynes and Murris, 2012, 2013). This kind of philosophical listening helps carve out new and fairer ways of working (Haynes, 2008, 2009a, b). Moreover, when listening to children's 'voices', we must move our attention away from individuals and concentrate more on the 'spaces' for 'freedom' to 'appear', as Biesta suggests, but these 'spaces' are not only discursive, but also unbounded, material and include the nonhuman.[12] How we observe and listen to children is informed by how we view objects and spaces as having active agency (Lenz Taguchi, 2010).

A posthuman approach helps to theorise the legitimacy of including young children's often magical, anthropomorphic and fanciful contributions (those of a 'stranger') to philosophical enquiries (Haynes and Murris, 2013), and is sympathetic towards the multiple materialdiscursive ways in which organisms construct knowledge and understanding. The posthuman stranger is however (in)determinate, that is, not a state of being, but dynamic, and 'the surprise, the interruption, by the stranger (within) re-turning unannounced' (Barad, 2014, p. 178).

(In)determinate subjectivity

The idea of (in)determinate subjectivity troubles the notion of a voice 'attached' to a singular indivi-dual. Inspired by Deleuze and Guattari's concept of the 'Body without Organs' (thinking without subject), Lisa Mazzei (2013, p. 733) has developed the notion of 'Voice without Organs' 'to describe a different kind of human being that enables one to think voice differently' – and by the same stroke – think 'listening' differently: a Listening without Organs (LwO; see Chapter 6).

We have seen in Chapter 1 that for Deleuze and Guattari (1987/2013, 1994) a human being is not a singular subject (or product), but multiple. Mazzei (2013, p. 733) explains this multiplicity as an 'assemblage, an entanglement, a knot of forces and intensities that operate on a plane of immanence and that produce a voice that does not emanate from a singular subject'. This also means that agency and intentionality are not located 'in' a person, but are always produced in relation with materialdiscursive human and nonhuman others. In particular in the second part of the book the implications of 'non-indivi-dualised' agency for education will be unpacked.

In summary, with a wave-like motion, I have read Biesta's notion of subjectification through a posthuman perspective, thereby not *negating*, but seeing through the discursive and also the material involved in his notion of subjectification (like two waves rolling closely together to the shore adding to each other's force and creating new patterns – a 'superposition' – in which the old is still 'present', but has become entangled in new formations). This posthumanist reading enables an inclusion of Biesta's original idea, but also extends it and makes the original 'apparatus' (Barad, 2007, p. 183) more powerful through the additional non-anthropocentric ontology. I use this diffractive 'version' of subjectification to justify a curriculum that includes the material, and that sees learning as part of being (as always becoming).

As we shall see in much more detail in the next chapter, a relational materialist subject is not an individual with distinct boundaries, but 'spread out', like 'a flow of energies, constituted in a total inter-dependence with other humans and the matter and physical intensities and forces around us' (Palmer, 2011, p. 7). An individual is not a 'centred essence' who remains the same through time and space, but instead comes into existence *through the encounter* with other materialdiscursive agencies (Petersen, 2014, p. 41). It is this move from the discursive to the materialdiscursive that constitutes a posthuman ontology with far-reaching implications for teaching and learning. Relational material subjectification as an aim of education justifies the inclusion of philosophy with children and Reggio Emilia as intra-active pedagogies for our own teaching in the university classrooms, as well as justifying approaches to childhood education in our primary schools, preschools, nurseries, centres and crèches. In Chapter 7 I will read both approaches to teaching and learning diffractively through one another to add force and vitality, and to create something new as part of that process.

The case for childhood studies

In educational settings, adults' responses to children's contributions to philosophical conversations are influenced by prevailing psychological and social perspectives both on child and on ways of knowing. Through their own experience and memories of being child, sibling and perhaps a parent, our current educators have been socialised in particular hegemonic discourses about child and childhood. During their initial teacher training, students' role models are the teachers they encounter in teaching practice, but often teachers' unexamined beliefs about the young child, their own school experiences and deep-seated emotions connected with freedom, control, power and social status influence how they conceptualise education, what is worthwhile and who is worth listening to from an epistemic perspective.

It is crucial for relational material subjectification that educators learn about 'developmentality' (Dahlberg and Moss, 2005): the essentialisms involved and the implied generalisations about what individual children as a matter of fact are capable of as a result of existing age prejudice. Knowledge about shifting views of child and childhood (e.g. by including a subject such as childhood studies in the curriculum) should therefore be a core component of foundation phase and primary teacher education. Opening up new ways of thinking about child, also outside of the academic world, makes different educational practices and relationships possible, and could produce events that enable educators to speak with their 'own' voice, rather than with 'a' voice that represents the still dominant developmental discourse. In Chapter 5 there is explicit guidance in how to diffract with various figurations of child and childhood.

Thus far I have presented a case for focusing on the relational material subjectification of (student) teachers by diffracting with Biesta's idea of subjectification. I have argued for inclusion of childhood studies in curricula that aim to prepare early years, foundation phase or primary teachers. The purpose of childhood studies is for students to learn the required skills and knowledge (qualification) to socialise them into practices that position child *as* citizen, not as citizen-to-be, and to be critical of the idea of the indivi-dual child of developmental psychology and social constructivism that still informs current school and teacher education curricula, policies, and school practices (File, Basler Wisneski and Mueller, 2012). Educators should therefore be introduced to a wide variety of pedagogies and educational approaches, including those that express postdevelopmental views of child (Nolan and Kilderry, 2010). What is involved in this shift philosophically is the subject matter of this book.

Entering the labyrinth

The challenge of shifting current hegemonic figurations of child and childhood in teacher education has been to write a book that has an unambiguous path, a clear journey for readers to travel so they do not get lost. The book's structure resembles a labyrinth with a single path to its centre[13] (Figure 2.1).

I do not use labyrinth as a metaphor; its 'stratification' (Pedersen drawing on Deleuze, 2013, p. 727) is physical and corporeal. Every year I walk this path with my students in my childhood studies course, and in the last week we spend a day on a local beach using sand and the sea to materialise and bring about new perspectives on ideas we have been building together during the year. They also create a labyrinth in sand (after they have drawn a labyrinth in class the day before) and walk it (see Figure 2.2). The year's course should have left marks on their bodyminds and 'erased' modernist assumptions about child as subject, as Foucault put it, 'like a face drawn in the sand at the edge of the sea' (Foucault quoted in Biesta, 2006, p. 39).

My childhood studies course is carefully organised to maximise transforma-tion possibilities; the journey through the labyrinth is like making your way through the chapters of this book. The sequence of the chapters is structured as a materialdiscursive force to engage students with various figurations of child

Figure 2.1 Photo of a labyrinth brooch belonging to Di Donaldson (photo by John
        Donaldson).

Figure 2.2 Student teachers creating a labyrinth in the sand at Clifton Beach, Cape
        Town (author's own photo).

and childhood during the year. It is what Barad (2007, p. 183) calls 'an apparatus' – a *doing*, not a thing. They are *boundary-making practices*:

> apparatuses are the material conditions of possibility and impossibility of mattering; they enact what matters and what is excluded from mattering. Apparatuses enact *agential cuts* that produce determinate boundaries and properties of 'entities' within phenomena.
>
> Barad, 2007, p. 148

We have seen at the beginning of this chapter that agential cuts are specific intra-actions: they are about matter and meaning at the very same time. Boundaries become determinate through the agential cuts and the intra-actions; and it is here that the responsibility of the educator becomes clearer. The trajectory of the labyrinth has as objective for educators to notice – to make note of, to mark – their own differing ideas about child and childhood without indoctrination or moralising. The concepts they hold in their imagination of child and childhood are part of the apparatus, as is the community of philosophical enquiry pedagogy that we use. This intra-active pedagogy is non-judgemental and characterised by divergent questioning, with the educator acting as a pregnant stringray,[14] and as a community we create new ideas together. As a result, students change and transform their practices without anyone being able to predict the outcome beforehand. The use of 'pedagogical documentation'[15] is instrumental to achieving this primary aim of the course in the form of a collaborative diffractive journal.

'Diffractive pauses'

Either before, or after, each chapter in this book 'diffractive pauses' have been included. Sometimes they have been integrated in the middle of a chapter. They sometimes contain entries of students' journals to illustrate the methodology, for example. At other times they have been included to add force to a theoretical idea. They form transitional spaces woven within the chapters, and although many practical teaching ideas for educators can be found there, sometimes more or less directly, each diffractive pause escapes the label 'practical'. No particular formula for these pauses has been used, but the guiding idea has been to support the practical implementation of a relational materialist philosophy in teacher education. For the sake of clarity, the diffractive pauses are indicated with grey shading. Strictly speaking, these pauses do not have to be read to follow the thread of my arguments, but I do believe that if not, the overall experience will be the poorer for it as it is in these diffractive pauses that the emotions 'cling themselves' to the arguments and an imaginary starts to develop of what might be possible in the (university) classroom. They are not prescriptive, and the idea is to diffract with them and in the process creating something new each time.

Not a maze

A labyrinth is not a maze – the difference is vitally important. A labyrinth has only one path, which goes forwards and 'backwards': the past cannot be left behind; it will always remain part of the present. In contrast, a maze is complex and has many different paths. One can easily get lost and not be able to go back. The purpose of this book requires a clear journey and a systematic approach for educators, while at the same time making room for the open-ended, ambiguous and divergent nature of philosophical enquiry. With Biesta we can say that it is radically beyond our control how our students will take up our beginnings as teacher educators. Educators' freedom to 'come into the world' is always shaped by the intra-actions with others, including nonhuman others.

The theory and practice of philosophy with children is mobilised in this book as an agential cut. As a 'boundary-drawing practice' (Barad, 2007, p. 140), it determines what gets included or excluded and opens up a philosophical space to examine how differences and binaries such as, for example, nature/culture, child/adult, emotion/cognition, inner/outer are produced and enacted in educational theories and practices. As such, philosophy with children is not just an 'educational tool' or a 'thinking skills programme', but a radical 'apparatus' and diffractive methodology with which to enquire into 'how differences are made and remade, stabilized and destabilized, as well as their materializing effects and constitutive exclusions' (Barad, 2012, p. 77). Differences are made, not found. As teacher educators 'we' are responsible and accountable for the entanglements '"we" help enact and what kinds of commitment "we" are willing to take on, including commitments to "ourselves" and who "we" may "become"' (Barad, 2007, p. 382).

The labyrinth structure of the book offers a temporary 'channelling', with clear 'boundaries' and obstacles built into its smooth surface *in order* to produce new insights about child and childhood. It is therefore advisable to use the chapters in the sequence of the book's layout.

As teacher educators, we are responsible for all three aims of education as explored in this chapter, including relational material subjectification. Like Barad's philosophyphysics, the motivation for the labyrinth is inspired by *justice*, not just *social* justice, but justice of an ontoepistemic kind. She explains:

> (Doing justice is a profound yearning, a crucially important if inevitably unachievable activity, an always already inadequate attempt to respond to the ethical cry of the world.) Or, rather, perhaps I can put it this way: It is the very question of justice-to-come, not the search for a final answer or final solution to that question, that motivates me. The point is to live the questions and to help them flourish.
>
> (Barad, 2012, p. 81)

The overall idea of the book is to help transform current institutionalised discriminatory practices in education – not only in schools, but also in the institutions that prepare teachers. Philosophy with children is one of my apparatuses. Philosophy with children *as a practice* asks profound questions about engrained, deep dualistic assumptions about children's capabilities as thinkers, and has materialised a relatively new interdisciplinary subject, 'philosophy of childhood' (Matthews, 1978, 1993, 1994, 2009; Lipman, 1993; Kennedy, 1996b, 2000, 2006, 2010, 2013; Kohan, 1998, 2002, 2011).

The relational materialist conceptualisation of philosophy with children that I offer is new to a heterogeneous field (philosophy for/with children, or sometimes abbreviated as 'P4C' or 'PwC') that also accommodates, for example, Cartesian realists, rationalists, American Pragmatists, poststructuralists, postmodernists (see e.g. Rollins, 1996). Its lack of homogeneity is challenging for researchers who are trying to re-present the field and who struggle with the idea of philosophy with children as an apparatus, which in the Baradian sense, is an open-ended practice without an essence or intrinsic boundaries (Barad, 2007, p. 146).[16]

The posthuman philosophical orientation informs the carefully layered educational opportunities for educators to be *directly* affected by people's materialdiscursive philosophical practices. The idea is to draw the reader *into* the writing, to think *with* and *alongside* the reader (the reader I *am* at the same time) and not to talk *to* the reader.[17] In most chapters, children's or students' philosophical ideas are central for readers to engage with experientially and differentially. Each time students and their teachers create and walk their labyrinth, new beginnings emerge that cannot be predicted, imitated or represented. Not despite, but *because* of this structure, each year the course is very different in practice, with infinite variations possible; the mutual materialdiscursive entanglement produces different knowledges and different entangled materialdiscursive experiences. I will also argue in Chapter 9 that the use of picturebooks is not incidental, but central in my endeavour to do justice to relational material subjectification as one of the aims of teacher education.

The Posthuman Child is a book about ontoepistemic injustice: the structural and systemic discrimination of children, particularly as knowers and the ones featured in this book are between three and eleven years of age. It offers educational support in how to challenge this discrimination through engagement with philosophy with children as a transformative educational practice. There are two major causes of ontoepistemic injustice done to child, which I will explore in detail in Chapter 6 when I read feminist philosophers Karen Barad and Miranda Fricker diffractively through one another.

The educational transformation proposed here is about a transformation of 'our-selves' as educators (our imaginations, desires, beings). It is a transformation of our relationships with students, with children, and other nonhuman others, including things of the world, a world we ourselves are also part of, our institutions, our societies (Barad, 2007, p. 383). This transformation is mobilised by thinking *with others* through philosophical enquiries about child and childhood. Philosophy with children is the apparatus that can help materialise this change if the labyrinth is walked with an 'open' bodymind.

The twists and turns in the labyrinth

The following is a brief summary of all the remaining chapters and 'diffractive pauses' interwoven between them.

Posthumanism as a navigational tool is a response to what has gone on before in the history of Western metaphysics and epistemology. In order to fully understand this response, Chapter 3 engages with the 'root' of the problem that humanism poses for justice: the Cartesian dualisms that exclude the other than 'fully-human' 'earth dwellers': females, slaves, animals, children and matter. By reading the natural and social sciences diffractively through one another, Karen Barad's knowledge of quantum physics informs an unprecedented radical contestation of Western metaphysics and offers an egalitarian, alternative ontoepistemology that forms the philosophical framework for the rest of the book. Two photographs that can be downloaded from the Internet of a 'statue–breast–infant–woman' offer diffraction opportunities.

Chapter 4 starts with a *diffractive pause* containing some ideas for use with educators about the implications of this new post-metaphysical ontology for childhood education. These examples from practice are followed by an exploration of what child *is* (and is *not*) in this new light. The new thoughts that emerged/are emerging in my diffractions with Karen Barad's relational materialism include use of the pronoun 'iii' to express subjectivity or 'bodymindmatter'. Instead of 'I' or even 'i', the neologism 'iii' is used as a continuous materialdiscursive reminder to challenge the binary discourses we inhabit, in order to help open up alternative, non-dichotomous understandings of child. Moreover, the new ideas in this chapter are put to work on a series of photos made by a six-year-old at his sister's wedding (in the *diffractive pause* that follows). The photos are explored from the perspective of child as 'i', 'I', 'ii' and 'iii' (including how each position assumes a different kind of observerteacherresearcher).

In Chapter 5, I use two strategies to do child and childhood differently. The first explores the notion of 'child's voice' from a relational materialist perspective; the second a reconfiguring of child and childhood through a genealogy of six well-known configurations: 'developing child', 'ignorant child', 'evil child', 'innocent child', 'fragile child', 'communal child'. Each configuration assumes the nature/culture dichotomy and particular teaching practices. I argue that for justice's sake, these configurations need to be disrupted and therefore embedded in this chapter is a practical activity – making bodymind maps. The activity is explained in the *diffractive pause* part of the chapter, and two examples are given of how the body can be a 'transformer'. A new posthumanist figuration of child is offered in the shape of rich, resilient and resourceful child (e)merging through materialdiscursive relationships.

This reconfiguration moves beyond the contemporary distinction between competent-incompetent child.

Chapter 6 starts with a quote that summarises one of the leading threads of this book: children are denied on three counts: 'ethically for being wrongfully excluded, epistemically for being wrongfully mistrusted, and ontologically for being wrongfully positioned as a lesser being'. Here, I turn more explicitly to knowledge, and how 'identity prejudice' discriminates and otherises child. The entanglement of knowledge, ethics, justice and transformation is given a new perspective by reading Miranda Fricker and Karen Barad diffractively through one another. Barad's philosophyphysics intra-acts with Fricker's notion of 'epistemic injustice', thereby creating the new idea of ontoepistemic injustice. Inclusion of 'age' in categories of discrimination necessitates an interrogation of what *counts as knowledge* in order to 'allow' young (black) child 'in'; I finish by arguing for increased epistemic *modesty*, epistemic *equality* and epistemic *symmetry* to make Listening without Organs possible. The arguments put forward are entangled with the *diffractive pause* of analysing a transcript of a philosophical enquiry with children (available on YouTube) that is at the heart of this chapter.

In this second part of the book, I focus more explicitly on the implications of a relational materialist philosophy for teaching young children, and read two approaches to teaching and learning diffractively through one another: philosophy with children and Reggio Emilia. Both intra-active pedagogies do justice to the ontology of child as 'inhuman becomings' and reconfigure child 'as' rich, resilient and resourceful (e)merging in relationships. This 'superposition' (Barad, 2007, p. 76) created by the diffraction is not critical, but adds force to both pedagogies, creating something unique in the process as exemplified by a brief example in this chapter's *diffractive pause*.

Chapter 8 proposes the image of a pregnant stingray as the superposition or interference pattern of a diffractive reading of three images: the midwife, the stingray and the pregnant body. I situate my radical proposal in the current South African literacy education 'crisis', and offer five responses: a critique of the apparatuses that measure; the power relationships assumed by the grammar of language; a rethinking of the role of the teacher; rethinking the languages s/he makes available to learners; all these in order to liberate child from her status as Fool. The fifth response is an interruption of what is meant by comprehension; the chapter maps the questions a pregnant stingray could ask and the ontoepistemologies they presuppose. The ethicopolitical implications of the intra-active pedagogy are explained, and suggestions made for how a philosophy with children session can be set up in the classroom. The support for teacher educators offered in this chapter's *diffractive pause* consists of a YouTube clip of a pregnant stingray in action, introducing philosophical questioning to a group of five-year-olds from the Cape Flats near Cape Town.

After briefly outlining in Chapter 9 some (now) well-established arguments for the use of picturebooks to explore abstract concepts philosophically, I explore in more detail the complex decisions picturebook author Anthony Browne made about censorship and child protection when creating the text and images in his book *Little Beauty* (2008). My analysis foregrounds the author's provocative play with the discriminatory binaries nature/culture, science/art, animal/human, fantasy/reality, machine/life, child/adult. The entangled relationship between his autobiography, his beliefs about children and his aesthetic choices creates rich material for educational institutions, because *they destabilise the core adult/child binary*.

Binaries in picturebooks can be 'pushed to their limits' with students of all ages, and examples from the work of one educator have been integrated within this chapter as a *diffractive pause* to show how the nonhuman and the text's materiality (in one particular case the colour red) a(e)ffect how *Little Beauty* can work as a text in philosophical enquiries. The chapter finishes with an idea of how to start a 'destabilising binary project' using a variety of Anthony Browne's picturebooks.

In the final chapter I propose that philosophy with children can help decolonise education through a new 'post'-metaphysical beginning. I diffract with poststructuralist colleagues who are critical of my choice of *Tusk Tusk* by David McKee, and the particular way I have used this picturebook in a South African Grade 2 class. The *diffractive pause* integrated within this chapter includes a relational materialist analysis of five literacy lessons. The interference patterns created by using the diffractive methodology include the valuable insight that 'teacher-proof' texts do not exist, that the training in philosophy with children should explicitly include the complex role of the teacher in reading 'against' 'the' text, and that such sessions should not be contained to one-hour isolated lessons, but be made part of larger projects. Finally, the diffractions expose the humanist metaphysics of the poststructuralist critique: to prevent dogma, unequal relationships and a restriction of freedom of expression, a posthumanist orientation towards such picturebooks troubles linear time, includes all earth dwellers, and breaks with the binaries that discriminate.

Humanism has created a 'two-world view' – of childhood and adulthood – that posthumanism brings together in common natureculture worlds (Taylor, 2013). The pedagogical implications of these metaphysical differences for 'post' colonial education are explored through two Socratic figurations of the educator, the 'gadfly' and the (pregnant) 'stingray'. The gadfly keeps child firmly in its marginalised childhood place with the humanist focus on the discursive, social power, *identity* and critical agency; therefore ontoepistemic injustice is done to child. By contrast, the pregnant stingray focuses on *differences* that matter in 'one' 'self'. The latter lets child 'in'; the former does not. The book will finish by showing that a radical move away from the exclusive anthropocentric focus on the psychological, social or discursive in education is particularly urgent to enable more just educational encounters with people who are not only young, but who might also live in poverty and not have English as their 'home' language.

A diffractive pause: the diffractive journal

Diffraction[18] as an emergent research methodology is core to the documentation we use as a core part of the overall assessment of the childhood studies course. One of the course requirements is to keep a *diffractive journal*[19] in groups of three using computer technology.[20] Educators need to be 'attentive to those bodymind faculties that register smell, touch, temperature, pressure, tension and force in the interconnections merging in between matter, matter and discourse' (Lenz Taguchi, 2012, p. 267). Importantly, this kind of documentation does not re-present what happened during the course, or 'mediate' (Barad, 2007, p. 231) learning, but, 'as a printed, tangible material entity, as apparatus', it intra-acts with educators 'each subjecting one another, each constructing one another' (Larson and Phillips, 2013, p. 20).

The various modalities of the course (e.g. PowerPoint presentations, readings, YouTube clips, philosophical dialogues) make marks on their/my/our/ other bodies, and the documentation maps the *effects* of difference (Barad, 2007). A body needs to be understood as in physics: 'any kind of body; a human body, an organ, and artefact or any kind of matter' (Hultman and Lenz Taguchi, 2010, p. 529). They are overlapping forces that intra-act and I have included two examples in Chapter 5 (Figures 5.1 and 5.2). Diffraction is not about *any* difference, but about differences that *matter* (Barad, 2007, p. 378), and it is here that responsibility and accountability for 'the new' produced by the educators comes into play. Barad reminds us that the new cannot be owned, because it is not located in time and space; rather as material entanglements they 'extend' across different times and spaces. The future and the past are always open, never closed, so the 'new is the trace of what is yet to come' (Barad, 2007, p. 383). The copyright sign (©) for Barad is not a symbol of ownership, but a symbol 'of the responsibilities entailed in producing differences (for whom and at what costs?)' (Barad, 2007, p. 383).

We have seen in this chapter how Barad (2007, p. 74) uses the term 'diffraction' from physics to describe how water, sound or light waves combine when they overlap (Figure 1.1). In the childhood studies course, each materialdiscursive intra-vention causes ripples or waves, and put together these waves (when meeting) constitute new waves that make marks on bodyminds (without ever leaving the 'original' waves altogether 'behind'). Waves are not singular entities with boundaries, but disturbances (Barad, 2007, p. 100), and new materialdiscursive interventions during the course (like rocks or body boarders in the sea) produce further effects. When two or more waves come together, unexpected new waves appear and 'boundaries' between waves and waves 'in themselves' are fluid.

Like waves, the boundaries 'between' human subjects are also fluid. At the micro level[21] all materials (including humans) are made of the same matter: atoms which have agency. As we will see in more detail in the next chapter, the present, dominant classical Western ontoepistemology starts from the wrong (human) optics.

So, the pedagogical documentation is an agential cut that maps 'the' history of the multitude of intra-actions as the educators travel the course, rather than just observing their learning from a distance (as in reflection). The point is not just that 'knowledge practices have material consequences', but that 'practices we enact *matter* – in both senses of the word', and that these practices of knowing are 'part of the world's differential becoming' (Barad, 2007, p. 91; my emphasis).

Making knowledge is not about the production of facts, but about 'making worlds', 'in the sense of materially engaging as part of the world in giving it specific material form' (Barad, 2007, p. 91). The journal enables students and lecturers to see how childism[22] is produced, that is, in fact any apparatus that creates differences and produces 'objects' and 'subjects'. These enactments or agential cuts matter as they are *normative* (Barad, 2007, p. 380).

The phenomena child (the conceptual and the physical) is constituted and embodied by particular apparatuses to the exclusion of others (Barad, 2007, p. 120); pedagogical documentation helps educators map how these apparatuses constitute the meaning of 'child'. The twists and turns in the labyrinth (e.g. the movies we watch, the readings we discuss, the drama we do, the art we make, our experimentation during teaching practice) have been carefully structured to produce new 'waves'; and the agential cut of each small group of educators is materialised in the collaborative documentation, their joint product (that is always process) making a difference that matters. This philosophical work is not subjective in the sense that this would already assume the objective/ subjective binary (Barad, 2007, p. 91), which in turn is parasitic on mind/body dualism. Instead, Barad (2007, p. 91) argues for an objectivity that is accountable to the 'specific materializations of which we are a part', and that the diffractive methodology is attentive to the finest details and 'makes manifest the extraordinarily liveliness of the world', that includes, but is not limited to, the psychological, the biological or the social as is often the case in early childhood education.[23]

As the lecturer, I also intra-act with their philosophical work through mutual dialogue (as a *pedagogista* would do in Reggio-inspired practices – see Chapter 7) and by sharing and discussing some of the images and video-recordings I regularly make on my iPad. The students' words, images and sometimes movements (if they use, for example, augmented realities[24]) form only a glimpse of the richness of their continuous intra-actions during the year. The art lecturer also intra-acts with the students with the knowledge and skills to help them materialise (and extend) their own ideas about the course content – as an *atelierista* would do in Reggio-inspired practices.[25] Then in preparation for their final exam, they 'walk back where they came from' out of the labyrinth, but this time on their own. They read (and feel) through their collaborative work, and document the materialisation of new thoughts and feelings in a final 'art installation' supported by an explanation in a written essay (see Figure 2.3[26] for an example of an installation).

The installation is an opportunity for the students to express, two- or three-dimensionally, their own transformed view of child and childhood, also materialised in construction of a miniature classroom. Displayed in their final end-of-year exhibition (the formal exam of the course), the students engage with fellow students, lecturers, family, friends and the external examiner about their art installation (which is filmed). In turn, the event itself materialises new ideas through the materialdiscursive entanglements.

Figure 2.3 Nabeela Kidy's final childhood studies installation in 2014.

Notes

1 Although focusing on *teacher* education, my philosophical exploration of the aims of education also holds for other levels of education.

2 Interestingly, Canadian educationalist Kieran Egan also argues that there are three aims of education, but claims that they are inherently incompatible as each purpose demands, for example, a different attitude towards assessment (qualification – the academic realm – should not be assessed at all, but socialisation should, he says, because we need to get it right). See: www.youtube.com/watch?v=0QFDzRkmiUE (accessed 16 December 2014). Egan derives his aims from *describing* how existing schools work (unlike his own philosophy of education). For Biesta they are ideals, therefore normative. The third aim for Egan is Rousseau's introduction (deeply influenced by Spencer) to educational theory – the idea of children's natural development that is not unlike Biesta's notion of subjectification, but there is no child agency or freedom, only a natural unfolding in what is 'there' innate and good 'in' the child at birth. See Egan, 2002.

3 Therefore a teacher's identity is not absolute, but 'sporadic', that is, 'only emerges at those moments when the gift of teaching is received' (Biesta, 2014, p. 54). Receiving the gift of teaching is to welcome the unwelcome, to give a place to inconvenient truths and difficult knowledge and it is at precisely that 'moment that we give authority to the teaching we receive' (Biesta, 2014, p. 55).

4 It is difficult to extract a coherent notion of subjectivity from his writings. For example, against the idea that a teacher is a facilitator of learning, Biesta argues that the teacher has 'to bring something new to the educational situation, something that was not already there' (Biesta, 2014, p. 44), and teaching can therefore not 'be entirely immanent to the educational situation but requires a notion of transcendence'. His arguments are complex and not directly relevant for my key arguments in this chapter, but there does seem to be a tension between his conception of a teacher and the subjectivity it presupposes and the notion of 'coming into the world'.

5 There is no space in this book to do justice to the complex topic of 'practical judgements' or '*phronesis*' (Aristotelian). For Joseph Dunne and Shirley Pendlebury (2003), practical reason leads to wise actions only if the thinker exercises various virtues, such as reciprocity, mutual respect, openness and a willingness to give reasons and to listen to others. The common thread is willingness to give-and-take. They understand *phronesis* as characterised by a habit of 'salient focusing', which involves 'the ability to see fine detail and nuance'—partly constituted by cognitive dispositions and partly by a person's perceptions of and emotional responses to situations (Dunne and Pendlebury, 2003, pp. 207–8). Emotions are involved in the perception (*aisthesis*) of the necessary details of a particular situation. Joseph Dunne and Kristjan Kristjansson insist that *phronesis* is not just the *application* of theories to particular cases (Dunne, 1997, p. 157). The implications for teaching are that the 'teacher's capacity for reasoning cannot first be taught 'in theory' and then applied 'in practice' (Kristjansson, 2007, p. 166).

6 In reality, most foundation phase teacher training focuses on subject knowledge. In South Africa it is currently literacy, numeracy and life skills (not childhood studies). When conceptualising the new programme at my current university I put childhood studies as part of *methodology* and not *education studies*, as it is fundamental for the *practice* of teaching. One quarter of teaching time in methods is allocated to childhood studies (that is one morning a week).

7 See Chapter 1.

8 In Chapter 6, I also argue that this relationship is symmetrical.

9 That is, disrupts the nature/culture binary. An on-doing of identity.

10 See Chapter 1.
11 For example, moral education tends to be more about socialisation than subjectification (Murris, 2012).
12 Or the 'inhuman' as Barad prefers in her later work (see: chapters 4 and 5 and Barad, 2012, p. 81).
13 A labyrinth is a single path which one enters through its 'mouth' and then walks to its centre. Unlike a maze there are no alternatives. When the goal has been reached, that is in the centre, one has only gone half the distance. One has to turn around and walk back out. See: www.labyrinthsociety.org (accessed 13 January 2015).
14 See Chapter 8.
15 The term 'pedagogical documentation' comes from an approach to teaching and learning called Reggio Emilia. This is explored further in Chapter 7, where I read Philosophy with children and Reggio Emilia diffractively through one another.
16 Philosophy with children is often misunderstood as a result (see e.g. Ecclestone and Hayes, 2009; Vansieleghem, 2006; De Suissa, 2008; Hand, 2008) and in Oxford, 31 March–2 April 2009, a group of colleagues held a symposium at the Annual Conference of the Philosophy of Education Society under the title 'What Philosophy with Children is not'. For download: https://uct.academia.edu/KarinMurris/Conference-papers.
17 Just as much as the 'other' is *present* when I am writing. I try to resist the reader/writer binary (for a brief discussion see Jackson and Mazzei, 2012, p. 138).
18 See also Chapter 1.
19 I have not come across this idea before, only the keeping of *reflective* journals.
20 We use Google docs for the intra-actions, which gives me useful tools to ascertain students' contributions and opportunities to intra-act with them.
21 Although it would be wrong to suggest a micro/macro binary here (Barad, 2014, p. 174).
22 Childism is a particular form of ageism. Like sexism and racism, it is prejudice on the basis of a person being young. See Chapter 6; and Elizabeth Young-Bruehler (2010).
23 See Chapters 4 and 5.
24 With the help of tablets and cell phones (e.g. audiotaping a discussion or videotaping some role play), reality is modified through augmentation. This use of computer technology enhances pedagogical documentation (Chapter 7) by adding real movement and 3D to 2D writing. When a journal is augmented, the 3D images and videos come to 'live' by using, for example, one's cell phone.
25 An *atelierista* is a particular kind of art educator and is explained in Chapter 7. The students are engaged in creative art sessions as part of the Life Skills course. The lecturer and I try to work together as closely as possible, although time constraints and other institutional constraints can limit the emergent nature of this work in practice.
26 Nabeela Kidy's installation is further explored at the beginning of the next chapter.

Chapter 3

This is not a child

I see the posthuman turn as an amazing opportunity to decide together what and who we are capable of becoming and a unique opportunity for humanity to re-invent itself affirmatively, through creativity and empowering ethical relations and not only negatively, through vulnerability and fear. It is a chance to identify opportunities of resistance and empowerment on a planetary scale.

Rosi Braidotti (2013, p. 195)[1]

Figure 3.1 'This is not a child' by Nabeela Kidy.

'This is not a child'

In 2014, as part of the final installation of her childhood studies course, student teacher Nabeela Kidy drew and displayed *Ceci n'est past une Enfante* – 'This is not a child'.[2] She explained that she made the drawing because it is so difficult to capture or pinpoint what it means to be a child. Inspired by Magritte's painting, *Ceci n'est pas une pipe*, she chose to draw a *picture* of a girl in school uniform at work, because a picture will always be an *interpretation*. She concludes: 'It might sound simple, but it was a profound realisation I came to after this course'.

For philosopherphysicist Karen Barad (2007, p. 360) the point of Magritte's painting is not only that the image of a pipe is a *representation* of a pipe and not *really* a pipe, but rather that the whole idea that words stand for things and that language re-presents (makes present) the world 'out there', is problematic. It is this question 'what do words or concepts refer to?' that drives this chapter. This is a salient question for educators as we saw in Chapter 1 when exploring the example of Laika and her thinking being slow (according to her teacher). The implicit or explicit answers we give to the question shape how we think about knowledge and the relationships we build with ourselves and nonhuman others. They inform our pedagogical theories and practices and our claims of knowledge about child and childhood. Moreover, these philosophies of mind and language are materialised in the institutions that use them to educate teachers. In order to appreciate how our practices as teachers express and already assume certain naturalised ideas about knowledge, this chapter focuses on how Ancient Greek metaphysics has influenced our thinking about words and concepts, and how these refer to 'the' world. This knowledge serves a deeper understanding of posthumanism as necessary for justice (Barad, 2007), and some would go as so far as to argue that it is essential for survival of the planet as human and nonhuman habitat (Braidotti, 2010), as the quote that started this chapter suggests.

Limited by space, this brief introduction to classical Western metaphysics aims to show in particular how contemporary theorists have problematised the 'deep dualism'[3] (Leal and Shipley, 1992, p. 35) associated with inherited and current engrained habits of thought as we already started to explore in Chapter 1. This dualism is 'deep' as we will see, because it has created binaries that are now part of the structure (including grammar) of the everyday and academic languages we think, feel and live with. Important binaries for educators are, for example, nature/culture, mind/body, emotion/cognition, inner/outer, girl/boy, teacher/learner. Philosopher of education Michael Peters describes how mind/body dualism has 'developed as an instrument for 'othering': of separating boys from girls, reason from emotion, minorities from the dominant culture, and classes from each other' (Peters, 2004, p. 14). These assumed binaries in education shape discriminatory ageist practices. Posthumanism deeply troubles the anthropocentric nature of binary thinking, and offers a new ontology that enables a re-evaluation of child. It does so by removing language as the main hub of knowledge production and with it the 'fully-human' sophisticated language speaker of age as the sole producer of knowledge.

The 'post' in 'posthumanism' does not suggest that we can or should leave 'humanism' behind – even if this were possible. The past is not fixed (like static events 'in' time and space without always being part of the present and the future[4]). Humanism refers to 'something essential and universal, with a defining quality' that is shared by all human animals, and identity is a 'humanist signifier' (Jackson and Mazzei, 2012, p. 68). As a signifier it helps to stabilise meaning about categories of people, such as children. Humanist ideas about child and childhood continue to shape how we think about and treat children; the idea of the posthuman child mobilises an openness and critical alertness to the different ways in which our categorisations and own childhood experiences shape educational theories and practices.

Indivi-dualism: the story written into our bones

Posthumanism is a response to what has gone on 'before' in the history of Western metaphysics and epistemology. For the reader unfamiliar with academic philosophy, the Cartesian dualisms that poststructualism, postcolonial theory and posthumanism are rejecting so fervently and profoundly,[5] can be understood only by using the apparatus of 're-turning[6] (to) the past' (Barad, 2014, p. 169), by going 'back' to the 'root' of the problem that humanism poses for justice – not just *social* justice; care for the other *also* includes nonhuman animals. As Barad herself puts it (2007, p. 378), posthumanism welcomes 'females, slaves, children, animals, and other dispossessed Others (exiled from the land of knowers by Aristotle more than two millennia ago) into the fold of knowers'. I also read Barad as saying that she includes other bodies, such as *matter* among the 'dispossessed Others'.

How is it possible that in humanism the not 'fully-human' animals (e.g. women, children, disabled) and the nonhuman (matter) were excluded from the 'fold of knowers'? Posthumanism provides not only a philosophical answer to this question, it also offers an 'alternative' philosophy, with profound ethical and political implications for action. Otherwise referred to as 'critical', 'new' or 'relational' materialism, posthumanism focuses on the interdependence between human animals, animals and nonhumans (e.g. machines).[7] It redefines the meaning of the human animal previously assumed in knowledge produc- tion. For feminist philosopher Rosi Braidotti, posthumanism is not a concept, but a navigational tool, that helps us to rethink the place of human animals in the bio-genetic age known as anthropocene (Braidotti, 2013, p. 5). In short, the posthuman animal is not the indivi-dualised 'fully' human at the centre of the epistemological and ontological universe, but a human animal that is both self-organising and materialist (a concept, as we will see, that includes both nature *and* culture). Now slightly rephrased, let us re-turn to this urgent question of how the indivi-dualised human has been at the ontoepistemological centre of our thinking and being for so long? And why is this so important for how we think about child and childhood?

Many people are still unknowingly Cartesian dualists; an important tenet of this chapter is to show how well 'we know this story' (Barad, 2007, p. 233), and that despite attempts to deconstruct Cartesian binaries (e.g. by social constructivists, poststructuralists, postmodernists) this story is still 'written into our bones', and 'in many ways we inhabit it and it inhabits us' (Barad, 2007, p. 233). The challenge is 'to unlearn what we have learned' (Lyotard, 1992, p. 117) and to distance ourselves from 'outworn vocabularies and attitudes' (Rorty, 1980, p. 12).

The term 'Cartesian dualism' refers to French philosopher René Descartes (1596–1650), who is often referred to as the 'Father' of modernity. He settled the notion of the mind as a separate entity located in 'inner space' more radically than ever before in the tradition of Western thinking (which, for example, inspired the development of the social sciences and their methodologies, or what has become known in popular culture as the 'Age of Me'). He proposed the idea that the mind is a 'substance' in which mental processes occur. To quote one of Descartes' most famous passages:

> I am a thinking thing, or a *substance* whose whole *essence* or nature consists in thinking. And although . . . I have a body to which I am very closely united, nevertheless . . . it is certain that I, that is to say, my mind, by which I am what I am, is entirely and truly distinct from my body, and may exist without it.
>
> Descartes, 1968, p. 156

Of the two substances, the mind is privileged over the body, in the sense that '. . . self-knowledge of the mind is superior and indubitable (in fact incorrigible), whereas knowledge of the body (by the mind) is hypothetical, uncertain and derivative' (Leal and Shipley, 1992, 42fn16) or, put differently, contemplative life is superior over active life.[8] Also, not the body, but the mind guarantees existence, as expressed in his well-known dictum: 'I think therefore I am' (*cogito ergo sum*). Building on Aristotle's notion of 'substance', Descartes uses it as one of the categories with which we structure reality. Anything that has independent existence, or can 'stand on its own', such as stones, chairs or trees, is a substance, as opposed to skills, emotions or colours. For Descartes the world consists of two different kinds of substance: *res cogitans* and *res extensa*. The latter is '. . . the normal Aristotelian kind, the material object', whilst the former is '. . . consciousness or mind – in Kant's celebrated phrase, 'this I or he (or she) or it which thinks' (Leal and Shipley, 1992, p. 35). This transcendental self[9] is what people often refer to as their 'fundamental "me"', their 'core', their 'I', the 'whatever-it-is that makes them the person they *are*' (Leal and Shipley, 1992, p. 35). For Foucault, self is an empirical being among other beings while at the same time it is the transcendental condition of the possibility of all knowledge.

Freud's 'house' with three stories

In Descartes we find the most extreme expression of the dichotomous split between 'subject' and 'object' that characterises modernity. Separation has become foundational (Barad, 2007, p. 137). Knowledge of the 'outside' world is obtained on the 'inside' of the knowing subject (as conscious, self-aware, self-contained, independent, rational, mature). The innate structure of the human mind mirrors the unchanging structure of reality (Jackson and Mazzei, 2012, p. 68). Nature for Descartes is inactive (unless acted upon) and the body is regarded as 'housing' the mind, as, for example, in Sigmund Freud's case a 'Vienna house of three stories' (Steiner, 1993). In a televised interview, philosopher George Steiner (1993)[10] notes that Freud's house accommodates a basement ('Ego'), the living quarters ('Id'), and 'the attic with all the secret objects, memories and haunting dust' ('Super-Ego'). He comments that Freud construed 'the consciousness of men in terms of middle-class, Austrian, Central-European architecture'.

The idea that consciousness is singular[11] and consists of different layers and different depths (e.g. 'subconscious') is expressed in the material metaphors 'we live by',[12] but what is significant is that these metaphors do not tell us much about how the world *is*. Of relevance to the development of psychotherapy and psychology were the great geological discoveries of the first half of the 19th century (Jaynes, 1990, pp. 2–3). In geological terms, a record of the past is 'written' in layers of the earth's crust. When chemistry took geology's place as the popular science in the middle of the 19th century, there was another shift in our metaphorical thinking about the mind: '. . . subconscious as a boiler of straining energy – when repressed pushes up and out into neurotic behaviour' (Jaynes, 1990, p. 3). Our prejudices about 'the' mind and what 'it' 'is' are directly related to our thinking about the physical world 'we' are part of.

For most people, the way in which material objects exist is the paradigm for deciding whether or not something exists (is real). How we think things *are* in the world and how we conceptualise their relationships inform how we *know* them. In other words, ontology informs epistemology. Posthumanism is a response to classical Western ontology. Although called 'Western', to signify its 'roots' in the philosophies of Ancient Greece, its influence has been global and Ancient Greek ontology is now deeply entrenched in how most people think about them-selves, others and the world wherever they are geographically. Our languages express the idea of an individualised human 'I' (e.g. with attributes and properties[13]). The natural and social sciences are built on its basic structure, and the Enlightenment project has Cartesian dualism between body and mind at its core.

To use the way material objects exist as a paradigm becomes a problem when categorising very small objects, such as molecules or atoms, or very large objects such as the earth or the universe (Leal and Shipley, 1992, p. 35). We cannot simply dismiss this problem as a minor nuisance. As Karen Barad (2007) forcefully argues, this seemingly minor 'problem' of categorisation reveals the problematic nature of Western metaphysics to use (geometric) optics as the 'potent imagery' (Sehgal, 2014, p. 188) to decide what *is* and *is not*. Put differently, at the micro level things are not what they seem at the macro level, although it would be wrong to propose a micro/macro binary (Barad, 2014, p. 174). Human vision as an epistemological tool helps to distance the knower from the object of that knowledge, by making human experience of the world the standard by which to judge how the world *is*. In contrast, in physical optics differences are distributed differently as we have seen when using a diffractive methodology.[14] As a result, knowing is more about direct material engagement, and knower and objects of knowledge are entwined or entangled (Barad, 2007).

Barad's exciting project involves a radical thinking through of the implications of quantum physics for a new ontology and therefore epistemology that queers a damaging indivi-dualist, unegalitarian and undemocratic Western metaphysics. Other feminist materialists have also used Barad's ideas and those of one of her key inspirations, Donna Haraway, to inform new research methodologies (diffraction), theories and practices (Lenz Taguchi, 2010; Van der Tuin, 2011; Jackson and Mazzei, 2012; Kaiser, 2014; Thiele, 2014).

Western epistemology

In order to understand posthumanism, it is necessary to 'tunnel' briefly (always partial and changing understanding as I go along) like an 'earthworm' (Barad, 2007, p. 231) and 'visit' the history of Western epistemology, without closure – even the past is open (Barad, 2014, pp. 180–1). For the sake of clarity, I will first describe my understanding of some key terms in this chapter. Ontology is the study of what *is* (it constitutes the 'what' of knowing) as, for example, in Ancient Greek philosopher Democritus' theory of atoms. His influential theory of atomism postulates that the world consists of independently existing things with separately attributable properties – even the smallest units (atoms) exist in such a way. Democritus' atomism (and Newtonian physics) has been challenged by Danish physicist Niels Bohr, whose quantum model of the atom excludes the idea that things have determinate properties (Barad, 2007, pp. 137–8). Heavily influenced by Bohr's philosophy of science, Barad draws the ontological (and ethical) implications of his epistemology (something Bohr himself did not do).[15]

Epistemology means 'theory of knowledge' (from the Greek '*episteme*') and it studies how we come to know anything (e.g. atoms). Its fundamental questions include the origin of knowledge and the place of experience and reason in generating knowledge. Metaphysics refers originally to Aristotle's notes that were literally written after (*meta*) his book the *Physica*. Metaphysics now means any enquiry that raises questions about reality that lies 'beyond' or 'behind' those capable of being tackled by the empirical methods of science. Importantly, Barad's interpretation of quantum physics relies on the empirical facts that show that there is direct, not *mediated* (e.g. through language or measurement) epistemological access to 'the' world.

Much of Western epistemology is a response to the idea that there is nothing permanent except change. This has been famously expressed by Heraclitus' (c.535–c.475 BC) in his claim that 'You cannot step twice into the same river'. After all, the world as accessed through our senses monitors continuous change. Now if this is so, a key epistemological question emerges: 'How can we have certain (true) knowledge of a world that is in constant flux, therefore is always unreliable, uncertain, deceptive?'[16] This quest for certainty has (roughly speaking) led to two key epistemological theories: rationalism and empiricism. Plato and Descartes are good examples of the former, whilst Aristotle spearheaded the latter. For a rationalist, knowledge is acquired through reason and for an empiricist through the senses. See Figure 3.2 for a visual representation of this metaphysical structure.

Both rationalism and empiricism assume access to an unchanging reality 'behind' all changes. As beautifully expressed visually in Raphael's painting *The School of Athens*, for Plato (pointing with his finger up to the sky) certain knowledge of concepts (the objects of thought) can be found only through the use of reason. The world of physical objects in space and time, the world of sense-perception is always changing. On the other hand the *Forms* (which for Plato had ontological existence) are unchanging, non-physical, non-spatial and non-temporal as, for example, the concept Dog in Figure 3.2. In contrast, in Raphael's painting, Aristotle's hand is pointing down, indicating that truth is acquired through the senses and the particular, concrete details of a situation – including dogs we can see and touch.[17]

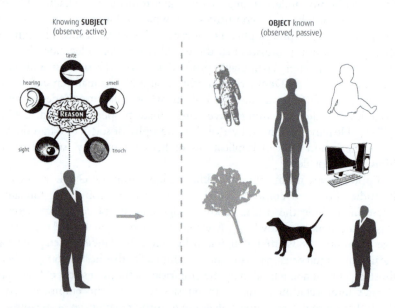

Figure 3.2 The Western metaphysical template of indivi-dualism, by Conor Ralphs.

Of course, how we conceptualise what the world is made of (ontology) influences how we claim we know that world. Following Barad, I will therefore use the concept 'ontoepistomology' throughout this book. In both classical philosophical orientations (rationalism and empiricisim) the ontoepistemology is indivi-dualistic: the knowing subject is a discrete individual in space and time[18] that 'does' the thinking – a thinking that can be measured and judged as being 'fast' or 'slow', as in Laika's case (Chapter 1). The ontoepistemology is also (*fully-*) human centred, as we have seen earlier. Both Plato and Aristotle were far from egalitarian thinkers. The 'stick figure' in Figure 3.2 is distinctly white, male, and not female, child or slave (Turner and Matthews, 1998).

So, how is knowledge possible if there is an ontological 'gap' between the left and the right hand side in Figure 3.2? What is the nature of the metaphysical 'dividing line' between the two? The classical Western metaphysical template necessitates a theory that 'bridges' the gap between subject and object for not only philosophical, but also psychological reasons (with significant implications for teaching and learning). Educationalist A.V. Kelly (1995) points out that the *psychological* need for certainty (cognitive) and security (emotional) has led, for example, to a curriculum that is focused on content knowledge and separate learning areas (mathematics, literacy, etc.). So in a sense, by introducing deep ontological dualisms into its metaphysics, classical philosophy has ended up with significant epistemological problems of knowledge, objectivity and truth. As Irish philosopher and Bishop George Berkeley provocatively comments on the history of philosophy:

> Upon the whole, I am inclined to think that the far greater part, if not all, of those difficulties which have hitherto amused philosophers, and blocked up the way to knowledge, are entirely owing to ourselves – that we have first raised a dust and then complain we cannot see.
>
> Berkeley, 1977, p. 46

The dust that has been raised for a couple of millennia is the difficulty of securing (philosophically as well as psychologically) knowledge that is certain and true in a world that is always changing. However, as we have seen, the issue only emerges as a *problem* within an ontoepistemology that assumes a subject/object divide. As Barad (2007, p. 137) puts it: 'representationalism is a prisoner of the problematic metaphysics it postulates'. Interestingly, both rationalists and empiricists do not regard the metaphysical relationship (that is the nature of the line that divides them) between the subject (knower) and the object (known) as *causing* the problem in the first place. They cannot get closer to solving the problem because 'they are caught in the impossibility of stepping outward from their own metaphysical starting position. What is needed is a new starting place' (Barad, 2007, p. 137) – a relational ontology that includes a performative[19] account of human and nonhuman bodies (Barad, 2007, p. 139).

The new ontoepistemology of quantum physics

For relational materialists, nature cannot be reduced to a mere object of human knowledge. Nature does not exist 'out there', passively, to be discovered by humans' thinking about or experimenting on 'it'. For Barad it is impossible to separate or isolate practices of knowing and being: 'they are mutually implicated' (Barad, 2007, p. 185). The physical world is not at a distance, on the other side of the line in Figure 3.2, but all 'knowledge-making practices, including the use and testing of scientific concepts, are material enactments that contribute to, and are a part of, the phenomenon we describe' (Barad, 2007, p. 32). Deeply influenced by both feminist theorist Donna Haraway and quantum physicist Niels Bohr, Karen Barad's significant contribution to both physics and philosophy is to see the ontological implications of what Haraway and Bohr before her thought were mainly epistemological issues. Bohr's famous two-slit diffraction experiment[20] (Barad, 2007, pp. 81–4) made evident that under certain conditions light behaves like a particle (as Newton thought) and under other conditions it behaves like a wave, described by Bohr's influential complementarity theory. Electrons are neither particles nor waves – 'a queer[21] experimental finding' (Barad, 2014, p. 173). Wave and particle are not inherent attributes of objects. But, 'the nature of the observed phenomenon changes with corresponding changes in the apparatus' that measures it (Barad, 2007, p. 106). Electrons and the differences 'between' them are neither here nor there, this or that, one or the other or any other binary type of difference; and what holds for an electron also holds for a human animal (Barad, 2014, pp. 174–5). Knowledge is constructed through 'direct material engagement with the world' and not by 'standing at a distance and representing' the world (Barad, 2007, p. 49). One must perform in order to see: 'you learn to see through a microscope by doing not seeing' (Barad, 2007, p. 51). The ontology of entities emerges through their relationality, and not only at quantum level (Kaiser and Thiele, 2014, p. 165). Quantum physics gives *experimental* evidence that subject and object are inseparable non-dualistic wholes (Barad 2007). As feminist materialists Kaiser and Thiele (2014, p. 166) put it: 'Onto-epistemology departs from discrete, given entities as units of analysis and considers agential forces (selves, cultures, objects, etc) as processually, relationally and asymmetrically produced (all at once)'.[22]

The God trick of seeing everything from nowhere

So a relational quantum epistemology removes human agency and responsibility from its classical metaphysical 'attachment' to an individualised body. There is not some-thing, a bounded entity that exists in, and moves through, time and space before it is measured. Another way of putting it is that posthumanism removes the metaphysical dividing line in Figure 3.2. The measuring (by the subject) and the becoming of 'the' object and 'the' subject all happen at the same time through intra-action. It is not possible to offer a new re-presentation for this radically new ontoepistemology – one that would follow (on) from Figure 3.2. A *visual* representation is impossible of the 'flattened out'[23] (Lenz Taguchi, 2010, p. 43), non-hierarchical ontoepistemology of a relational materialism that is inspired by Barad's reading of quantum physics. After all, such an image would imply 'the god trick of seeing everything from nowhere' (Haraway, 1988, p. 581) – as of course is the case in Figure 3.2.

Although such a transcendent, 'meta' point of view from nowhere is not possible (that is, the 'god trick' assumed in Figure 3.2) the imagery of optics remains a powerful one for Haraway. Arguing against the disembodied infinite vision of modernity, she makes a powerful call for a vision that is particular and embodied and avoids binaries (Haraway, 1988, pp. 581–2). Not universality, but *particularity* makes *objectivity* possible, she claims. Eyes are 'active perceptual systems', not passive or morally and politically innocent, but 'specific *ways* of seeing, that is, ways of life' (Haraway, 1988, p. 583). The eyes of different organisms or machines 'see' differently. Therefore, objectivity involves understanding 'how these different visual systems work, technically, socially, and psychically' (Haraway, 1988, p. 583).

Dualism has given rise to a notion of objectivity that is historically, socially and culturally naïve, because of its mistaken assumption that it is possible to re-present the world through knowledge systems (the dividing line) and claim that knowledge is not embodied and particular with a knowing subject whose eyes represent while escaping representation (Haraway, 1988, p. 581). Barad builds on Haraway's proposal to reclaim vision from how it has been used 'to signify a leap out of the marked body and into a conquering gaze from nowhere' (Haraway, 1988, p. 581). For Barad, location is also not about a 'fixed position', and she rightly points out how Haraway's notion of 'situated' has been profoundly misunderstood,[24] that is, conflated 'with the specification of one's social location along a set of axes referencing one's *identity*' (Barad, 2007, p. 470Fn45; my italics). 'Location' does not mean the same as 'local' or 'perspective'. For example, my email address is specific *in* the Internet, but this net itself is always fluid and becoming, and so are identities (Barad, 2007, p. 470Fn45). For Barad location is about 'specific connectivity' (Barad, 2007, p. 471Fn45) and has to do with how bodyminds intra-act with the world.

Objectivity is an ontoepistemological issue, not just the epistemological one it was for Haraway. Barad's knowledge of quantum physics and her diffractive methodology of reading the natural and social sciences through one another inform an unprecedented radical contestation of Western metaphysics.

What other earth dwellers tell us

For Barad, scientific study of small organisms calls into question the individual/group binary and problematises the nature of identity and individual existence. These tiny creatures show behaviours and ways of thinking that traditionally would have been located in the brain but in organisms that have none, for example the brittle star. Barad (2007, pp. 369–84) argues that the brainless and eyeless brittle star is a 'living testimony' of the idea that knowing, being and doing are inseparable (Barad, 2007, p. 369). This cousin of the starfish, sea urchin and sea cucumber has no eyes as such, but its entire skeletal system functions as a visual system, and its superior visual capacity has been used as an inspiration for scientists, for example, to build tiny lenses for optical computing (Barad, 2007, pp. 369–70). Brittle stars do not have eyes, but *are* eyes – it *is* a 'visualizing apparatus' (Barad, 2007, p. 375). Although brainless, the brittle star (as its name suggests) breaks off limbs when in danger of being captured by a predator and in doing so continuously reworks its bodily boundaries (Barad, 2007, p. 375), not as an individual object 'in' space and time, but always intra-actively produced and entangled with other phenomena. Boundaries are 'there', but never determinate or permanent, always changing and becoming. Barad explains that brittlestars are not 'pure bits of nature or blank slates for the imprinting of culture . . . [or] mere resources for human interventions' (Barad, 2007, p. 381). They *are* 'lively configurations of the world, with more entanglements than arms' (Barad, 2007, p. 381). They are more than 'knowledge-making and product-making projects' (Barad, 2007, p. 381). They *are* the world, not 'in' it, but *part of the world – like all other organisms and matter.* For example, the powerful documentary *In the Mind of Plants*,[25] directed by Jacques Mitsch, shows how plants have consciousness and intra-act with the world. They respond to music, have an active and dynamic social life, act as a community and perceive the space around them without eyes, ears, brains or a nervous system as we know it. Plants move and have agency, in that they can carry out chemical attacks and wage wars. The refusal of assigning agency to them has to do with the use of human time as criterion for the concept 'movement'.[26]

Like any other beings (earthlings) or matter, nonhuman others, such as brittle stars and plants, are *part* of the world. Barad's notion of 'entanglement' expresses the idea that reality and language, nature and culture, matter and meaning are inextricably entwined (Barad, 2007, p. 3). So, how is it possible to conceive of my body or a child's body as ontologically without boundaries, without visual 'edges'?

Indeterminate boundaries or edges

From a quantum physicist point of view (so not using the *human* eye as a paradigm for knowing), there is an 'inherent ambiguity of bodily boundaries' (Barad, 2007, p. 155) – boundaries that become determinate through particular practices. Bohr gives the following example of holding a stick in a dark room:

> When the stick is held loosely, it appears to the sense of touch to be an object. When, however, it is held firmly, we lose the sensation that it is a foreign body, and the impression of touch becomes immediately localized at the point where the stick is touching the body under investigation.
>
> Bohr quoted in Barad, 2007, p. 154

These two different practices determine whether the stick is 'part' of the subject (used as an 'extension' of the arm) or the object (of observation and study). An obvious objection might be to say that this is just a matter of how humans *experience* the world subjectively, and not how things *are* in the world? Barad counters this possible objection; worthy of quoting at length:

> At first glance, the outside boundary of a body may seem evident, indeed incontrovertible. A coffee mug ends at its outside surface just as surely as people end at their skins. On the face of it, reliance on visual clues seems to constitute a solid empirical approach, but are faces and solids really what they seem? . . . physics tells us that edges or boundaries are not determinate either ontologically or visually. When it comes to the 'interface' between a coffee mug and a hand, it is not that there are x number of atoms that belong to a hand and y number of atoms that belong to the coffee mug. Furthermore, as we have seen, there are actually no sharp edges visually either: it is a well-recognized fact of physical optics that if one looks closely at an 'edge', what one sees is not a sharp boundary between light and dark but rather a series of light and dark bands – that is, a diffraction[27] pattern.
>
> Barad, 2007, pp. 155–6

So for Barad the production of bodily boundaries is not a matter of someone's individual, subjective experiences, or about how we *know* the world, but the way the world is put together *ontologically*. Barad is not just making the point that it is an empirical fact that there are 'clear boundaries' only for the human eye (therefore subjective), and that this is *not* the case from a physical optics point of view. She is also claiming that for a blind man a stick is not just part of his body, but that the way he negotiates the stick *as part of* his body is the 'result of the repetition of (culturally and historically) specific bodily performance' (Barad, 2007, p. 155). Only when the man, for example, loses his stick or it breaks will the stick will be noticed as an apparatus that is part of an ongoing negotiation with the world with an image of '"normal embodiment" in mind' (Barad, 2007, p. 158). It is only then that the integral entanglement of the material and the discursive gets *noticed* (which does not mean that in *reality* this is not always the case).

Matter and meaning are intricately entangled as *a matter of fact*. And so is the indeterminate location of the subject. Barad (2007, p. 159) illustrates this idea with an example of Stephen Hawking's motionless body when he gives a talk through an artificial speech device. Without the device (the box in his lap) there is no talk, no Hawking. Hawking does not stop at the edge of his body (Barad, 2007, p. 159).[28] Also, there is more to Hawking's subjectivity than his body, that is, he has privileged access to his own thoughts. He can lie, conceal his thoughts, have secrets, but as philosopher Ludwig Wittgenstein (1971, p. 157: para. 293) already pointed out through his well-known 'beetle-in-the-box' metaphor, it does not follow that Hawking therefore 'has' a mind, as a substance, as *res cogitans*. The authority he has in accessing his own thoughts is epistemological (about *how* he knows) and not ontological (about the *material* that he knows) (see Murris, 1997). His mind is not an entity in this world, 'he' *is* bodymind (or 'iii' as iii[29] will argue in the next chapter) and so *is* the brittle star.

Posthumanism is not *anti*-humanism; it does not reject humanism's secular emancipatory agenda of 'solidarity, community-bonding, social justice and principles of equality', nor does it leave behind altogether liberal individualist values such as 'autonomy, responsibility and self-determination' (Braidotti, 2013, p. 29). Its thinking is positive: 'and/and', not critical: 'either/or' logic (see Chapter 1). What posthumanism objects to is the 'epistemic violence' (Braidotti, 2013, p. 30) done to earth dwellers by humanism. As Braidotti (2013, p. 30) puts it: 'The acknowledgment of epistemic violence goes hand in hand with the recognition of the real-life violence which was and still is practised against nonhuman animals and the dehumanized social and political 'others' of the humanist norm' (Braidotti, 2013, p. 30). Humanism is full of intrinsic contradictions, strikingly expressed in Figures 3.3 and 3.4. On the one hand humanist social and scientific practices assume similarity between human animals and nonhuman animals. At the same time, 'they' are different enough to eat, imprison and mistreat (and the latter also in the case of young human animals *because* of their age when, for example, victims of corporal punishment[30]).

For an alien, earthlings all look alike. If earthlings or broader: 'earth dwellers'[31] were very different from 'us' there would be little point in experimenting on them. But if they are not very different, how can 'we' justify eating and mistreating 'them'?

This is *not* a child

My 'time travel' in this chapter involved going 'back to the future' (Barad, 2007, p. 168) through Ancient Greece in order to disrupt the individualism that lies at the heart of (age) discrimination. As 'there is no absolute boundary between here-now and there-then' (Barad, 2007, p. 168), thinking about the history of Western philosophy *in this particular way* is a materialdiscursive intra-action.[32] It has left its marks on 'my' bodymind (and hopefully also on the reader's), and I am never the same, always becoming and as such 'my' voice is a 'de-centred' voice with fluid boundaries.[33] Voice needs to be understood as 'attributable to a complex network of human and nonhuman agents, including historically specific sets of material conditions that exceed the traditional notion of the individual' (Barad, 2007, p. 23). Like 'voice', notions such as 'agency' and 'intentionality' are also no longer positioned 'in' individual subjects as knowers and thinkers.[34] But, one might object, is this not problematic for transformation and social justice in the case of children? This unusual perspective of human beings' agency generates many questions. Surely, attributing voice and agency to *individual* children through children's rights discourses[35]

Figure 3.3 The problem with earthlings is that they all look alike (drawing by Joey Carroll).

Figure 3.4 We experiment on other earth dwellers, because they are like us (drawing by Joey Carroll).

is empowering? Thus, is the posthumanist 'removal' of child from the ontological centre of meaning-making and knowledge construction[36] therefore problematic? Are hard-won gains of autonomy at risk of being lost perhaps?

This book is about reciprocal and responsive listening to the voice of other earth dwellers (especially child as a non indivi-dualised 'stranger') in a community of philosophical enquiry and how challenging this can be for adults' listening. Educational transformation from a posthuman perspective moves 'beyond' the individual, and troubles the assumed Cartesian dividing line between subject and object. Educational intra-ventions express particular assumptions about the nature of this 'line' – a line that informs teaching and learning. The world can be either *represented* or *presented* to the learner (Lenz Taguchi, 2010, p. 44), and it is this distinction that informs figurations of child and childhood, and the pedagogies teachers enact.

Nabeela Kidy's poignant and beautiful artwork, *Ceci n'est pas une enfante*, inspired the key question that structured this chapter: 'What do words or concepts refer to?'. Her installation made it possible to explore the humanist ontoepistemological relationship between words, things, what it is that keeps them apart (the dividing line) and what puts them 'back together in relationship with one another' (through linguistic and symbolic representations), as we will see in particular in the following chapters. Importantly, what is assumed is that there is no *direct* access to reality; human animals are kept at a distance from what things *are* and this includes 'child' and the difficulty, as Nabeely put it, to capture or pinpoint what it means to be child.

'This is not a child' is not just about disrupting representationalism. It also disrupts a particular kind of difference implied – what Deleuze would call *negative* difference.[37] By italicising the 'not' in 'This is *not* a child' I indicate that by assigning the concept 'child' to child ('this' being 'in' the world), it is *not* the case that child is therefore separated out from its 'opposite' 'adult' *in order* for the concept to have meaning (Hultman and Lenz Taguchi, 2010, p. 529). In the case of negative difference, the system of signifiers in language brings into existence child subjectivity. It does this by positing 'child' in opposition to 'adult'. Child subjectivity is therefore an *effect* of language. This negative difference relies on something always out of reach, 'something absent that signifies a promised or deferred presence outside our language system' (Hultman and Lenz Taguchi, 2010, p. 529). For Barad, child is also not just a linguistic construction, but a discursive *and* iterative dynamic and material production (Barad, 2007, p. 151). It is when we focus on negative difference that deficit models of child and childhood emerge: child is still developing, not complete and is unfinished, immature. Child is compared to adult, that is, the 'trans-cendental signifier': mature, developed, complete . . .

Positive difference, by contrast, is about difference 'within' bodies (not as compared to something 'outside itself' like adult). But because of the differ-ences made by the connections within and between other bodies, a child always already finds her/himself as *part* of the world. It is about 'bodies that differentiate *in themselves*, continuously [like life itself] – one singular event after the other' (Hultman and Lenz Taguchi, 2010, p. 529). So, whenever we say 'child' or 'childhood', what difference does it make to what we do as teachers? Each time we pinpoint, point *at* a child, what is the effect on the body? What difference does it make to how we think about these bodies in the room? What difference do my intra-actions with 'them' and other bodies (the chair I sit on, the picturebook I am holding, the ants on the window sill, my hungry stomach) make on 'my' body? In the next chapter, the implications of a posthumanist philosophy for subjectivity and what child *is* will ripple on. Chapter 5 will engage with various well-known figurations of child and childhood.

A diffractive pause: statue–breast–infant–woman

I have found the following activity very useful for practising a relational materialist analysis in the diffractive journals. We use a widely available downloadable image from the Internet: Google search for 'baby sucking statue'. The image is available on the following links:

http://brog.engrish.com/wp-content/uploads/2009/02/baby-sucking-statue.jpg
http://cdn-ugc.mamaslatinas.com/gen/constrain/500/500/80/2013/01/08/12/9b/gn/pozc2ouio0.jpg
www.weirdasianews.com/wp-content/uploads/2008/04/statue-breast-feed.jpg

The download comprises two photos (on some sites only one photo) of a woman (mother?) and infant in what looks like a museum. As the mother stands near a topless female statue, the infant leans over and suckles the breast. The mother laughs. In class we diffract with the two photos in groups of three and discuss the new ideas that (e)merge. We start by 'brainstorming', or 'chimney sweeping', questions about the photos on a large piece of paper in groups first, for example, before and after working with this chapter, and then explore collaboratively the difference the philosophical work has made. An example of a group of student teachers' initial responses is in Figure 3.5 (this was before they started to diffract in their journals). It is very difficult to move away (especially on your own) from a humanist analysis, the anthropocentric gaze, that is, a focus *only* on the humans in the photos.

In educational analyses, the role of the material is usually reduced to how it serves human ends (e.g. intentions, design and drives). The students (the 'Mangoes') were typically interested in the woman and what or who she was looking at, and the infant: for example, how old he was, whether he was hungry

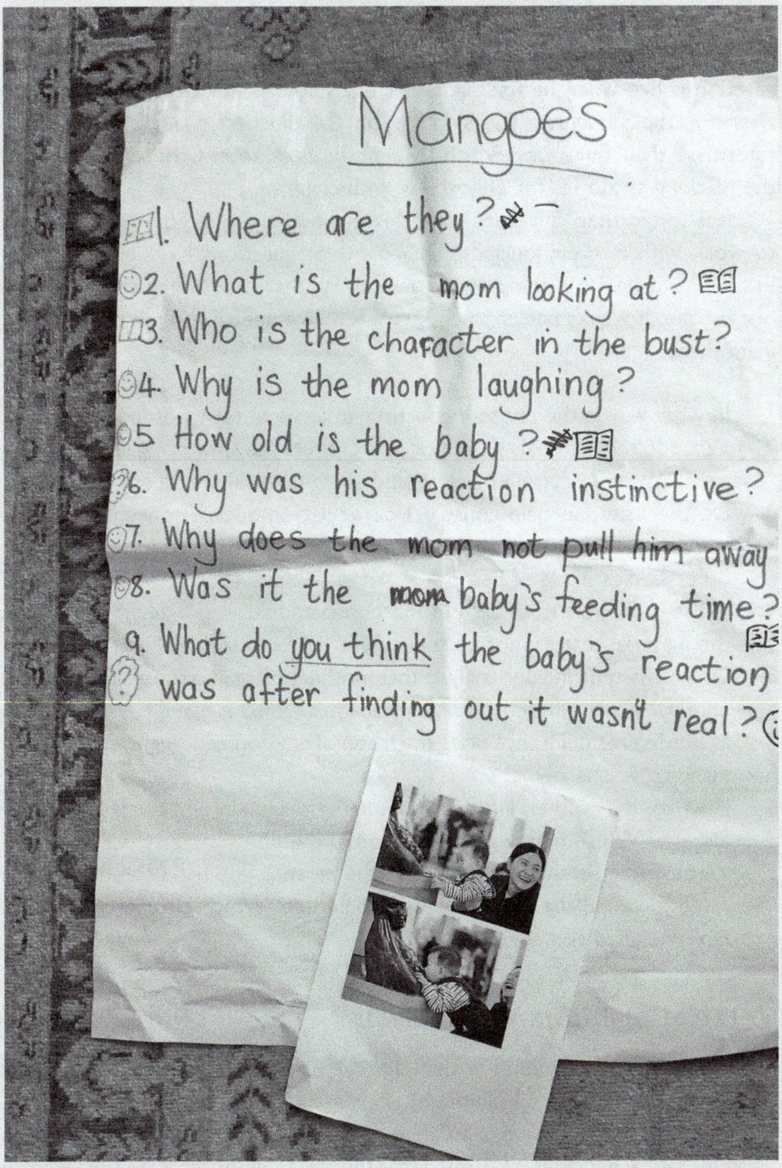

Figure 3.5 The students' initial questions about the statue–breast–infant–woman photographs.

or breastfed, and whether his behaviour was instinctual. The statue is only 'in' the picture when they ask who the character is that is depicted and whether it is art (also an anthropocentric question). Finally, the statue is assumed not to be real in their question nine, which invites peers to speculate what his reaction is like when he finds out that the statue is not real (which seems a given for the students). The symbols on the flipchart paper were used to categorise their questions, which I will come back to in Chapter 8 as one of the teaching strategies for philosophy with children.

Ideas for further diffracting with this material are offered to the students to work with in their journals. The following questions have proved to be helpful,[38] but *not* as a comprehension activity, that is, working through them one by one. It works better to choose a few that appeal and take the enquiry from there:

1   In what way is the photo a constitutive force in terms of identity?
2   What do the materials permit or prevent? Do they invite, exclude, regulate participation in certain material and socio-cultural practices?
3   Do the materials help construct particular emotions, concepts, ideas or knowledges? Does it matter that the statue is made of bronze and the other bodies made of flesh?
4   What is invisible/not heard in the photo and still has agency? How does the material that cannot be seen affect your reading of the photo?
5   Do you assume in your analysis that mother, infant and statue are separate entities? What difference for your analysis would it make to regard them as one? What difference does the material environment (light, space, time) make to your analysis?
6   How are the mother, infant and statue performed into becoming an entity/identity? Which binaries are assumed in the photo's construction?
7   What matter in the photo matters the most? If you had been holding the camera, would the shot have been different? Which binaries would you have included and excluded?

Vertical or humanist analysis[39]

One possible interpretation is that the child does not know the difference between real and not real (animism), as is assumed in the students' question nine in Figure 3.5. Animism is a deficit view of child. Attributed to child is an epistemological deficit: it is assumed that the child cannot separate fantasy from reality. The focus of humanist analysis will be on what is happening 'in' the child and 'in' the mother. For example, the child has the natural urge to drink from the breast. Neurologically speaking his brain is 'hardwired' to do this for survival or instinct; or it could be seen as culturally learned behaviour. We can assume he is, or has been, breastfed.

Psychological analysis relies on the subject/object divide. We 'see' a 'mother' and a 'child' and (therefore) assume a relationship of dependency. Less value is attached to the statue than to the human animals. The statue is passive, inactive. Baby and mother have agency and intentionality, but the statue does not. We see a child and a mother, who is laughing. She seems happy. The rest is 'backdrop'. The event is an experience and makes a difference, but the difference is within the people involved psychologically. Mother feels happy, the baby frustrated perhaps? Speculative questions could emerge about what caused her laughter. Perhaps she felt embarrassed? We might speculate how sincere she is in how she expresses her emotions. How do we know? Perhaps she has suppressed her real emotions? How binaries (nature/culture, inner/outer) dominate this analysis: choice, human agency, intention . . .

When diffracting with students in their journals, some of the following ideas have helped to move more towards a posthumanist analysis of the photos. One novel idea (e)merged in one group's diffractions, which in turn, materialised many new ideas: What if the statue was made of chocolate? How would that change our reading of the image? (see below).

Horizontal or relational materialist analysis

What are the opportunities here for a diffractive seeing? The formal setting and the encounter materialise fun, laughter: the laughter is 'in' the space, not just 'in' the woman, but in the relationship between woman, child, statue, the space, the light . . . The relationships between the bodies in the photo are non-hierarchical and need to be 'flattened'. The infant and the statue are doing something to 'each other'. They transform as an effect of the intra-actions that emerge 'in between' them. The statue offers certain possibilities to the baby. The statue does not 'end' where the baby's lips touch the statue, or the hands hold the baby. The infant's eyes are focused on the face/eyes of the statue once he started sucking. The hands are put on the statue as if it were a human. The statue's topless body and facial expression invite the baby to do the sucking. The woman, statue and the infant have no agency on their own. In the intra-action between the infant and the statue, a situation emerges when the infant moves his muscles towards the statue to suck the nipple. In order to do this the infant has to balance his weight carefully as he is held up by the woman's arms. He feels her body, her muscles holding him, clothes touching, the warmth of the bodies permeating the fabrics. Balancing the weight carefully, both bodies adjust to make sure that the infant does not hurt himself when reaching out to the statue. Statue, woman, child, the museum – all are overlapping forces and continually becoming.

Note the statue's colour, shine, and feeling to the touch (is it made of chocolate?). The statue must feel quite warm to the touch. It looks as if the sun is shining on it. The baby is not wearing a coat, so it cannot be too cold. Also, is it inside a museum? In what way does the apparently formal setting and the age of the infant's body bring about the laughter? What are the complex material conditions that work in the images? What are the discourses about traditional maternal relationships we bring to our readings?

Moreover it is a *photo*, not just 'a window on the world'. It expresses choice and agency and is an apparatus – not a thing, but a *doing*. The statue is matter that equally matters in the photo. It begs the question: Who and what is left out by focusing on the woman and infant? Who is making the photo? Who or what is she looking at? How does the photo materialise the woman's identity as the mother of the infant? And what is the difference made by having the two photos? (the face of the statue and the shoulder have a different force in the second photo[40].) After three weeks working on their collaborative journal at home, weaving individual sentences into one fabric, one group (the 'Educats') concludes:

At this moment in time and space the infant explores by using his mouth. In passing held at waist level he is at the ideal height to connect, or could he just be hungry or seeking comfort. Is this his mother, would he explore and suckle a bust whilst in his mothers arms. Has he been breastfed, has he been weaned. Why do we assume this is a gallery could it be in an embassy, official building, shopping centre or why not even a display of 'chocolate' creations? Would this have happened if the woman holding the child had passed from another angle? What matters most is that all that constitutes this event as depicted in this image came together at that exact moment in time to make it happen. Nothing can be singled out to matter more, all within this space and time hold the same importance. Notice all that immediate and beyond, past and present, all constitute meaning. All within this space is given agency because of their intra-action. Being what we are and in particular the way we have been educated does not lend itself to easily recognise this and adopt this approach when conducting analysis. What I have observed in all the observations is that we continually slip in and out of the humanist and posthumanist model. What cap do we wear and where do we place ourselves is there a right or wrong approach?

A diffractive pause: an idea that needs legs and mouths and ears to spread

After a student teacher had read Chapter 3 and discussed it in class, the following entry was written in the collaborative diffractive journal about the difference between diffraction and reflection, and the usefulness of the journaling process:

> Diffracting, and looking out rather than in, for me has been a bit tricky as so much of what we have been trained to do in the past has been us looking in and *reflecting* back in towards ourselves. And after having reread the article 'This is *not* a child', I feel that like the dualism between diffraction and reflection, there exists somewhat of the same bond between diffraction and reflection. Posthumanism doesn't suggest that we leave humanism behind, if it were at all possible, but rather we need the ability to see beyond that refined and defined perspective and to see the bigger picture. I think the same can be said for diffraction and reflection. To reflect certainly has its strong points, but to diffract gets us out of this inward looking perspective, one that is very centred on us as an individual, and instead look out and see how it impacts others around us. For me at least this helps understanding one concept in relation to another. It's so tricky and at times awkward for me to get out of this humanist perspective, and I think that it's because we are just so accustomed to it, very much like we are to reflection. In this way I can see that posthumanism does work. However what is bugging me is how do we get the whole world to see life in this way? How can we transfer what we have learnt to the bigger and broader social setting outside of our classroom? Surely this idea needs legs and mouths and ears to spread it? Perhaps it started as a thought but how did it grow beyond that? Just want to see what you guys think?
>
> Entry in the diffractive collaborative journal of the
> 'Peanut Butter and Jelly Sandwiches' group, 9 April 2015

I was particularly struck by the force of the particular language of 'legs', 'mouths' and 'ears' to spread the message – so apt, as well as humorous. The aim of Chapter 4 *is* to be such legs, mouths and ears. I also very much liked the description of diffraction as looking 'out', rather than 'in' and the difficulties involved in breaking away from our established ways of educational thinking and doing.

The movie Spring, Summer, Autumn, Winter, Spring

The introduction to posthumanism had also made a real impact on other preservice student teachers in that same 2015 course. As I do every year, part of the course is viewing and discussing a South Korean movie called *Spring, Summer, Autumn, Winter, Spring* directed by Kim Ki-Duk. I usually timetable this session as part of their preparation for their first Teaching Practice (three months into the programme). For most of the day we spend time thinking together about selected readings concerning classroom discipline and punishment (and the conceptual difference between the two concepts that are often confused), using the community of enquiry pedagogy of philosophy with children. We explore the legal requirements and the complex meaning of being in *loco parentis*, and we lay the groundwork for the philosophical work we do later in the year when we investigate their own moral dilemmas arising from their placement experiences in the schools (Murris, 2014b). So, why have I chosen this film in particular?

The film is about a Buddhist monk passing through the seasons of his life in solitude on a wooden hut floating in the middle of a lake in a forest. Living with him is a young orphan. Regularly they take their small rowing boat to the shore to pick some herbs and vegetables and walk and swim. One day the boy ventures on his own and teases three animals, a fish, frog and a snake, by putting a stone at the end of a string and tying it to their bodies – clearly enjoying their discomfort. Without the boy noticing, he is watched by his master who does not intervene. The boy returns home without removing the stones. That night when he is asleep the master ties a large stone to the boy's back and when he struggles to get up, his master tells him that he will not untie him until he saves all three animals. If it is too late, he warns, the boy will have 'to carry the stone in his heart forever'. The boy eventually finds all three animals, but only the frog can be saved – the fish and the snake are dead. When he picks up the snake covered in a pool of blood he bursts into tears. At this point I stop the film before it continues with the next period in their lives ('*Summer*'). Usually after a brief moment of private thinking time, I ask them to work in groups of three to develop questions for philosophical enquiry. But this year I noticed that the students were deeply moved, some were crying. The atmosphere was heavy. I do not think that this was a coincidence; it was the first year that I worked explicitly from a relational materialist perspective, and some had become particularly sensitive to the plight of other earth dwellers. In previous years, not all students had embraced the master's actions positively. Some had argued that the master had been cruel, even though they appreciated the life lesson the boy must have learnt through experiencing the consequences of his own actions. For many of them, he had gone too far and they concluded that at some point the master should have intervened and saved the animals. It is always impossible to predict what direction a philosophical enquiry will take, but the students' interest helpfully opened up an enquiry about intervention in teaching and learning: who should intervene, why, when and how.

Dominant influences on views of child

Of the three major orientations in teaching and learning, the *interactionist* is often the most popular in teacher education, although probably empiricist practices are most common in South African schools. Waldorf, Montessori and Froebelian education are all examples of interactionist teaching; they are positioned on a continuum between the *empiricist* and the *nativist* lens through which child is viewed (Bruce, 1987/2011). On one end of this continuum is the empiricist epistemology that draws on Aristotelian developmental thinking (Stables, 2008), with John Locke (1632–1704) as a major voice, claiming that the child's mind is a *tabula rasa*, or blank slate, and teachers need to 'fill' the child's mind with knowledge. Locke famously held the view that the child's mind at birth can be compared to a *tabula rasa* or 'white Paper, void of all Characters, without any Ideas' (Locke quoted in Archard, 2004, p. 87). It is the teacher's job to 'write' on this paper or slate and stock the child's mind with experiences, meaning both 'sensory awareness of the world' and 'reflective awareness of the mind's own operations' (Archard, 1998, p. 87). So, learning proceeds from acquiring concrete, specific concepts (e.g. different shades of red) to more abstract ones (e.g. 'red'). The other extreme, the *nativist* or '*laissez faire*' approach, is influenced by the philosophy of education of Jean-Jacques Rousseau (1712–1778), and assumes that the child is seen as preprogrammed to unfold in predetermined directions (Bruce, 1987/2011, p. 2), but ultimately is as old as Plato's Theory of Reminiscence. The idea is that the biological structure of the adult is already present from conception; cognitive development is the making manifest of cognitive structures that are latent (Matthews, 1993, p. 154). This position assumes that child is seen as genetically preprogrammed to unfold in predetermined directions. This natural, maturational process should not be hastened, and teachers should let themselves be guided by child who '"naturally" learns at his own pace, according to the dictates of his own curiosity, unfettered by the imposition of assumptions, preferences, expectations, or desires of others' (Simon, 1998, p. 107).

As for the empiricist, development for the nativist is individualised and separate. The same holds for the interactionist approach that draws its inspiration from German philosopher Immanuel Kant (1724–1804) (Bruce, 1987/2011, pp. 2–11). For this Enlightenment philosopher, all humans have autonomous agency and capacity to act on their own reasons; but although he believed that children are agentic from an early age, their agency is not the same as that of mature, rational, adult agency (LaVaque-Manty, 2006, pp. 365–7). Kant's epistemology includes a sophisticated interaction between knowing the limits of knowledge acquisition as a result of the structure of the rational mind (e.g. humans are limited to order their thinking in terms of the categories of time and space) and the content provided for by sense experiences. The role of the teacher is therefore critical in ensuring that children make maximum use of

Figure 3.6a The 'Philosopher's Washing Line' in 2014.

Figure 3.6b The 'Philosopher's Washing Line' in 2014.

Figure 3.6c The 'Philosopher's Washing Line' in 2014.

their environment by helping them to 'develop their own strategies, initiatives and responses' (Bruce, 1987/2011, p. 8). Swiss psychologist Jean Piaget was a Kantian in that he believed that children have 'schemas', that is, cognitive structures that shape their understanding of the world with increasing complexity (and as we will see later, this development is in 'stages'). But Piaget also focused on children's real and direct sensory experiences of that world (Bruce, 1987/2011, pp. 8, 53).

In order to help their learning of historical dates and names, I encourage educators to make a philosopher's chronological timeline where they hang up their ideas on a 'washing line' with pegs (see Figure 3.6). The first photo shows a materialdiscursive expression of Aristotle's developmental philosophy of education. They continue to add to this material line during the year as they learn more about each philosopher and their theories multimodally (including visits to a Montessori and Waldorf centre later in the year).

Presupposing the nature/culture binary

The continuum sketched above is indeed a helpful apparatus to categorise teaching practices that usually are somewhere on this scale, as being more or less empiricist, nativist or interactionist. Crucially though *all these lenses* assume the nature/culture binary. Child is associated with nature that either will unfold (Rousseau) or needs to be developed (Locke), or interacted with (Kant) in order to become 'fully-human'. As Maria Kromidas (2014) points out, not even Darwin's theory of natural selection 'lays humanism to rest', despite his concern about human exceptionalism: the child for Darwin is the *origin* of the human, and, in that sense, is 'the last savage' (Kromidas, 2014). The nature/culture dualism has, and continues to, shape our imageries of child and childhood, as we will explore in more detail in the next chapter.

Early childhood teacher educator Tina Bruce sums up her preference for the interactionist approach and the critical role of the educator:

> children are not seen as nativist sole instigators of their knowledge, pre-programmed to learn naturally, and held back or helped as the case may be by variations in the environment and culture. They are instead supported by adults and other children, who help them to make maximum use of the environment and cultural setting.
>
> Bruce, 1987/2011, p. 8

At first sight, the idea of maximising the use of one's environment and cultural setting seems plausible and unproblematic, but the lens through which the interventionist approach views the child troubled some of the students (as expressed later in their journals). They had made creative lateral connections between a lecture by Tina Bruce, the film and their reading of the previous chapter. They were concerned about the anthropocentric perspective of both the interventionist teacher and the master, who – it was suggested – should make 'maximum use of the environment and cultural setting'. It left them worried about the instrumental use of the environment and the nonhuman animals in the film for the sake of the child's education. There was disturbance in the room as they were feeling the implications of their newly acquired knowledge for teaching and classroom management, although interestingly during the dialogue itself (see below) most still expressed an empiricist view of child – a child with a mind that needs to be filled with the right kind of knowledge about concepts – even in the case of a concept such as death. These discourses are resilient and 'written into our bones' (Barad, 2007, p. 233).

Does anyone know the concept 'death'?

The following dialogue emerged when the students selected the following question out of a wide range they had generated about the film: 'Should we shelter children from death?':

Yaya:[41] 'I know that experience is the best teacher, but to what extent should the master not have exposed the kid to that situation, shouldn't he have been sheltered from that?'

Teenah: 'I hadn't thought of that before, because you are right . . . I thought it was just good, because it was experiential, but it wasn't just death, it was like . . . murder, to kill these animals . . . he really could have intervened, like, but then wouldn't he have had that lesson? I think it is a difficult balance'.

Katusha: 'We are used to see animals, small vertebrates, as less important life. That is another dimension. Are those deaths different?'

Yaya: 'No one ever told me that my pets die. It was always like they were going to a farm and then I thought but why? Don't they love me anymore? What is the matter with me? It would have been better if my parents would have told me what happens when you die. Is it in better place now, that sort of thing'.

Me: 'What would you say though? When a child asks you that question, what do you say?'

[laughter]

Yaya: 'I should have known about the concept, to prepare. I would have been prepared more'.

Tobogo: 'It is something they should think about and explore. You shouldn't shelter them from it. That goes back to the image of the child as innocent'.

They continued their enquiry by giving reasons for why it is important to understand what death is. The kind of knowledge, most of them thought, adults do have, but children either do not, or should be sheltered from. Despite the fact that Yaya didn't appreciate not having been told herself that her pet animals had died (but gone to a farm), she kept saying that she would shelter young children from that knowledge, as if we were talking about two different things. I challenged the class and pushed for strong reasons, asking them why children should be sheltered from such conversations.

Rowan: I was at a school the other day and the children were five and six and one of the children in the school was actually dying, had just died, and it was too abstract for them, they didn't understand it. The kids kept saying: 'When is she coming back?'. They didn't understand she was actually gone. Theoretically heaven is there, but I don't know whether they really understand what happens.

Bronwen: Yes, in one of the schools where I was observing, the children were drawing themselves and one girl had made a drawing of herself on the swing but there was someone else there as well, and when I asked the teacher later she said that it was her brother and the teacher told me later that her brother had died last year. He is in all her pictures. She doesn't really understand.

Me: What does it mean to understand the concept death? Are you saying that at a particular age you only understand death in a particular way?

Katusha then returned to her original comment about more or less important deaths.

Katusha: Yes, and I feel we make a distinction between important death and animal death, because the children eat meat, so they know about death, but that is perhaps not the same as your grandpa dying. Do we have two sets of death and only shelter them from the one? And where do you draw the line? Can you say that an ant is less important?

Vursha: But they don't know it is a cow, or a chicken they are eating.

Me: So should we in the foundation phase take children to a slaughterhouse, as part of life skills?

[some look horrified; sounds of muttered protest]

The question is an important one of course. Why should we shelter young children from such experiences? But more is at stake here than a consideration of whether *children* should be protected from encountering animals that already have been killed or are on their way of being murdered. What is at stake for *all* human beings visiting such places? What springs to mind is Helena Pedersen's (2013) haunting ethnographic article about a study visit to the slaughterhouse with a group of Swedish veterinary students. Accompanying the group in her role as educationalist, she describes in much detail how animals and human animals' bodies are regulated through the spatial-material organisation of the slaughterhouse. She describes how in the case of ensuring a 'smooth' transition when transporting sheep to the slaughterhouse, a 'Judas sheep' is used, that is a substitute for a live sheep by draping a sheepskin over a cart (training a 'real' sheep to encourage other sheep to move their bodies to the place of slaughter is no longer allowed). This decoy animal (a 'betrayal' and 'deceit') makes the sheep also part of the 'slaughter apparatus' for an audience sensitised to 'the idea of "humane" slaughter' (Pedersen, 2013, p. 722). When arriving at the slaughterhouse itself, Pedersen comments on a salient moment of the study visit for her:

The moment we enter this passageway marks a shift of character in our study visit, a shift from detached discussions of animal protection measures and productivity figures to a physical experience with the animals going to their slaughter. In the narrow passageway we proceed slowly side by side with them, at a similar pace, with only a low fence between us that allows for eye contact between us and them. Physically, the distance between us is only a few decimeters, but in all respects this distance equals the perimeter of Earth minus these decimeters. We and the cows enter parallel universes. The radical species-coded separation, demarcating who of us will be killed at the end of the line and who will not, makes the momentary intimacy between us and them appear almost obscene.

Pedersen, 2013, p. 722

This passage resonates deeply with me. I 'am' staring in the cows' eyes 'in' my vivid imagination – feeling for and being *with* the cows. It reminds me of Katusha's remark about 'two sets of death'. It also sheds a different light on our question about whether we should include slaughterhouses as suitable for school trips. From a relational materialist perspective the observer-observed dichotomy is no longer possible: 'we' are 'in' 'it' together. The cows and I are all *part* of the same world and the slaughterhouse apparatus produces subject-ivities where the flesh of one is consumed by the other. Therefore, I could not eat their corpses, and intra-acting with them in a slaughterhouse would make me complicit in their murder.

Being there would *make* me response-able. For Barad (2014) matters of fact, matters of care, matters of concern all come together, because of how the world *is* (empirically), that is, not a collection of indivi-dual atomistic entities. I am convinced that the disturbance in the university classroom after seeing the movie, when one human allowed animals to be killed for the sake of the education of another young human animal, was directly related to their increased sense of speciest egality.

Now would I allow/invite children to be involved in encounters that sensitise them to 'humane' killings? The answer to that question, and the broader one about whether we should shelter children from death, depends very much on context, pedagogical tact and questions about what knowledge is, as well as what child is (Haynes and Murris, 2013). The former topics re-emerge in various ways in Chapter 6 and Part II. In Chapter 4 we start with the latter question: What is child? The philosophies of education we enact in our practices as educators, implicitly or explicitly, assume a particular view of child.

Notes

1 With thanks to Rouxnette Meiring for reminding me of this passage.
2 See Chapter 2; her use of the feminine spelling of the 'normal' masculine *un enfant* is deliberate. As Nabeela drew a girl, she argued, the language should therefore reflect this fact and *une* and *enfante* should be used instead of *un* and *enfant* – 'correct' French.

3 Fernando Leal and Patricia Shipley call it *deep* dualism, first because it has such a 'profound grip on us', but also, they claim, because it underlies all other dualisms (Leal and Shipley, 1992, p. 35).

4 As Trinh puts it: 'Every gesture, every word involves our past, present, and future'. It is '[w]hen history separated itself from story, it started indulging in accumulation of facts' (Trinh quoted in Barad, 2014, p. 182).

5 Without necessarily claiming that humanism can be 'left behind', erased from the past and an imagined future (by humans theorising). As this would mean subscribing to control and agency to humans, which in and by itself is a humanist assumption (see Braidotti, 2013, p. 30).

6 Returning as 'turning it over and over again' in the making of new diffraction patterns (Barad, 2017, p. 168).

7 Posthumanism is different from transhumanism, which is not a critique of the Enlightenment self, but a humanist celebration of the ego (often achieved through techno-pharmaceutical means). In contrast, the strand of posthumanism embraced in this book rejects anthropocentrism and sees human and nonhuman as always already entangled in the multiplicity of mutual relations.

8 This Cartesian privileging of the mind over the body profoundly influences the choice of classroom resources. See especially chapters 5 and 7.

9 'Transcendental' for philosopher Immanuel Kant means 'the-condition-of-the-possibility-of' having this or that kind of experience. For example, without 'time' and 'space' I could not do any mathematical sum (see *Der transzendentalen Aesthetik* in: Kant, I. *Kritik Der Rheinen Vernunft*, pp. 66–94).

10 *Memento*; George Steiner in an interview with Joan Bakewell. Broadcast by UK Channel 4, 13 May 1993.

11 See Chapter 1.

12 We have seen in Chapter 1 how George Lakoff and Mark Johnson (1980) argue that metaphors not only structure our everyday language, but also our thoughts, attitudes, actions and *ontology*.

13 For example, philosopher Bertrand Russell has argued how '"Substance", in one word, is a metaphysical mistake due to the transference to the world's structure of the structure of sentences, composed of a subject and predicate' (Russell, 1970, pp. 196–7). A concept like 'substance' might be *linguistically* useful, but it does not tell us anything about what 'things are like in the world'. So, in Laika's case in Chapter 1, the structure of a sentence like 'Her mind is slow' makes us believe that there is this thing (mind) in the world that has a quality (slowness), and that this quality exists apart from the substance (mind). But in reality this is not the case.

14 See chapters 1 and 2 (e.g. how to use diffractive journals for assessment of learning).

15 See Barad, 2007.

16 Note that this is a different question from: 'There are so many opinions and beliefs about things, so who am I to decide what is true? (epistemological relativism).

17 For an excellent introduction to Aristotle's notion of *phronesis* see Joseph Dunne (1997).

18 Time is understood to be continuous and linear, which has split nature and culture (Barad, 2007, p. 231).

19 Barad has been influenced by Judith Butler's theory of performativity, but is also critical of her reinscribing matter 'as a passive product of discursive practices rather than as an active agent participating in the very process of materialization' (Barad, 2007, p. 151).

20 For a helpful basic explanation of the experiment: www.youtube.com/watch?v=Iuv6hY6zsd0

21 As we have seen earlier, with 'queer' Barad does not just mean 'strange', but it disrupts the nature/culture binary and is therefore an 'undoing of identity', because waves and particles are ontologically different entities. It raises the key question how is it possible that an electron can be both? See: www.youtube.com/watch?v= cS7szDFwXyg (accessed 21 February 2015).

22 The key question is: Is there some-thing, a bounded entity *before* it is measured? Interestingly, for Heisenberg the answer is about *uncertainty*, and for Bohr (and Barad) it is about *indeterminacy*.

23 The idea of 'flattened' (horizontal) as opposed to hierarchical (vertical) comes from John Frown (see: Hultman and Lenz Taguchi, 2010, p. 529).

24 The idea that knowledge is 'situated' is often used to argue for an inclusion of indigenous knowledge systems in curricula.

25 See: www.youtube.com/watch?v=W2zyOpv_SHo

26 See, e.g. www.youtube.com/watch?v=CrrSAc-vjG4. There is a salient difference between anthropomorphic humanist projection of consciousness onto nonhuman animals and plants and the dehumanisation of intelligence, agency and intentionality characteristic of posthumanism.

27 For more on diffraction see chapters 1 and 2.

28 For Hawking talking about how 'he' talks: www.youtube.com/watch?v= UErbwiJH1dI

29 See Chapter 4 for an explanation of my use of 'iii' instead of 'I'.

30 Corporal punishment is still a common practice in South African schools despite being illegal since 1996 (Murris, 2012, 2014b).

31 With thanks to Simon Geschwindt, who suggested this term to me. 'Earthlings' suggests the inclusion of nonhuman animals as, for example, in the drawing. 'Earth dwellers' is more 'horizontal' and includes, for example, roots, brittle stars and matter.

32 What I have 'brought' to my readings of relational materialism is my acquaintance and affinity for the ontology of German philosopher Martin Heidegger in his groundbreaking work *Sein und Zeit* (1927/1979). The profound contribution he has made to the history of ideas and the development of posthuman thought is the radical idea that *bodily existence* (being) and not the individual (beings) is ontologically prior (not to be confused with *chronologically* prior, that is, one thing preceding another in time and space) – that is, individuals always already find themselves surrounded by beings (including others). This shift in thinking has made the development of posthuman and other non-dualist relational pedagogies possible. Heidegger also argues that 'thinking' cannot be *defined*, since asking the question, 'what does it mean to think?' can be answered only by thinking (Heidegger, 1968, p. xii). We *are* thinking. Not this subject (mind) imprisoned in this object (body) is thinking *about* the world, but we are always already 'there', that is, *in* the world. *Dasein*, usually translated in English as 'being-there' 'replaces' the subject (mind) (Heidegger, 1927/1979, para. 2). Since *Dasein* is always thinking about its own thinking – an *activity* rather than a thing – it cannot take a detached (subject/object) view of itself (that would mean regarding itself as a thing). It is for this reason that thinking does not need external justification: it is not a means to other ends. Thinking is always *underway* (*Unterwegs*). For Heidegger the teacher–student relationship should be like that between master and apprentice in the medieval guilds – to let 'learning occur' (Heidegger, 1968, p. vi). What is salient for teaching and learning is that the 'in', in 'being-*in*-time' and 'being-*in*-space', is not understood in a *psychological* sense, but in an *ontological* sense. Psychological methods tend to rely on individuals accessing their experiences with the help of the senses and/or introspection. What is needed is a post-metaphysical beginning that acknowledges Being, not a metaphysics of indivi-dualised beings (Thomas and Thomson, 2015).

33 It is in this sense that I am also included in the 'readers' of my own writing. See also Chapter 2.

34 See in particular Chapter 4.

35 As, for example, the participation rights in the United Nations Convention of the Rights of the Child (www.unicef.org/crc/files/Participation.pdf, accessed 19 February 2015).

36 Although admittedly, children are seldom involved in knowledge *production*, only knowledge *consumption* in formal education.

37 See Hultman and Lenz Taguchi's (2010, pp. 528–9) helpful clarification of negative difference.

38 These questions benefitted from a Webinar presented by Denise Wood in 2014 as part of the NRF *Posthumanism and the Affective Turn* project, run by Vivienne Bozalek from the University of the Western Cape, and from an email exchange with Carmen Blyth on 21 February, 2015.

39 The distinction between the two analyses has greatly benefited from my discussions with colleagues in our weekly Posthumanism reading groups, and an article by Hultman and Lenz Taguchi (2010). See also Chapter 4.

40 It was Vivienne Bozalek who alerted me to this.

41 Their names are pseudonyms.

Chapter 4

Posthuman child

This particular chapter has been structured by an exploration of what child *is* (and is *not*) in the light of the ontoepistemology of the previous chapter. The new thoughts that emerged/are emerging in my diffractions with Karen Barad's (2007, 2014) relational materialism are to use the pronoun 'iii' to express subjectivity or 'bodymindmatter'. Instead of 'I' or even 'i', the proposition is to use the 'iii' as a continuous materialdiscursive reminder to challenge the binary discourses we inhabit in order to help open up alternative, non-dichotomous understandings of child subjectivity. Perhaps these neologisms can be the legs, mouths and ears my student was suggesting (see the diffractive pause on p. 64)?

Chris Jenks (2005, p. 3) also observes how 'child' appears still locked within binary reasoning. Unlike gender and race, child is not 'deconstructed into the post-structuralist space of multiple and self-presentational identity sets' (Jenks, 2005, p. 3). But the solution for me is not a poststructuralist or postmodernist one – a problem that can be solved at the level of discourse ('child-as-ii' as we will see below). My argument is for a relational materialist move from child-as-nature (the 'last savage'), or child-as-i, to child as 'inhuman-iii'. The following quote is a good summary of what this chapter sets out to achieve. Maria Kromidas explains the materialdiscursive, ontoepistemic turn beautifully:

> Rather than argue for extending the boundaries of the human to encompass those children presumably waiting at its gates, posthumanism encourages us to rethink the human itself through the child, and recuperate the human's remainder into a new vision of the human being in the world.
>
> Kromidas, 2014, pp. 426–7

Moreover, the new ideas in this chapter can be put to work on a series of photos made by a five-year-old at the occasion of his sister's wedding (see the diffractive pause in this chapter on p. 94). The photos can be explored from the perspective of child as 'i', 'I', 'ii' and 'iii' (including how each position assumes a different kind of observerteacherresearcher).

The scientific, cognitive child – child as 'i'

Broadly speaking there has been a shift in childhood studies from psychology of childhood, to sociology of childhood, to philosophy of childhood, although psychology is still the dominant discipline in early childhood education policies, practices and curriculum design globally (File, Basler Wisneski and Mueller, 2012). For example, Hatch (2012, p. 43), in her research of textbooks at teacher training institutions, shows how child development theory still strongly influences 'the materials, programs, and policies that drive the early childhood education mainstream'. The 'DAP brand', as she calls it, is carefully marketed by the American National Association for the Education of Young Children (NAEYC) and adopted by 'countless programs, policies and products in the US and around the globe' (Hatch, 2012, p. 43). 'DAP' stands for Developmental Appropriate Practice, and this developmental orientation is informed by a number of theories about physical and psychological development, including Piaget's theory of cognitive development and Gesell's theory of maturation (Linington, Excell and Murris, 2011). Piaget's '"genetic epistemology" seeks to provide a description of the structuring of thought' and constitutes 'a particular system of scientific rationality' that is both 'natural' and 'universal' (Jenks, 2005, p. 21).

Humans develop innately, according to general laws, through clearly identifiable stages of intellectual growth[1] that are 'chronologically ordered but also hierarchically arranged along a continuum from low status, infantile, "figurative thought" to high status, adult, "operative" intelligence' (Jenks, 2005, p. 22), unless a child has some abnormality (Dahlberg, Moss and Pence, 1999/2013, p. 49). Figurative thought is concrete and in the here and now, and young children struggle to abstract and transfer experience from one situation to another. Figurative thought is seen as childish (Jenks, 2005, p. 22) and underdeveloped. Each decentring stage of the individual child's intellectual growth is 'characterised by a specific "schema" or well-defined pattern and sequence of physical and mental actions governing the child's orientation to the world' (Jenks, 2005, p. 22).

Child's transformative process of 'decentring' from birth to adult is characterised by 'a change from solipsistic subjectivism to a realistic objectivity; a change from affective response to cognitive evaluation; and a movement from the disparate realm of value to the absolute realm of fact' (Jenks, 2005, p. 22). The child's maturation process and the project of genetic epistemology are completed when child's mind is scientific and rational, that is, capable of 'abstraction, generalization, logico-deductive process, mathematization and cognitive operations' (Jenks, 2005, p. 23).

Although not an educationalist, Piaget's influence on education has been, and still is, paramount, despite profound and continuous critique from many disciplinary quarters. As a result, teaching has become a process that should proceed from the simple to the complex, from the particular to the general, from the concrete to the abstract and from the empirical to the rational (Egan and Ling, 2002, p. 94).[2] The developmental 'milestones' children need to reach before they are 'ready' for the next stage informs DAP, which focuses on what is known by experts other than the child about their developmental needs, interests, strengths and abilities (Linington, Excell and Murris, 2011). The metaphor is that of the individual 'child-becoming-adult' climbing a ladder, accomplishing successive stages or milestones (rungs on the ladder) with increasing autonomy (Dahlberg, Moss and Pence, 2013, p. 48). I touch upon some major concerns about this theoretical position, before exploring the social child.

Critique of developmentalism

Piaget's influential theory is a prime example of what is called *developmentalism*, which has its grounding in the Aristotelian idea (Stables, 2008) that the individual child's mind/psyche (and body) is in a process of being formed (Cregan and Cuthbert, 2014, p. 10) according to its innate potential: in the same way that an acorn flourishes (*eudomonia*) when it becomes an oak tree. Major concern has been expressed about the conceptual confusion that occurs when these natural metaphors are applied to humans and education: the mind is understood as if it were a physical body (see Chapter 1) that grows 'naturally' and matures in stages (Murris, 1997; Egan, 2002, pp. 79–82). Multidisciplinary critique of developmentalism can be summarised under the following headings: lack of methodological validity, a normative process, complexity reduction, preparation for a capitalist economical workforce, evolutionary bias and otherising child. We will look at each in turn.

Lack of methodological validity

Much effort by psychologists has been put into reinterpreting Piaget's conclusions drawn from psychological experiments. Margaret Donaldson argues that it is not his findings that are suspect, but that the conclusions drawn from those findings are wrong (Donaldson, 1978, p. 23). For example, in an attempt to demonstrate how egocentric children are, Piaget conducted an experiment to show that children in the foundation phase (under the age of eight) do not have the ability to take account of someone else's point of view – literally. In his experiment, a child sits at a table with three different mountains on it. A doll is placed somewhere else round the table. Most children cannot describe what the doll sees. Donaldson contests Piaget's conclusion that children are 'unable to "decentre" in imagination' (Donaldson, 1978, p. 20), which is a crucial requirement for rational thinking and reasoning. This is because if a child cannot shift between different points of view, s/he cannot make valid inferences (Donaldson, 1978, p. 41). Empirical evidence for rejecting the conclusion of this experiment has been given by constructing similar experiments, but in situations that make sense to the child (Donaldson, 1978, p. 23; Sutherland, 1992, p. 15).

A normative process

Canadian educationalist Kieran Egan points out another problem with conceiving of development as a largely linear process 'of increasing differentiation that recognizes no losses attached to cognitive gains . . .' (Egan, 2002, p. 105). He argues that it is not clear to what extent this biological model is *descriptive* or *prescriptive*, that is, 'when someone describes "the developmental process", we have to ask how far they are giving us an account of some natural, spontaneous process or how far they are describing a process shaped by our previous educational prescriptions' (Egan, 2002, pp. 79–80). So the argument is this: even if it were true that children's minds develop, grow and mature like a physical thing in the world, it still needs to be argued that developmentalism is indeed desirable as an *educational theory*, especially because the implications for practice in the early years are profound – the metaphor shapes how educators perceive children as thinkers (Murris, 1997), how they regard the purpose of play and how they theorise their role as pedagogues generally (as either empiricist or nativist educators).

Complexity and diversity reduction

The scientific, biological child is not only 'cut up' into different stages through which s/he develops, but this development itself is 'cut up' into, for example, the social, the cognitive, the emotional, the moral and the physical, with each separate category having its own development (so a child can be in a pre-operational stage for his/her emotional development and in a concrete operational stage for his/her cognitive development). This development can be measured, thereby 'isolating complex processes and viewing them dichotomously' (Dahlberg, Moss and Pence, 2013, p. 49). This 'complexity and diversity reduction' does not respect otherness, and turns 'the Other into the Same (Moss, 2014, p. 42). For posthumanists, binary thinking about child misses important knowledges (Jackson and Mazzei, 2012, p. 114).[3]

Interestingly, for anthropologist Maria Kromidas, these comparisons between child and adult 'savage' (historically or geographically) do not hold any longer: 'even' racialised Others and women are now theorised as 'fully-human', therefore only animals and children remain (Kromidas, 2014, p. 426). Child as not fully-formed-human and developing is evident in biomedical and bio-psychosocial approaches to early childhood education (e.g. their focus on age, weight charts, language, gross and fine motor skills) (Cregan and Cuthbert, 2014, p. 10). However, all developmentalists are Cartesian dualists, so the mind/psyche/intellect is regarded as having priority over the body, although both child's mind *and* body are object of observation and surveillance (Dahlberg and Moss, 2005).

The unquestioned assumption in developmental theories is that the goal of the process is maturity – each stage is followed by one that is 'better', more 'mature'. This is what philosopher of childhood Gareth Matthews calls 'evolutionary bias' (Matthews, 1994, p. 17). Developmentalism is a *recapitulation theory*: child's intellectual development is compared to ('recapitulates') the development of the species (with the child as nature, as the origin of the species') from 'savage' to 'civilised'. Developmentalism and empiricist, or nativist or interactionist pedagogies go hand in hand. They all assume the nature/culture dichotomy, in that child's mind (nature) has to be 'filled' by culture (e.g. knowledge and information) according to the empiricist educator, or 'allowed to unfold', according to the nativist educator, or 'interacted with', according to the interactionist educator. Importantly, an underlying philosophical assumption of Piagetian theory is that children's thinking will develop automatically as they get older. An attempt to hasten this process is simply a waste of time – perhaps even an educational malpractice (Gazzard, 1985, p. 11). But as Matthews points out, the *philosophical child* is not the scientific, cognitive child. Having more knowledge is not always an advantage when doing philosophy with children, for example. The better handling of philosophical questioning is not guaranteed by simply growing up and/or by knowing more. Maturity, Matthews argues, often brings 'staleness' or 'uninventiveness' to the exploration of philosophical ideas, whereas children are often 'fresh and inventive thinkers' (Matthews, 1994, p. 18).

Each generation has to find its own answers to philosophical questions (Van der Leeuw, 1991, p. 13); therefore philosophy as a discipline has something to learn from children doing philosophy (Matthews, 1994; Murris, 1997; Kohan, 2002, 2015; Kennedy, 2006; Haynes, 2008; Haynes and Murris, 2012). Academic philosophy, for Matthews, is the epistemological pursuit of 'starting all over again', that is, finding out for myself '. . . that I really do not know whatever it is I claim to know' (Matthews, 1994, p. 18). For philosophy with children pioneer, Matthew Lipman (1993, p. 141), making space for philosophy of childhood as a legitimate field of academic philosophy might help adult philosophers acknowledge the significant role the philosophical beliefs they held as children shaped their adult philosophies. One necessary condition for a philosophical being-in-the-world-with-others is the abandonment of cherished beliefs and assumptions, something that is much harder for older people, whose beliefs often have become firmly fossilised habits of thought (Murris, 2000).

Otherising child

Gareth Matthews (1994) argues that the universalising tendency of Western developmental psychology encourages educators to 'distance' themselves – 'both from the children around us and from our own childhood selves' (Matthews, 1994, p. 66). Such distancing often leads to 'condescension', which Matthews argues is 'morally offensive' (Matthews, 1994, p. 67). He suggests that teachers should engage with *individual* children as rational, active, collaborative participants in knowledge construction, as their 'simple directness' often 'brings us back to basics' (Matthews, 1994, p. 67). Generalising about children's abilities fails to do justice to the capacities of individual children, especially their imaginative meaning-making capabilities when philosophising (Murris, 1997; Haynes and Murris, 2013; Haynes, 2014).

The developmentalist holds the scientific, cognitive child at a distance. Child is seen as an *object* of research, to be 'measured, compared, controlled and actively formed' (Cregan and Cuthbert, 2014, p. 11). In other words, child is positioned as an indivi-dual, an 'i', like the adult researchers that measure them (but they themselves are not an 'i', but an 'I' – a fully-formed-human). Child is a self-contained, bounded object of study – the not fully-human subject of humanism. Kromidas (2014, p 429) warns that when developmentalism is combined with neuroscience the child is doubly disadvantaged as not-yet-human, for example, when a particular stage of childhood is determined by a hormonal surge. When children are treated as 'i', teaching or research is 'paternalistic' (Christensen and Prout, 2002, p. 480). The child is regarded as *passive* – a person acted upon by others, rather than a subject acting in the world. Children are seen as dependent on others and are not social persons in their own right. So, as a teacher working with children, any research that assumes a child subject as 'i' will involve the perspectives of adults (parents, carers) and not necessarily the views of the child (Christensen and Prout, 2002, p. 480).

The child with human rights – child as 'I'

A 'quantum leap' in the contemporary construction of the normative global child has been the adoption of the United Nations Convention on the Rights of the Child (UNCRC) in 1989 (Cregan and Cuthbert, 2014, p. 56). Articles 12 and 13 include respect for the views of the child and their right of freedom of expression. This includes child's freedom to speak and to receive and impart information and ideas of all kinds 'in any way they choose, including by talking, drawing or writing'. Article 14 stipulates children's freedom of thought, conscience and religion: 'Children have the right to think and believe what they want'.[4] The Convention is ratified by all countries except Somalia and the United States, and articulates childhood as a phase of life that requires special provision and protection. The kind of rights assigned to children was previously reserved for adults only.

The UNCRC is not without its critics. For some, it does not go far enough as it is still developmental;[5] the Convention assumes the 'not-yet-fully-developed responsibility for those under 18', but with civic and political dimensions now added to the understanding of child and childhood (Cregan and Cuthbert, 2014, pp. 6, 17). Despite its contradictory, universalist stance, the UNCRC is often praised for helping to enculturate respect for child as competent, elevating child's status to a liberal rights-bearing individual. The Convention states explicitly that 'the end goal of childhood is the formation of an adult citizen competent and capable of living individually and contributing productively to a Western-style liberal democracy' (Cregan and Cuthbert, 2014, p. 17). Kantian traces are clearly visible. The adult is the accepted valued norm, and child therefore as a lesser, still maturing, adult-in-the-making: childish, less competent, and less useful – the ultimate 'Other'. 'Immaturity' becomes synonymous with childhood (Jones, 2009, p. 39).

At the same time, the Convention advances a normative version of child as having rights 'not as proto-adults or as the property of parents' (Jones, 2009, p. 6), and also claims respect for cultural and other diversity (a clear contradiction here with the universalist claims of the UNCRC). However, it is to be welcomed that the UNCRC positions child more as leaning towards that end of a continuum that regards child as 'capable, active, visible, powerful, valued and attended to in the present, an individual with their own capacities' than at the other end of the continuum that regards child as 'incapable, passive, invisible, vulnerable and needy, seen and attended to as an investment for the future, a mini-adult lacking in full adult capacities' (Jones, 2009, p. 29). So, another way of putting this is that the relative emancipatory progress made with the UNCRC is a move from 'child-as-i' to 'child-as-I' (even if in spirit). One could argue that child is positioned as an agent with power (e.g. participation rights) and an increased equality between the status and authority of parents and children, even though in practice adults are pivotal in how these rights are interpreted and whether children can exercise them. Marg Sellers (2013, p. 74) argues that attributing rights assumes 'expert-adult knowledge of children's needs and desires . . . there is an underlying assumption of a conceptual vulnerability that exacerbates inequitable, inferior positioning in both family and society'. Some are indeed sceptical of endowing children with rights that are so dependent on others for their execution, as well as dependent on variables such as age, capacities, language and access to resources (Cregan and Cuthbert, 2014, p. 56).

It does not come as a surprise that implementing and incorporating these changing ideas about child in practice is difficult, especially in families and societies that are patriarchal (Jones, 2009, p. 7). Attaching rights to individual human beings is 'both ethnocentric and morally imperialistic' (Cregan and Cuthbert, 2014, p. 15), as not all nations conceptualise citizens in such an anthropocentric and humanist manner: assigning rights that are attached to individual human beings. Relevant for us working and living in Africa is the African Charter on the Rights and Welfare of the Child (ACRWC, 1990) – a critical response to the cultural bias of the UNCRC (Cregan and Cuthbert, 2014, pp. 69–70). Article 31 of the Charter has added the responsibilities African children have towards their parents and communities in return for the rights they have been assigned (something the UNCRC does not do). Children's freedom in Africa is 'balanced' by making explicit that children need to respect their 'parents, superiors and elders at all times and to assist them in case of need', serve national and international communities, and 'preserve and strengthen African cultural values . . . in the spirit of tolerance, dialogue and consultation'.[6] Although the ACRWC might be valued as a situated response to the imperialist imposition of a Western (indoor) child as the global norm, the possible conservative interpretation of the Charter significantly reduces the political gains made on behalf of children worldwide. My experiences in teaching ethics to large groups of student teachers at two different African universities suggest that – for my sample of South Africans at least – 'respect' means 'obedience' (Murris, 2012). Applied to education, such an interpretation of respect means a continuation of the current *status quo* whereby teaching is authoritarian and corporal punishment is, albeit against the law, frequently justified as being 'part of black culture', thereby confusing moral values with cultural values (Murris, 2014).

The individualistic nature of the UNCRC is also of concern to post-humanists, but not because child needs to be put back in its place in a hierarchical universe. As we have seen, for posthumanists in a monist universe all earth dwellers – mutually entangled and always becoming, are always intra-acting with everything else (Barad, 2007). Posthuman child *is* relational. There is no prior existence of individuals with properties, competencies, a voice, agency, etc.[7] Individuals materialise and come into being through relationships; and so does meaning. There is ontological, as well as epistemological equality between species and between different members of each species.

Social constructionists, linguistic constructionists, poststructuralists and postmodernists are also critical of any childhood theory that assumes a Western individualised child as norm – a child that is positioned as competent, autonomous and strong and in the process of *becoming adult*.[8] The problem, they say, is that it decontextualises children from their socio-economic, linguistic, cultural and historical environments. Child is not an 'I', but an 'ii'.

The social child – child as 'ii'

The key idea of the social child is that of society's influence and the interactions with others on the formation of self and identity, drawing in particular on early sociologists James, Cooley and G.H. Mead (Cregan and Cuthbert, 2014, p. 12). Like developmental psychology, early expressions of this theoretical model were more concerned about socialisation as a process of child becoming (the better socialised) adult, without regard for child as social agent (Cregan and Cuthbert, 2014, p. 12). It was not until the late 1970s that sociologists and anthropologists started to ask questions about the dominant empirical positivist research in early childhood education; research methods were descriptive, focusing on truth and what *is*, rather than what *ought* to be (Bloch, Swadener and Cannella, 2014). A growing number of scholars expressed concern about the dominant positioning of child as object of cognitive science, and started to critique developmentalism as reductionist from a sociological perspective (Jenks, 1982; Walkerdine, 1984; James, Jenks and Prout, 1998). Developmental psychology, they argued, ignored the role of political, economic and social power relations and the politics of cultural, racial and gendered identities, inclusions and exclusions (Dahlberg, Moss and Pence, 1999/2013; Moss and Dahlberg, 2005). Questions were also raised about the way developmental psychology and hegemonic notions of child development were used for curriculum construction (Nolan and Kilderry, 2010; File, Basler Wisneski and Mueller, 2012).

For postmodernists Gunilla Dahlberg and Peter Moss, developmentalism is 'a narrative game' played in early childhood education; but 'those within such narratives often cannot see them for what they are – stories' (Dahlberg and Moss, 2005, p. 166). Developmentalism is a story that uses scientific knowledge to tell so-called universal truths about children. The psychological stages through which children develop are articulated in these theories, but they ignore the social cultural contexts in which children live. Postmodernists view child as *decentred*, that is, existing through his or her relationships with others and always in particular contexts. 'The child' or 'childhood' does not exist, because 'there are many children and many childhoods' (Dahlberg, Moss and Pence, 1999/2013, p. 46). Of course, Philippe Aries' seminal work from 1962 (*Centuries of Childhood: A Social History of Family Life*) was a significant marker in disrupting biological imaginings of child and childhood by proposing that childhood is a social and cultural invention, which has been a major influence on sociologists of childhood. So, for example, Leena Alanen's (1988) groundbreaking work in rethinking childhood was a major inspiration for a sociology of childhood that can be characterised as regarding childhood as a social construction, childhood as a variable of social analysis, that children's culture and social relationships need to be taken into account in research and lastly, that children are active agents with a voice of their own (Dahlberg, Moss and Pence, 1999/2013, pp. 52–54; Cregan and Cuthbert, 2014, p. 12). The claim that is made is that although childhood is 'a biological fact, the way in which it is understood is socially determined' (Dahlberg, Moss and Pence, 1999/2013, p. 52). Children are not just passive, not just child as 'becoming adult' (with the adult the active agent), but a 'being child'. Currently the theorising in sociology of childhood has shifted even further in that both child and adult are now seen as always in a state of 'being *and* becoming'. Kate Cregan and Denise Cuthbert explain:

> That is, children have an experiential reality 'in the moment' of childhood that is a valid site of agency (and object of study) and they are also aware of and can articulate their experience as a state of progression to a future self.
>
> Cregan and Cuthbert, 2014, p. 13

Expressions of such agency in the global South, they argue, include a child deciding to be involved in armed conflict, or taking paid labour to support a family whilst attending school.

On the whole, the focus of early childhood researchers has shifted to matters of discourse and language (with Burman's deconstruction of developmental psychology as a powerful example), from the psychological to the social, the political and the cultural. Qualitative, ethnographic research methods and critical discourse analysis have become more common in the field (Bloch, Swadener and Cannella, 2014).

The concept 'child' became increasingly researched using feminist, poststructuralist, postcolonial and postmodernist lenses focusing on how the binary categories female/male, black/white, poor/rich, etc. marginalise and exclude. The idea started to take root that childhood (like race) is a social construct (social constructionism) – currently a pervasive theoretical lens in the context of race in postcolonial South Africa.

Critique of social constructionism

Referring to Prout, Affrica Taylor (2013, p.xviii) warns against regarding childhood as a cultural and social construction and as a semiotic autonomous system, because *social constructionism* then runs the risk of becoming a 'reverse discourse', replacing nature for culture (society), and thereby repeating modernist dualisms.

The oft-made and rarely questioned assumption that childhood is a social construction is an expression of a humanist perspective with profound implications for our practices in early childhood education (e.g. combatting gender and racial stereotyping by restricting children's access to certain stories (see Chapter 10). Philosopher David Archard (2004) would agree with Taylor; he argues that it would be a simplification to claim that childhood is a social construction – a concept that can be deconstructed and reconstructed – even though childhood has been understood in different ways across cultures and different historical periods. Influenced by political philosopher John Rawls, Archard makes a helpful distinction between *concept* and *conception* (Archard, 2004, pp. 27–31). He argues that the concept of childhood is necessarily linked to that of adulthood: childhood as the absence of adulthood. It is also necessarily linked to age – 'children are young human beings' (Archard, 2004, p. 29).

What is salient in his argument is that whether we believe that children's development involves progress, for example, from wild savage to mature scientist, or whether it can be characterised as a gradual demise of imaginative, metaphorical, embodied and original thinking (Egan, 1988, 1991, 1992, 1993, 1995, 1997), these theories depend on one's *conception* of childhood. Moreover, for Archard, childhood is *also* a biological phenomenon, but biology that is not understood as a set of facts, immutable across time and space. They are not merely brute facts of the given, but 'represent the claims of particular scientific discourses' and 'social, political, geographical, and economical factors have caused the construction of "immaturity"', i.e. 'a child's physical nature relative to adults' (Archard, 2004, p. 26). So, all societies have a *concept* of childhood, but their *conceptions* differ, according to the extent (when does it finish?), its nature (what exactly constitutes the difference between child and adult?) and the significance adults attach to these differences (Matthews, 1994; Archard, 2004, pp. 28–31). In Archard's critique, however, there is no theoretical space for the body that child also *is*, and the agency of the material world child is also part of.

The idea that childhood is a social construction is symptomatic of the 'linguistic turn'. Barad argues that 'matters of "fact" (so to speak) have been replaced with matters of signification' (Barad, 2007, p. 132). Language has been granted too much power. The power of language has not only been substantial, but also 'substantializing', allowing linguistic structure to determine our understanding of the world (Barad, 2007, p. 133). Barad explains:

> Language has been granted too much power. The linguistic turn, the semiotic turn, the interpretative turn, the cultural turn: it seems that every turn lately every 'thing' – even materiality – is turned into a matter of language or some other form of cultural representation.

Posthumanism breaks with the assumption that there is no direct 'access' to child, that child is not *present*, and can only be *re-presented*. Unwittingly child is still objectified in social constructionist approaches, that is, positioned on the 'other' side (on the right hand side of Figure 4.1 below) as object or subject

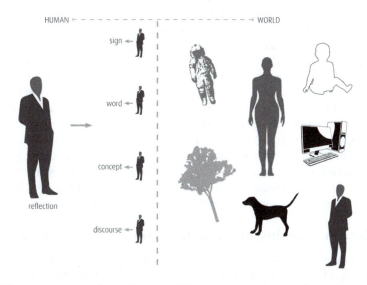

Figure 4.1 The representationalism of humanist Western metaphysics, by Conor Ralphs.

of study and mediated more or less successfully through language or other means of representation that are seen to determine what is real.

The materiality of child (child as *part* of the world) is seen not to matter (enough) in meaning-making. The new ethicoontoepistemology of post-humanism exposes how sociological approaches to childhood study are also humanist (and thereby Cartesian dualist). In contrast, the posthuman child is also the material child, the body that child not just 'has', but also *is*.

Since the 1980s, various poststructuralist thinkers and postcolonial theorists have drawn attention to the significance of power differentials in (childhood) education. Concerns about gender, race, class, 'et cetera' are now routinely interwoven into foci for educational research and teaching. But there are risks attached to paying so much attention to the binaries that exclude (usually race, class and gender in South Africa, in that order). Ironically, an emphasis on such binaries can reinforce children's use of them, and thereby possibly increase their discriminatory force (as I will exemplify in Chapter 10). It is of concern that the category 'age' is not often listed among lists of power differentials commonly used in academia and public discourse and amongst the 'et ceteras' above (see Chapter 6). It is an interesting exercise to think about the 'et ceteras', and what they might or not include, and why. Not many would disagree about 'disability' or 'ethnicity' as an 'et cetera'. But what about 'nonhuman animals, or non-'living' things, or 'child'? Poststructuralist and postcolonial theories are clearly humanist, in that regulatory regimes or social structures are human made. Visually expressed in Figure 4.1, the metaphysical dividing line, that is, the structures (language, signs, discourses) produce the subject. So the arrow is not from subject to the right, pointing to reality, but there is an arrow from the dividing line back to the subject, and *the metaphysical dividing line itself is a human construct*. For poststructuralists words have meaning as a result of a *shared value* that is *constructed* through shared language (Jackson and Mazzei, 2012, p. 70). For relational materialists matter does not matter (enough) in this picture (that is, in Figure 4.1). For example, showing a *photo* of a pile of shoes that belonged to Jews in a concentration camp has a different force, tells a very different story than merely mentioning the *number* of Jews killed in the camp.[9] Signs matter, but signs themselves are *also* and *always* made of (but not reduced to) matter, and their particular matter has implications for meaning. Hence the posthuman choice of 'materialdiscursive' or 'materialsemiotic'. Susan Hekman (2010, p. 22) argues that postmodernists, or 'linguistic constructionists', also have not fully deconstructed the language/reality dichotomy. Language for them constructs not only the social world, but also the natural world: 'We humans, in short, are the creators of all we survey' (Hekman, 2010, p. 1). The method of deconstruction is a good example of linguistic constructionism.

Deconstructing adult as transcendental signifier

In Chapter 3 we have seen how the phrase 'this is *not* a child' is not only about disrupting the logic of representation, but also what Deleuze calls *negative* difference. This is the idea that a concept such as 'child' has meaning, because of what it is *not*, that is, 'adult'. 'Adult' and 'child' are what philosopher of childhood David Kennedy calls a 'mutually necessary contrastive pair', 'child' is unthinkable without 'adult' and vice versa (Kennedy, 2000, pp. 215–16). So, in other words, the system of signifiers in language brings into existence child subjectivity; therefore child subjectivity is an *effect* of language. This negative difference relies on something always out of reach, and here *deficit* models of child and childhood emerge: child is still developing, is not complete, and is unfinished and immature. Child is compared to adult, with the latter as the 'transcendental signifier' (Hultman and Lenz Taguchi, 2010, p. 529): mature, developed and complete. Importantly, difference is associated with atomistic indivi-duals moving (as substances) through space and time.

Deconstructing adult as transcendental signifier, Kennedy (like Braidotti) argues how the self is multiple, nomadic, without one singular stable identity or being firmly located geographically, historically, ethnically, or fixed by a particular class structure. Braidotti also proposes a 'nomadic subject' that is continuously 'becoming' – a corporeal entity that has spatio-temporal force, that is, embedded and embodied, and therefore immanent and dynamic (Braidotti, 2006, pp. 151–2; Braidotti, 2013). As we will see in Chapter 8, the nomadic subject is also an 'epistemological orphan' (Braidotti, 1991, p. 2) – there are no longer epistemological or ontological Fathers (read: Descartes) to turn to. The key idea here is that self is not 'subject-as-substance', but always 'subject-in-process', and always produced involving contradiction (and diffractions). Crucially, this means that in a sense 'adult has become child . . . a being who is incomplete, always on-the-way, who is never finished developing' (Kennedy, 2006, p. 10). The implication of understanding subject-as-always-in-process for adult: child relationships is that child becomes a 'fellow traveller' rather than being treated as a 'future-worker-consumer-citizen' (Kennedy, 2006, p. 11). Similarly, for Argentinian philosopher of childhood, Walter Kohan, childhood is not just a period in a human life, but also a particular relationship with and experience of time (*aion*) – as associated with play and power (as in empowerment, not power over), and in this respect adults can learn much from children (Kennedy, 2006, pp. 11–12; Kohan, 2015). Kohan argues that each conception of childhood presupposes a particular concept of time. So, childhood conceptualised as the period of time at the start of a person's life presupposes a quantitative chronological concept of time (*chronos*). By contrast, *aion* 'designates the intensity of time in human life – a destiny, a duration, an un-numbered movement, not successive, but intensive' – a particularly forceful and intense experience of being in time: childlike (Kohan, 2015, p. 57). As such, the concept 'child' shifts from noun to verb, something all of us can do: to child (Kennedy and Kohan, 2008).

But transformational agendas that focus on deconstructing concepts suggest a self that can remove itself meta-cognitively and *reflect* on its linguistic self; and this assumes that emancipation and educational change can be brought about (mainly) by challenging the discourses people inhabit. Despite being a major inspiration for relational materialism, even postmodernists and poststructuralists are trapped in the binaries contained in the language we speak and think with, and the humanist discourses we inhabit. In a sense, even in postmodernism, the material world has been reduced to the social. By the same token (with the nature/culture binary as mechanism), science studies have reduced the social world to the material. Even 'child' has become a re-presentation in social constructionist approaches to childhood. The act of representing is an act of mediation between knower and known, that displays for Barad 'a deep mistrust of matter, holding it off at a distance' (Barad, 2007, p. 133).

Posthuman child – child as 'iii'

The natureculture orientation of Karen Barad's posthumanism challenges the idea that language can represent pre-existing things (including 'child' or 'childhood'). Thinking, observing and theorising about child are 'practices of engagement with, and as part of, the world in which we have our being' (Barad, 2007, p. 133). Approaches to childhood education that focus on *discourses* only about child ignore how 'matter matters' (Barad, 2007, pp. 132–85). The idea of *denaturalising* childhood is linked to the 'linguistic turn' in the history of ideas (Taylor, 2013). A further shift in theorising child and childhood is the contemporary 'material turn' that attributes agency (also) to the material world (Barad, 2007; Bennett, 2010; Hekman, 2010; Braidotti, 2013; Snaza and Weaver, 2015), and that problematises all binary opposites, including the theory/practice (Lenz Taguchi, 2010), child/adult (Semetsky, 2006), animal/human (Pedersen, 2013; Miller, 2015) and nature/culture (Taylor, 2013; Rotas, 2015) divides. Posthumanism enables a re-evaluation of child as competent meaning-maker. It does this through an explicit monistic ontoepistemology.

As we have seen in Chapter 3, posthumanism, or 'relational materialism', profoundly democratises the 'playing field' in many directions – nothing is considered to stand 'outside', 'above' or take a true privileged transcendental position. It understands the human body as an unbounded organism that exists in an entangled network of human and nonhuman forces. Diffracting with philosopher of science Andrew Pickering, Susan Hekman proposes the term 'mangle realism' (Hekman, 2010, p. 23) to describe a posthumanist world full of material agency: an agency of matter that cannot be reduced to the agency of humans and subverts the human/nonhuman distinction and correspondence theories of truth.[10] Mangle is both a noun (the entity without clear boundaries) and a verb (the action) (Hekman, 2010, pp. 24–5). Although human made, machines (e.g. cameras, video recorders) are also part of what Hekman refers to as the mangle.[11] They structure the outcomes of educational research and play a key role in creation of scientific reality, also accepting that this reality is always socio-political (Hekman, 2010, p. 24). Posthumanism[12] opens up a very different kind of 'being' and 'knowing'. Here we investigate the implications of this ontoepistemology for child subjectivity: What *is* posthuman child?

Posthumanism is critical of the human-centredness of what has gone on 'before' – at the same time acknowledging that humans inhabit humanist discourses that cannot be got rid of, other than through the continuous use of neologisms (e.g. 'intra-action') or the bringing of new meanings to existing concepts (e.g. 'agency'). It is for this reason that I will introduce my neologism 'iii' instead of 'I'. Queering[13] 'I' with 'iii' foregrounds child subjectivity as 'bodymindmatter' – an 'iii' that is *part* of the world, not 'in' it as an object 'in' space and time. The neologism should serve as a continuous materialdiscursive challenge to the binary discourses we inhabit, and aims to open up alternative, non-dichotomous understandings of child. Using different shades of grey and black for printing 'iii' indicates that a self is not a bounded singular organism, and that a posthuman analysis is not the same as simply adding the material to the discursive (adding 'i' to 'ii' = 'iii', but not 'iii'). After all, the relational ontologies of the linguistic turn still assume humanist binaries. The human is in charge of knowledge production and meaning making through language and discourses (see Figure 4.1). A posthuman ontoepistemology disrupts this human-centredness (expressed through a dispersed, indeterminate 'iii'[14]) and re-presentation is no longer possible – no 'god trick of seeing everything from nowhere' (see Chapter 3; Haraway, 1988, p. 581). The empirical findings of quantum physics create new decolonising possibilities for conceptualising child subjectivity, including what it means to know 'child' and how to understand, observe, listen to and relate 'to' young children. Child is an entanglement; constituted by concepts *and* material forces, where the social, the political, the biological, and its observing, measuring and controlling machines are interwoven and entwined – all elements intra-act and in the process 'lose' their clear boundaries. Each element has agentic force and regarding child as a mangle opens up possibilities to include a much wider selection of causal factors for understanding what is going on in an educational encounter. So, child *is* an unbounded mangle – an inhuman materialdiscursive becoming 'iii'.

Barad, who only 'relatively recently dared to speak about this publicly', proposes 'inhuman' – 'as an infinite intimacy that touches the very nature of touch, that which holds open the space of the liveliness of indeterminacies that bleed through the cuts and inhabit the between of particular entanglements' (Barad, 2012, p. 34). Describing child as such is not an attempt at a definition; that is not the objective of this chapter. To define, MacLure (2013, p. 661) points out, is 'to return to the logic of representation, where words "refer" to entities as if they were separate and distinct from one another'.

Relations, not relata

For relational materialists, the ontological and epistemological starting points for theorising are the *relations* 'between' individuals and nonhuman others, not the *relata*. Relations are always materialdiscursive and *constitute* the individual – not the other way round. Ontologically prior to indivi-duals are the *processes of individuation* (Mercon and Armstrong, 2011, p. 252). The monism of 17th-century Dutch philosopher Baruch Spinoza (1632–1677) continues to be an inspiration for many contemporary posthumanists, including Deleuze and Guattari (see in particular Deleuze, 1970/1988), especially as an alternative to Rene Descartes' much more influential dualism in modernity. Recall how for Descartes the body and mind are entirely different substances – for Spinoza they are one and the same thing. Relational materialist Jane Bennett (2010, p. 2) describes how, for Spinoza, human *and* nonhuman bodies have 'a peculiar vitality' or 'conatus' – a power present in every body. Quoting Spinoza, she explains how 'Each thing [*res*], as far as it can by its own power, strives [*conatur*] to persevere in its own being' (Bennett, 2010, p. 2). In that sense, all things (including the human body) are equal, and therefore form an ontological *continuum*, not a difference of *kind*. Although for Spinoza (like Descartes a rationalist) human beings strive to live by the guidance of reason, *all* things have vitality and are able to persist in existing 'with the same force whereby it began to exist'; for Spinoza even a falling stone strives to continue its motion (Bennett, 2010, p. 2). Spinoza's main inspiration for posthumanism is the monist idea that not only human bodies, but also their minds, are *part* of nature, not in control of it, or in command of it (through culture), so characteristic of the anthropocentrism of humanism (and developmentalism). As we have seen, the humanist assumes that the transcendental positioning of the human subject has epistemic and other kinds of power over all nonhuman things, including nonhuman animals. Posthumanism offers a creative alternative to regarding children as objects of study, and frees childhood education from the normativity of objectifying and essentialising children as indivi-dual objects in the world.

'iii' – 'just like a new pair of shoes'

Posthumanism has given new meanings to existing terms, such as 'diffraction', 'matter', 'meaning', 'agency', 'knowing', 'being', 'cause', 'intentionality', 'realism'. We have also seen how neologisms are constructed to do justice to a new ontoepistemology, such as 'intra-action' and 'agential realism'. Finally, there are also certain concepts that have become problematic or confusing as they express the wrong hierarchical (transcendental) ontology. Therefore, discussions about the right meaning of words are not just a matter of semantics,[15] but a matter of ethics and politics. To be more precise, they are a matter of *justice*, because the Western ontology mapped out in the previous chapter is embedded in the languages and discriminatory discourses we inhabit; they are never innocent. Classical humanist ontology assumes a clearly bounded indivi-dualised subject in space and time, that is, the 'I' capable of constructing knowledge *of* the world through representational systems the 'I' has put in place: the languages of the sciences, everyday languages, etc. (see Figure 3.2 in Chapter 3).

For philosophers Gilles Deleuze and Felix Guattari, everything in our thinking flows from the habit of saying 'I'. The self is named and cut apart from other selves and things (Lenz Taguchi, 2010, p. 57). The not 'I' is in opposition, different *from* the 'I' that has not only been cut apart from other animals and things, but an 'I' that has also been put *above* nonhuman others celebrating a higher ontological status (e.g. *homo ludens*, *homo faber* or *homo rationalis*). This 'I' is *normative* and also includes or excludes the other 'I's – a distancing or cutting apart from the 'other' human that is not 'fully' formed or developed (as yet) – the 'I' who is 'disabled', 'female', 'child', 'black', 'poor'.

The use of the capital word 'I' as a pronoun to describe 'me', 'self', the 'subject' does not do *justice* to an ontology that assumes that there are 'no individual independently existing entities or agents that pre-exist their acting upon one another' (Barad, 2012, p. 77). Barad explains: 'individuals do not preexist as such but rather materialize in intra-action'. It is the entangled *relationships* that materialise individuals. One of the challenges is to innovate and to find new ways of expressing this different subjectivity linguistically. So the question has become: how can a new language express best the ontological inclusion of the material and materiality of a posthuman subjectivity that also includes the excluded and marginalised?

It is for this reason that the neologism 'iii' has been introduced in this chapter. The pronoun 'iii' does justice to an ethicoontoepistemology that attributes equal status to the other (the second 'i' or 'ii')[16]. The 'other' also includes 'the sexualized other (woman), the racialized other (the native) and the naturalized other (animals, the environment, or earth)' (Braidotti, 2013, p. 27). Although not explicitly mentioned by Braidotti, I take the 'naturalized other' to include the developing, thereby 'less than fully-human', child and the material world (the third 'i' of 'it'). The 'it' that 'I' also *am*, 'this' being 'amongst' other beings *is* a body with 'fluid' boundaries – a body that is part of the world and not 'in' space or time, but always emerges 'in' relation (spacetime). 'I' am 'bodymindmatter', or, 'iii'. What is needed to 'overcome' humanism is not another theory, but literally an '*approach* . . . a different attitude or philosophical *ethos*', an experimental '*transgression*' (Foucault referred to and quoted in Biesta, 2006, p. 41). Biesta explains what is at stake: 'the development of *different* ways of 'being, doing or thinking what we are, do, or think' (Biesta, 2006, p. 41).

The use of the posthuman 'iii' is a proposal to help bring about a different way of being, doing and thinking. Its use 'might chafe at first, just like a new pair of shoes' (Lenz Taguchi, 2010, p. 64). Living without bodily 'borders' or 'boundaries', 'the' 'iii' as quantum entanglement is not a 'new' unity but it is like 'a' sea that as a 'unit' troubles the very nature of one-ness, two-ness, three-ness . . . the use of the pronoun should provoke 'a different sense of a-count-ability, a different arithmetic, a different calculus of response-ability' (Barad, 2014, p. 178). The pronoun 'iii' is like the Tardis in the *Dr Who* series, troubling classical spacetime conventions.

The way iii have read Biesta and Barad through one another (Chapter 2) is that it is not so much *what* the (knowing) subject *is* (e.g. his or her identity or essence), but *who* and *where* the subject as a unique and singular being with

A diffractive pause: Liam's photos at/of his sister's wedding

Karin Hultman and Hilleva Lenz Taguchi (2010) offer helpful examples to illustrate the difference the agential nature of matter makes for research, teaching and learning. iii will use one of their examples at length to emphasise the significant contribution made by posthumanist *theorising* to childhood education *practices* (without setting up a false binary). My students' diffractive journals testify to the power of one example in particular. One student explains how diffracting their small group analysis of the statue in the museum (in Chapter 3) with Hultman and Lenz Taguchi's 'girl in the sandpit' example greatly helped their analysis. She wrote:

> I would say that our group analyzed the pictures from both a humanist and posthumanist interpretation. I feel that it is extremely challenging to remove the humanist lens from the way we perceive the image. However, I do believe we were able to do it in some ways. From a post humanist perspective, neither the statue nor the child have agency. From this, we can see that the child and the statue are intra-acting creating an enmeshed agency. Neither can operate in isolation. They are not separate, but rather, enmeshed together intra-acting as one producing the image that the viewers see. The child is inviting the child in and in this, it can be understood as a cause in relation to each other. This became more clear to me after the example of the little girl playing in the sandpit. The way the 'sand and the girl are doing something to each other simultaneously' so are the statue and the child.

The girl in the sandpit

Hultman and Lenz Taguchi's posthuman analysis of a young girl playing in a sandpit with a bucket is fascinating. They first describe how the photo could be analysed (somewhat simplified as they declare) through a humanist lens as follows:

> What we see with a habitual anthropocentric style of seeing is a girl in a sandbox who is playing with sand. The girl as the subject of the photograph is separated and detached from the sandbox, which merely becomes the backdrop. In this way of looking, our reading of the image relies on a subject/object binary divide. This also applies to the researcher as the subject of seeing who understands herself or himself as separated and detached from the photograph as the object to be analysed. Moreover, this constitutes a foundational division between subjects understood as humans (subject-humans) and objects understood as part of nature (objects-

nature) (Mol 2002, 33). This division is asymmetrical in terms of value, that is, the girl playing with sand is given a far greater value and is seen as superior to the sand, the bucket and the sandbox. She is active and the sand is passive. As a subject she acts out her intentions and competences.

Hultman and Lenz Taguchi, 2010, p. 527

From a humanist perspective, the material in the photo is merely the backdrop to what really matters. Physical objects are discrete, clearly separated, in a causal relationship with other objects and 'acting only when acted upon by an external agent' (Jackson and Mazzei, 2012, p. 111). Hultman and Lenz Taguchi (2010, p. 529) suggest an alternative to this 'vertical', hierarchical reading of the photo above. Their reading is 'horizontal' or 'flattened' – in line with the ontoepistemology explored in Chapter 3, and the implications for child subjectivity as explored in this chapter.

A posthuman methodology resists starting out by focusing on the human in the picture, as we have seen in reading the image of the infant drinking from the statue's breast. Hultman and Lenz Taguchi (2010, p. 530) offer us the following unusual – therefore again worthy of quoting at length – *horizontal* reading of the photo:

... the sand and the girl are doing something to each other simultaneously. They transform as an effect of the intra-actions that emerge in between them. Thus, all bodies in the event are to be understood as *causes* in relation to each other (Deleuze 1990, 4). In another way of understanding this, the sand offers certain possibilities in its relations with the girl. In the intra-action between the girl and the sand, new problems to be solved *emerge* as an effect of their mutual engagement ... The girl and the sand have no agency of their own. Rather, what is understood as 'agency' in a relational materialist approach is a quality that emerges *in-between* different bodies involved in mutual engagements and relations: muscles lifting the arm and hand which slowly opens up and lets go of the sand, which by the force of gravity falls with specific speed into the bucket, where it lands – one grain upon the other with force causing it to roll over and down and simultaneously constructing a hill of sand in the middle of the bucket. The uneven foundation of the sandbox forces the body of the girl to adjust to find the perfect balance to be able to perform her task. She directs her whole body around the sand ... The force of gravity, the uneven foundation, the bucket and the quality of the grains of sand are all active forces that intra-act with her body and mind and that she has to work with and against.

From the perspective of a relational materialist methodology, the sand is active and has agency. There are no absolute boundaries between the two bodies: sand and girl. They are overlapping forces. The girl plays with the sand

and the sand plays with the girl. Both child and sand are continually *becoming* (Hultman and Lenz Taguchi, 2010, p. 530). The girl certainly has agency, but as an 'iii', not an 'I', that is, an intentional superior autonomous humanist subject (Hultman and Lenz Taguchi, 2010, p. 530).

Now imagine if the object of the researcher's gaze had not been a photo, but an observation in the actual sandpit of the child talking to other children. Also, imagine the researcher videotaping the intra-actions and transcribing the encounter, followed by a discourse analysis with data coded and categorised. Then it would have been even more obvious how *human-centred* the analysis would or could have been – *even if embodied socio-cultural relationships* had been foregrounded when analysing the data when child is 'ii'.[18] But by putting so much emphasis on language and discourse, the *material* has been forgotten and its role as discursive practice ignored. Drawing on philosophers Deleuze and Guattari, Maggie MacLure argues how qualitative research is committed to revealing patterns and regularities, but that this is 'a retroactive, knowledge-producing operation that makes things stand still, and the price of the knowledge gained is the risk of closure and stasis' (MacLure, 2013, p. 662). She suggests researchers should resist representation, and expose the limits of rationality's reductive explanation' (MacLure, 2013, p. 663); and instead 'surf' the intensity of the event, consider how the material world intra-acts with children, 'in order to arrive somewhere else' (MacLure, 2013, p. 662).

The differences made in this chapter between child as 'i', 'I', 'ii' and 'iii' can be put to work on an example from my own experiences as a mother when one of my sons was five years old.[19]

Liam and his sister's wedding

Key for a posthumanist analysis is to engage more fully with the materiality of language and how it affects the body. Language is 'in and of the body; always issuing from the body; being impeded by the body; affecting other bodies' (MacLure, 2013, p. 663). Discourse analysis misses the 'tears, sneers, sighs, silences, sniffs, laughter, snot, twitches or coughs that are part of utterances', and Maggie MacLure continues:

> Interview transcripts seldom record what eyebrows, hands, shoulders or crossed legs are doing, and if they do attend to such features, the aim is usually to point to what they 'mean' – that is, to bring them within the compass of representation. And fieldnotes certainly cannot register the body's automatic responses in the unfolding scenario – the slowing or speeding of the pulse, the spasms of the bowel, the changes in skin conductivity and the dilation of the pupils.
>
> MacLure, 2013, p. 664

As we have seen, the posthuman 'child' is not an independently existing object of study (on the right hand side of Figure 4.1), objectified by the critical teacherresearcher who stands outside and separate from 'the data', 'digging behind or beyond or beneath it, to identify higher order meanings, themes or categories' (MacLure, 2013, p. 660). MacLure points out that:

> Data have their ways of making themselves intelligible to us. This can be seen, or rather felt, on occasions when one becomes especially 'interested' in a piece of data – such as a sarcastic element in an interview, or a perplexing incident, or an observed event that makes you feel kind of peculiar. Or some point in the pedestrian process of 'writing up' a piece of research where something not-yet-articulated seems to take off and take over, effecting a kind of quantum leap that moves the writing/writer to somewhere unpredictable. On those occasions, agency feels distributed and undecidable, as if we have chosen something that has chosen us.
>
> MacLure, 2013, p. 660

MacLure describes this kind of encounter in terms of 'the data beginning to "glow"' (MacLure, 2013, p. 661). MacLure's graphic description re-minded me of the following example that sort of 'chose me' – a perplexing incident with one of my sons. iii have used it several times with educators, and it provokes fascinating comments and questions about child and childhood.

The wedding

In the summer of 2007 my daughter got married. We were living on a remote farm in West Wales at the time and the paddocks were an ideal setting for the wedding reception. Our children were used to having 'strangers' on the premises as we used four of our cottages as holiday lets. Despite that, we never locked the farmhouse, or our cars. Theft was and still is rare in rural Wales, and it never occurred on our farm during the 12 years we were living there. Many people had to travel from far away for the occasion, and the drive up to the farm was a single, narrow track up the hill. Some guests had travelled from as far as Spain, and my best friend from Holland had also come over for the occasion. Our youngest son Liam (then six years of age) was given the task of showing people where to park their car (in the paddock next to the farmhouse; Figure 4.2).

On the piece of paper he has drawn an arrow to the right (barely visible on the photo).

About three months after the wedding, my Dutch friend emailed me asking my permission to delete the photos Liam had made of the wedding. Unbeknown to me he had asked her if he could borrow her camera (probably after she

Figure 4.2 Liam directing cars to the car park with an arrow to the right.

had made this photo of him herself?) and she had happily obliged. She had noticed his photos before, but had only now got round to sorting them. They were 'strange', she said, not really photos *of* the wedding, photos that were out of place really. Intrigued, iii asked her to email them to me and when iii saw them they turned into 'data that glow' (MacLure, 2013). Liam had made numerous photos, but of cars only, not of people at all, and *all* the photos feature the cars' registration plates (see Figure 4.3).

My friend, her camera, the computer, myself, my son – we were all what Barad (2007, p. 148) calls *apparatuses*, that is, 'the material conditions of possibility and impossibility of mattering; they enact what matters and what is excluded from mattering'. They are open-ended practices without intrinsic boundaries, and not 'passive instruments for observations', but part of the ongoing intra-activity of the world (Petersen, 2014, p. 33). In other words, the apparatuses *produced* the phenomena; the data did not exist prior to the email. It is the relations that bring the *relata* into existence, not the other way round.

The material had agency in what was said and done and how the photos worked. Expectations of what wedding photos *should* look like were a critical causal factor making the data; a better word for it is 'creata' to emphasise the constructed nature of data (Petersen diffracting with Stainton-Rogers, 2014, p. 34). Curious about the photos, iii asked him many questions that he answered, but these boundary-making practices also excluded others through my choice of questions (Petersen, 2014, p. 33). So let us have a look how the analysis of the creata changes according to whether iii position Liam as 'i', 'ii' or 'iii', and the difference it makes in terms of justice.

Liam as 'i'

Analysing the photos from a humanist indivi-dualised perspective would involve a range of explanations and search for meanings. *Why* did Liam make these photos? What might have been the *cause* or *reason* for him making them? The impression from the photos is one of loneliness and detachment. Does he feel invisible? Is that why he puts the piece of paper in front of his face when someone makes the photo of him? He is all on his own and seems not to relate to his sister, his four brothers or anyone else at the party. His sister who got married is not once in his photos, only cars. She seems not important to him. Why isn't he involved in what normal children are interested in? What is wrong with him? What do they tell me about him, who he *is*, his *personality*, his *character*, his *essence*. How could iii code or theme these photos as a motherteacherresearcher? What were these photos a sign of? Perhaps he feels excluded and is jealous of the attention his sister is getting. Does he want to

Figure 4.3 The photos Liam made of/at the wedding.

own a car himself? Much (all?) is speculation. It is essential to interview him and to find out what the photos mean, and what they *represent*. An interview will be of no help in getting to the truth as he is still so young, and does not really know himself because he cannot take a detached perspective in his own reasoning, that reflects his own motives and intentions. He might also have suppressed his true, inner feelings.

Liam as 'ii'

Analysing Liam from a social constructionist and poststructuralist perspective, we could say that Liam's interest in cars shows a clear gender bias in how he experiences the world: boys tend to like cars and girls do not, in the same way that boys like guns and girls do not. Even when avoiding giving guns to boys as toys they will make them from bananas, Lego or sticks. This has been socially, historically and culturally constructed by his upbringing and education. Liam has played with cars from a very early age, imitating and inspired by his older brothers around him. Liam clearly moves his body around comfortably in a middle-class environment living on a farm with frequent visits by holidaymakers who often come with expensive cars. He is familiar with people owning cars, being identified by their cars as status symbols (especially men). Cars express and affirm relationships of power. Men usually drive the cars when couples or families are in a car. Born at home in the farmhouse and spending the first eight years of his life on the farm means that being in this rural environment comes naturally. Using a paddock as a car park is normal for a child grown up between the cows, the sheep, the tractors and frequent visitors. He seemed to enjoy the task and responsibility of directing the adults to the paddock by holding up this piece of paper he designed himself. Such confident actions are the result of a particular upbringing, and of having internalised social-cultural practices he is familiar with, including how to relate to adults in such situations.

In both analyses iii am involved at a distance as a teacherresearchermother, ontologically and epistemologically. The use of my knowledge in both cases is used to evaluate and interpret the situation and his actions. In the second analysis, binaries are a salient apparatus: boy/girl, adult/child, rich/poor, rural/city *and by doing so the adult/child binary is reinforced*. Liam is firmly kept at a distance through the adult knowledge used to reflect on the meaning of his photos. It is almost a closed, hermeneutical system that needs to be deconstructed and reconstructed. Whatever Liam says is absorbed into this system of meaning making, and is simply an example of how he has been positioned as a rural, middle-class boy. We are not listening to *Liam* in such cases. Justice is not done to *him* (see also chapters 6 and 10). So, is this indeed all we can say about these photos? How can we look at them differently from a posthumanist perspective? As MacLure (2013, p. 663) comments: 'these moments . . . frustrate the workings of representation and expose the limits of rationality's reductive explanations. They push us to consider how the material world "intra-acts" with children'.

Liam as 'iii'

From a relational materialist perspective, the salient question to ask is not 'What does it mean?', but 'How does it work?' When 'intraviewing'[20] Liam informally, he told me the photos worked as evidence *in case of theft*. He explained that he would be ahead of the game and able to show the police everyone who had been on the property, as everyone had arrived by car. Furthermore, even without theft, he would be able to identify the people by their cars if he went to the supermarket later on and saw their car in the car park. Both were highly imaginative and also logically possible scenarios. iii was amazed. How clever: photos of number plates to secure identification! Did he want to protect us all? Liam had not really taken part in our conversations about issues of security, but he must have been present and must have felt the nervousness in the space. Some of the wedding guests were or had been serious drug users and the adults and older siblings had wanted all precious possessions hidden away during the wedding. Normally speaking the front doors of the farmhouse and the cottages were never locked, neither were the doors in the farm (many did not have a lock). But suddenly some of them were bolted, just for the occasion. He would have noticed this, as it was very unusual. The materiality and discourses intertwined (e.g. bolted doors, removal of precious possessions, my friend's camera) and were mutually constitutive of the taking of the photos. More is at stake in understanding his actions than just consciousness, language or discourses (what can and cannot be said). What were the material conditions that produced the creata, but also created matter that mattered – data that glow? How did his body work? For example, it is fascinating to see how Liam 'hides' his face behind the piece of paper (Figure 4.2), *becoming* a road sign by this bodily gesture and the particular use of a piece of paper. He positions his body right in the middle of the lane, and the car behind him as well as the shed on the right help him prevent cars from passing him. The agential force of the material is for the cars to move to the right into the paddock – knowing that the paddock is an 'overflow car park' as suggested by the sign on the piece of paper and therefore also discursive. It is a wedding, therefore it is likely that there will be many people who need to park their car, hence a shortage of space. Parking is clearly not possible on the property itself, as can be seen on the left of the picture. The gate is shut, no more space left – also for the car parked on the lane. All the relata create the data. Resisting an anthropocentric lens, and not focusing on the human animals in the photos only is very difficult

– it does not come 'naturally'. But when Liam played with toy cars as a child, he *was* the car, moving it around spaces as if he were the car, and in the same way he likes dressing up smartly, it is important to him that cars are aesthetically pleasing. Nowadays, he *is* also the car he plays in his computer games, and, importantly, this is not age bound. A good driver, claims my husband, *is* his or her car – you know exactly how big 'you' are when navigating your 'self' through the world and as part of the world.

So what *difference* does it make to read Liam's photos from a relational materialist perspective? Any analysis already includes me as the mother-researcherobserver and other intra-active materialdiscursive forces. The human and nonhuman are understood as performative agents making themselves known to each other (Lenz Taguchi, 2010). Each analysis constitutes particular relationships, and, in the first two, the relationship performed depends on binaries that exclude children as knowledge bearers. Donna Haraway (1988) reminds us that binaries reinforce hierarchical thinking, since each part of the binary otherises the other in fixed positions. The third analysis is marked by not applying prior knowledge to explain the situation and being moved into the not-yet-known, thereby de-territorialising the power structures between my son and me, and changing both of us in the process (Petersen, 2014, pp. 38–41). Liam's story was not a description, but an enactment constituted of many diffractions, and came to matter through the apparatuses used, including the questions iii asked him and the theories iii inhabit. In Chapter 6 iii will argue the importance of a posthumanist orientation for disrupting ontoepistemic injustice. But first we will explore in the next chapter how certain figurations shape, and continue to shape, our humanist understandings of child and childhood, including our own.

fluid boundaries comes 'into' the world (as an *event*) and *how* these beginnings are taken up and materialised in intra-action (with other human animals, and nonhuman others). The implications for teaching and learning are how, when, where and who takes up these beginnings (but not as indivi-dualised moments, events or units). What does 'taking up' mean and is it material? discursive? or both, always at the same time materialdiscursive? What is the role of the teacher (the learners) in this process of 'taking up', and could/are teachers also learners, and vice versa, learners also teachers?[17]

Notes

1 Piaget himself was not interested in educational theories, but in how the mind works, and less concerned with a strict application of developmental stages (Dahlberg, Moss and Pence, 2013, p. 49).

2 See Chapter 10 for a critique focusing on children's imaginative meaning-making capabilities.

3 See the diffractive pause at the end of this chapter of an example to illustrate this.

4 For a helpful summary to use with educators, download from: www.unicef.org/crc/files/Rights_overview.pdf

5 See, for example, Article 12: 'Children's ability to form and express their opinions develops with age and most adults will naturally give the views of teenagers greater weight than those of a preschooler, whether in family, legal or administrative decisions'.

6 See http://pages.au.int/acerwc/documents/african-charter-rights-and-welfare-child-acrwc, accessed 29 April 2015.

7 See Chapter 5 for an exploration of voice and agency from a relational materialist perspective.

8 This model liberal adult is guided by self-determination, self-governance, independence and individual decision making.

9 See, for example, in Chapter 9 how the colour red in a picturebook materialises a particular philosophical enquiry.

10 Correspondence theories of truth assume an ontology, as mapped in Figure 4.1.

11 I prefer not to use 'mangle' the noun, which means a 'wringer'; the verb means 'to destroy by ripping apart'.

12 What is interesting about posthumanism is the 're-turning' to materialism without slipping into essentialism and reductionism. The philosophy is different from transhumanism, which is not a critique of the Enlightenment self, but a humanist celebration of the ego (often achieved through techno-pharmaceutical means). In contrast, the strand of posthumanism embraced in this book rejects anthropocentrism: it sees human and nonhuman as a quantum entanglement in the multiplicity of mutual relations (Barad, 2007).

13 'Queering' is to radically question identity and binaries. See Barad, 2012, p. 34.

14 In the next chapter the subtlety of Barad's relational materialism will become more visible. It is not correct, for example, to talk about 'blurring' or 'losing' boundaries. Importantly, entanglements are not unities, as each bit of matter, each position in space, at each moment of time, is not 'a blending of separate parts or a blurring of boundaries, but in the thick web of its specificities, what is at issue is its unique material historialities and how they come to matter' (Barad, 2014, p. 176).

15 Posthumanism's rejection of old (dualist) meanings of key ontoepistemological terms has been a real challenge in writing a book that is intelligible to a reader who might be new to posthumanism or academic philosophy.

16 I am indebted to former colleague and friend John Colbeck for the idea of using 'ii'.

17 We will find these questions again in our labyrinth in Chapter 7.

18 As, for example, poststructuralist, feminist, social constructivist theories subscribe to.

19 The example iii share with his permission.

20 This neologism is from Petersen, 2014.

Chapter 5

Figurations of child and childhood

This again makes this question go around and around in my head . . . What is child and what is childhood? I don't know if I truly have an answer to this question any more because what I thought I knew and was happy to accept as my childhood is all upside down and all over the place! These binaries have not only influenced my childhood but my adult life too and I now think about how I will let these binaries shape the lives of my own children or the children I teach in the future?

A student teacher's diffractive journal entry after making her bodymind map, March 2015

Fear of losing autonomous agency

Posthumanism has opened up creative possibilities for rethinking child subjectivity. In Chapter 4, we enquired into the meaning of 'child' and explored what child 'is'. With posthumanism as my 'apparatus' (Barad, 2007, 2012, 2014), some key distinctions emerged: child-as-'i', 'child-as-I', 'child-as-ii' and 'inhuman-as-iii'. The latter includes both child and adult as bodymindmatter – a materialdiscursive quantum entanglement. After all, matter is seen as always entangled with meaning in posthumanism (Barad, 2007; Alaimo and Hekman, 2008; Coole and Frost, 2010; Hekman, 2010).

My proposal to understand childadult, or better put, the 'inhuman' (Barad, 2012, p. 34) as the neologism iii, involves non-dichotomous ways of valuing young children's thinking in its post-Cartesian redefinition of (organic and inorganic) matter as 'agential', non-inert and having force. Although it 'might chafe at first' (Lenz Taguchi, 2010, p. 64), I will use the posthuman 'iii' for child (and adult) because it helps to disrupt human-centredness in knowledge production, and thereby makes room for the not-yet-fully-human of humanism, that is, 'child'.

Salient in this chapter is the notion of *difference* instead of *identity*. Moving beyond the semiotic and returning to the distinction between negative and *positive* difference (see in particular Chapter 3), the latter is about difference 'within' bodies (not as compared to something outside itself like 'adult'). These differences are made by the connections within and between the other bodies a child always already finds her/himself 'in'. It is about 'bodies that differentiate *in themselves*, continuously [like life itself] – one singular event after the other' (Hultman and Lenz Taguchi, 2010, p. 529); and from a philosophical perspective of objects' 'ontological inseparability' from one another (Barad, 2007, p. 128). These are like waves when they overlap and create diffractive patterns ('superpositions') that show the effects of difference within. As iii asked in Chapter 3, whenever we say 'child' or 'childhood' what difference does it make to what we do as teachers or researchers? How can we break with the 'old', produce something radically new and resist looking for the same and the familiar? Each time we pinpoint, point *at* a child, differentiate child from adult, what is the effect on the bodymind? What difference does how we position these bodyminds 'in' the room make for our theorypractices?

The neologism iii might induce fear. Relational materialist Samantha Frost (2010, p. 158) reminds us that fear is an a/effect that spurs us into action as 'a response to the limits of epistemology . . . a response to the obscurity of the unknown'. Diffracting with philosopher Thomas Hobbes, she acknowledges the risks attached to portraying subjects as materialist selves, wholly embodied and without non-physical elements (like minds or spirits) as agents of those bodies that *set it apart from its environment*. The main fear, Frost says, is to lose the notion of autonomous agency (Frost, 2010, p. 160), something child has gained only recently (politically at least) in the form of the UNCRC. But the problem is that the idea of child as autonomous agent (child-as-I), that is, self-governing, is a metaphysical illusion that does not do justice to the 'immense range of causal factors', the many 'chains of events' that cause an action (Frost, 2010, p. 161). This is the case for all human and nonhuman animals, including child. Doing justice to children means taking into account a much greater complexity of 'causal'[1] factors when 'reading' their actions. However, this will inevitably bring with it insecurity and uncertainty, as it does not fit particularly well with hegemonic notions of knowledge and truth in education.

Two strategies for educational transformation

We have seen in the previous chapter how the concept of childhood is not only historically contingent, but also culturally and philosophically problematic. Philosopher of childhood Gareth Matthews points out that we cannot see 'child' except through some intervening social, cultural, religious or philosophical lens – in other words, with the help of some kind of narrative (Kennedy, 2006, p. i). For philosopher of childhood David Kennedy, child is constituted through Western modernist discourse – a humanist discourse that is preoccupied with 'self' (Kennedy, 2006, p. 1), which is '. . . the illusion of the internally sovereign "I" as a metaphysical given . . .' and constituted through language (Kennedy, 2006, p. 3). Highly critical of schools, Kennedy argues in a Foucauldian manner that these sites of oppression position child as the original wild body that needs to be tamed and rendered docile, domesticated (Kennedy, 2006, p. 6) through 'systems of surveillance, normalization, and location in the resource grid', with child–adult relations marked as inauthentic, manipulative and psychologically exploitative (Kennedy, 2006, p. 7). This raises the question of how educational transformation is possible. David Kennedy offers two possible strategies. The first is deconstruction of the notion of 'child's voice'; and the second is deconstruction of conceptions of child and childhood. Although these strategies are not posthumanist by themselves, they have been put in the labyrinth to open up creative relational materialist ways forward – a different *doing* of child and childhood. We look at each strategy in turn.

De-centred voice

We have seen in Chapter Two how 'subjectification' is one of Gert Biesta's three aims of teacher education. Subjectification is about speaking with one's 'own' unique-as-irreplaceable voice and bringing something new into the world. In teacher education we often socialise student teachers into speaking with a representative voice, that is, we socialise them into developmental or social constructivist learning theories, and when doing so (e.g. through particular kinds of assessments) it does not matter *who* speaks. Recall how Biesta's subjectification is not individualised: learning is not 'in' the individual, but always *in relation* with other human animals. His ontology and that of social constructivists, constructionists and poststructuralists, is relational: there is a clear move from 'I' to 'ii'. However, as we have seen, relational materialists take the ontoepistemological 'liberation' from binary thinking one step 'further'; from 'ii' to 'iii'. This is not simply *adding* the material dimension. Of course, the idea that the body is part and parcel of knowledge construction and acquisition, although perhaps not mainstream, is not really new as such (see, e.g. Ellsworth, 2005; Shotwell, 2011). Neither is a focus on the visual, the material or physical spaces in teaching and learning (see, e.g. Ceppi and Zini, 1998; Clark, 2010; Larson and Marsh, 2014). What is new, however, is the radical move from 'ii' to 'iii', that is, the 'removal' of the metaphysical dividing line between the knowing subject and the world (as in Figure 4.1 in Chapter 4), leaving a 'picture' of reality that cannot be visualised, because we are part of the picture. So, it is not simply a matter of 'widening' the circle of 'stakeholders' because that would assume beings as self-contained atomic units existing in spacetime (Barad, 2012). Now, if the boundaries of a human (e.g. the biological) are 'blurred' in an entangled ontology of the social, the cultural and the natural, then what are the implications for 'the' child as 'object' of study, and how should 'voice' be conceptualised? What *is* 'voice'? And what is different about voice from a posthumanist point of view from that assumed by the UNCRC?

David Kennedy argues how developmental psychology and mainstream pedagogies involve a notion of listening that is a form of 'ventriloquism' (Kennedy, 2006, p. 7); teachers already know beforehand what is being said (what Bronwyn Davies [2014] calls a 'listening-as-usual'[2]). Such a relationship expresses adult domination, as the educator claims in advance to understand the educated better than s/he understands her or himself (Kennedy, 2006, p. 7). When this happens, ontoepistemic injustice is done to child, as iii will explore at great length in the next chapter. Challenging this kind of injustice involves a decentring of voice from the autonomous indivi-dualised subject. Inspired by Deleuze's idea of 'thinking without organs', Lisa Mazzei (2013, p. 733) has developed the notion of 'Voice without Organs' (VwO) to describe a voice that does not emanate from a singular subject, but pre-exists individual expression. Language is already 'collective, social and impersonal' (MacLure, 2013, p. 660). Voice, and therefore agency and intentionality, are always produced in relation with materialdiscursive human and nonhuman others.

Child, as we have seen in Chapter 4, is a 'phenomenon', an entanglement of various materialdiscursive apparatuses (Barad, 2007), and child's agency is not of the individualised kind as assumed in the children's rights discourse. In Chapter 2 iii have argued how observing and listening to children is informed by whether we regard objects and spaces as having active agency (Lenz Taguchi, 2010), and by whether voice is 'attached' to an indivi-dual. The implications of a de-centred voice are that agency and intentionality are also not located 'in' a person, but are always produced in relation with material-discursive others. Nikki Rotas reminds us that is a real challenge to un/learn and 'to theorise agency as located outside the acting, human body' (Rotas, 2015, p. 94). The implications for childhood education are that 'voice' is not 'attached' to individual children's 'organs', that is, no single voice can be linked to 'its' expression in, for example, a transcript of a philosophical enquiry with children, as we shall see in the next chapter. Voice emerges as part of its 'milieu' and does not emanate 'from' an individual child as a bounded organism that is present, conscious, and coherent and 'knows who she is, says what she means and means what she says' (MacLure quoted in Mazzei, 2013) and speaks with a mouth (Deleuze and Guattari, 1987/2013). For visual researcher Pat Thomson (2008, p. 4) '. . . the notion of voice suggests both a particular point of view and also one that is not universal'. She reminds us that just like adults, 'children and young people don't speak as one . . . they have different experiences, opinions and modes of expression'. Besides, each individual uses more than one voice (Thomson, 2008, p. 4). Mazzei (2013, p. 734) concludes that we need to 'decouple voice' (spoken and written words) from the bounded, inten-tional, agentic subject of humanism. Child from a posthuman perspective exists in a complex (always) already entangled network of human and nonhuman forces.[3]

Reconfiguring child and childhood

The second strategy David Kennedy suggests is to deconstruct conceptions of child and childhood in order to become aware of the glasses, metaphorically speaking, one cannot take off as teacher and researcher. It is this latter strategy that is the focus of the remainder of this chapter.

Kennedy (2006, p. 8) states that '[t]he eye and the brain work by culturally and historically mediated interpretation; there is no such thing as simple registration'.[4] A salient element of educational transformation is to map with (student) teachers the various imageries we have of child in our collective imagination. Rosi Braidotti (2002) uses the term *figurations* as an alternative to metaphors. These figurations are embodied imaginings, cognitive assumptions and beliefs (Jackson and Mazzei, 2012, p. 137), and in this case about (but not limited to) younger people. Braidotti (2001, p. 2) explains that 'figurations are not figurative ways of thinking, but rather more materialistic mappings of situated, or embedded and embodied positions'. They are not metaphors, but social-material positions: 'living maps, a transformation account of the self' (Braidotti, 2011, p. 12). Although iii have changed her example and applied it to child, the idea is the same: subjectivity is not singular and not metaphorical, e.g. a child is a migrant, a learner at Kensington primary school, a son living with his mother in a township, a soccer player for Landsdowne football club, a surfer at Muizenberg beach, a refugee from Malawi, a victim of xenophobia, someone who is HIV-positive, a fluent reader of English, a good friend of Tebogo, a chess player. Teaching and research that involves children always enact (sometimes contradictory) figurations, that is, acts of shaping into particular figures; and they always express particular locations and power relations (and are therefore political). Unlike metaphors, figurations demand a sense of 'accountability for one's locations' and a 'self-reflexivity' that is not an individual activity, but an intra-active process that 'relies upon a social network of exchanges' (Braidotti, 2002, p. 69). Braidotti explains:

> The figurations that emerge from this process act as a spotlight that illuminates aspects of one's practice which were blindspots before. By extension, new figurations of the subject ... function like conceptual *personae*. As such, they are no metaphor, but rather on the critical level, materially embedded, embodying accounts of one's power-relations. On the creative level they express the rate of change, transformation of affirmative deconstruction of the power one inhabits.
>
> Braidotti, 2002, p. 69

These subject positions are hybrid, multilayered, often internally contradictory, interconnected and web-like. Current discourses about child and childhood are shaped by non-linear, often contradictory, figurations of child and childhood. Drawing on Deleuze, Braidotti (2002, p. 78) argues that the transformational project is to develop alternative 'post-metaphysical' figurations (or 'reconfigurations'[5]) and new images of subjectivity that break with theoretical representations, and that creatively express active states of being, such as 'bodies without organs', 'flows of energy', 'forces', 'becomings', 'rhizomes'. In the case of child subjectivity, 'post-metaphysical' means a rejection of the nature/culture binary and rethinking and redoing how, for example, voice in the (university) classroom is conceived, encouraged, and evaluated.

Bodymind maps

The way iii have used these ideas above in my childhood studies courses is to create with my students 'bodymind maps' that express dynamic reconfigurations of (child) subjectivity. In this case, diffracting with how figurations of child and childhood (see Table 5.1) has 'left' marks on 'adult' bodyminds. They are 'politically informed maps', that is, a 'cartographic weapon' (St Pierre quoted in Sellers, 2013, p. 9). The map-making activity involves 'disentangling' some of these entangled figurations, theoretically, but also at a personal level through multimodal mark-making 'on' a piece of paper (for two examples see *the diffractive pause* that is part of this chapter). The activity aims to be diffractive, rather than reflective,[6] because it does not focus solely on a 'self-referential glance back at oneself' (Barad, 2007, p. 88), but instead encourages students to engage critically and creatively backwards *and forwards* multimodally through their intra-actions with each other (e.g. talk or drama), the lecturer and various materials (e.g. fabric, paint, play dough, stones, thread, wool, photos, readings, furniture and bodyminds in the room or the lighting).

Braidotti (2002, p. 21) reminds her readers that what is meant by 'the body' is never 'pure', natural, biological, but that the body is a complex interplay of highly constructed social, affective and materialsymbolic forces. The bodymind mapping activity does not involve a therapeutic 'going back into the past'. The

Table 5.1 A map of figurations of child

Figurations of child	Theoretical influences	What child lacks by nature	What culture needs to provide child
Developing child	Aristotle, Darwin, Piaget, Vygotsky	Maturity	Maturation, guidance
Ignorant child	Plato, Aristotle, Locke	Rationality, experience	Instruction, training
Evil child	Christianity esp. Protestantism	Trustworthiness, natural goodness	Control, discipline inculcation, drawing in
Innocent child	Romantics (Rousseau)	Responsibility	Protection facilitation
Fragile child	Psycho-medical scientific model	Resilience	Protection, medication, diagnoses, remediation
Communal child	African philosophy, Ubuntu	Social relationships, norms and values	Socialisation by elders, inculcation

'post' in posthumanism does not suggest that we have or can leave the past 'behind' or go back in time and have direct access to the past – not even one's 'own'. Braidotti (2002, p. 21) insists that we need to think 'of the body as an entity that inhabits different time zones simultaneously, and is animated by different speeds and a variety of internal and external clocks which do not necessarily coincide'. And as we have seen in Chapter 4, for Walter Kohan, different configurations of childhood presuppose different conceptions of time: *chronos* and *aion* (Kohan, 2015, p. 57). How could remembering childhood also involve *feeling* this childlike and intense experience of being 'in' spacetime? What are the marks *aion* has 'left' on one's bodymind? The idea of having true access to the past assumes indivi-dualistic agency and intentionality with memory as the methodological tool. But memory is not a matter of the past. 'It' recreates the past each time it is invoked (Barad in interview with Dolphijn and Van der Tuin, 2012, p. 67).

Cutting–together–apart

In the process of making these maps, educators diffractively engage with theoretical ponderings about voice (and agency) and figurations of child and childhood. These two strategies are not meant to be critical (separating into differences), but are supposed to be creative by offering new beginnings – what Barad (2014) refers to as a 'cutting–together–apart'. Diffraction as a methodology troubles notions such as identity and difference and queers (as opposed to 'normal' or 'natural') binaries (Barad, 2014, p. 171). Diffraction breaks through the tyranny of thinking in terms of identity that cuts us apart from other earth dwellers (a concept that includes matter) – it sees difference as difference between two or more *entities*. But in the same way that electrons are neither just wave, nor particle, but both, iii am also both male *and* female, nature *and* culture, white *and* black. These differences are not ignored or erased by thinking and being in this way, but seen as relations of *difference within* (Barad, 2014, p. 175) – a 'material multiplicity of self'. Differences are not 'givens' (attached to a person), but are formed through intra-activity in the making of 'this' or 'that' within the phenomenon that is constituted in the entanglement (e.g. a bodymind map). Importantly, entanglements are not unities, as each bit of matter, each position in space, at each moment of time, is not 'a blending of separate parts or a blurring of boundaries, but in the thick web of its specificities, what is at issue is its unique material historialities and how they come to matter' (Barad, 2014, p. 176). These superpositions, not *oppositions*, are the effects of agential cuts.

Key to understanding the distinct posthumanist character of the bodymind maps is Spinoza's monist notion of difference (a philosophy of *immanence*). It posits a difference *without* identity, that is, a difference that assumes being without substance and subject, 'the establishment of a relationality that is affirmative – structured by positivity rather than negativity' (Dolphijn and Van der Tuin,

2012, p. 127). The active, creative process of 'pushing dualisms to the extreme' (Dolphijn and Van der Tuin, 2012, p. 127) also pushes difference to the limit and instead of looking for the same in the other, it involves looking for difference in the other, which is not *evaluative*, but *performative* (Dolphijn and Van der Tuin, 2012, p. 127). For Elizabeth Grosz, 'revolutions in thought' cannot be brought into being by *negating the past* but only through a radical rewriting of modernity in the present (in order for a past and future to unfold) (Dolphijn and Van der Tuin, 2012, pp. 120–1). This philosophical act of creation can take place only by using the language and concepts that currently exist. As Foucault poignantly puts it: 'the self is not given to us . . . we have to create ourselves as a work of art' (Foucault quoted in Dahlberg, Moss and Pence, 1999/2013, p. 165). Therefore the bodymind maps are not 'self-fascination and self-absorption', but instead 'self-disentanglement and self-invention, the construction of self rather than self-consciousness' (Dahlberg, Moss and Pence, 1999/2013, p. 165). The exercise is not a Romantic form of sentimentalising using the method of introspection and transparency to learn about one-self, one's inner nature and unique essence (Dahlberg, Moss and Pence, 1999/2013, p. 48).

The relationship between posthumanism and humanism is neither *negative* nor *critical*. The point of the activity for (student) teachers in this chapter is to 'go back in time' and become aware of the discriminatory nature/culture dichotomies of humanism. The use of these dualisms is discriminatory if child is assumed by nature (his or her essence) to *be*, for example, immature, innocent, or fragile, as transcendental philosophies assume – and is now 'buried . . . deep in the minds . . . of scholars today' (Dolphijn and Van der Tuin, 2012, p. 94).

The purpose of making bodymind maps with students is not to produce *absolute separations*, for example, by rejecting how certain binaries (e.g. being a 'good girl') have shaped one's understanding of self. Students are also still child (and so *am* iii). We have seen in Chapter 4 how child is a *mangle* – constituted by concepts *and* material forces, where the social, the political, the biological, and its observing, measuring and controlling machines are interwoven and entwined. All these elements intra-act, and, in the process, 'lose' their 'boundaries'. The past always remains threaded through the present. The diffractive activity of bodymind mapping is a 'cutting together–apart' as one move. The making of the map is an agential cut, but the subject remains entwined, because the difference exists within 'itself'. As Barad (2014, p. 168) explains: 'the quantum understanding of diffraction troubles the very notion of *dicho-tomy* – cutting into two – as a singular act of absolute differentiation, fracturing this from that, now from then'.

We now turn to the core dichotomy, nature/culture, that underpins all figurations of child and childhood and current discriminatory childhood theories and practices. Diffractive engagements with the dichotomy should help materialise fresh imaginings of alternative educational possibilities. It paves the way in the labyrinth to consider and get excited about two intra-active pedagogies in Chapter Seven that regard children (and their parents and communities) as a rich resource, not as troubled or troublesome, or with minds as empty slates that need to be 'written on', or who are 'immature'.

Child as immature: 'savage' or 'little angel'

'Immaturity' has become synonymous with childhood and – according to poststructuralists – meaning is assigned to the concept by 'those who hold social and political power: adults. In the past, and within the aspects of a number of contemporary societies, this is often adult, white, able-bodied, heterosexual-identified males' (Jones, 2009, p. 39). In other words, maturity is adult masculinity (Jones, 2009, p. 40). Immaturity has become an umbrella term for a period in a human's life that is *lacking*: lacking cognitive ability, moral responsibility, emotional independence and rationality. The label is therefore morally offensive and the injustice of its use can cause anger (Murris, 2011b). Child is seen as vulnerable, fragile and in need of adult surveillance and controlled opportunities and experiences, 'given' by teachers whose empiricist teacher-directed pedagogies[7] rob children of opportunities to show what they know and can do – ontoepistemological injustice is routinely done to children (see Chapter 6). Interestingly, there is the same ontoepistemic distancing move[8] from child by adult when childhood is conflated with idealised 'pure' nature (Taylor, 2013), for example child as 'little angel'. Influenced by Rousseau, positioning child as innocent means that s/he needs to be protected from the corrupting influence of adult society, and is therefore separated off from the rest of humanity (Taylor, 2013, p. 62). Critically, the way the concept childhood is used in teaching, research, policy-making and curriculum design presupposes the nature/culture dichotomy, with child associated with nature and adult with culture. Anthropologist Maria Kromidas (2014, p. 429; my italics) argues that children have been neglected, 'taken for granted as appendages to adult society, or cocooned from the world and thrown out of society, children can only be of *nature*, which is to say, *outside the human* . . .'. She points at the lone position child takes up, the 'last savage', since people of colour and women have found their legitimate place in society (by law, although not necessarily in practice iii hasten to add). She puts it beautifully:

> Humanism, with its discourse of progress and perfectibility theorized as a movement out of nature, no longer holds the racial Other or prehistoric man as the representative of ground zero – that position is now solely the child's.
>
> Kromidas, 2015, p. 429

So child is either positioned as good or as bad (e.g. immature) by nature, and therefore, adults needs to protect child, or adults need to be protected *from* child. In both cases, it prevents children to be seen as *part* of the world they share with other earth dwellers, and prevents them from building 'real common world relationships' (Taylor, 2013). This, Taylor (2013, p. 62) points out, is the 'biggest cost of all'. Diffracting the ideas of biologist and feminist social scientist, Donna Haraway, she argues that the real world gets lost. 'Common worlds' (a term from Bruno Latour), she explains, are 'down-to-earth' . . . 'worlds full of entangled and uneven historical and geographical relations, political tensions, ethical dilemmas and unending possibilities' where crucially nature and culture come back together again (Taylor, 2013, p. 62). So, as a result of the ontoepistemological nature/culture divide, our complex, 'messy' real worlds have been kept away from our sanitised classrooms (see also Chapter 10).

For educational transformation to be possible, the suggestion was made to use two possible strategies. The first was to rethink voice; the second was to reconfigure child and childhood. To disrupt the core dichotomy nature/culture is central to both. We will now focus in more detail on these figurations of childhood and their genealogies, before exploring, in the second part of this book, the implications these figures of child have had on educational practices.

A genealogy of figurations of child and childhood

As part of the ongoing process of making bodymind maps, Table 5.1 includes some key figurations of child and childhood as a starting point for further research. These figurations have made, and continue to make (always fluid, *emergent*, never 'finished'), material discursive marks on educators' bodyminds: child as 'innocent', 'evil', 'ignorant', 'developing', 'communal' and 'fragile'. My apparatus for choosing these particular figurations has been the nature/culture dichotomy each presupposes, hence positioning child that is *deficit*. As Rinaldi puts it: we are always living with certain images of child and the child of psychoanalysis and 'various branches of psychology and sociology' identify child as deterministic, as 'a weak subject, a person with needs rather than rights' (Rinaldi, 2006, p. 123). Hence the need to explore these images at length with educators. iii briefly comment on each figuration below.

As a very brief genealogy its aim is not to be historical,[9] chronological or linear, but maps several key strands of philosophies, beliefs or theoretical developments (Davis, 2004, pp. 3–4) as relevant for these six figurations of child and childhood. Although the rigid structure of a table has been used for the sake of clarity, these strands are overlapping and always entangled.

How each figuration presupposes particular conceptions of the teacher is also briefly referred to.

Developing child

Philosopher of education, Andrew Stables (2008, p. 9), argues that all our assumptions about children and childhood are rooted in the Aristotelian tradition, so it is a good idea[10] to start with Ancient Greek philosopher Aristotle (367–347 BC), whose major contribution to childhood has been the idea that child's biological development is central to the development of the person and requires careful observation and testing of theories. As 'emergent adult', child is 'reliant on appropriate environmental conditions to thrive' (Stables, 2008, pp. 30–1). The child is an ontological individual *substance* that grows and develops to completion as a human adult. This idea of child as person in formation locates this young human animal in the early years of life. Until child has grown up into an adult, s/he is unknowing, irrational and immature. The maturation process therefore is like that of animals. Philosopher Daryl McGowan Tress (1998, pp. 19–21) explains that for Aristotle the child is 'unfinished' in that the child *is* something of a natural kind from the beginning – that kind being a nonhuman animal, but it is incomplete. The human form is there from the start, and this determined process will be realised naturally and successfully as long as the child is cared for properly and is protected from harm (e.g. is shielded from morally corrupting influences).

Stables (2008, p. 36) points out that Aristotle did not theorise children in isolation; as each generation matures, they carry the responsibility for the formation of future generations. The child develops naturally and purposively like an acorn grows into an oak tree. The human essence is always there potentially – eternal and unchanging, and needs to be actualised through the right circumstances (culture). As this hierarchical, developmental process is in phases – each with their own *telos* – children have no choice or agency, and are incapable of flourishing (*eudaimonia*) until they are mature (McGowan Tress, 1998, pp. 19–20). Without the right training and education children can never flourish, but if their natural inclinations are supported and channelled properly, young children as potential adults are hugely important for society (Stable, 2008, pp. 34, 39). Culture's role is to guide and help mature what child is by nature.

It is not surprising that Aristotle's potentiality–actuality thesis sounds very familiar. It is the material discourse we inhabit, despite most never having read Aristotle. For example, the schools we know are organised around a sequential fixed curriculum, same-age groupings and age-appropriate practice – all expressions of Aristotelian thought (Stables, 2008, p. 48). His influence on modern education more than two millennia after his lifetime has been phenomenal, and still is. The materialdiscursive influence of his writings still shapes the relationships we form with our children and the responsibilities we bear as adults to provide the supportive environment we think children need to develop biologically and psychologically into flourishing adults. Influential 20th-century psychologists Lev Vygotsky and Jean Piaget were both Aristotelians and so was Charles Darwin (see under developmentalism in Chapter 4). For the latter, humans are basically animals, although interestingly Darwin was a humanist: the child is the *origin* of the human. We have seen how developmentalism normalises children in accordance with (universal) developmental 'milestones' and age and development-appropriate practice (DAP). There is no room for collaborative meaning making. Although social constructivism (Vygotsky) does not essentialise children, a biologised psychology is assumed.

As a biological entity in the world, child is governed by natural laws, and therefore an object of science. By nature the mind matures (unfolding ontogenesis), a process which can be 'scaffolded' or 'mediated' through culture by a more knowledgeable (mature) teacher. Hence, adults need to be careful not to demand too much – not more than their current level of maturity allows (Lenz Taguchi, 2010, p167). The medium for teaching and learning is linguistic. Unlike Piaget, Vygotsky was interested in interpersonal processes. Learning involves habituation to social practices through participation in those practices. All cognitive processes are an internalisation of external processes. Even children's first symbolic operations need to be acted out first before slowly becoming internalised, 'from the outside to the inside, from culture to the individual' (Davis, 2004, p. 135). The teacher is 'the *expert* or *master*' and teaching is a matter of *mediating* ('to be in the middle' in Latin) (Davis, 2004, p. 135).

Ignorant child

The key influence here is, again, Aristotle with his faith in rationality, and with it a clear hierarchy among different forms of life and among people (Stables, 2008, p. 32). Child lacks rationality and intelligence; besides, reason is understood as universal, timeless and context independent, hence neutral of gender and ethnicity. For Aristotle, child is ignorant in the sense that child needs *experiences* in order to claim knowledge that the path to flourishing is a reasonable life (Stables, 2008, p. 37). Influenced by Aristotle, John Locke believed (as we have seen in Chapter 4) that children are born as 'blank slates' or 'empty vessels', with an innate (but not yet developed) capacity for reason. There is a hierarchy of reason, with 'eudaimonia' ('flourishing') accessible only by the adult. For empiricists, learning should focus on what is observable and quantifiable (changes in thinking are impossible to measure), so on changes in behaviour as a result of changes in the environment (Davis, 2004, p. 88). For an empiricist, teaching is what effects such changes: *training* and *conditioning*, that is, 'doing what must be done to increase the probability of a desired response to a set of conditions' (Davis, 2004, p. 88). For Plato, child is also ignorant, and gains knowledge through remembrance of the Ideas of Forms (concepts) that child innately possesses, but can only be accessed through rational means guided by absolute truth. For a rationalist like Plato, teaching concerns itself with direct *instruction* (from the Latin 'straight', helping to set learners' understandings straight; Davis, 2004, p. 78). For both Aristotelians and Platonists, reasoning only gradually develops over time as child gains more experiences with reason, and development is the realisation of *potential*, not *alteration* (Stables, 2008).

Evil child

Catholicism was the core influence on child in the Middle Ages, but Protestantism took its place after the mid-16th and 17th centuries. The influence was especially from Protestants continuously resisting Catholicism, and even disputes within Protestantism shaped childhood (Cunningham, 2006, p. 62). Especially for Puritans (e.g. Quakers), child is born essentially sinful and can therefore not be trusted. The influence was strong in Europe, but also spread to the USA with the settlers (Stables, 2008, pp. 51–2). Stables explains that although a small sect, some of 'the key ideas embody the Protestant spirit to the extent that it is justifiable to characterise a mass movement in attitudes towards children as "Puritan"' (Stables, 2008, p. 53). Similar influences can be detected in South Africa through colonialism – for example, the influences of the Calvinistic and exceedingly conservative Dutch Reformed Church introduced to the Western Cape initially through the Dutch settlers (Afrikaners) and also, to a much lesser extent, the influences of the Anglican Church brought by the English settlers. The leading idea is that child is born with sin, and the soul needs to be purified through prayer, good work, devotion and a rejection of worldliness. Essentially corrupt, or easily corruptible by nature, the objective of any intervention (culture) is salvation. Some children can even be possessed by the Devil (Cunningham, 2006, p. 62). Strict regulation and direct instruction is necessary – the earlier in a child's life the better. The preferred method of teaching is *inculcation* (in Latin 'force upon' or 'stamp in') (Davis, 2004, p. 85). The educational context should be one of *discipline, austerity* and *simplicity* (Stables, 2008, p. 55). However, in Western religious traditions, these are not the responsibilities of the learner but the duties of the teacher (Davis, 2004, p. 58). Importantly, as in the current meaning of *disciple*, the aim is to surrender one's authority to someone else, a Truth outside oneself; teaching is a *drawing in* to established systems of thought (Davis, 2004, p. 58).

Innocent child

Stables (2008, p. 51) argues that the Romantic Movement is also a response to the Aristotelian notion of 'the incompleteness of child' (the question of Original Sin). For the Romantics, child is innocent by nature and even adult can retain their 'inner child', playful and uncorrupted (Stables, 2008, p. 48). Of major influence here is Jean-Jacques Rousseau's *Emile* (1762) – a key text offering a 'natural education', meaning, for example, that a learner can 'indicate the pace, subject matter and course of study' (Simon, 1998, p. 105). As we have seen in Chapter 4, for nativists such as Rousseau, childhood is a special time (the Golden Age) of vulnerability, with child uniquely gifted with imagination and fantasy by nature that needs to unfold naturally with as little intervention as possible. Child lacks responsibility and needs to be protected (often meaning removed from) dangerous adults and environments outdoors. Key concepts are risk, danger and hazard. Children out of sight are more at risk than when they are within sight. Adults need to know, protect and control children's lives (Burke, 2008, p. 23). The figuration, innocent child, points at child as cognitively different from adult and progressing through different stages of development. These earlier stages of innocence are not negative, but to be celebrated and nurtured with the teacher *facilitating* and instilling a passion for learning (Davis, 2008, p. 134). The role of the teacher is to let children play, use their imagination and fantasy and shelter them from the corrupt surrounding world, a world that is violent, oppressive, commercialised and exploitative. Child needs protection from adult secrets, such as sex, death, violence or addiction. The contexts teachers need to provide for children should offer 'protection, continuity and security' (Dahlberg, Moss and Pence, 1999/2013, p. 49). Affica Taylor (2013) queers the Romantic relation between childhood and singular nature, and proposes a denaturalisation of childhood. This, of course, would have implications for all figurations of childhood, not only innocent child.

Fragile child

Around the beginning of the 20th century, teaching became increasingly concerned with notions of the normal child and normal development. Guided by these norms, educational research started to focus on 'newly invented categories as hypo- and hyperactivity, retarded and advanced intelligence, introversion and extroversion, and other forms of deviation. Schools responded by developing new categories such as 'special needs' or, more recently, 'barriers to learning' (Davis, 2004, pp. 87–8). Activities such as *diagnosing* and *remediating* (Davis, 2004, p. 87) became important for teaching. Rights-based discourses, such as the UNCRC, and policies that focus on welfare, also position child as fragile. Although, on the one hand, the UNCRC assumes that child is a capable, active agent responsible for his or her decisions, child is in contradictory fashion at the same time regarded as an object of concern – fragile, and therefore in need of protection by the expert (Cregan and Cuthbert, 2014, pp. 15–16). The management of children is increasingly professionalised, medicalised and psychologised (Cregan and Cuthbert, 2014, pp. 15–16). And although it is indeed sometimes necessary to help or protect a child (sometimes even from his or her own parents), there is growing critique of current trends to extensively intervene in children's lives (Jones, 2009, p. 32). Health and safety concerns in the West are a good example of these. In schools, for example, some teachers avoid emotional upheaval and discussion of controversial or taboo topics (Haynes and Murris, 2012). Children are seen as vulnerable and in need of protection and medication for normalisation. Anecdotal evidence gives rise to real concern about the dramatic increase of the use of medication (such as Ritalin) in local South African schools and universities for conditions such as attention deficit (hyperactivity) disorder (ADD/ADHD), or simply to help to focus better on the tasks in hand. Philosopher of education Kristjan Kristjansson argues that this global trend depoliticises and decontextualises social issues, raises unrealistic expectations of a life without pain and suffering, pathologises the individual rather than the school, is non-inclusive and puts teachers in the role of 'sickness-brokers: disease spotters and drug administrators'

(Kristjansson, 2010, pp. 200–9). Important voices against the figuration of the fragile child are liberal educationalists Kathryn Ecclestone and Dennis Hayes (2009). They warn against the current therapeutic trend in schools and universities as it endangers, what they term, the liberating effect of quality education and argue that educators do not so much avoid controversial issues, but tend to focus on activities that are emotionally engaging at the expense of intellectual rigour (Ecclestone and Hayes, 2009). The 'diminished self' it presupposes lowers one's own expectations of one's self as well as others and creates dangerous dependency on experts, such as counsellors, psychologists and psychiatrists. Students of all ages start to perceive existential, which are not necessarily *psychological*, problems associated with uncertainty, disagreement, new challenges, conflict and so on as 'feeling stressy', 'disengaged', 'having an anxious morning' or 'being got at' (Ecclestone and Hayes, 2009, p. xi). In particular, the figuration of child as fragile positions an individual, Western, indoor child/student.

Communal child

Although there is very little published about children in Africa from a critical theory perspective (Wells, 2009), what can be claimed is that the figuration of the African child is not 'fragile', but a person with responsibilities (sometimes even for warfare; see Twum-Danso, 2005) and part of a larger community: African child is *communal* child. This is not a romantic idea of agency, but an idea intricately related with race and poverty and basic survival. For example, in South Africa, it is only since 1994 that *all* children *in principle* have had access to the same education (Wells, 2009, pp. 9–10), but in a country with stark socio-economic inequalities and black and coloured children considered during apartheid to be less than human, equal access is still a dream, not a reality. Especially in a continent plagued with HIV/AIDS there is a distorted picture of what childhood is like for many children, obscuring their capacities and the contributions they make in caring for siblings and other family-members (Kesby, Gwanzura-Ottemoller and Chizororo, 2006, p. 186). In all literature about young children the central assumption is that children grow up in a benign environment where the family will look after them, but child-headed households are not uncommon in Africa (Penn, 2005, p. 111).

'Children's resilience, solidarity, capacity for sharing, their stamina, their sense of time, place and the future, are rarely conceptualized or investigated' (Penn, 2005, p. 111).

The idea often written about in African philosophy is that African societies are characterised by communal interdependence – in particular the existence and flourishing of the extended family (children, parents, grandparents, uncles, aunts, cousins, nieces and other distant relatives), with the latter being a microcosm of the wider society (Letseka, 2013). Hierarchies are written into the nature of the universe, with child low in the hierarchy – subservient (obedient and respectful) to adults and ancestors. There is a connection between the still 'alive and thriving' notion of communal interdependence and the Ancient African worldview of *Ubuntu* 'unumtu ngumumntu ngabantu', the humanist idea that: 'I am, because we are; and since we are, therefore I am' (Bonn, 2007). Humanness finds expression in a communal context[11] (Le Grange, 2012). According to Mbiti (quoted in Letseka, 2013, p. 748), it therefore follows that 'whatever happens to the individual happens to the whole group, and whatever happens to the whole group happens to the individual'. Teaching is seen as *socialisation*, as *inculcation* – firmly locating the transmission of correct social and cultural values (what child is lacking) in the hands of the elders and the extended family (Ajayi, 2000). Child's place is to serve this extended family, with obedience as a prerequisite and reinforced through physical punishment (Penn, 2005, p. 110). Girls have even less status and authority than boys, and are expected to be more domesticated and more compliant, also sexually (Penn, 2005, p. 110).[12]

Child as iii – 'rich, resilient and resourceful child'

Apart from communal child, what these figurations of childhood above foreground is Western 'adultlike' knowledge; knowledge as asocial, apolitical and rational (in a disembodied manner), so deeply dualistic in a Cartesian sense. However, although not individualistic, *Ubuntu* is also a humanist worldview that locates learning *in* individuals mediating between (hierarchical) nature and culture. Not only does the nature/culture dichotomy essentialise child, but by the same token essentialises adult. When removing language as the hub of *all* knowledge production, and with it the fully-human sophisticated language speaker of age, posthumanism offers a forceful new ontology, therefore epistemology, and therefore ways of valuing children's capacities to construct knowledges. Room is made for the material – even for *the material nature of language itself* and how discourses materialise and work (Jackson and Mazzei, 2012, p. 113). The ethicoontoepistemology (Barad, 2007) of posthumanism makes possible a re-evaluation of child. It does this, because *for the very first time* (despite postmodernism wrongly claiming this victory), the binaries of Western metaphysics are made redundant (through a new ontoepistemology). Child emerges as 'rich' (Dahlberg, Moss and Pence, 2013, pp. 53–5), resourceful and resilient (see Chapter 7). Especially in the context of South Africa, with dominant discourses referring to child as 'poor', 'disadvantaged' and attending 'under-resourced' schools, the figuration of *all* our children being rich and resourceful has a strong appeal. Drawing on Loris Malaguzzi's belief in children as *rich in potential*, Gunilla Dahlberg, Peter Moss and Alan Pence explain that teachers have a choice to regard children as 'rich':

> The rich child produces other riches. [In Reggio Emilia] [t]hey argue that 'if you have a rich child in front of you, you become a rich pedagogue

and you have rich parents', but if instead you have a poor child, 'you become a poor pedagogue and have poor parents'. In this construction of the 'rich' child, learning is not an individual cognitive act undertaken almost in isolation within the head of the child. Learning is a cooperative and communicative activity, in which children construct knowledge, make meaning of the world, together with adults and, equally important, other children: that is why we emphasise that the young child as learner is an active co-constructor.

Dahlberg, Moss and Pence, 2013, p. 53

In this reconfiguration, child (or any other human animal for that matter) is not 'poor', waiting to passively receive culture's epistemic input, like Lockean blank slates (nature) that need to be written on by the teacher. Instead, the teacher allows herself to be 'childlike' (see Chapter 7), that is, to seek encounters with children that assume a rationality that does not sever thought from action, emotion from the intellect, form from content or abstract from the concrete. For teaching and learning, it implies a relational approach that emphasises an attentiveness to the presence of the bodies in a classroom, bodies without 'insides' and 'outsides', but engaged in lived experiential encounters.

The nature/culture dichotomy and intergenerational justice

Binary thinking about child misses important knowledge – it cuts things in two: 'a singular act of absolute differentiation, fracturing this from that, now from then (Barad, 2014, p. 168). It cuts child away from adult, mind from body, nature from culture, boy from girl. By positioning intelligence in the mind (or that part of the body *only* called the brain) it also makes it possible to call children *competent* or *incompetent* as if children's capabilities can be separated out into different competencies – the human animal is still indivi-dualised and dicho-tomised. As Jackson and Mazzei (2012, p. 114) explain: the artificial divisions between the biological and the cultural, the material and the semiotic, the natural and the human, genes and the environment blind us to the knowledge 'at the intersection between things and people, between feats of engineering and social structures, between experiences and bodies'. As a matter of *fact*, knowledge cannot be acquired from a distance. Observing child, being with child, *is* always an entangled relationship. As Affrica Taylor puts it: children are already enmeshed within the 'common worlds' they inherit and inhabit with a whole host of human and nonhuman others. The idea of becoming-other with learners is not only a matter of epistemology or pedagogy, but also a matter of justice, as 'questions of ethics and justice are always already threaded through the fabric of the world' (Barad in interview with Dolphijn and Van der Tuin, 2012, p. 69). It is a matter of *intergenerational justice* (Braidotti in interview with Dolphijn and Van der Tuin, 2012, p. 24).

Not like changing one's clothes

At any one time, a plethora of assumptions about child and adult manifest themselves in teaching and research practices. The *doing* of childhood is profoundly complex and contradictory as we will see in the next chapter. But structured efforts in disentangling some of these figurations and how they inform practice make it possible to start imagining other possible ways of doing childhood that are also ethical. What we have seen in the analysis in this chapter is how the nature/culture dualism affirms the adult/child binary, but is ontologically redundant in posthumanism as a navigational tool. Posthumanism does not offer just another 'conceptual' framework for teaching and research from which educators can *choose* out of a range of other options (like the choice of clothes to wear when waking up in the morning). It would presuppose a notion of intentionality that assumes a humanist subjectivity – theories as mere *discursive* tools freely chosen by human animals. But human animals are neither in charge of nature, nor of culture. As a matter of *fact* they are *part* of nature-culture and cannot take a transcendental, detached point of view (from 'nowhere' in particular). It simply is not an option (Haraway, 1988). We cannot simply change our *stories* about child.

The figurations of child and childhood presented in this chapter are the apparatuses we think and feel with and enact in our (educational) encounters with children. These collective images shape our teaching and research practices and the historical, socio-cultural discourses and practices have material a/effects on bodies. Hence the vital work of examining these entangled figures of child diffractively, and mapping the marks they have made (and continue to make) on our bodyminds. This work is always emergent and bound by the language and concepts of the past. The new can only emerge against a background of the present (Dolphijn and Van der Tuin referring to Elizabeth Grosz, 2012, p. 120). During the childhood studies courses iii teach, the students continue in their collaborative journals expressing new diffractive patterns of inclusion and exclusion, of 'othering' as they emerge during the year. Their bodymind maps are forever 'under construction', forever becoming and *moving* (Dolphijn and Van der Tuin, 2012, p. 111), exposing increasingly fine nuances of difference in being, knowing and doing, culminating in their final installation at the end of the year (see Chapter 2). The main objective of this formative assessment is for students to think *and* feel how discriminatory and unjust early year's practices are as a direct result of the binary thinking that excludes the 'other' (child), through the different values adults attach to one side of each binary. The binaries that dominate modernity are structured by a relation of negations (e.g. immature, undeveloped, ignorant, savage and evil). Relational materialists Rick Dolphijn and Iris van der Tuin (2012, pp. 126, 127) explain how through 're-affirming these negations' it is possible to create new concepts as an ontoepistemological activity that is also ethical and political. The concept 'iii' introduced in the last chapter is such a 'concept'. It is the expression of

A diffractive pause: child-in-the-making – creating bodymind maps

The students had been doing their own further research provoked by Table 5.1 and bringing their findings to class. They then worked in small groups, sometimes on their own on their maps or, at other times, discussing discourses that position child materially, socio-culturally and historically within the Western system of binaries, such as 'savage/domesticated', 'good/evil', 'dangerous/safe', 'male/female', 'egocentric/selfless', 'sexual/innocent', 'mature/immature', 'developing/developed', 'fragile/resilient'. iii intra-acted with each group, asking probing questions and offering further ideas to diffract with.

A wonderful example to illustrate the power of creating bodymind maps is Hlengiwe Mkhize's map. She explains that it was made of brown paper 'to show that I am black (race)' (Figure 5.1). It was just by chance she had found what was, for her, the right material to express this difference – a bit of cardboard in the room. Other materials to construct new ideas multimodally are always available in the room: different kinds of fabric, wool, play-dough, clay; natural materials such as stones, twigs and leaves; waste and recycled materials (e.g. bottles, egg boxes and toilet roll holders); art materials (e.g. paint, glue, pencils, thick felt-tip pens and old newspaper). Students add to our collection as the year progresses.

Hlengiwe continues in the collaborative journal:

> The wooden cross represents my religion. Which played a huge role in my childhood, Sunday school was part of my life. The reason why my favourite childhood story book, is the story of Adam and Eve which can be found in the bible. The pink skirt shows that I was raised to know that there are differences between boys and girls, girls wear pink boys wear blue etc. However I grew up in an inclusive society which accepts and encouraged freedom of expression. This has made be behave in the way that I choose to behave. The big pink heart with soft wool inside shows that I have been raised to forgive, and love unconditionally. Growing up in a big family has made me a giving person as sharing has always been part of my childhood practices. The soft wool shows that my heart can be easily broken. In my body map I am standing on rocks and shells which can be quite uncomfortable. This shows that, I have been raised in a way that has made me strong enough to fight and overcome challenges, and still have a big heart. Rules like you need to be indoors by no later than 5:00 pm, no boyfriend until you're 21 years etc., have made me a very disciplined and focused young woman. The yellow sun like shape in my head shows that I am an open minded person.

So far, Hlengiwe's narrative uses the more familiar humanist methodology of reflection and symbolic representation. From an educational point of view, allowing this helped the students engage also at a personal level with the theories of childhood in their research that covered philosophers as diverse as Plato, Aristotle, Lock, Rousseau, Darwin, Deleuze and Guattari and Barad. The historical dimension helped to 'fracture' and 'open up the past' in order to 'bring forth the new' (Rotas, 2015, p. 98) – an 'affirmative approach that undoes binary logic by thinking and doing simultaneously' (Rotas, 2015, p. 101). Almost

Figure 5.1 Hlengiwe Mkhize's bodymind map.

without exception the students understood how these philosophies were profoundly entangled personally and institutionally, and had left their marks, not only in respect of how they had been treated at home, in their communities and at school, but also how they continued to leave their materialdiscursive marks on their bodyminds. Diffraction makes it possible to see child-in-the-making; it maps the *effects* of difference, including the intra-actions with others in the past, present and future. Hlengiwe also mapped how language in particular had, and continues to have, a materialdiscursive force, and how it shapes her endless becoming and differentiating. She writes:

> I grew up in a very supportive family and my dad has always told me that '*Mntanami uhlakaniphile and ayikho into efundwayo eyokuhlula*'. Which means 'My child you are a star and smart and, there is nothing that needs to be studied that you will not be able to study'. This has made me think beyond human boundaries and encouraged me all the times. The wide open eyes in my body map indicates that I have explorative imagination. In my early foundation phase years, my father used to tell me that I need to keep my eyes open and never sleep until I have what I want. That has made me think out of the box and always keep my eyes open for new opportunities. Over the years I have been involved in a number of leadership positions and been involved in things that develop and grow me. Keeping my eyes and mind open for new opportunities.

Hlengiwe's bodymind map, as shown in Figure 5.1, was her first powerful effort. Her use of materials made me think of the limitations of written and verbal language. Her use of the stones at the bottom of her page expressed materially the corporal punishment she was subjected to as a child. She had been given a choice to work on it during the rest of the year or find other multimodal ways of expressing new ideas that would emerge.

For example, after introduction to the Loris Malaguzzi's Hundred Languages poem (in Chapter 7) the group called the 'Looney Tunes' write in their diffractive journal:

> For next term, we discussed coming together at some point to work on our body maps using different creative languages (i.e. through making sculptures, full body-size maps, or through music) in order to further reflect on our upbringing/identity and to create more meaningful material to diffract on. Then, during the term we will draw on this material (which I suppose we will document here) when we do our diffractions.

My response in their journal was that iii thought these were excellent ideas, and suggested making photos and recordings of these different creative languages, and adding them to their journal. They could also make sure others can access this information through augmented realities.[13]

Another student, Tarryn Welsh, created a bodymind map that was very different from Hlengiwe's, also at the start of the year (Figure 5.2). She wrote in her group's collaborative journal:

> I found this to be an interesting activity. I enjoyed looking at my childhood in this way and seeing how much of it was shaped by the way I was viewed by my parents, siblings, teachers, and the world in general, constructed by stereotypes and confined by these binaries. I always felt repressed for my gender. I was always the fragile innocent little girl that needed to be more protected and looked after than by brother who was my opposite in everything. Where I was good, he was evil, where I was fragile, he was not. I feel this shaped us both to perceive ourselves and others through these lenses. These were not always true however they shaped my experience and my reality which was my truth. This has shaped me in many ways, the most pronounced being the anxiety I have around being in the world. It always feels like a space that is unsafe for me or that I am unable to handle it because I am fragile. On my body map I framed the feminine, using a light coloured material over the features on my face, because I felt I could not talk about or see the world in any other way than through this lens, this binary, and because of this, I felt caged. I stuck the netting over my body to display this feeling. It shows how my gender was seen as my weakness and how I was hugely limited in the things I wanted to do that were perceived as unladylike or unsafe. It is symbolic of feeling trapped or caged by these figurations of child or childhood.

Again, the medium of the material afforded a unique means of expression. Her use of colour (pink flowers) and the netting forcefully express in a materialdiscursive way how the binaries had left marks on her bodymind, had caged her as a child, and continued to restrict her freedom. The work of these student teachers shows how binaries of race and gender work(ed) in their lives. For Hlengiwe, the phrase *Mntanami uhlakaniphile and ayikho into efundwayo eyokuhlula* had materialdiscursive force in how it shape(s)(d) her child-in-the-making. This initial provocation[14] started to take on a life of its own when the students continued to mark the *differences* our emerging philosophical work had made on these maps.

The next time we met, iii offered a further provocation by engineering an intersubjective materialdiscursive 'event of difference', a performative, embodied act that challenges representational models of knowledge acquisition (Rotas, 2015, p. 93). I started the session by asking questions about their bodymind maps, and asked whether they thought they might have been working in a more

Figure 5.2 Tarryn Welsh's bodymind map.

humanist, representational and symbolic way. The need to do this was generated in particular by one student who had objected to, what she called, the 'regressive' nature of the exercise, conducted in 'an uncontained environment'. Diffracting with this student was imperative, and took place mostly outside the collaborative sessions. The exercise had touched her at a very deep level, creating many unwanted memories of her childhood past that were still present.

The body as transformer

A relational materialist way of working with bodymind maps takes account of the complex interrelations between the 'inside' and the 'outside' of a subject, and between self and society, opening up possibilities for radically critiquing power and the humanist subject (Braidotti, 2002, p. 20). Rosi Braidotti (2002, p. 20) argues that the embodied or enfleshed subject is no longer the Cartesian *cogito ergo sum*, but a *desidero ergo sum* – a subject whose thinking is 'enlarged to encompass a number of faculties of which affectivity, desire and the imagination are prime movers'. The students had observed, not just how difficult, but how impossible it was not to 'slip into symbolic ways of thinking' or to use the much more familiar psychological discourses, especially for some of our students who are psychology graduates. One student suggested we look again at Figure 4.1, which indeed we did. iii also decided to post a few passages from Braidotti's *Metamorphosis* for them to diffract with in their collaborative journal:

> I take the body as the complex interplay of highly constructed social and symbolic forces: it is not an essence, let alone a biological structure, but a play of . . . social and affective forces . . . This is a clear move away from the psychoanalytic idea of the body as a map of semiotic inscriptions and culturally enforced codes. I see it instead as a transformer and a relay point for the flow of energies: a surface of intensities . . . [Inhabiting different time zones the body refers to] simultaneously incorporating and transcending the very variables – class, race, sex, nationality, culture, etc. – which structure it . . . The body remains a bundle of contradictions: it is a zoological entity, a genetic data-bank, while it also remains a bio-social entity, that is to say a slab of codified, personalized memories.
>
> Braidotti, 2002, pp. 20–1

'Transformer' could be taken to mean an appliance that changes the voltage in an electric circuit, or the Hollywood creation of robots who can take humanoid form, or transform themselves into vehicles (and vice versa). Either way, the idea of a transformer expresses the desire, vitality and high-voltage energy generated by reconfiguring child and childhood. Even the smallest agential cut matters in their diffractive journals: a short passage, a question, PowerPoint slides or the suggestion to watch a YouTube clip. My responsibility as a lecturer then, is my ability to respond, and to 'listen for the response of the other and an obligation to be responsive to the other, who is not entirely separate from what we call self' (Barad in interview with Dolphijn and Van der Tuin, 2012, p. 69).

iii was involved in (not 'witnessing' as this would assume iii was at a distance of what happened) a complex entanglement of the theoretical and the practical with unclear boundaries and emerging new knowledges constructed by the students. By selecting texts, and asking probing questions, was iii 'facilitating' their learning? Was iii 'mediating'? We return to these questions in Chapter 8. Nikki Rotas explains how teaching in this way 'disrupts the repetition of reason' and provokes a shift from asking questions that are problem-solving based to those that are curiosity-generating and divergent,[15] 'questions that foster a transdisciplinary praxis that is effected by the past but not determined by it' (Rotas, 2015, p. 93). Such events have 'an intensive quality of experience that fosters an emergent praxis that bears material implications' (Rotas, 2015, p. 97), and an experience that 'desires crisis . . . if students are to become affected' in spaces that are 'chaotic and disruptive' (Rotas, 2015, p. 94). Therefore, students' resistance to being affected/effected can be expected; lecturers need to accommodate exploration of these disturbances[16] as part of their teaching. The most typical form of student resistance is to use, in their journal, previously acquired knowledge about child development as the truth or last word about children (students who become foundation phase or primary teachers are often acquainted with developmental psychology and social constructivism, or are learning it at the same time from other lecturers in the same institution). Another form of resistance encountered is students' refusal to participate in the task, because the exercise can generate painful memories. Because the context is not conventionally therapeutic, and therefore maybe seen as 'unsafe' (as mentioned above) or too public (they work collaboratively on their journals), alternative ways of working need to be generated. This is not so much a case of 'something has gone wrong' requiring 'intervention' by the lecturer in order 'to repair the damage', but as Rotas observes, the classroom has its own 'ecological capacity' – alive and breathing – 'to un/learn through its own int-e(r)vent-ion' (Rotas, 2015, p. 95). Classrooms as living, breathing ecosystems resonates with the two intra-active pedagogies we read through one another in Chapter 7.

the *continuous process of individuation* that any subject *is* (including child and other earth dwellers). The posthuman child *is* 'iii', bodymindmatter and *at the same time* linguistic, social, political, natural, material and cultural. We have seen in Chapter 4 how child *and* world are entangled becomings, and child is *part* of the world, not *in* it (Lenz Taguchi, 2010, p. 47). Lenz Taguchi (2010) shows the profound implications of this new insight for pedagogy and content in schools and universities. In Part II we will start exploring the implications for pedagogical practice, but first in Chapter 6 iii read philosopher Miranda Fricker's notions of 'identity prejudice' and 'epistemic injustice' diffractively as a means to justify different pedagogical practices.

Notes

1 iii return to the ontology involved in causality later in this chapter.
2 See Chapter 6.
3 The implications for child agency are further explored in chapters 7 (practical suggestions for intra-active pedagogies) and 10 (the context of controversial topics children chose to think about philosophically).
4 See, for example, Maria Kromidas (2014), where she argues against the idea of 'colourblindness' in the context of race and disagrees with the idea that children just 'see' black skin naturally.
5 See Taylor, 2013.
6 With thanks to Veronica Mitchell, who helped me make some important distinctions in the context of this exercise in particular.
7 See: Chapter 4 and chapters 7 and 8.
8 My position is here slightly different from Taylor's. For her, this distancing is 'at least' semiotic, at the level of language and discourse – for me it is ontoepistemic. In her *Reconfiguring the Natures of Childhood* (2013), Affrica Taylor argues how Rousseau's focus on nature – and how since then nature is used as teacher – casts childhood in terms of pure and innocent. Taylor's method of disruption is deconstruction and reconstruction (reconfiguration) – a *doing* of nature and childhood differently (Taylor, 2013, pp. 62–83). My method of disruption is the diffractive methodology of relational materialism as set out in this book (and inspired by the educational philosophies of Reggio Emilia and philosophy with children).
9 Although iii am diffracting with Andrew Stables' argument that Aristotle's notion of development has been a key influence on conceptions of child and childhood in Western civilisation, my mapping is not historical but uses the nature/culture dichotomy as its apparatus, thereby creating a 'superposition', something new.
10 Often academic literature in childhood education does not go far back enough in the history of ideas in order to disentangle current hegemonic educational discourses and related practices.
11 Le Grange (2012) disagrees with the claim that Ubuntu is a humanist notion, and argues for a posthuman understanding of African philosophy, but without a philosophy of *immanence*, and therefore a non-hierarchical relationship between, gender, elders and ancestors, and between species, it is unclear how this claim could be true.
12 In Chapter 8 we will return to South African education and the figuration of child in the context of early literacy.
13 See Chapter 2, note 24.
14 In Chapter 7 we will see how project work (*progettazione*) in Reggio Emilia starts with a provocation. Similarly, in my Reggio-inspired teacher education practices iii start with a provocation, and the students are invited to continue to explore the topic further through various 'languages' in their diffractive journals and by using augmented realities (introduced later in the year) in non-predefined childhood studies tasks.
15 See in particular chapters 7 and 8.
16 See Chapter 8 about the teacher as pregnant stringray.

Chapter 6

Ontoepistemic injustice and Listening without Organs

> They are thus denied on three counts: ethically for being wrongfully excluded, epistemically for being wrongfully mistrusted, and ontologically for being wrongfully positioned as a lesser being.
>
> Carmen Blyth 2015, p. 145

This quote from Carmen Blyth's doctoral study sums up beautifully the thrust of the first part of this book by disentangling three threads: the ethical, the ontological and the epistemological in the context of how children are treated in educational settings. So far we have seen how figurations of child wrongfully position children as lesser beings ontologically – the reason why they have been, and still are, excluded from practices and many decision-making processes in education. This intergenerational injustice has been foregrounded, and a posthumanist reconfiguration of child (inhuman becoming) has been argued for. In this chapter, the *epistemological* thread is picked up and woven into a new fabric by reading the philosophies of Miranda Fricker and Karen Barad diffractively through one another.[1] New Materialist, Iris van der Tuin (2011, p. 22), argues that reading diffractively 'breaks through the academic habit of criticism and works along affirmative lines'. Like waves of water closely rolling towards the beach, 'interfering' with each other, adding to each other's force and without clear boundaries,[2] at least two key ideas have agency in this chapter.[3] Barad's ontoepistemology intra-acts with Fricker's notion of epistemic injustice, thereby creating the new idea of ontoepistemic injustice.[4]

These ideas are intra-acting through Miranda Fricker's relatively influential notion of *epistemic injustice* – a kind of injustice that is woven into the fabric of social injustice. For educational transformation this is important, because much injustice is inflicted on children on the basis of adult claims of what counts as true knowledge, and therefore what is educationally worthwhile. Epistemic injustice is done to children when they are wronged specifically in their capacity as a *knower*. Knowledge is offered by the child, but not heard by the adult, because of identity prejudice (ageism). This kind of prejudice is in turn related to figurations of child and childhood (Chapter 5), and needs to be reconfigured by queering the nature/culture dichotomy that all these well-known figurations presuppose.

Fricker's philosophy concerns mainly race, class and gender, but not child. This is not surprising as including age as a category for discrimination is still unusual, and Fricker is not an educationalist. In the past (Murris, 2013b), iii have used her powerful 'conceptual apparatus' (Code, 2008) by making the 'circle' wider[5] as it were, and to include child as a social type that is also excluded and discriminated against – even more so when child is also black (a 'double whammy'). But in this chapter iii diffract with my earlier position in that inclusion of 'age' also necessitates an interrogation of *what counts as knowledge* in order to 'allow' young (black) child 'in', and iii finish by arguing for increased epistemic *modesty*, epistemic *equality* and epistemic *symmetry* in order for emergent listening to become possible.

'Worthwhile' educational practices

Oft-quoted analytic philosopher of education, R.S. Peters, states that educational practices are 'those in which *people try to pass on* what is *worthwhile* as well as those in which they actually succeed in doing so' (Peters, 1966, p. 26; my emphasis). But is it indeed necessary for practices to count as educational only when people try (and succeed) in 'passing something on'? And what does it mean for knowledge to be 'worthwhile'? Routinely in schools adults are positioned to 'pass on' knowledge, and to determine what is 'worthwhile' learning. A brief example below will illustrate the urgency of these questions, and lead to an exploration of the notion of *ontoepistemic injustice*. Opportunities to critically explore epistemic injustice in practice are offered through transcripts of a televised philosophical enquiry with children. The chapter will conclude with an alternative definition of teaching that does more justice to relationships of ontoepistemic trust, modesty and equality as part of emergent listening characteristic of philosophy with children.

An example from a Grade 1 classroom

One of my students during teaching practice engaged her five-year-olds in creating 'plants' out of recycled materials. The children were encouraged to use a wide range of materials freely to construct their understanding of the various parts of a plant (stem, root, leaf, seeds, flower and fruit) as they wished. After the 1-hour life skills lesson (observed by me) the children went out to play, which marked the end of the lesson. After their return they had to move on with a literacy lesson (insisted upon by the student's mentor teacher) with no connection at all to the previous life skills lesson – either in planning or execution.[6] Despite the children being used to this 'silo approach' to education, some of them expressed a clear disappointment about not being able to continue with their project after the break. As the classroom had been filled with purposeful activity and deep immersion in the task by most, my student teacher made a wise judgement and promised the children[7] to pick up the work again some other time soon. A few days later, when there was an opportunity to continue with their projects, she found out that their work had been thrown away 'in case the parents saw it' (her mentor teacher explained). My student was clearly upset, in particular because she had promised the children that she would keep their work. My student's mentor teacher had made a decision on the basis of a particular classical conception of knowledge that clearly excluded the use of children's 100 languages.[8] She explained that she felt under institutional and parental pressure to make sure that her children in class produced *beautiful* things to display. She was unfamiliar with the idea of using 'junk' materials (Odegard, 2012) or the arts as a powerful medium for knowledge construction. Nor was she acquainted with the proposal that children's work can and should be displayed as emergent work that is (always) in progress (Vecchi, 2010; Davies, 2014).

The children's installations were varied and fascinating, but the 'problem' was that they were not 'pretty' in any 'conventional' sense. Although the aesthetic value of the work was not part of the objective of the lesson, the children's creative use of material stood out as an experience for me as observer. Also, the diversity of expression through the recycled materials stood in stark contrast with other examples of children's neat work displayed around this and other classrooms in the school. As elsewhere, the products of children's art (or other) lessons (carefully mounted) in schools look disturbingly similar.[9]

Learning *with* children and *with* materials can be educationally transformative, if, and only if, the adults in authority also regard the new knowledge produced as worthwhile. And this of course depends on the figuration of child and childhood we bring as educators to our listening practices. Identity prejudice (who and what is child?) influences what counts as worthwhile knowledge. This salient concept for doing justice is explored below.

Stereotyping and identity prejudice

Epistemic prejudices[10] are related to adults' implicit and explicit assumptions and prejudices about child. Fricker introduces the helpful notion of 'identity prejudice' as 'a label for prejudices against people *qua social type*' (Fricker, 2007, p. 4; my emphasis). The academic literature is still remarkably silent on how the category child and age, as its criterion of identification, influences what adults regard as 'real' knowledge and therefore by implication what it means to hear child's 'voice'[11] – to use a current metaphor. Although much academic critique focuses on the social and cultural normativity of knowledge claims when deconstructing Cartesian dualist oppositions, their focus is almost exclusively on race, class and gender,[12] and Fricker is no exception. Children are still invisible in mainstream academic philosophy[13] as well as other fields of academic enquiry. Although Fricker does not explicitly include any reference to age in her writings, she has acknowledged in conversation[14] how relevant her arguments are for how we think about and treat children. Child is just as much a relevant social type for epistemic injustice as race, class or gender.

In her book *Epistemic Injustice: Power & the Ethics of Knowing* (2007), Fricker focuses on human practices through which knowledge is gained (epistemic practices) and their social situatedness, which exposes their inevitable ethical and political dimension. In the context of race, class and gender, she argues that:

> identity prejudice gets into hearers' judgements of speakers' credibility, often despite, rather than because of, their beliefs. I suggest that such prejudices typically enter into a hearer's credibility judgement by way of the social imagination, in the form of a prejudicial stereotype – a distorted image of the social type in question.
>
> Fricker, 2007, p. 4

The ethicopolitical issue here is how the prejudicial stereotype *distorts* a social perception, a perception that is epistemically loaded. Now for Fricker, the use of stereotypes might be 'entirely proper' or they can be 'misleading' (Fricker, 2007, p. 17). Stereotypes are more than 'hasty generalisations' (Code, 2008), and Fricker defines them as 'widely held associations between a given group and one or more attributes' (Fricker, 2007, p. 30). Although they can be 'neutral', in the sense of 'reliable', and therefore a 'proper part of the hearer's rational resources' (Fricker, 2007, p. 30), hearers are 'perpetually susceptible to invoking stereotypes that are prejudiced' (Fricker, 2007, p. 30). A stereotype is misleading when the prejudice 'works against the speaker'. Two things might follow, she continues, 'there is an epistemic dysfunction in the exchange – the hearer makes an unduly deflated judgment of the speaker's credibility, perhaps missing out on knowledge as a result', and secondly, the 'hearer does something ethically bad' – 'the speaker is wrongfully undermined in her capacity as a knower' (Fricker, 2007, p. 17). Importantly, it is the *attributes* that make a stereotype positive, negative or neutral. And it is the meaning (always situated) given to an attribute (e.g. attributing 'immaturity' to a child) that is morally significant.

Now, stereotyping involves empirical generalisations about a given social group (here, children), sometimes even resulting in universal claims, such as, 'All children are immature'. Fricker points out two necessary conditions for the identity prejudice in the claim to be prejudicial. First, the attribute (immaturity) needs to be a reliable generalisation, and second, it should not be a 'prejudgement', that is a judgement made without proper evidence (Fricker, 2007, pp. 32–3). She continues that many attributes assigned to historically powerless groups are often associated with a lack of 'competence or sincerity or both' (Fricker, 2007, p. 32), and the attributes she mentions also apply to child historically: 'over-emotionality, illogicality, inferior intelligence, evolutionary inferiority, incontinence, lack of 'breeding', lack of moral fibre, being on the make, etc.' (Fricker, 2007, p. 32). These prejudices of deficit are often held 'unchecked' in the collective social imagination, and do their damage, especially, iii claim, when child is not only young, but *also* female, black and lives in poverty. Prejudice runs deep and operates 'beneath the radar of our ordinary doxastic self-scrutiny' (Fricker, 2007, p. 40). Despite this awareness, Fricker is hopeful that social transformation is possible through corrective force at individual and social level.

However, cutting through the inappropriate use of identity-prejudice when assigning epistemological credibility to a *young* speaker, adds an additional layer of complexity with far reaching implications for educational praxis *and* for Fricker's philosophical analysis itself. The action of including child in her list of epistemically marginalised social types forces the reader to consider *what is meant by knowledge*, whether it is *worthwhile* and *who* can make truth claims about the worthwhileness of knowledge. What iii am arguing for here is that my philosophical proposal to include child *at the same time* exposes the still individualistic and humanist orientation of Fricker's notion of epistemic injustice, despite her feminist focus on epistemic *practice* and situated knowledge (Code, 2008). Consider, for example, our discussion of the 'who' of Stephen Hawking when 'his' box speaks in Chapter 3.

Epistemic challenges of social transformation

Educators embody many of the ideas of educational institutions – their theories and their practices. Pedagogies and what counts as content knowledge are shaped by conceptions of child and childhood, which prescribe the boundaries of what counts as valuable knowledge and learning. Characteristic of most communicative exchanges between adult and child in school is children presenting to adults what the latter want to hear, not necessarily what children themselves genuinely believe in (Haynes and Murris, 2012). We will see in Chapter 8 how the routine asking of closed, rhetorical questions by teachers is a mere symptom of a deeper engrained epistemic orientation that profoundly influences how we speak and regard what it means to think *with* children. Even when a serious and well-intentioned effort is made by teachers to encourage children's authentic speculations, the listening might be a listening out for, or rehearsal of, what teachers already know – a 'listening-as-usual' (Davis, 2013). Teachers' self-identity as epistemic authorities constitutes a serious barrier to listening to children even when room is deliberately made in class to listen to their philosophical ideas. The example from practice in this chapter has been chosen deliberately to show how even educators committed to philosophy with children can be prejudiced. We have indeed seen in previous chapters why this prejudice runs so deep and why the attributes assigned to child are still structurally embedded in educational policies and in curriculum design.

Not just someone's accent (Fricker's example), but in most educational systems, children's medium for knowledge construction and representation is written or verbal language only.[15] Of course young children's linguistic abilities are emergent, but despite this, their thinking tends to be judged by their ability to express themselves linguistically (Murris, 1997). Philosophereducator Loris Malaguzzi (1998) reminds us that schools value one language only and have forgotten the other 'nine-nine'. As we shall see in Chapter 7 when reading Reggio Emilia and philosophy with children diffractively through one another, opportunities for multimodal expression of ideas emerge in communities of philosophical enquiry – opportunities that do more justice to children's meaning-making capacities. This is even more urgent when children are not very familiar with the Language of Learning and Teaching (LoLT) when they start school at the age of four or five (as is the case for the majority of children in South Africa). Moreover, as we will see in Part II, children's imaginative play with ideas when philosophising challenges the exclusive requirement of rationality when doing philosophy (see also Haynes and Murris, 2013).

Fricker's sophisticated distinction between hermeneutical and testimonial injustice helps to clarify the different ways in which child is ontoepistemically marginalised even further through adults' claim to what counts as true knowledge.

Hermeneutical and testimonial injustice

For Fricker (and relational materialists) the ethical is not divorced from the epistemic. They are mutually entangled (Code, 2008). She argues that social identity and social power[16] are involved in 'two of our most basic epistemic practices: conveying knowledge to others by telling them, and making sense of our own social experiences' (Fricker, 2007, p. 1). These two forms of epistemic injustice involve a moral wrongdoing to a person in their capacity as a knower (Fricker, 2007, p. 1). The 'immediate wrong' done to a child as a speaker is to be on the receiving end of epistemic injustice, because the child is wronged in her capacity as a knower (*hermeneutical* injustice) and/or as a giver of knowledge (*testimonial* injustice) and when 'one is undermined or otherwise wronged in a capacity essential to human value, one suffers an intrinsic injustice' (Fricker, 2007, p. 44). Epistemic injustice, as such, is woven into the fabric of social injustice' (Fricker, 2007, p. 100).

In cases of *testimonial* injustice, a prejudice (e.g. accent) will cause a hearer to give a deflated level of credibility to a speaker's word, and 'sometimes this will be sufficient to cross the threshold for belief or acceptance so that the hearer's prejudice causes him to miss out on a piece of knowledge' (Fricker, 2007, p. 17). Credibility deficit is related to age, in that being a particular age has significant impact on how much credibility a hearer affords a speaker, and when and how she is silenced systematically. She explains:

> When someone is excluded from the relations of *epistemic trust* that are at work in a co-operative practice of pooling information, they are wrongfully excluded from participation in the practice that defines the core of the very concept of knowledge.
>
> Fricker, 2007, p. 145; my emphasis

Of the two kinds of epistemic injustice, *hermeneutical* injustice is even more difficult to detect. Fricker defines it as: 'the injustice of having some significant area of one's social experience obscured from collective understanding owing to a structural identity prejudice in the collective hermeneutical resource' (Fricker, 2007, p. 155). That is, the power relations and structural prejudice undermine child's faith in their own ability to make sense of the world, and constrain their ability to understand their own experiences. Children's situated lived experiences of learning, their friends, family or community are irrelevant to the 'real' work in class (that is, dominant discourses about knowledge). As a result, child will lose confidence in his/her general intellectual abilities, to such extent that s/he is genuinely hindered in his/her educational development.

Fricker suggests that we need to change 'our philosophical gaze' through 'the negative space that is epistemic injustice' (Fricker, 2007, p. 177) in order to fully understand the injustice done to other human beings in everyday epistemic practices. Her proposal is a powerful promise – especially in the context of how children in schools are routinely treated. However, social transformation is not straightforward. Being wronged in one's capacity as a knower 'can cut deep' (Fricker, 2007, p. 44), and involves denying certain categories the 'capacity for reason' (Fricker, 2007, p. 44). Apart from the 'attributes' child shares with other historically marginalised groups (see above) – according to widely held prejudices in the collective social imagination – we have also seen in Chapter 5 how figurations of child can be used for excluding children.

Elsewhere, Fricker argues that 'the perspectives in which the powerless may view the world can appear less rational than they are, owing to an uneven discursive terrain' (Fricker, 2000, p. 160).

In this uneven 'discursive terrain', figurations of child regulate how adults listen to child. These are summarised in Table 5.1 in Chapter 5, and make clear how the nature/culture dichotomy structures our imageries of child, implying certain conceptions of knowledge and therefore of teaching. When child is seen by nature (Taylor, 2013) as primarily and exclusively 'innocent', 'evil', 'ignorant', 'fragile', 'developing', or 'communal', educators will respond in a discriminatory manner to their knowledge claims. Examples include cultural responses such as: protection, control, discipline, instruction, development, socialisation, medication, empowering and guidance. Epistemic injustice is done when the individual is treated as a *typical* example of a particular social type, *before* s/he has been allowed to show who or what s/he is, and before interventions are negotiated democratically.

As argued elsewhere (Murris, 2000), a typical category mistake made by academic philosophers who claim that children cannot think philosophically (Kitchener, 1990; White, 1992) is to compare the abilities of children philosophers (who are new to philosophy) with adult philosophers (who are trained in academic philosophy). Of course, this is like comparing apples to pears. The only *fair* comparison would be between two different groups of people (with age as the only variable) and *both* groups being *new* to philosophy. Moreover, the research would also need to include a wide variety of material multimodal meaning-making opportunities when doing philosophy (to not disadvantage emergent literate children) and include the imagination as part of rationality (Murris, 1997; Haynes and Murris, 2013).

Disrupting how adults 'listen-as-usual' (Davies, 2014) to children involves diffracting these figurations of child and childhood, the underlying nature/culture binary and the notions of teaching we have become so used to. These actions set in motion alternative ontologies (therefore epistemologies) and ethical *responsive* listening practices. As opposed to *polite* listening,[17] *responsive* listening requires adults to think about what a child is saying *as well as* being fully aware of the other materialdiscursive elements of the situation (Barad, 2007), and to respond not just to the *words* used by the child (see Chapter 7). Carlina Rinaldi (2006, p. 65) uses the notion of *emergent* listening, which requires a suspension of 'our prejudices' and opens up 'new ways of knowing and new ways of being' (Davies, 2014, p. 21). This kind of emergent listening is a Listening without Organs, as iii will show in the analysis of the philosophical enquiry.

Prejudices and conceptions of child are part of humans' (including children themselves) habits of thought, and from which we can never fully free ourselves, nor would this always be desirable because, *to a certain extent*, child is *also* in need of protection, guidance, socialisation, experiences, maturation, discipline and so forth. They are morally wrong only when they are used to *exclusively* listen-as-usual children, that is, when they are used to producing 'individual selves who have an identity that can be grasped through already existing categories' (Davies, 2014, p. 34) – categories structured through the dominant nature/culture binary in our thinking about teaching and learning (Taylor, 2013) (see in particular Chapter 5).

An example of epistemic injustice

The main objective of the subject childhood studies in my teacher education curriculum[18] is to become more aware of the figurations of child and childhood we all bring to our educational practices and observations. In this chapter, a critical incident in my own practice as teacher educator is used diffractively to explore Fricker's notion of 'epistemic injustice' and to foreground the identification of 'identity-prejudicial credibility deficit' (Fricker, 2007). A child receives this deficit when s/he is taken less seriously than s/he ought to be, because it is *child* who is speaking (child is *prejudged*). The example offered in this chapter is not so much about the dialogue between children as such, but my experiences of using the dialogue with educators in preservice and inservice teacher education, including my explicit identification of identity-prejudicial credibility deficit. iii have used it to provoke 'a'[19] philosophical enquiry by showing the DVD first, and then reading the transcript and my comments out loud together as a starting point for enquiry. It is strongly recommended also

A diffractive pause: how to read *Granny and the Goldfish*

We read together a publically available dialogue that took place between a girl called Charlotte (aged 6) and her teacher. It was published by Jane Pascal.[21] iii usually ask participants to record their own responses using a medium of their own choice (e.g. drawing, writing, play-dough, existing images) before talking to others in their group and to share their findings when they are ready.

> Teacher: Do you have a pet?
> Charlotte: Yes. I have a cat and a guinea pig. And a goldfish. The cat is called Zephyr and the guinea pig is called Gip.
> Teacher: Do you like them?
> Charlotte: Of course. Everyone likes their pets.
> Teacher: How would you feel if something awful happened to one of your pets?
> Charlotte: Really sad. I had a rabbit once, but a dog got in and ate it. I cried.
> Teacher: Have you heard of Africa?
> Charlotte: It's a long way away. They have jungles there, and wild animals.
> Teacher: There are people there as well. Millions of them.
> Charlotte: I know.
> Teacher: Would you care if someone in Africa were hit by a bus?
> Charlotte: Not much. It probably happens all the time.
> Teacher: Would you rather someone you didn't know in Africa was hit by a bus, or your goldfish died?
> Teacher: How about 10 people killed in a bus crash?
> Charlotte: I still don't want my fish to die.
> Teacher: What if the choice is between your goldfish and a thousand people killed in an earthquake? What if you were magic, and had to choose?
> Charlotte: Maybe the people are more important.
> Teacher: What if it's between the people and Zephyr?
> Charlotte: No way. I love Zephyr.
> Teacher: What if its either 10 people in Australia killed in a bushfire or Zephyr hit by a car?
> Charlotte: People I don't know?
> Teacher: Yes. You don't know any of them.
> Charlotte: Then I'd pick Zephyr not to be hit by a car.
> Teacher: What if it's between Zephyr and grandma?
> Charlotte: Um. Grandma's very old. She might die anyway.
> Teacher: What if its either grandma dies in 6 months before she would have, or Zephyr is hit by a car?
> Charlotte: Are you going to tell grandma what I said?

Teacher: I don't know. Probably not.
Charlotte: I think grandma is more important.

. . . .

We then watch a philosophical enquiry of children thinking together about this dialogue. James Nottingham, the Year 5 class teacher, has been involving his learners twice a week in 1-hour philosophy with children (P4C) sessions over a period of time. It is not clear for how long he has been teaching P4C to this particular class. It is available at: www.youtube.com/watch?v=CkeEjZVaEqk. Again, iii ask participants to record their own responses first and to take note of the parts of the published dialogue that were broadcast and which ones were not. iii suggest they speculate why this might have been the case and ask what difference it has made. They then discuss it again with the same group.

Subsequently as a whole group we take turns in reading aloud together a short transcript of part of the dialogue as edited and broadcast on British television. Each participant is reading a few sentences, but it is possible to 'pass' and not read aloud. The particular part of the dialogue iii have chosen goes as follows:

. . . .

Boy 1: Princess Diana . . . you only knew her name, but you didn't really meet her like, when she died people were sending her flowers and everything, but in a way she was a stranger, but I cared for her.
Boy 2: What is a stranger?
Girl 1: You haven't met them, but sort of not communicated with them.
Girl 2: I rather wish a stranger died than my family and friends, because you don't really know other people . . . they might be horrible.
Girl 3: Yes, but you are saying that just because you don't know them it is better that strangers die, just because you don't know them.
Girl 4: If there were such a thing like God, why would he like make horrible people in the world, like the people in Kosovo? Why does he make people suffer?
Boy 3: I don't agree with you Amy, because God might like some bad people on the earth, because He might think it's too peaceful, so he might say you have to have some bother sometime.
Girl 5: It's impossible to have a perfect world . . . I mean you have to have bad people in the world, coz if we did have a perfect world we would go round saying 'hiya' drinking cups of coffee all the time . . . always being nice to each other that wouldn't be right, that wouldn't be comfortable at all.

We continue reading together two incidents from my practice below.

Two critical incidents

First example: the dialogue between the teacher and Charlotte

When showing this YouTube clip as an introduction to philosophy with children at a conference some years ago, one teacher (with a background in psychoanalysis) expressed his deep disturbance about using this transcript (based on a real conversation) as a text in class. He pointed out that, by doing so, educators sanction a child making such admissions about their grandmothers in public. 'In this case, Charlotte', he claimed, 'will have to carry that guilt for the rest of her life'. Such a statement is a clear example of credibility deficit as a result of identity prejudice. Without knowing her, so not based on prior acquaintance, he makes this *prejudgement* and assigns the attributes fragile, vulnerable, ignorance and perhaps even innocence to this six-year-old. This stereotyping prevents him from listening responsively, and therefore from taking her seriously as knowledge bearer. The teacher's reasoning must have gone something like this: Charlotte cannot *really* believe that she cares more about Zephyr, her cat, than grandma. When she grows up and is more mature, she will come to realise that she cares more for her grandma (because children love their grannies more than cats) *and in the meantime* it is the adults' responsibility to protect her. But Charlotte as-a-matter-of-fact *says* that she would choose Zephyr. However, the teacher is not prepared to even contemplate the truth of this possibility, hence *testimonial* injustice is done to Charlotte. *Hermeneutical* injustice is harder to detect, but let us look again at the following exchange:

> Teacher: What if it's between Zephyr and grandma?
> Charlotte: Um. Grandma's very old. She might die anyway.
> Teacher: What if its either grandma dies in 6 months before she would have, or Zephyr is hit by a car?
> Charlotte: Are you going to tell grandma what I said?
> Teacher: I don't know. Probably not.
> Charlotte: I think grandma is more important.

Only *after* asking whether grandma might find out what she has told her teacher, does she say that 'grandma is more important'. Before the intervention, it was very clear that she loved Zephyr *more* than grandma (perhaps she does not love grandma at all!). However, Charlotte is not *allowed* to love nonhuman animals more than human animals without running the risk of feeling guilty (especially after grandma has died). The original dialogue includes many thought experiments that put increasing pressure on Charlotte to prioritise human animals over nonhuman animals. The choices she has to make are between the death of a goldfish over one person killed in Africa, then 10, then 1,000 people, and finally the comparison between her grandma (a human animal she has a relationship with) and Zephyr the cat. Here, the power relations between teacher and child, and structural prejudice could well undermine Charlotte's own faith in her ability to make sense of the world, and constrain her understanding of her own future experiences. Over time, her responses might increasingly conform to the expectations of her adult educators (including adopting the humanist prejudice that human animals are always more loveable or at least worth saving more than nonhuman animals). Interestingly, the teacher in the transcript is not pushing her to give *reasons*. It would have been fascinating to hear what Charlotte's reasons were for all her choices.

Second example: the documentary

This documentary is often shown in pre-service or in-service teacher education courses in philosophy with children. Despite an audience sympathetic to the philosophy with children ethos and generally holding young children in high regard as thinkers, the documentary invariably prompts adult laughter (Haynes and Murris, 2012). Even when teachers are very familiar with P4C, they smile, laugh or claim that Charlotte cannot possibly be telling the truth, and must be making it up. I have also heard teachers exclaim 'How sweet', or 'Cute' after watching the DVD. This endearment, which involves attributing innocence to child, is in itself far from innocent. When teachers smile knowingly to one another or laugh as children express novel ways of understanding the world, this endearment usually allows them to avoid any re-examination of their own beliefs and assumptions. Sentimentality and endearment seem to presuppose vulnerability and *inequality*. Children's speculations are seen as unusual, sweet, perhaps foolish, but *harmless*. Children's philosophising does not lead to adults' changing their minds about important matters. So what would it be like to listen responsively in this particular example?

Through being and thinking together, the children problematise the idea that peace is a desirable goal we should 'naturally' strive for. By doing that, the children pose an interesting challenge to peaceful existence as the 'overarching aim' of citizenship education (Joubert, 2009, p. 12) – as designed and concept-ualised by adults. So what are the missed opportunities here? Taking the children's playful challenge, that living in a 'perfect world' might be boring and not all that blissful, could lead to new understandings of concepts by examining together the meaning of a 'perfect world' or even 'boring' for that matter. But also, what *is* meant by 'peace' – the exclusion of armed conflict, such as wars, or also other kinds of conflict? What is so uncomfortable about always drinking cups of coffee together?

> The philosophical potential of the enquiry for a deeper understanding of the issues involved is exciting. Does 'peace' mean 'being always nice to each other' – as suggested by one of the children? Or does it mean 'disarmament', or 'abandonment of fighting'? If so, does this include *all* fighting, including play-fighting or fighting for a just cause? And what is the difference between the two? What about verbal arguments, or other kinds of conflict?
>
> What is important here is the prejudice that when children grow up, that is, develop into more mature, rational adults, they will come to understand that perfect worlds are peaceful (whatever that might mean) and grandmas *should be* loved more than cats.

to use Table 5.1 (Chapter 5) diffractively – for example, on a separate hand-out or displayed on the interactive whiteboard. The idea is for new thoughts and ideas to emerge – not for educators to agree with my comments, but for them to respond in enquiry mode and to document their ideas multi-modally as part of their ongoing assignment during the year in their diffractive journals.[20]

Further diffractions . . .

The teacher in the documentary seems guided by the children's interests. He is not invisible,[22] although it is clear that the children are used to be listened to responsively and feel comfortable speaking their bodyminds. So what does he *do*? He has made sure that their bodies sit in a circle on chairs, so they can all see each other's faces. Importantly, he writes down their philosophical questions on the white board for easy access and with their names after the questions as an aide memoire. They might be kept to start off future enquiries or hang up on the wall. It signals importance to the children – their questions *matter* to their teacher. Writing them down makes it less likely that they will be forgotten and therefore (arguably) has more *agency* than if only spoken.

As viewers, we have no access to the one question that starts off the enquiry and that the children must have voted for. It is unclear how much the teacher is involved in the process of recording the questions. He does use his voice to express his appreciation for the question 'Do animals have feelings?', but it is unclear whether the children were given 'thinking time' or worked in pairs or small groups first. It is possible to speculate from the resultant enquiry that they are discussing the children's question, 'Why would you want to save someone you don't know?'.

The teacher takes little part in the content of the dialogue, but, because the DVD has been heavily edited, much is speculation. And without having access to the unedited version, it is unclear how the agential cuts[23] of the DVD bring about a particular perspective of the intra-actions.[24] My agential cut, that is, choice in extract and critical incidents, brings into focus not only epistemic injustice, but also *onto*epistemic injustice, in that child is treated epistemically in a particular way because of identity prejudice, that is, the association with a particular being-in-the-world (child).

The ease by which the children engage with each other (and with the knowledge that it will be televised) suggests the establishment in that class of a more or less self-sustaining democratic practice where the children have learned that taking risks in dialoguing is permissible and valued. Epistemic trust seems to have been established and the adult in charge must have shown respect for their ideas and experiences in the past, or they would not have been thinking aloud in this manner. By not intervening (too) much, the dialogue unfolds. But also, something else is going on. The 'teacher' here is not one person; the children (teachers?) are listening responsively to each other and constructing new thoughts together. The physical boundaries of turn-taking hide the collaborative negotiation of the knowledge that is under construction, and the *language* that is available to analyse the transcript almost forces us to stay with an individualistic subjectivity. A child asks the probing question, 'What is a stranger?' and a definition of 'stranger' follows (although this might not have happened). Then the implications of what it means not to know a stranger are drawn: why save strangers if they might be horrible? (What a wonderful counter-example!) The belief that families have moral priority in one's who-shall-I-save-first list is challenged: why should 'knowing someone' be a salient criterion? The responsibility for the existence of horrible people in the world is put in god's lap and his or her intentions are questioned. A solution is also proposed: we need the bad, not just the good, and it leaves me curious about what the reasons for this might be, other than having to contemplate how boring it would be to live in a world where you always have to be nice to other people! The children's voices were *without organs* – not just coming out individual *mouths*. Deleuze and Guattari poetically prescribe the way forward:

> Is it really so sad and dangerous to be fed up with seeing with your eyes, breathing with your lungs, swallowing with your mouth, talking with your tongue, thinking with your brain, having an anus and larynx, head and legs? Why not walk on your head, sing with your sinuses, see through your skin, breathe with your belly . . . Where psychoanalysis says, 'Stop, find your self again', we should say instead, 'Let's go further still, we haven't found our BwO [Body without Organs] yet, *we haven't sufficiently dismantled our self*'. Substitute forgetting for anamnesis, experimentation for interpretation. Find your body without organs. Find out how to make it. It's a question of life and death, youth and old age, sadness and joy. It is where everything is played out.
>
> Deleuze and Guattari, 1987/2013, p. 175;
> my emphasis

A posthumanist orientation 'dismantles' the self and understands bodies as sets of practices. Voice is produced in relation with materialdiscursive others in a complex (always) already entangled network of human and nonhuman forces, and is thereby located 'outside' acting, human, and nonhuman bodies. This has of course implications for how educators should *listen* to voice and what this means: a Listening without Organs (LwO).

Listening without Organs

LwO disrupts the common practice in schools of 'listening-as-usual' (Davies, 2014), that is, listening as *evaluating, interpreting* –listening out for the *same*, thereby confirming what we already know. Instead LwO involves listening-as-experimentation and is always emergent – listening out for the effects of *difference*, what makes me as educator think and feel *differently*. Children's bodyminds transform me when iii listen without organs.

The children's wonderings in the philosophical enquiry were genuinely thought provoking in the Heideggerian sense: we can learn to think only by '*giving* our mind to what there is to think about' (Heidegger, 1968, p. 4; my emphasis). This 'giving' is possible only when educators are 'open-bodyminded' and have *ontoepistemic modesty*, that is, accept that their (and all) knowledge is limited and constructed 'between' children, adults and nonhuman others, and that, therefore, they can learn (also) from children. They need to be open to what they have not heard before, and to resist a listening-as-usual. What, for example, were the girl's own experiences she was drawing on when claiming that drinking cups of coffee all the time and being nice to each other would not be comfortable? As Maybin puts it:

> Meaning-making emerges as an on-going dialogic process at a number of different, interrelated levels: dialogues within utterances and between utterances, dialogues between voices cutting across utterance boundaries and dialogues with other voices from the past.
>
> Maybin, 2006, p. 24

For this reason, concepts such as 'speaker' (sending a message) and 'listener' (receiver of the message) are inappropriate metaphors as they do not do justice to the materialdiscursive entanglement of the encounter. Listening is not only with the ear and the brain, but with the entire unbounded body, as we will explore in the next chapter with the metaphor of a Hundred Languages, and in particular with the teacher listening as pregnant stingray in Chapter 8.

Early childhood educator, Carlina Rinaldi, reminds us that the physical space is another strong language that constitutes thought, although its 'code is not always explicit and recognisable' (Rinaldi, 2006, p. 82). She points out how reading 'spatial language is multisensory and involves both the remote receptors (eye, ear and nose) and the immediate receptors for the surrounding environment (the skin, membranes and muscles)' (Rinaldi, 2006, p. 82). The children's experience of re-doing the concept of a 'perfect world' is therefore a materialdiscursive sensory activity of thinking together, and goes beyond the confines of a material indivi-dual body. Rinaldi also emphasises young children's 'high level of perceptual sensitivity and competence' (Rinaldi, 2006, p. 82) – one reason for taking utmost care in the use of light and colour in teaching.

In philosophical enquiries the meaning of ethical concepts (here: 'perfect world') are shaped by normative beliefs and bodily practices. In the examples above, hearers' prejudices can cause them to miss out on knowledge offered by the children, for example, the depth of Charlotte's love for Zephyr, or their challenge to the idea that a 'perfect world' should be desirable. Clearly, children cannot be trusted to have access to the truth here, as they are usually not regarded as epistemic authorities. This stereotyping has to do with how educators view knowledge, as much as child, and is even more extreme when child is *also* female, black and lives in poverty (but of course we do not have such important situated details at our disposal in this example).

One form of disciplinary power, according to Foucault, is 'normalisation': schools define what is normal and desirable, and in this case norms are applied to how teachers interpret children's interpretations of reality. Such dominant discourses exclude other ways of thinking and of understanding the world (Dahlberg and Moss, 2005, p. 17). When thinking *alongside* children (Haynes and Murris, 2013), *everyone* needs to 'give' their bodymind to what there is to think about, which is possible only when adults are also 'open-bodyminded', have *ontoepistemic modesty* and *ontoepistemic trust*. If what children say (the content) is not heard (but laughed at) – *ontoepistemic equality* is absent.

Ontoepistemic equality is different from *political* equality or symmetry, in that adults clearly have more active and passive power[25] over children. Teachers have the capacity to control the actions of children *actively* (e.g. administer tests), but also *passively*, that is, there is always the possibility that teachers might use their capacity to regulate the children's behaviour. Similarly, in the case of ontoepistemic equality, teachers have the power to actively and passively use ontoepistemic trust and modesty in their classrooms. These intellectual virtues are about an openness to the possibility that when a child speaks she might not only contribute to the pool of knowledge (the possibility of which should not be prejudged), but also that knowledge contributions are indeterminate, and therefore cannot be quantified.

Letting child 'in' by rethinking what knowledge is

Re-turning to where we started in this chapter, ontoepistemic equality is possible only when teaching is not regarded as 'people trying and succeeding in passing on what is worthwhile' (Peters, 1966, p. 26). Teaching, more broadly and in less humanist terms, can be any object or event that makes a difference, that *disturbs* (Bateson in Davis, 2004, p. 51). The word 'teach' is derived from the

Old English 'tacn', meaning something like 'sign' (Davis, 2004, p. 51), and therefore broader than the use of words only. Also, as we have seen in Chapter 4, in the case of *philosophical* knowledge, child is in a distinct *advantageous* position as s/he is less likely to take the everyday use of abstract concepts for granted (Murris, 2000) – as long as the criterion for 'worthwhile knowledge' does not exclude children's narrative and imaginative materialdiscursive practices (Haynes and Murris, 2013).

For a humanist, knowledge is representational: knowledge is possible *of* the world from above or outside and the knowing subject stands outside the physical world the subject seeks to know (Barad, 2007, pp. 341–2). In contrast, for a posthumanist, knowledge is not 'ideational', but part of being. Knowing is a material practice, that is, 'a physical practice of engagement', a specific entangled, open and ongoing reconfiguration of the world of which it is a part (Barad, 2007, p. 342).

So we have seen that it is indeed true that philosopher Miranda Fricker's sophisticated 'conceptual apparatus' (Code, 2008) adds force to the idea that child should be included in knowledge construction. However, just adding 'age' to 'race', 'class' and 'gender' – the more common categories of exclusion and discrimination – is insufficient. In this chapter iii have shown that it is also necessary to disrupt what counts as 'worthwhile' knowledge in order to include child ontoepistemically. Ironically, the ethical move to allow child 'in' ontoepistemically *also* means that children should be allowed to challenge adults' political agenda that sometimes prevents children from using binaries that exclude and discriminate such as race, gender and class. One of the aims of education (see Chapter 2) is for children and students to bring something new to the world as an event ('relational material subjectification'). This can take the form of openly exploring topics or concepts that some people might not find 'politically correct' (Browne, 2006). So adding 'age' to 'race', 'class' and 'gender' as a category of discrimination exposes such moves as reestablishing a hierarchy in teaching and learning practices because *what knowledge is* and *whose knowledge matters* remain unquestioned.

By reading Barad's posthumanism and Fricker's notion of epistemic injustice through one another, new knowledge was created. Not just epistemic, but also *onto*epistemic injustice is done to child as the intra-actions change how child is part of the world.[26] Although Fricker admits that concepts are not necessarily linguistic[27] and that making sense of one's experiences (hermeneutical injustice) is possible without expressing one's thoughts and ideas verbally, multimodal means of knowledge construction and awareness of space and the material in teaching and learning need to be considered in order to be able to 'allow' child 'in'. As recognised by my student teacher, but not understood by her mentor teacher in the example at the beginning of this chapter, junk materials can be used forcefully to 'break boundaries, open up realms of thought and create new connections' (Odegard, 2012, p. 398), otherwise teachers 'may be in danger of reproducing what they have already seen or thought in an unending circle of recognition and repetition' (Odegard, 2012, p. 396). And the ethicopolitical commitment to emergent listening implies being open as an educator to what they have not heard before, and to resist the urge to translate of what iii hear into what is familiar (Haynes and Murris, 2012). This transformation is particularly urgent for more just educational encounters with people who are not only young, but might also live in poverty and are unlikely to have English as their home language. In the next chapter, iii will read philosophy with children diffractively with Reggio Emilia – another intra-active pedagogy that disrupts existing age prejudice and 'flattens' the ontoepistemological hierarchy in the classroom.

Notes

1 I have argued elsewhere (Murris, 2013) that listening to children using the individualistic ontology of classical Western epistemology hides the learning that takes place in the space 'between' child (as educator) and adult (as learner). In this chapter iii re-visit, or what MacLure (2013) would describe as 'being pulled back', by the data, that is, iii re-turn using a diffractive methodology to a previous analysis of a publically available philosophical dialogue between children. This leads to a reconsideration of some of my earlier arguments and develops this relational ontoepistemology further to include not only *child's* agency in knowledge production, but also the material, including the fact that the dialogue was filmed and broadcast.
2 Waves of course are not individual 'things'. Waves can overlap at the same point in space. When two waves of water combine, the 'resultant wave is a sum of the effects of each individual component wave, that is, it is a combination of the disturbances created by each wave individually. This way of combining effects is called *superposition*' (Barad, 2007, p. 76).
3 Building on Deleuze, Lenz Taguchi (2012) explains how reading texts diffractively foregrounds questions such as 'Does it work?' and 'How does it work?' instead of 'What does it mean?'. This chapter exemplifies how a diffractive reading of Fricker has generated questions about including age as a category of discrimination and marginalisation, but also questions about the politics of knowledge, what it is, who it is for and the kind of relationships it keeps in place.
4 With thanks to Vivienne Bozalek, who pointed this out to me when presenting a draft version of this chapter in a Webinar for the South African National Research Foundation project *Posthumanism and the Affective Turn.*
5 I argued elsewhere that it was a matter of adding as another category, but iii understand that differently now. See: Murris, 2013.
6 Even if the lesson had been planned separately, it would still have been possible to adapt the lesson in the moment to connect with what had gone on before.
7 The student teacher's complex role during teaching practice is not always easy to manage, and the 'being a guest in school' status combined with the 'locus parentis' role of teachers can give rise to the most complex of professional moral dilemmas (see Murris, 2012, 2014).
8 See Chapter 7 in particular.
9 Many classrooms look very much alike: they materialise a particular empiricist idea of 'worthwhile' education. As *tabula rasa* or empty vessel, the child as passive recipient of culture and knowledge needs to be 'filled' (Bruce, 1987/2011, pp. 3–4) with the information hung up in, for example, posters around the room.

10 This kind of prejudice leads to what she calls 'testimonial injustice' – see below.

11 Of course, in Chapter 5 it is argued how a reconfiguring of child and the decentring of voice ('Voice without Organs') are the two strategies that are necessary for transformation (to seeing the body as 'a transformer'). See also the analysis of a philosophical enquiry below.

12 And in that order of priority, at least in South Africa.

13 Academic philosophers such as Matthew Lipman, Gareth Matthews, David Kennedy, Walter Kohan, Karin Murris and Joanna Haynes have argued for 'philosophy of childhood' as a distinct field of philosophical enquiry.

14 In private conversation at the Social Equality conference, held at the University of Cape Town in August 2014.

15 Students who do not have English as their mother tongue do not only benefit from, but also should be allowed to benefit from, Reggio-inspired practices in teacher education from a justice point of view.

16 She makes a distinction between active and passive social power. Power is the socially situated capacity to control the actions of others, and, applying her ideas to education, this is the case in schools when teachers have active power over their learners by, for example administering punishment, but also in a more passive way: the mere capacity that a teacher can hand out punishments influences and regulates learners' behaviour (Fricker, 2007, pp. 9, 10).

17 Tina Bruce (1987/2011, p. 166) points out the damage done to children by 'herding' them in large groups, for example, by letting three- and four-year-olds sit for long periods of time in assembly. Such practices require children to sit still and to listen *politely*. If they cannot do that and 'misbehave' they will be accused of being 'naughty' and they will learn – Bruce points out – that 'naughtiness is simply not doing what an adult wants', or, in other words 'what inconveniences the system'. This then becomes blurred with a naughtiness that is *moral*, not just rule-breaking, and involves wrong-doing to other humans or nonhuman animals.

18 See Chapter 1.

19 Although a philosophical enquiry has a beginning and an end 'in' time, the entangled intra-actions are not unities (Barad, 2014, p. 176) and 'are' always present, past and future.

20 See Chapter 2.

21 See http://members.ozemail.com.au/~jpascal/intro.htm (accessed 27 December 2014).

22 Unlike an earlier analysis of this dialogue (Murris, 2013), iii now acknowledge the significant role the teacher's body plays *as part of* the facilitation and the materiality. Knowing is a material practice, that is, 'a physical practice of engagement' (Barad, 2007, p. 342), a specific engagement with the world of which the teacher is also a part. Knowledge construction is always an entangled, open and ongoing reconfiguration of the world.

23 Agential cuts are specific intra-actions and always within relationships (Barad, 2012, p. 77).

24 The neologism 'intra-action' has been created by Barad (2007) to avoid the dualisms involved in 'interaction' (two separate entities acting upon each other).

25 See Chapter 1, note 10.

26 Moreover, the diffractive methodology itself works with 'positive differences', and therefore supports children's confidence to make sense of their own experiences. Diffraction is an affirmative method and central in intra-active pedagogies, as we will explore further in Chapter 7.

27 In private conversation during the 'Social Equality' Conference held at the University of Cape Town in August 2014.

Part II

Posthumanist intra-active pedagogies

Plates 1a–c
The 'Philosopher's Washing Line' in 2014

Plate 2a Hlengiwe Mkhize's bodymind map

Plate 2b Tarryn Welsh's bodymind map

Plate 3 Giving and taking: Shel Silverstein's *The Giving Tree*

Plate 4a Upset about King Kong's death scene, Gorilla smashes the television set

Plate 4b The kitten's tail points towards the Fall of Icarus, who drowned in the sea because he flew too high and his wings melted

Chapter 7

Reading Reggio Emilia and philosophy with children diffractively through one another

... The child has
a hundred languages
(and a hundred hundred hundred more)
but they steal ninety-nine.
The school and the culture
separate the head from the body ...

> From 'The Hundred Languages', a poem by
> Loris Malaguzzi (translated by Lella Gandini) –
> Founder of the Reggio Emilia Approach[1]

In Chapter 7 iii have used the diffractive methodology with very different philosophical texts and ideas – those of Miranda Fricker and Karen Barad. What emerged was the new notion ('superposition'[2]) of *ontoepistemic injustice*: a child is not listened to, because of its very *being* of child, and therefore can make no claims to knowledge, because s/he is (still) innocent, (still) fragile, (still) immature, (still) irrational and so forth. Child is denied ethically, epistemically and ontologically.

Recall how child (and also adult) is a relational entanglement – an inhuman materialdiscursive becoming 'iii' (Chapter 4). 'The' subject as a unique being with indeterminate boundaries comes 'into' the world as an *event*. This 'uniqueness' of the subject manifests itself in the materialdiscursive *relationship* with others (Chapter 3). It is not a property, essence or quality of an individual ('child as 'i' or 'I'), but it is the relationship with human and nonhuman others that is necessary for uniqueness to be articulated, for a subject to become singular in an ethical sense (Chapter 2). So, the salient ethicopolitical issue in Part II is *who*, *where* and *how* are child's materialdiscursive beginnings taken up and materialised in intra-action in schools (with other human animals, and nonhuman others). What are the response-abilities of early childhood educators in these complex situations? iii suggest that the answers to these questions revolve around two intra-active pedagogies that do justice to the ontology of child as inhuman becomings, and child's reconfiguration 'as'[3] rich, resilient and resourceful in relationships (Chapter 5).

In this chapter I read philosophy with children and Reggio Emilia diffractively through one another using a relational materialist orientation.[4] What emerge are new diffraction patterns that include, and do not reduce, one of these intra-active pedagogies to the other. The 'superposition' (Barad, 2007, p. 76) created by the diffraction is not critical, but adds force to both. iii will simply call it 'Reggio-inspired philosophy with children'; and after this chapter it is assumed that when iii refer to 'philosophy with children' that it is indeed this superposition iii am referring to, unless explicitly stated otherwise.

Reggio Emilia

Reggio Emilia is a city in the Emilia Romagna region of northern Italy. It is famous for its development of an early education system, often referred to simply as 'Reggio'. It is not a method or prescribed curriculum to follow and to copy, but a socially and culturally embedded educational approach and philosophy (Stremmel, 2012, p. 134). According to its founder Loris Malaguzzi, its history started six days after the end of the Second World War, in the Spring of 1945 (Malaguzzi, 1998, p. 49). He had heard that a group of mothers in nearby Villa Cella wanted to build and run a school for young children, so, a teacher himself, he literally jumped on his bike and joined them. In an interview, Malaguzzi (1998, p. 57) beautifully describes the force of the material in that process of starting a school: '. . . you have to agree that seeing an army tank, six horses, and three trucks generating a school for young children is extraordinary'. They had been left by the Germans and the first preschool was built by their own hands and financed by selling these (Malaguzzi, 1998, pp. 49–51). Run by parents in the poorest parts of this village, they struggled at first to communicate well with the children, who were often hungry, in poor health and spoke a local dialect. But these socio-economic and cultural factors became a positive opportunity. In Loris Malaguzzi's own words: 'A simple, liberating thought came to our aid, namely that things about children and for children are only learned from children' (Malaguzzi, 1998, p. 51). It was the 'first spark' (Malaguzzi, 1998, p. 50) of a now globally well-known and admired (secular[5]) approach to early childhood education. The first municipally funded preschool opened in 1963.

Pedagogies as living organisms

Concerned about Italy's political role during the Second World War and its fascism, a philosophical practice developed (and is still developing) that regards schools as places for democratic conversation, critical and creative thinking and caring relationships (Stremmel, 2012, p. 134). Reggio and philosophy with children are *living organisms* – they shape themselves according to the various psychological, sociological and philosophical theories that theorists bring to the practice. The kind of education they inspire cannot simply be replicated or imitated in other settings. In effect, to avoid domination by hegemonic theories of child and childhood, Reggio practitioners continually engage with educational theories critically and overtly in collaborative dialogue with important others: parents and colleagues.

The literature suggests that both approaches do not exclude developmental psychologists, social constructionists, social constructivists, pragmatists, phenomenologists, poststructuralists and postmodernists, although the relational pedagogies certainly resonate more with some than with others. It would be wrong to suggest that practitioners of a Reggio-inspired philosophy with children should feel at *home* in their practices; on the contrary, the educator should remain 'nomadic' and continuously question educational theories with other teachers, practitioners, authors, parents, materials, ideas, traditions (Kennedy, 1996a).

Theories and practices are constantly on the move, evolving, shifting and changing. In fact, the 'rhizomatic' nature of the school curriculum (see below) is echoed in how the schools are run and managed. As with philosophy with children, beliefs are held tentatively and knowledge about children, schooling and the adult/child relationship are regarded as always incomplete – resisting temptations for closure and including a normalisation and celebration of conflict and disagreement (Haynes and Murris, 2012). In that sense, the interrogation of the figure of child in both pedagogies is as much about child as it is about the figure of adult and their relationship (Kennedy, 1996a).

In other words, childhood educators as nomadic subjects think for themselves (importantly *through* thinking with others) about their educational ideas and ideals as they situate their understandings of the pedagogies in their own sociocultural contexts, and infuse the practice with their own identities and philosophical beliefs. In a Wittgensteinian sense, they are united in the way members of a family share certain resemblances (such as noses or ugly toes) – any generalisation (or capturing of an essence) fails to do justice to what is unique about each family member, and not one characteristic is shared by everyone. My own practice is a constantly shifting and changing superposition of both (and other) philosophies and pedagogies, and recently also from a posthumanist orientation that is still rare, but gaining traction.

There are some key ideas that characterise members of 'this' family, and the main objective of this chapter is to express some of these, as they are salient for transforming classroom practices. My overall argument that drives this chapter is my desire to show how matters of ontology and epistemology have implications for ethical relationships in our educational institutions, and that they cannot, and should not, be reduced to apolitical governmental concerns about efficacy and standardisation.

My proposal is for educational practices that are ethical and do ontoepistemic justice to posthuman child as well as adult (and other nonhuman others). Reggio-inspired philosophy with children should put a stop to current discriminatory ageist practices routinely inflicted on earth dwellers in our homes and institutions.

The following core ideas can be found in this section of the labyrinth: the 'Hundred Languages', building a democratic community of enquiry, education as relationships, the figuration of child, Child as Fool, a rhizomatic curriculum and knowledge as a 'tangle of spaghetti'.

The Hundred Languages

Loris Malaguzzi's metaphor of 'The Hundred Languages' came out of a political discussion in the 1970s in Italy about the reasons for, and consequences, of privileging two languages only: reading and writing (Dahlberg and Moss, 2010, pp. xviii–xix). The metaphor refers at one (practical) level to the introduction of materialdiscursive tools for meaning making in schools, such as visual arts, physical movement, video, digital cameras, augmented realities and computers. At a symbolic level, the Hundred Languages are, as Carlina Rinaldi (2006, p. 175) puts it: a 'metaphor for crediting children and adults with a hundred, a thousand creative and communicative potentials'. Creativity exists in all languages, including mathematical and scientific languages (Rinaldi, 2006, p. 176), and Reggio-inspired schools employ artists/art-educators (*atelieristas*) who orchestrate a wide range of cognitive and poetic languages (especially the visual, see Vecchi, 2010). The practices of the early education centres in Reggio Emilia – as well as the many educational centres around the world that are now 'Reggio inspired' – trouble the still-dominant humanist focus in education on the written word – this one dominant (human) language. As a result we fail so many of the world's children.

Including the oral language of philosophy with children

Philosophy for children (P4C)[6] was pioneered[7] by philosopher Matthew Lipman (1988, 1991) in the late 1960s, whose passion to effect real change in the world was also ignited by the Second World War and its after-effects; he had served as a soldier on foreign soil in Europe. Moreover, lack of critical thinking about the Vietnam War by his fellow Americans[8] (including his own undergraduate philosophy students) gave rise to his inspirational idea to start with teaching philosophy in childhood. Essential for a well-functioning truly democratic society, he speculated that early intervention through a specially written curriculum[9] would tap into children's original curiosity, sense of wonder and enthusiasm for intellectual enquiry, and strengthen their philosophical thinking. In his autobiography, Lipman (2008, p. 53) explains the salient influence on his philosophy of education by Russian psychologist Lev Vygotsky and the philosophy of, and personal relationship, he had with John Dewey. Lipman was particularly attracted to studying philosophy as an academic discipline by its concerns with *thinking about thinking* (Lipman, 2008, p. 58). He also describes the sophistication required of philosophical conversations – 'a language of languages', a focus on 'something greater than the judgments', that is, the criteria for those judgments' (Lipman, 2008, p. 59). These criteria, in turn, interlock with other criteria that are interlocked with other criteria and so on, and, although no answers yet emerge, the process is 'intriguing, exciting, illuminating' (Lipman, 2008, p. 59). They generate enquiries that focus on meaning, rather than learning; on understanding, rather than truth. This language, he writes, makes us more *reasonable*, more *questioning* and more *conceptually* adept (Lipman, 2008, p. 60).

The Institute for the Advancement of Philosophy for Children (IAPC), which he founded at Montclair University in 1974, is the intellectual hub that supports the training of teachers and philosophers all over the world in establishing philosophy with children in their own countries. David Kennedy (2011, p. 96) describes the revolution Lipman brought about as 'the radical reconstruction of philosophy as dialogue, and dialogue, moreover, among children'. This revolution – the emergence of philosophy of childhood – was also supported by philosopher Gareth Matthews, who questioned Piagetian developmentalism and argued for child as 'natural philosopher'. His highly accessible books (1980, 1984, 1994) are littered with arguments and dialogues with children that exemplify that children's thinking is similar to that of adult philosophers.

Advocates of philosophy with children disagree about their views of child[10] (Murris, 1997, 2000, 2008, 2015; Haynes and Murris, 2012, 2013). For example, Walter Kohan (1998) has been a strong voice in arguing against efforts to include children in the rational world of adults. The encounter between philosophy and childhood opens up the challenge for adults of a different form of reason and knowledge, resulting in different philosophies that children may bring to academic philosophy itself.

Despite these differences, childhood became the site for a radical democratisation of academic philosophy, and educationally Lipman combined the ideas of Paulo Freire (democratic dialogue) and John Dewey (education as enquiry) into the *community of enquiry* pedagogy. It is an elusive concept, impossible to define, because it 'takes on new aspects and dimensions as teachers and students apply it and modify it to their purposes. A community of enquiry is at once immanent and transcendent: it provides a framework which pervades the everyday life of its participants and it serves as an ideal to strive for' (Splitter and Sharp, 1995, pp. 17–18).

The pedagogy has been inspired by the oral Platonic dialogues featuring Socrates, and characterised by the metaphor of thinking as 'inner speech' (Matthews, 1980, p. 42). The Vygotskyan assumption is that children will learn to think for themselves if they engage in the social practice of thinking together (Cam, 1995, p. 17). By the same token, the teachers are to 'internalise' the procedures of intellectual imaginative conversations (Bleazby, 2012). The social constructionist and social constructivist idea is that the 'internalisation' of the 'outer voices' that build on each other's ideas in a community of enquiry will lead to a richer, more varied 'inner' dialogue, and as a result a better, more reasonable thinking, through 'self-correction' (Splitter and Sharp, 1995, pp. 32–3).

Advocates of this relational approach to the teaching of thinking sometimes struggle to resist the pressure of governments to evaluate and measure the 'progress' of the philosophical work in community of enquiries in *individualistic* terms – for example, in order to get funding, or to get the approach established in a school (Haynes and Murris, 2011). Reggio strengthens the relational dimensions of philosophy with children. Therefore, a Reggio-inspired philosophy with children does not limit itself to the teaching of philosophy as a separate subject – for example, 'philosophy' as a one-hour per week lesson, in one particular class, or a particular phase. Instead, the philosophical practice infuses the entire curriculum, as a whole-school approach and also involves parents and other members of the community. In that way, a school becomes an enquiring, inexhaustible and dynamic 'living organism' (Malaguzzi, 1998, pp. 62–3). Reggio-inspired philosophy with children should be part and parcel of everyday good-quality early years provision (see e.g. Sara Stanley's [2004, 2012] groundbreaking work on philosophical play).

Materialdiscursive relationships with human animals and nonhuman others

Building good relationships between children and their teacher is built into the notion of a community of enquiry. Reggio's metaphor of 'education as relationship' extends the more democratic, less hierarchical circle to include parents and other community members – the Reggio triadic relationship of child, teacher, parent (Malaguzzi, 1998, p. 65). Carolyn Edwards (1995) reminds us that the Reggio metaphor of relations also stands for relations other than between people: relations between things, between thoughts, between concepts, with the environment.

As we have seen in Chapter 1, a relational materialist ontoepistemology does not understand relationships as connections that are made between independently existing ontological units (like the more familiar 'inter-action'), as this would assume that there *are* bounded subjects and objects 'in' the world moving through space and time (Barad, 2007, 2013, p. 815). Instead, the pro-position is that it is impossible to say where the boundaries *are* of each child, or the teacher, or the parent, or the gecko on the wall, or the furniture, or the drawings, and so forth (not only from an *epistemological*, but also from an *ontological* point of view). For relational materialists, the ontological and epistemological starting points for theorising are the intra-actions – the *relations* 'between' individuals and nonhuman others, not the *relata*[11] (see Chapter 4). Intra-action is *mutual relationality*: things 'are' because they are in relation to and influencing each other. It involves giving up the idea that a teacher can be an objective observer at a distance watching, recording and evaluating children's thinking or behaviour according to a predetermined framework of expectations and norms (Dahlberg, Moss and Pence, 2013, p. 154).

The pedagogical documentation used in Reggio does not pretend to describe the truth, but always involves a value-laden choice: selective, partial and contextual and demanding that teachers be 'response-able' (Barad, 2007) for their observations, descriptions, interpretations and explanations, and to dare to see the ambiguities (Dahlberg, Moss and Pence, 2013, p. 155). It is the documentation that emerges 'in' relationship with the child, both as content and process (the same can be said about the diffractive journaling process), bringing *'forces* and *energies'* to the project work (Dahlberg, 2003 cited in Olsson, 2009). The content is the concrete, visual or audible material itself in the form of, for example, handwritten notes, photographs, or videos – a living record of the pedagogical practice (Dahlberg, Moss and Pence, 2013, pp. 156, 162).

As a process, the relations (including the material and the dialogues with parents, children and other teachers) make the documentation possible, and always project forwards, opening up further avenues for exploration (Dahlberg, Moss and Pence, 2013, p. 156). Interestingly, the new is created by diffracting with what happened 'in' the past. Crucially the documentation is not only about the *children*, but is an opportunity to diffract with the configurations of child that have been brought into existence through the materialdiscursive practices, including the documentation (or the diffractive journal as iii use it in higher education).

Mutual relationships when thinking together

In a community of philosophical enquiry, everyone (including the teacher) becomes aware of a horizon of meaning larger than the perspectives of any one individual (Kennedy, 1996a), a kind of distributive thinking, 'a mind of the whole group' (Kennedy, 2006, p. 9) or what *atelierista* Vea Vecchi (2010, pp. 28–9) calls 'collective intelligence'.[12] This collaborative and authentic thinking generates and nurtures feelings of culture and solidarity, responsibility and inclusion, and helps to develop thinking and actions that are not only critical, but also creative and caring.

Conceptual work benefits greatly from alternating the use of the 'language of languages' (philosophical language) with the other 'ninety-nine languages'. The physical properties of various media influence how a concept can be expressed, for example, by the use of string, blocks or clay to express 'love' (Forman, 1994, pp. 37–8). Typically, extended projects (*progettione*[13]) start with 'verbal outpourings' that allow easy access to memories and a 'free reign to thought' (Edwards, 1995, p. 42), aided also by removal of the obstacle of having to read or write. In turn, regular philosophical enquiries have other affordances, for example, formulating new theories and hypotheses out of these oral exchanges, real or imagined, which in turn can be put to the 'test' through drawing what they know (see, for an example, Chapter 10). Then when drawing they might discover 'gaps' in their knowledge and have to readjust the theories

(Forman, 1994), thereby continuously building on and refining earlier thinking. Each transformation generates something new, making the situation more complex, making understanding more precise. By drawing, for example, learners get rid of excessive, superfluous or misleading ideas: 'With each step, the child goes farther and higher, as a spaceship with several stages, each pushing the rocket deeper into space' (Malaguzzi, 1998, p. 92). A drawing needs to be able to communicate; learners need to make their ideas visible to others in a much simpler, more direct way. Thus, the different languages diffract with one another and create new understandings in the process. The imagination is part of the cognitive process here by ex-pressing what is not there, sometimes in 2D, other times in 3D, simultaneously creating a kind of eco-system, and, in the process, creating deep empathetic understanding for other earth dwellers.

The Giving Tree

Take, for example, the following philosophical work by a group of educators. They were exploring the picturebook *The Giving Tree* (1964/1992) by Shel Silverstein.[14] This old favourite is about an apple tree that gives everything to a little boy. A close materialdiscursive relationship is drawn in black and white pencil. The tree clearly has agency: the boy swings from her branches, they play hide-and-seek together, and he sleeps in her shade. He loves the tree and the tree is happy. As the boy grows older he sees the tree less and less, but he still needs her: she gives her branches to him to make a house, and later in his life also her trunk so he can make a boat and sail away. She is now only a tree stump. Years go by, and finally the boy returns – now an old man. She says: 'I am sorry, Boy, but I have nothing left to give you . . . I wish that I could give you something . . . but I have nothing left. I am just an old stump. I am sorry . . .'. The boy answers: 'I don't need very much now . . . just a quiet place to sit and rest'. The tree responds: 'Well, an old stump is good for sitting and resting. Come, Boy, sit down. Sit down and rest. And the boy did'.

After reading the story, the group wrote down the following abstract concepts on a large piece of paper: 'greed', 'choices', 'captivation', 'consequences', 'anxiety', 'presumptuous', 'potential', 'empathy', 'guidance', 'unfulfilled', 'thoughtlessness'. In two small groups they expressed their questions with playdough and pebbles as in Figure 7.1.

It struck one group that the picturebook was a journey into the unknown, materially expressed as a river. On the river is a little boat with the boy in it. The boat is the tree carrying the boy and the boat is of the same colour (red) as the river, to indicate that the boat needs the river to move. The final destination is still uncertain, hence the question mark outside the picture. The tree is 'content, but sad' and so is the boy, who although grown up, is 'more childlike now' – content with little. One participant remarked that 'the story is more for the reader – to learn from. There is more than one story here: the story of the reader reading the story'.

Figure 7.1 Giving and taking: Shel Silverstein's *The Giving Tree.*

The other group expressed their puzzlement about the polarity and entanglement of the tree and the boy in the second photo in Figure 7.1. The concepts 'giving' and 'taking' (be)come together, like 'transformation', one participant said. In the giving is always the taking. The tree was not only giving; at the same time she was also receiving. One participant problematised the idea of the tree always giving. To be able to give you need *agency*, actually *doing* something, so the title is misleading; the tree is not a *giving* tree at all. Her agency was more in terms of affordances: the tree had made it possible for the boy, for example, to swing on her branches, to climb her and to cut her down. One participant concluded that the choice of gender for the more 'passive' character in this story was far from incidental, and was 'typical'.

After unpacking each other's ideas plenary, the enquiry soon focused on a question that (e)merged out of the question of the first group ('What does it mean to be selfish?') and the second group (Is giving always a good idea?): 'Can you be a selfish giver?'. To answer that (e)mergent question we needed to investigate the relationship between 'needs' and 'wants' – after all, the former leads to the latter and some needs are more authentic than others. For example, can you trust your body to indicate what you need?[15] They agreed that you cannot draw a physical line and say: '*that* is too much'. They continued to discuss the difficulty of quantification, for example – how much love do you *really need* and how much do you *want*? (and why is love not a children's right?, someone asked). Then the Internet was offered as an example: is that something you need or want, or both? Their conceptual wanderings increased the complexity of answering the question that had provoked the enquiry (whether it is possible to be a selfish giver), but they decided that some other (second-order) questions had to be answered first (what does 'giving' mean). They discovered the difficulty of deciding what makes a gift, a gift. It is not necessarily something you *do*; it is not necessarily a *thing* (you can give time, for example), so what is it?

A Reggio-inspired philosophy with children emphasises oral language, and iterative intra-actions with the materialdiscursive body, the material environment (e.g. sitting in a circle), texts, emotions, questions, ideas, each other, the teacher, and even silences. The practice includes questioning contestable, but significant concepts, and 'listening without organs' (LwO) to the answers to these questions. LwO involves listening out for the new and unfamiliar – and distributive thinking without decentred voice (Chapter 6), enabling reconstruction of adult/child relations in education – that is, a disruption of practices of power (Kennedy, 2006, p. 9). Part of LwO is not listening with a particular part of the body, for example, the organ 'ear', but manifests itself in the relationship through *action* (e.g. asking a question in *response* to what a learner says or does) and making the learning visible through documentation, mind maps, recording questions on paper – continuously intra-acting and diffracting. Taking the image of a Body without Organs *literally* as a body in the world without organs would entirely miss the point of what Deleuze and

Guattari are trying to say (Jackson and Mazzei, 2012, p. 85) – that is, the neologism provokes us to move away from the One language that interprets, represents and defines what a concept *is* – assigning it an essence, like pinning a dead butterfly to a display board. As we saw in the enquiry above, definitions are not the endpoint of a philosophical enquiry, but the starting point: what does it mean to give?

In Reggio-inspired philosophy with children, participants initiate long-term open-ended investigations with teachers working alongside other teachers, who intra-act and collaboratively create the right materialdiscursive environment. New conceptual knowledge is created in *ateliers* (classrooms) – metaphorical places where 'brains, hands, sensibilities, rationalities, emotion and imagination all work together' (Vecchi, 2010, p. 2).

To incorporate the ideas of the Hundred Languages and mutual relationality into education is certainly a challenge, especially as we are so used to the ideal of objective truth and the fragmentation and segmentation of knowledge and social relations in schools. To that end iii have found it helpful to use Malaguzzi's poem[16] as a starting point for philosophical enquiries. It opens up space to think together about the ideas it provokes and their implications, and for educators to make their own materialdiscursive connections. Moreover, their own questions provide valuable information about what they seem to know and do not know. See, for example, in Figure 7.2, question 2 that was posed by one small group (who had named themselves 'One'): 'What is the one language they don't steal from children?' The educators started answering this particular question, which in turn led to an enquiry about language, what it is, and whether only humans have language. Their thought-provoking questions produced many hours of enquiry, including an investigation about the existence of objective knowledge (provoked by question 5).

Figurations of child: some tensions and contradictions

Both philosophy with children and Reggio Emilia assume child as competent, rich, agentic and with rights. But, as Marg Sellers rightly observes, these figurations 'are entangled in western assumptions of children as essentially weak, needy and embryonic adult' (Sellers, 2013, p. 76), because both assume the nature/culture dichotomy, as we have seen in the previous chapter. Peter Moss reminds us that Loris Malaguzzi's configuration of 'child as rich' 'does not deny that many children are poor in the sense that they live in material poverty, have lives and prospects blighted by inequality, and have to contend with other conditions that deny any hope of a flourishing life' (Moss, 2014, p. 88). For him, the reconfiguration of child from needy and deficient to rich and resourceful is 'a constant reminder of *potentiality*, dwelling on what each and every child brings to early childhood education and what early childhood education can contribute to the realisation of that potentiality' (Moss, 2014, p. 88). With this emphasis on potentiality, the reconfiguration of 'child as rich, resilient and resourceful' is within the context of a relational materialist orientation and *not* an essentialising *abstraction*, as Erika Burman (2013, p. 230) warns when, for example, using the figure 'child as educator'. This figure may appear to reverse

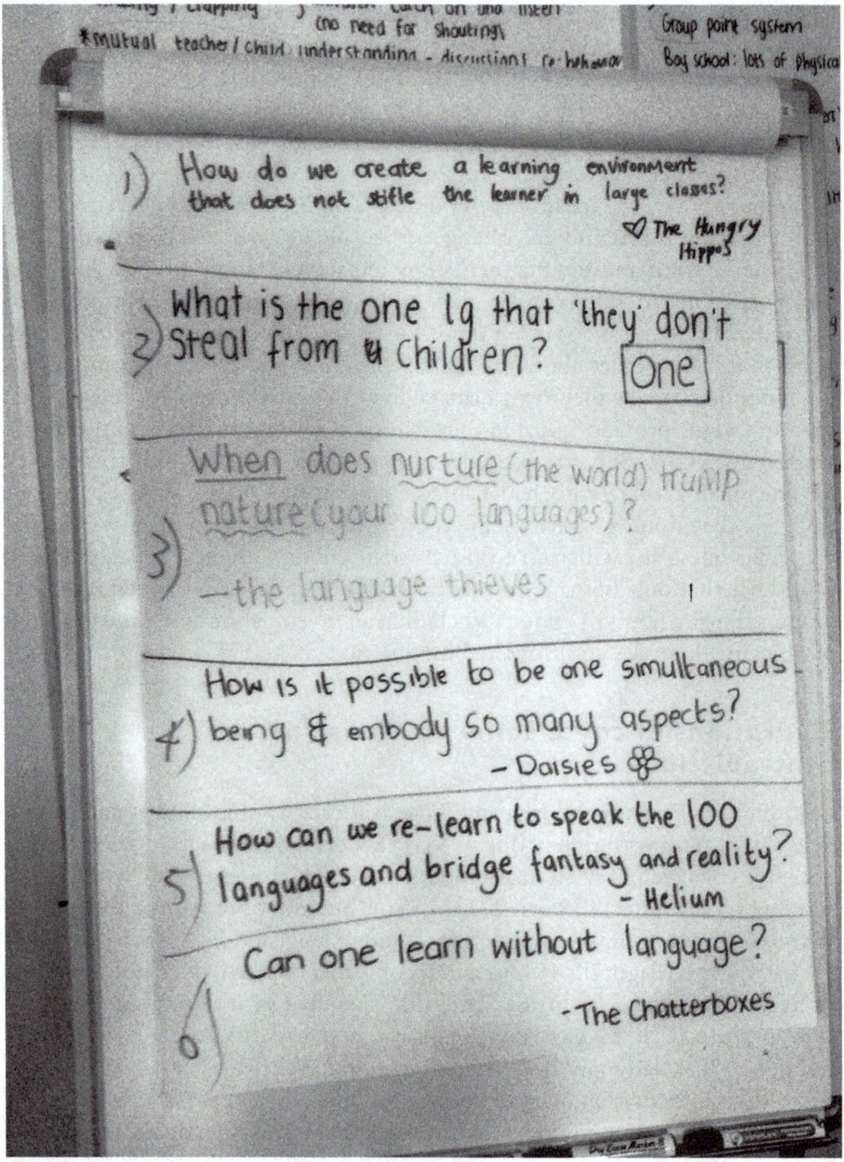

Figure 7.2 Questions about Loris Malaguzzi's poem 'The Hundred Languages'.

power relations between adults and children, she argues, but in fact could repeat that 'the' child of the child-centred pedagogy of 'progressive education' is compatible with both liberal left-wing and right-wing neoliberal policies. Drawing on Fendler and De Vos, Burman (2013, p. 231) argues that the figure or motif of 'child' is heir to a philosophical and cultural heritage of individualism, 'which has become elaborated into a regime of individualisation and psychologisation'. Similarly, Peter Moss points out the contradictions involved when speaking of the 'competent child'. It could mean competence in the 'narrow, technical sense of acquiring certain specified skills or information through training' (Moss, 2014, p. 88), or assume an indivi-dualistic ontoepistemology as iii argued in Chapter 5.

Moss reminds us that a 'competent child' can also mean something different, especially when a Reggio Emilia specialist such as Carlina Rinaldi refers to the concept. She writes how child is rich, strong and powerful 'in potential and resources, right from the moment of birth . . . driven by the enormous energy potential of a hundred billion neurons' (Rinaldi, 2006, p. 123). She affirms that child wants to know and to grow, is curious, and wants reasons for everything. Each child, both individually and in relation with the group, possesses an 'ecological sensibility towards others and the environment'.[17] The child for her is patient and wants to show what s/he can do, has knowledge and has high expectations. This child is *competent*. The way Rinaldi explains how she interprets the concept 'competent' iii fully agree with and is worth quoting at length, as it is the figuration of child (any inhuman becoming in fact) that is assumed by the pedagogies iii enact and promote:

> Competent in relating and interacting, with a deep respect for others and accepting of conflict and error. A child who is competent in constructing, in *constructing himself* while he *constructs his world* and is, in turn, *constructed by the world*. Competent in *constructing theories* to interpret reality and in formulating hypothesis and metaphors as possibilities for understanding reality. A child who has his own values and is adept in building relationships of solidarity. A child who is always open to that which is new and different. A possessor and builder of futures, not only because children are the future, but because they constantly re-interpret reality and continuously give it new meanings. The child as a possessor and *constructor of rights*, who demands to be respected and valued for his own identity, uniqueness and difference. To think of a child as a possessor of rights means not only recognising the rights that the society gives to children, but also creating a context of 'listening' in the fullest sense.
>
> Rinaldi, 2006, p. 123; my emphasis

The key here is how any 'inhuman becoming' (instead of 'human being' or 'child') is capable of actively *constructing* knowledge through materialdiscursive relationships. Malaguzzi (1998, p. 73) urges educators to understand children as *producers* of knowledge, not *consumers*. Children should be taught nothing that they cannot learn by themselves, he adds. Children are capable of constructing *worlds*, constructing *theories*, constructing *rights*, constructing *knowledge* and bringing themselves into being each as an *event*.

Exploring how different the meanings of abstract concepts are, and constructing new conceptual meanings, is at the heart of the activity of philosophical enquiry. Fortunately, children have the privilege of being less attached to their own ideas, which they continuously reconstruct and reinvent (Malaguzzi, 1998, p. 75).

Abstract concepts are embedded in any human enquiry. So far in this book, how the concept 'child' works in our materialdiscursive practices has shaped our journey through the labyrinth. In turn, our enquiry into configurations of child is rhizomatically connected to a core concept such as 'knowledge'. Are children really producers of *knowledge*? 'Is *knowledge* indeed something that is constructed?' 'Is there no established 'body of knowledge' that children need to learn, and is it not our job as teachers to make sure we teach it? Do we not need a set curriculum for educators to teach, and if we do not, will we not run the risk that child initiated learning will not cover the 'basics'? The answers to all these questions depend on what we mean by knowledge and who has access to it and how.

Child as Fool

The only language not 'forgotten' by modern education is reading and writing, with the invention of printing a key event for the 'establishment' of childhood. This narrow meaning of literacy has enhanced adulthood (Stables, 2008, p. 45) and, at the same time, put child in its marginalised place (Kennedy, 1989). No wonder that introducing the other 99 languages as an authentic medium for communicating and constructing knowledge is met with resistance and suspicion. In Chapter 8 iii will argue how dominant this limited notion of literacy still is, despite the 'digital revolution', and how unjust these literacy practices are, especially for children living in poverty and who are often unfamiliar with the language of instruction at school.

Resistance to including the other languages is not just an issue of power, it is metaphysical (and of course the two are entangled). Language has been too *substantialising*, bringing into existence figurations of child as substance with essence, as if the subject-predicate structure of language reflects an ontology: independently existing child *with* competencies or attributes – the arrogance of the anthropocentric human animal one might say. Friedrich Nietzsche did warn us not to take grammar too seriously (Barad, 2007, p. 133). Deleuze and Guattari write:

> When knife cuts flesh, when food or poison spreads through the body, when a drop of wine falls into the water, there is an intermingling of bodies;

but the statements, 'The knife is cutting the flesh,' 'I am eating,' 'The water is turning red,' express incorporeal transformations of an entirely different nature (events).

Deleuze and Guattari, 1987/2013, p. 86

Language has been granted excessive power in determining what is real, and has instilled a deep mistrust of matter, figuring it as mute, passive, immutable (Barad, 2007, p. 133). Language and discourse have positioned us, human animals, as thinkers above or outside the (material) world (see Figure 4.1), and with that same move have distanced us, 'fully-human' adults, from both matter *and* child (and other so-called 'illiterates').

Philosopher of childhood David Kennedy (1989) compares child to the historical Fool – both are marginal to the adult hegemonic scientific Cartesian world-picture that favours language and literacy and a particular kind of rationality and subject/world relationship (one that is mediated through literacy). The oral, aural and the visual are the domain of child or the artist, where no real knowledge is located. Kennedy claims that what was once a fairly universal cognitive style becomes peculiar to young children' (Kennedy, 1989, p. 374).

Literacy, in its narrow meaning of reading and writing, requires isolated, formal and individualistic instruction from an early age, and is an activity highly valued by adults (Stables, 2008, p. 45). So, the transition from orality to literacy has left child behind. Child as Fool, says Kennedy, expresses a crisis, and points at what needs to be suppressed in order to keep the ontoepistemic *status quo*, so 'the King keeps a Fool, to remind him that he is not a god'. This Fool 'speaks in riddles', turning things sideways or 'on their heads'; showing 'the underside of what is being carefully avoided by normal people' (Kennedy, 1989, p. 374). He continues poetically:

> Hence, the Fool is *mana* – he reveals the secret language of the world by babbling and playing, for it can be revealed in no other way. And from his play the sacred emerges, the *involuntary whole* which the hegemonic situation has excluded, as an uninvited guest. The Fool's knowledge is both forbidden and necessary.
>
> Kennedy, 1989, p. 374; my emphasis

We have seen how, for Affrica Taylor (2013), child has been excluded from the 'common worlds' – the world where nature and culture come back together again – 'the involuntary whole' excluded and rejected by the scientific reality of the developmentalists as too subjective and irrational.

The metaphysics responsible for the discriminatory practices against the not-fully-human is held in place by humanism, individualism and representationalism (Barad, 2007, p. 134), and underpins our schools policies and practices. Posthumanism disrupts breaks with representationalism, with 'logos', the 'philosopher-king', the 'transcendence of the Idea', the 'interiority of the concept' (Deleuze and Guattari, 1987/2013, p. 24), in short, with the belief that words represent existing things in the world.

As a means of drawing the attention to this critical transition from orality to literacy with educators, iii sometimes use the Latin version of the picturebook *The Giving Tree* above (Silverstein, 2006). By making the images available on a document reader in Latin (a language no one understands) and *at the same time* reading it out loud in English, educators get a real experience of what it is like to have access to the images without being able to read the words. What is that like? How unnerving and unsettling is it to see words, but not be able to read them with meaning? Does our experience of such an event with the materiality of ink on paper (or projected on the screen) approximate those of children who are emergent readers and writers?

From a materialdiscursive point of view, it was interesting how one group (many years ago in Wales) responded to this activity. Because of my affiliation with the university, the assumption was that iii as a scholar could read Latin, so they felt foolish, but not for the reasons iii had hoped for. As an educator in such sessions iii never disclose my reasons for choosing one text over another at the beginning, so as not to influence what participants find important to talk about. My hope (and therefore how iii participate in these enquiries) had been that they would enquire into what it means to be '(il)literate', what it must be like to learn to read one's home language, or to learn a foreign language, or to be fluent in many languages at the same time (as is often the case in South Africa). In which language does one think, for example? Can anyone remember how we learned to read? Philosophy with children sessions are indeed always unpredictable, and the text's *performativity* is an important factor in this unpredictability (see also Chapter 9). Barad uses quantum physics as empirical evidence that discursive practices have *performative agency* in that thinking, observing and theorising are practices of engagement with, and as part of, the world in which we have our being (Barad, 2007, p. 133). A Reggio-inspired philosophy with children enacts Barad's agential realism[18], and disrupts current literacy practices. Knowledge production and expression merge and draw on *all* of child's materialdiscursive languages, thereby disrupting the ontoepistemic injustice routinely done to children. However, one of the 'problems' for implementation is that the 'other' languages are more difficult to interpret, assess and verbalise. See, for example, the image from Anthony Browne *Voices in the Park* (1998) in Figure 7.3.

It *shows* that visual art provokes thought and dialogue (but that this is not that easy to express in words). Also, the image on the cup – what David Lewis calls the 'the flesh' of the word – is itself 'pregnant with potential narrative meaning, indeterminate, unfinished' (Lewis, 2001, p. 74), especially if one is familiar with the picturebook. The connection between the poppy and the cup is uncertain (it connects multiplicities), and the idea of uncertain knowledge makes adults 'nervous' (Kennedy, 1996a), because of the desire for cognitive closure (Haynes and Murris, 2011, 2012). Malaguzzi (1998, p. 58) proposes that 'it is important for pedagogy not to be the prisoner of too much certainty'. He admits that they had many fears themselves when setting up the preschools, but that those 'reasonable' fears helped them to work cautiously and with care for relationships, especially those with children. Images can be read in multiple ways, also because children's engagement and experimentation with the aesthetic dimension (e.g. line, colour) might 'distract' from the task of more 'straightforward' knowledge

Figure 7.3 Anthony Browne, *Voices in the Park.*

construction (Thomson, 2008, p. 14). Similarly, the language of space is very strong in Reggio – 'a constituent element of the formation of thought', but its code is 'not always explicit and recognisable' (Rinaldi, 2006, p. 82). Furthermore, children's imaginative, narrative hypothesising challenges adults' linear, vertical (*aborescent*) understanding of what knowledge is.

A rhizomatic curriculum

Gilles Deleuze and Felix Guattari (1987/2013) write how 'aborescent' systems of thought and binary logic have dominated Western reality with its images of knowledge such as, for example, 'root', 'foundation' and 'ground'. Although the brain is 'much more a grass than a tree', they insist that many people 'have a tree growing in their heads': a thinking that is vertical and hierarchical with continuous binary cuts and nesting classifications (Deleuze and Guattari, 1987/2013, p. 15). They argue that the brain is not One, rooted, like a tree, but an assemblage of multiplicities. And 'thought and concepts can be seen as a consequence of the provocation of an encounter with difference' (Dahlberg and Moss, 2006, p. 8).

In Reggio-inspired philosophy with children, members of a community of enquiry make connections *horizontally*, not *vertically*, from one materialdiscurive language to another, like a *rhizome*.[19] Deleuze and Guattari (1987/2013, p. 25) explain that 'a rhizome has no beginning or end; it is always in the middle, between things, interbeing, *intermezzo* . . . The tree imposes the verb "to be", but the fabric of the rhizome is the conjunction, "and . . . and . . . and". Instead of starting from "the beginning", they "proceed from the middle, through the middle, coming and going rather than starting and finishing"' (Deleuze and Guattari, 1987/2013, p. 25).

Using a Hundred Languages in Reggio-inspired practices does away with foundations, nullifying endings and beginnings. It does not mean 'going from one thing to the other and back again, but a perpendicular[20] direction, a transversal movement that sweeps one *and* the other way, a stream without beginning or end that undermines its banks and picks up speed in the middle' (Deleuze and Guattari, 1987/2013, p. 25). The principles of the idea of knowledge as rhizome are connection, heterogeneity, multiplicity (Deleuze and Guattari, 1987/2013, pp. 7–8), and asignifying rupture, that is, 'a rhizome may be broken, shattered at a given spot, but it will start up again on one of its old lines, or on new lines' (like ginger root). There are only lines, 'no singular points or positions in a rhizome', such as those found in a structure, tree or root and 'any point of a rhizome can be connected to another' (Deleuze and Guattari, 1987/2013, pp. 7–9). Every rhizome contains stratification, territorialisation and signification, but also lines of deterritorialisation 'down which it constantly flees' (Deleuze and Guattari, 1987/2013, p. 9). Thought then becomes a matter of experimentation and problematisation (Dahlberg and Moss, 2005, p. 117), and these 'lines of flight' are part of the rhizome (thereby escaping dualism).

Deleuze and Guattari (1994, p. 25) suggest establishing a logic of AND, to do away with foundations, beginnings and endings. They suggest having 'short-term ideas' and to make maps (see the bodymind maps of Chapter 5). Maps have multiple entryways and dimensions, not units. They do not produce an unconscious closed in upon itself, but foster connections between fields. Maps are open and connectable. They can be torn, reversed, adapted to any kind of mounting, reworked by any individual or group, drawn on a wall, be a work of art, constructed as a mediation or be a political action (Deleuze and Guattari, 1994, p. 12).

Knowledge as an 'entanglement of spaghetti'

The rhizome figuration[21] is akin to Loris Malaguzzi's well-known culinary image of knowledge as a 'tangle of spaghetti' (Dahlberg and Moss, p. 117), or at other times is referred to as 'entanglement of spaghetti' (Malaguzzi quoted in Dahlberg 2003, p. 279).

Recall that we explored in Chapter 2 how each person's 'coming into presence' depends on how their beginnings are taken up by others, and, importantly, because others have the freedom to take up a subject's beginnings as they wish, a subject's *coming into world* is always shaped by the actions of others (Biesta, 1994, p. 143). These beginnings are never 'from the beginning', because knowledge has no endings or beginnings – as visualised imaginatively from a relational materialist orientation in Figure 7.4.

For Barad, the 'spaghetti', the material, also 'has' agency, not just the human animal sticking her fork in the spaghetti. The idea that agency is located

Figure 7.4 Knowledge as an 'entanglement of spaghetti' with agency, by Nabeela Kidy

'inside' a human animal assumes the humanist metaphysical illusion that individuals (also matter) exist prior to the worldly relationships of which they are always already a part, and does not do justice to the 'immense range of causal factors', the many 'chains of events' that cause an action, including the material (Frost, 2010, p. 161). The inspirational, thought-provoking image in Figure 7.4 has been specifically designed as a reminder (like a neologism such as iii) of the performative agency of matter for teaching and learning. Barad's point that 'matter matters' (Barad, 2003) is not the same as the current focus on embodied pedagogies, and taking physical environments or architecture seriously in teaching and learning. Particularly in feminist writing, the materiality of knowledge construction has been foregrounded; but not sufficiently[22] for material feminists, who argue that we should engage with 'affective physicality, human–non-human encounters and a keen interest in what emerges in mutual *engagements* with matter' (Alaimo and Hekman in Hultman and Lenz Taguchi, 2010, p. 526). For Barad, 'space is an agent of change, that is, it plays an active role *in the unfolding of events*' (Barad, 2007, p. 224; my emphasis).

The movement of the fork is an *agential cut*. An agential cut is a specific intra-action, semantic as well as ontic. So it is not the case that there are no separations or differentiations, but they are always within relationships (Barad, 2012, p. 77). Our pedagogical choices as teachers are agential cuts. So are the books we use for our teaching and the questions we ask. The 'linear', highly structured labyrinth (that is this book) is an example of an agential cut.

Knowledge as an 'entanglement of spaghetti' helps us *do* education differently. The image is not a signifier, a linguistic construct, like a metaphor. We should not ask: What does it mean? but: How does it work? (Deleuze and Guattari, 1987/2013, p. 4). How does the image change our pedagogical practices? The idea of knowledge as an entanglement profoundly challenges habits of thought about development, progression and the organisation and planning of lessons. With cooked spaghetti it is often not clear where one string starts and another ends – closely touching and sticking. In this case, the strings are not confined to a bowl. There are no boundaries, there is no map of the territory. The tangle of strings is infinite.

For Levinas, the idea of infinity 'disrupts and dislocates human subjectivity' (Dahlberg, 2003, p. 272) in that our knowledge of the Other is always limited and fallible. Like the Body without Organs (Chapter 6), it is an attempt to think without a subject. The BwO makes it possible to regard students' prior knowledge as a gift to extend our own knowledge and understanding as educators, rather than treating personal, private knowledge as a necessary starting point to lead the student down a well-trodden and predetermined path. As educators, we make a philosophical choice (an agential cut) between construing the primary aims of education as socialisation into an existing order, or that they bring something *unique* into existence as an event ('relational material subjectification'; see Chapter 2).

The spaghetti figuration opens up possibilities of pedagogical encounters that challenge the familiar constructionist approaches to teaching as mediation ('to be in the middle'), mentoring or modelling (Davis, 2004, p. 135), with the teacher regarded as the knowledge expert who helps the less knowledgeable novice (learner) to move one step at a time (like climbing the stairs to 'enlightenment') from the 'known' (everyday knowledge) to the 'unknown' (school knowledge). The image of knowledge here is that of a tree, with 'the roots as a point of origin from which everything else develops in a linear way' (Dahlberg and Moss, 2009, p.xix). Social constructivists 'scaffold' (Wood, Bruner and Ross,1976) learners, whereby the idea is not so much to impart established knowledge, but an enculturation into specific practices through internalisation of language and other cultural tools (Davis, 2004, p. 136).

In this chapter, iii have foregrounded an alternative intra-active pedagogy whereby teachers make room for 'all'[23] of the Hundred Languages, thereby opening up possibilities to think differently about what knowledge is, and who owns and constructs new knowledges. In this kind of scaffolding the building materials are not made of steel or iron, but of narrative, a use of the body, imagination and fantasy.[24] The shape of the construction is not necessarily square or rectangular, but undetermined. Every-one and every-thing in class helps to construct the scaffolding and plays on it – taking risks, encountering dangers, ignoring the warning signs, not wearing a crash helmet. Such alternative onto-epistemological relationships ask the question: what is learning in a rhizomatic curriculum?

Learning in a rhizomatic curriculum: becoming other in ourselves

Diffracting involves 'to break apart in different directions' (Barad, 2014, p. 168). There is no moving beyond or leaving the old behind. This forward movement always creates something new: it brings into being a *divergent* curriculum that centres on *difference*, rather than the same. It uses differences to diffract in a positive, affirming way, although this does not exclude criticality and a 'pushing for reasons' because we still need to assume responsibility for what we claim to know. In a philosophy of immanence, there is an entanglement of ethics and knowing; therefore teaching is not just an epistemic, but always simul-taneously an ethical practice (Simon, 2015). As Gilles Deleuze and Felix Guattari put it, learning is 'becoming other in ourselves – becoming transformed' (Lenz Taguchi, 2010, p. 173). Lenz Taguchi explains that as an adult-becoming-child iii am still an adult but iii change and become different in myself, that is, iii transform, *become other*, but not in relation to something *outside* myself. So the adult is not *acting as* a child (and later become adult again as if iii temporarily take on another role), nor am iii being child in the sense of being on the 'other side' of the binary. I am activating my imagination, and change as a result of the intra-actions with materialdiscursive events (Lenz Taguchi, 2010, p. 173).

In the next chapter, we look at the role of the teacher in a rhizomatic Reggio-inspired philosophy with children curriculum.

Notes

1 From: www.innovativeteacherproject.org/reggio/poem.php, accessed 26 February 2015.
2 'Superposition' is a combination of disturbances, or the effect, of the waves that have been created by the diffraction when two or more waves combine (Barad, 2007, p. 76).
3 See the discussion below about the troubled nature of the motif 'as' in 'child as . . .'.
4 iii am not looking for similarities or differences; iii make no comparisons or try to identify themes, but create new pedagogical practices by adding and strengthening certain characteristics and dimensions and diffracting both pedagogies with Karen Barad's relational materialism.
5 It was a break from the then dominant Catholic preschools carried out by nuns.
6 'Philosophy for Children', or 'P4C', refers to the curriculum initiated and developed by Matthew Lipman. It has been the backdrop and inspiration for theories and practices now more broadly termed 'philosophy with children', which includes philosophical enquiries with *all* ages and in a variety of formal and informal settings. For a lengthy discussion, see Haynes and Murris, 2012, Chapter 3.
7 To what extent do indeed individual subjects pioneer or start movements? With both Lipman and Malaguzzi, their agency was also in relation to the force, vitality and energy present after the Second World War that helped their determination to keep on going against all odds.
8 See the obituary by Douglas Martin in the *New York Times* on 14 January 2011: www.nytimes.com/2011/01/15/education/15lipman.html?_r=0, accessed 15 May 2015.
9 For a theorisation of this curriculum, see Lipman, Sharp and Oscanyan (1977). For a discussion of child as positioned by the P4C curriculum, see Murris (2015).
10 My PhD thesis (1997) reports on three important shifts I myself made in my views of child as philosopher.
11 Barad's relational ontology rejects the metaphysics of *relata*, or 'words' and 'things'. See: Barad, 2003, p. 812.
12 See the previous chapter's diffractive pause for an analysis of a philosophical enquiry arguing for this.
13 *Progettione* does not translate easily into English; it means something like 'to project ahead' (Stremmel, 2012, p. 139). For an excellent description, see Rinaldi's website: www.thinkers.sa.gov.au/thinkers/carlarinaldi/p513.aspx#P8
14 For very interesting philosophical readings of this picturebook, see Miller (2011) and Radeva (2011). In Jaques (2015a, pp. 126–31) there is a posthumanist reading of the story, but this reading is not post-metaphysical – one that troubles an individualist ontoepistemology. So it is more transhumanist in fact, and concentrates on symbolism and how, for example, characters represent deeper meanings. For readings from a relational material perspective, see especially Chapter 9.
15 See Haynes and Murris (2002) (The Web of Intriguing Ideas: Growing and Wanting) for ideas how to explore these philosophical concepts in class.
16 There are many sites on the Internet from where you can download the poem. There are also videos of the poem that can be used with children reading it aloud. See, for example, www.youtube.com/watch?v=174pYUcwn7w

17 From Rinaldi's website that describes succinctly the core principles of Reggio Emilia, and is very much worth a visit. See www.thinkers.sa.gov.au/thinkers/carlarinaldi/p513.aspx#P8, accessed 2 January 2015.

18 Agential realism is Barad's relational materialist philosophy of immanence. Things or objects are real, but they emerge through particular intra-actions (relationships), boundary-making practices that include or exclude. In agential realism the epistemological, the ontological and the ethical merge. See Barad, 2007, Chapter 4. It involves a reworking of poststructuralist notions of performativity (Barad, 2003, p. 811).

19 For a helpful interpretation of a 'rhizome' by John David Ebert, see www.youtube.com/watch?v=0pH—FtP0j4, accessed 5 April 2015.

20 When you pull a dog by its chain in an upward and rightward direction, then you are exerting an influence upon the object in two separate directions – an upward direction and a rightward direction. That is a perpendicular direction. From www.physicsclassroom.com/class/vectors/Lesson-1/Independence-of-Perpendicular-Components-of-Motion, accessed 14 May 2015.

21 The rhizome is not a metaphor, but an imaginary, a 'conceptually charged use of the imagination' (Braidotti quoted in Sellers, 2013, p. 9). A metaphor re-presents, or is symbolic for, something else, and assumes an atomistic metaphysics.

22 Poststructuralists fail to take account of nonhuman agency, writes Barad (2003, p. 807). Even Foucault does not 'offer an account of the body's historicity in which its very materiality plays a role in the workings of power' (Barad, 2003, p. 809).

23 Of course it is a metaphor and does not mean *literally* 100 languages.

24 With thanks to Joanna Haynes for developing these ideas further.

Chapter 8

Educator as pregnant stingray

We have seen in Chapter 7 how a Reggio-inspired philosophy with children is able to offer a rhizomatic curriculum that fits the posthuman child. With the help of Deleuze and Guattari's *A Thousand Plateaus* (1987/2013), I showed how knowledge as a rhizome works, and how we should think of 'learning' with a focus on *difference*, rather than *sameness*. iii concluded that a curriculum should be enacted that does away with foundations, nullifying endings and beginnings – a curriculum that would break with current unethical discriminatory practices in schools.

Although my ideas are more broadly applicable, in this chapter iii situate my analysis in the current South African literacy education 'crisis' to illustrate the relevance, but also the urgency, of my proposal for educational change. My five responses to this crisis include rethinking the role of the teacher, a critique of the apparatus that measures competency, a focus on the power relationships assumed by language itself, the privileging of reading and writing over all other 'ninety-nine languages' and the need to interrogate what comprehension means.

Before further exploring the role of the educator (especially for teaching comprehension), iii argue that the current 'expanding horizons curriculum' assumes developmentalism, and thereby neglects the important role of the imagination in knowledge construction, which has implications for the texts we chose for literacy.

A rhizomatic curriculum that caters for the logico-mathematical as well as the imaginative 'side' of the child's bodymind requires a reconfiguration of the educator, and iii offer a diffractive reading of three images through one another: midwife, stingray and the pregnant body. The chapter concludes by mapping the questions asked by a pregnant stingray and the necessary shift in ontoepistemology.

Early literacy in South Africa

In the last decade, the 'crisis' in education (Soudien, 2007; Fleisch, 2008, 2012; Bloch, 2009) in South Africa has attracted much attention, mainly as a result of national and international assessments. But the problems (and therefore the solutions) are less obvious, and are open for interpretation and debate.[1] It is claimed that despite substantial investment in education by the South African government over almost 20 years, many children in independent and government schools are still failing to achieve basic literacy and numeracy skills in the foundation phase (National Education Evaluation & Development Unit [NEEDU], 2013). For example, in all international literacy[2] tests South Africa scores almost the lowest of all participating countries – even in comparison to other African countries such as Morocco.

The basis of these written tests is reading comprehension; learners are expected 'to engage in a full repertoire of reading strategies, including retrieving and focusing on specific ideas, making simple and more complex inferences and examining and evaluating text features' (Howie *et al.*, 2007, p. 13). Using international benchmark tests as a standard (see e.g. Taylor, 2014, p. 6), none of the African language learners is able to reach the 'high level' at Grade 4 or even at Grade 5 level. Only 17 to 18% of South African learners in Afrikaans and English could be considered competent readers (Howie *et al.*, 2007, p. 28). All subsequent tests have produced similar results (Murris, 2014c). However, the results are unlikely to change soon, for a complex mix of reasons. In the literature these are mainly phrased *negatively*,[3] and they include: under- or unqualified teachers,[4] a majority of people living in poverty, the devastating effects of HIV/AIDS on households and schools, huge language barriers for learners and teachers,[5] lack of resources in schools,[6] little parental involvement, limited literacy practices in many African home and community settings (Alexander and Bloch, 2010), and insufficient attention paid to literacy instruction at the institutions that prepare teachers (Taylor, 2014).

The educational crisis has contributed to the introduction of a more prescriptive, revised curriculum – the Curriculum Assessment Policy Statement, or CAPS (Department of Education [DoE], 2011) – and annual testing of literacy and numeracy in Grade 3, for example. Prescription has taken the form of a highly 'specified, sequenced and paced guidance regarding the content that should be taught in schools and how this should be done' (Murris and Verbeek, 2014, p. 2). In addition, much agency has been removed from the teacher through teachers' guides for textbooks as well as specially written materials produced by the Department of Education, and providing teachers with 'scripted lessons in an attempt to cover for a lack of teacher content and pedagogic content knowledge' (Murris and Verbeek, 2014, p. 2). Like many governments globally, the dominant assumption in South African policies and practices is that literacy is about learning a set of neutral, value-free discrete skills that can be taught independently of people's experiences and of social, cultural, economic and political contexts (Larson and Marsh, 2014). Elsewhere (Murris, 2014c; Murris and Verbeek, 2014), iii have argued that teachers spend too much time on teaching the so-called 'big five' in early literacy instruction and in a linear sequence that is problematic; the key assumption is to start with phonological awareness, followed by phonics, vocabulary, fluency and comprehension. The idea is that children need to 'learn to read', before they can 'read to learn' (Fleisch, 2012; Taylor, 2013; Pretorius, 2014), so comprehension comes last on the chronological list (Howie *et al.*, 2012, p. 114) and is not really taught, only tested (Verbeek, 2010).

Five responses to the 'crisis' as a creative opportunity for transformation

One possible response to the low literacy results is to challenge the particular *sequence* of the 'big five' (see: Murris, 2014c), or alternatively, to extend this sequence by *adding* to it (e.g. Readers Response). iii continue by offering further brief responses to the dominant approach to literacy by highlighting the pedagogical, political and therefore ethical dimensions.

The impossibility of separating skills from pedagogy and relationships

A possible response is to challenge the assumption that the so-called 'basic reading skills' can be separated out *empirically* from 'sensitive and subtle pedagogical decision-making' (Davis, 2013, p. 17; see also Murris, 2014c). After all, even when teaching phonics in the other 10 official languages with less opaque orthographies such as English, teachers are required to make situated judgements. Therefore their practices cannot be 'teacher proof' through mechanistic, skills-based lessons (Alexander, 2012; Alexander and Bloch, 2010, p. 198). Philosopher of education Andrew Davis dismisses the idea that phonics teaches *reading*, because it already assumes readers' existing knowledge and understanding in order to *say* the word (Davis, 2013, p. 26). In a profound sense, phonics does not teach learners to read real words – as carriers of meaning – at all. He offers the following striking analogy: delivering a phonics skill out of context is like teaching an actor to be sad by showing her how to turn down the corners of her mouth (Davis, 2013, p. 31).

Power relationships assumed by language

iii have argued throughout this book that language itself is substantialising and dichotomising, and requires rupturing (see also Chapter 9). Power is not only attached to colonial languages such as English or Afrikaans, but to all languages, in that grammar tricks us into holding particular metaphysical beliefs (see e.g. Chapter 7), has instilled a deep mistrust of matter, and privileges the individualised human animal.[7]

The privileging of reading and writing over all other ninety-nine languages

A focus on reading and writing *at the expense* of the oral, visual and aural – all other 'Hundred Languages' in fact – has brought Child as Fool (childhood) into existence (Chapter 7). The digital revolution should be a useful lever to liberate child from its status as Fool, and to include literacy practices that involve all of their languages (Larson and Marsh, 2014). In other words, the current crisis is a creative opportunity to transform schools into sites for political action (Dahlberg and Moss, 2005) by changing how we teach and by reconfiguring child and childhood – by assuming child as rich, resilient and resourceful 'becoming-iii' – a complex thinker capable of asking and responding to cognitively challenging questions if given the right materialdiscursive opportunities (e.g. starting with children's oral capabilities in their home language). Unfortunately, the field of digital literacy in early years is under-researched, and the majority of the research assumes either a psychological-cognitive or sociocultural conceptual framework (Olsson and Theorell, 2014, pp. 216–33).

The subjectivity of the apparatus that measures

Measuring children's achievements through national and international tests takes no account of the *relations* 'between' earth dwellers. Child is taught and tested on *individual* achievements and performances only. But these measurement apparatuses are open-ended practices without intrinsic boundaries; they are not neutral, passive instruments of observation, measuring children's abilities objectively. They are instead 'the material conditions of possibility and impossibility of mattering; they enact what matters and what is excluded from mattering' (Barad, 2007, p. 148). Evaluating children's capabilities through universal, standardised testing assumes *instrumental rationality*: calculation of the most economical means to achieve certain ends. Success is measured in terms of efficiency; and discounting the measurement apparatus ignores the particular kind of ontoepistemic relationships presupposed in the measuring. Treatment of individuals as ends in themselves and as persons with dignity in their own right has been sacrificed to achieve a particular result and is justified by that result. However, the moral point of view is not optional – one among a competing set of perspectives an educator can choose from (when it suits). It always already asserts itself, because our relationships (and therefore the rights and interests of others) precede who and what we are, and what and how we measure. Ethics emanates from the realities of educational practice, rather than being applied to these realities (Campbell, 2003, p. 10). When we interpret the 'crisis' in education predominantly as a curriculum and public service issue (Moss, 2014), the apparatuses that bring the data into existence – how relationships *produce* the phenomena – remain invisible. Part of the apparatus that does the measuring is a particular view of literacy, of knowledge and figuration of child as deficit.

What is not acknowledged is the importance of relationships in teaching – the *ethics* of pedagogical practices (Dahlberg, 2003). 'Poor children' are not poor in the sense that they (e)merge[8] rich and resourceful in intra-actions. It was not despite, but *because* of the particular socio-economic circumstances in Reggio Emilia that an educational philosophy developed that foregrounds ethical relationships 'between' *all* humans and nonhuman others.

Interrogating the meaning of comprehension

The fifth response to the test results is to interrogate what is meant by 'comprehension'. Currently South African teachers rely on comprehension questions that 'assess immediate recall of information and that neither improve proficiency nor promote independent and effective thinking skills while reading' (Verbeek, 2010, p. 38). Rhetorical 'test'-like[9] questions are dominant in our schools (Brodie, 2007). The IRE[10] (Initiation Response Evaluation) framework is used, reducing children's responses to 'a-guessing-what-is-in-teacher's-head' approach that prevents children from *thinking* on their own terms about texts. The annual national literacy tests also contain comprehension exercises with simple stories followed by rhetorical recall questions.[11] They therefore do not prepare our learners adequately for the level of comprehension and inferential reasoning required in the international tests (Taylor, 2014, p. 6).

Later in this chapter we will look in much detail at the ontoepistemic assumptions of the questions educators ask, and explore the pedagogical role assumed in those practices. But first it is necessary to look at the wider context of literacy and the current curriculum in which developmentalism is nested. Cognitive psychology has left its marks on a curriculum that underscores the importance of good-quality narratives and the imagination.[12]

Contesting an 'expanding horizon curriculum'

As elsewhere (File, Basler Wisneski and Mueller, 2012), the South African curriculum is based on the figuration of child as *developing, innocent* and *ignorant*, and, as we have seen in Chapter 5, assumes the nature/culture dichotomy and binary thinking. Child is not only put at a distance from its more knowledgeable, mature and rational elders, as well as his/her body ignored in new knowledge construction, but his/her mind is further dichotomised into the 'logical-mathematical' and the 'imaginative' (Egan, 1993). Aristotelian philosophy, cognitive psychology and certain strands of sociology have informed a curriculum that includes pedagogical instruction from the 'simple' to the 'complex', the 'concrete' to the 'abstract' and the 'familiar' to the 'unfamiliar' (Egan, 2002; Stables, 2008). The assumption is that this is how children's minds develop cognitively.

Canadian educationalist Kieran Egan argues that the imagination, on the other hand, is stimulated and developed by the opposite: the *complex*, the *abstract* and the *unfamiliar* (e.g. aliens, monsters, mysteries and out-of-the-ordinary events). Current curriculum development focuses only on the logico-mathematical 'side' of 'the mind' (Egan, 1993), leaving the imagination starved of oxygen to breathe. However, for comprehension, the imagination is vital, as it is not just the capacity to form images, but 'crucially involves our capacity to think of the possible rather than just the actual' (Egan, 1992, p. 4).

Without introducing a dichotomy between reason and imagination, Egan argues that narratives set up a dialectical activity between the familiar and the everyday by featuring the extremes of reality and the limits of experience (Egan, 1992, p. 73). So, although Egan agrees with John Dewey that a curriculum should start with children's/students' own experiences, interests or environment (but transfigured through fantasy), an idea that has led to the currently mainstream 'expanding horizons curriculum' (Egan, 1995, p. 119), he stresses that especially in the foundation phase these experiences should *also include* children's knowledge of abstract concepts.

Relational thinking in a community of philosophical enquiry

Reggio-inspired philosophy with children uses 'both' 'sides' of children's minds (logico-mathematical *and* the imaginative), diffractive methodologies, divergent questioning into contestable concepts, embodied thinking moves and involves an ongoing experimentation with the Hundred Languages. This rhizomatic curriculum has no overall ordering principle with roots, trunks and branches like a tree (Rinaldi, 2006), but advances more like a sailing boat trying to tack into the wind (Lipman, 1991, pp. 15–16), making 'progress' by moving from side to side. Unlike ordinary conversation, a community of enquiry aims at a *disequilibrium* created through its dialectic 'reasonable judgments' that are never set in stone, but are 'temporary resting places' (Lipman, 1991, pp. 17, 65), hence contesting common notions of progression. The pedagogy gives rise to much uncertainty, and therefore insecurity, in the facilitation process (Haynes, 2005, 2007b).[13]

Lipman compares the movement of an enquiry with walking. When you walk you constantly shift your weight from your left foot to your right and so on, throwing yourself off balance in the process (Lipman, 1991, p. 229). The movement in a community of enquiry is not linear, nor circular, but rhizomatic and provoked by some-one or some-thing that raises philosophical questions.[14] The 'products' of an enquiry are 'reasonable judgments' (including emotions and moral judgements) and, as such, are never set in stone, but are 'temporary resting places' (Lipman, 1991, pp. 17, 65). Various humanist metaphors have structured our adult beliefs that arguments should have a goal, a beginning, and should proceed in linear fashion (see Chapter 1, Murris, 1997).

Unlike the modernist goal of rationality, the 'reasonableness' of the community of enquirers' judgements involves doing justice to the complexity of thinking together in a community of philosophical enquiry: the feelings in the room (Davies, 2013), the flesh of the bodies with snot, coughs, diluted pupils, raised heartbeat, the silences (MacLure, 2013), the words people use when talking, writing and the drawings they make, the school architecture and furniture (Lenz Taguchi, 2010), the way we regulate bodies to govern themselves (Dixon, 2010), the wider 'context': figurations of child, the curriculum (hidden and official), school's policies and practices, relationships with parents and other human and nonhuman others, and so forth. With all 'that' going on, what does 'community' mean, or 'enquiry', and what makes enquiries 'philosophical'? What are the relationships between people and other earth dwellers that we as educators make possible and not possible within all that complexity? What are our apparatuses, our boundary-making practices? Who and what do we exclude? What are our response-abilities?

Australian philosopher of education Laurance Splitter claims the relationship between the two – 'community' and 'enquiry' – is asymmetrical and inter-dependent: 'a community is not necessarily a community of inquiry, but inquiry necessarily presupposes an element of community' (Splitter, 2000, p. 12). He explains that communities may have powerful bonds of trust, collaboration, risk-taking and a sense of common purpose, but they lack necessary features of enquiry, such as reflection, dialogue and acknowledging alternative perspectives. Splitter insists that a community is a necessary condition for the teaching of enquiry, because as a mode of thinking, enquiry has a dialogical structure and as such is 'problem-focused, self-correcting, empathetic and multi-perspectival' (Splitter, 2000, p. 13).

Differences in practice depend to a large degree on one's philosophy of edu-cation (e.g. humanist or posthumanist, and the implications for a particular subjectivity), one's interpretation of both 'community' and 'enquiry' and the particular balance of the two. What it means to learn to 'think-for-yourself-through-thinking-with-others' as a shorthand for philosophy with children can easily become a useful *instrument* to achieve two aims of education only: the teaching of useful knowledge and skills and socialisation (to satisfy curriculum objectives, such as better speaking and listening skills, questioning and thinking skills, or even education for global citizenship). But we need to be careful not to 'forget' the ethicopolitical dimension of these practices, and the communal aspect is key to transformation and relational material subjectification as the third aim of education (Chapter 2). Philosophy with children disrupts practices of power as a continuous experimentation. Community, as we have seen in Chapter 2, is 'not so much a place, or a finite group of people', but 'a way of mattering, a way of engaging with the world, and of re-configuring that world as a place where self and other matter, and make a difference, to each other and with each other' (Davies, 2014, p. 12). In that way, 'community' and 'enquiry' cannot really be separated at all. They are not 'two', because the communal relations bring the enquiry into existence – the community is the condition of the possibility of enquiry.

A focus on abstract core concepts

Kennedy describes a community of enquiry as any group of people who communicate together regularly and whose common project is to enquire critically and creatively into something they find important, find out how things work, in short, create knowledge together (Kennedy, 1996, p. 2). A posthuman orientation includes the relations and intra-actions between human animals, nonhuman animals and matter as constitutive for the knowledge that emerges. Not one single person claims access to the Truth and takes up a position to transmit knowledge, not even the teacher, and they all hold their beliefs with epistemic modesty and equality, always open for deliberation and contestation, and dedicated to 'the ongoing reconstruction of the concepts that constitute our systems of belief' (Kennedy, 2012, p. 231).

These core concepts that philosophical enquiry targets are not only *common* (we all use them), *central* (to how we think about the world and ourselves), but always *contestable* as we need to *connect* with our own lived experiences (in a Deweyan manner) to know what concepts mean for *us*. A text book definition will not do (Splitter, 2000).

Kennedy (2012, p. 233) refers to the philosophy curriculum as a 'living thing, an emergent whole in ongoing reconstruction, because the concepts that form its nodes of intensity are in constant proliferation and reconstruction'. So deterritorialisation is part of the ontoepistemology of philosophy with children that moves in a horizontal manner, like a rhizome, through and across the disciplines, bringing the whole back to its parts, and at the same time problematising the whole. Concepts are not abstractions *from* the world, but an active force *of* this world (Thiele, 2014, p. 203). Routinely members of a community of enquiry enquire about how the same concepts with multiple meanings *work* across disciplines, or across contexts. What people themselves think is foregrounded; it is *their* connections that matter, often deterritorialising established understandings, such as 'child', 'knowledge', 'love', 'animal', 'human', 'truth', 'give' and 'take'.[15] These concepts 'afford multiple entries for emergent philosophical reflection within each academic discipline' (Kennedy, 2012, p. 233), with continuous diffractions ('between' human animals, the questions they ask, their bodyminds moving, the physical space, the texts they use).

The educator as pregnant stingray

For enquiry to be *philosophical*, participants think not only about a particular question or problem, but they enquire about the *procedures* of this thinking about a subject matter. This 'meta-thinking'[16] by the community, or what Lipman calls 'complex thinking' (Lipman, 1991, pp. 23–4), needs educators who can use a diffractive methodology – that is, diffract with others and also produce the assumptions, points of view, bias and prejudice each participant brings to the enquiry, including the educator him or herself. It is here that acquaintance with philosophers' dialogues that constitute the subject of philosophy is particularly helpful, and even judged by some to be necessary (Murris, 2015b), thereby creating anxiety in teachers who do not have a background in philosophy (Murris, 2008).

Furthermore, educators should 'resist representation, and expose the limits of rationality's reductive explanation' (MacLure, 2013, p. 663); and instead 'surf' the intensity of the event, consider how the material world intra-acts with children, 'in order to arrive somewhere else' (MacLure, 2013, p. 662). It is therefore necessary to position adult working alongside child as 'another kind of grown-up' than they are used to encounter at school – one that helps materialise a different kind of knowledge and produces a more equal relationship (Petersen, 2014).

The rigour and uncertainty that accompany a Listening without Organs (LwO)[17] in a community of enquiry involves listening out for the new and unfamiliar – a distributive thinking without de-centred voice (Chapter 6) enabling a reconstruction of adult/child relations in education. These relations are understood to be democratic, understood to include moral principles such as freedom and equality of opportunity, and imply that schools make space for children to actively participate as citizens in contexts that are meaningful to them. This includes challenging the way in which the authority of the school is deployed (Haynes, 2008). For example, opening up a space where children can ask questions such as: 'Is it fair always to choose the question for enquiry that gets most votes?', or, 'Can we talk about *anything* we want?'.

Treating children as democrats also includes presenting knowledge truthfully, as it *is*, that is, fallible, problematic and therefore always open to revision (Lipman, 1988, 1991). In philosophy with children, the teacher's authentic stance towards knowledge is evident in her/his problematising the meaning of abstract concepts.

The role of the educator is that of a co-enquirer, a participant that '*numbs*', asking questions that provoke philosophical enquiry, without knowing the answers to the questions s/he poses; and facilitating only where appropriate, that is, benefiting the community's construction of new ideas. Her/his role is to map out the territory of the dialogue, without manipulating or steering the course of the enquiry (Haynes and Murris, 2012). The image of the educator is that of a stingray – a famous image from Ancient Greek philosopher Socrates in the Platonic dialogue, Meno:

> *Meno*:   Socrates, even before I met you they told me that in plain truth you are a perplexed man yourself and reduce others to perplexity. If I may be flippant, I think that not only in outward appearance but in other respects as well you are exactly like the flat sting-ray that one meets in the sea. Whenever anyone comes into contact with it, it numbs him, and that is the sort of thing that you seem to be doing to me now . . .

Socrates: . . . if the sting-ray paralyses others only through being paralysed itself, then the comparison is just, but not otherwise. It isn't that knowing the answers myself, I perplex other people. The truth is rather that I infect them also with the perplexity I feel myself.

Meno, 80a–c; in Guthrie, 1956

So, for Socrates an educator is not just a 'stingray' (see Figure 8.1), but a self-stinging stingray.

In the sea, the stingray is dangerous; it numbs its victims. Socrates as stingray also numbs himself. In Socratic teaching the educator is as 'numb' and perplexed as the other members of a community of enquiry (Matthews, 1999, pp. 87–91). The figure of Socrates is well known as someone 'who questions others, not from a position of assumed knowledge, but rather from a position of self-confessed ignorance' (Matthews, 1999, p. 89). Typically his questions are not about difficult matters, but exactly those matters that 'most people think too simple and basic for a grownup to question' (Matthews, 1999, p. 89). The danger, therefore, of the stingray is that its paralysis undermines confidence and can start to shake the certainty with which people habitually take for granted the meaning of everyday abstract concepts, such as 'respect' or 'child' or 'knowledge'.[19] It can also cause embarrassment, because concepts investigated are often common words that adults claim familiarity with and certainty about their meaning; so they can be made to look foolish. Everyday abstract concepts, however, are always contestable, and everyone has ideas about what they mean by them, based on their own lived experiences. And it is here that the more

Figure 8.1 Socrates as Stingray. © Sharon Girard and proustmatters.com.[18]

positive figure emerges – the educator as a midwife, another famous character of Socrates, whose mother was a midwife.

Interestingly, stingrays give birth to multiple,[20] live[21] young.[22] The image of the midwife is introduced in the dialogue *Theaetetus*. Socrates, himself barren (of both child and wisdom, he claims), helps others to deliver their theories, insights and ideas about philosophical concepts (Matthews, 1999, p. 88). The educator assists in the process of giving birth ('labour'), so has a more productive role, even assisting in abortions and false pregnancies, that is, identifies 'sham theories, doctrines and analyses' (Matthews, 1999, p. 91). The power of it is that the educator is not seen as the *source* of the knowledge – understanding has to come from 'within' through reasoning (including the emotions and feelings). The educator has no wisdom to impart or transmit, but children 'discover within themselves a multitude of beautiful things, which they bring forth into light' (Socrates quoted in Matthews, 1999, p. 88). There is not one theory (baby), but multiple, like the stingray giving birth. This 'superposition' (Barad, 2007, p. 76) of the pregnant stingray connects with the reconfiguration of child as rich, resourceful and resilient in potentiality, and disrupts deficit views of child as ignorant and incompetent. Knowledge comes from 'within', not from without.

Now, despite the power of this concept of the educator, both stingray and midwife seem to assume individual subjectivity. Is the relationship that between two entities 'in' the world: educator and learner? However, there is something more that can be said of the stingray. As Barad (2011, p. 131) points out, the neuronal receptor cells in stingrays make it possible for these creatures to *anticipate* a message which has not arrived as yet – a kind of clairvoyance, one could argue, that strikingly describes the embedded and embodied listening of the posthuman educator. Confounding the logic of causality, stingrays unlock themselves before this is (apparently) necessary (Barad, 2011, p. 131).

Furthermore, an even more powerful figuration can be created through diffracting the created superposition of the pregnant stingray with that of another body that is part of this world: the female human animal. The pregnant female body (not as a metaphor) contests Western metaphysical assumptions about subjectivity.

The relationship between mother and unborn baby is not simply one of *containment*. We have seen in Chapter 1 how, drawing on the work by Lakoff and Johnson, the metaphors we live by shape all dualist mind/body relationships and psychological constructs of self.

They argue that containment is the underlying structure that works at a pre-conceptual level and shapes our (mostly universal) experience of embodiment and territoriality (Lakoff and Johnson, 1980, p. 29). Philosopher Christine Battersby is highly critical of the idea that everything is either *inside* a container or *outside* of it. When reading Lakoff and Johnson's account of embodiment she comments:

I register a shock of strangeness: of wondering what it would be like to inhabit a body *like that*. And that is because I do not experience my body as three-dimensional container into which I 'put various things' – such as 'food, water, air' – and out of which 'other things emerge (food and water wastes, air, blood, etc.).

Battersby, 1998, pp. 41–2

She argues that the containment model for bodily boundaries and selves might be more typical of male experience, which has shaped the Western metaphysical notion of self and self-identity: bodies as containers and selves as autonomous (Battersby, 1998, p. 54) – a body that is One and *not* the Other. In metaphysical constructions of self, philosophers have bypassed the female body which 'is messy, fleshy and gapes open to otherness – with otherness "within", as well as "without"' (Battersby, 1998, p. 59). Take, for example, the meaning of the concept 'innate'. When theorists use the concept, it is assumed that what is meant is 'before birth', not 'before conception'. The relationship the mother has with her unborn baby does not count. Intrapersonal relationships do not exist before the baby is born.

The female body is different from the male body. It has the potential of becoming more than one body out of its own flesh. Battersby concludes that there '. . . is no sharp division between 'self' and 'other'. Instead, the 'other' emerges out of the embodied self, but in ways that mean that two selves emerge and one self does not simply dissolve into the other' (Battersby, 1998, p. 8). In other words, the female was always already 'ii', not 'i', or 'I' (since women voting rights, for example) as she has been previously reduced to in Western metaphysics. The male body 'has acted as both norm and ideal for what is to count as an entity, a self or a person' (Battersby, 1998, p. 50).

Inspired by French feminist philosopher Luce Irigaray, Battersby proposes a different account of identity: a different understanding of boundaries leads to a different conceptualisation of (self)identity. She understands identity as emerging out of patterns of *potentialities* and *flow* (Battersby, 1998, p. 53). When there are no clear boundaries between 'self' and 'not-self', it becomes possible to think of *the self as always in flux*, and to privilege 'becoming' over 'being' (Battersby, 1998, p. 55). For Lenz Taguchi (2010, p. 95), the pregnancy image holds within itself 'a potentiality of new invention and new becoming from what already is'.

According to Socrates, the expertise of the midwife/educator is 'matchmaking' – to connect thoughts, to ask probing questions and to assist learners in giving birth to new ideas. In the language of knowledge as spaghetti (Figure 7.4), strings of pasta are linked and new entanglements are created. Every participant can put a fork in the bowl and twirl it. A community of enquiry is a living organism, with fluid spaces 'between' educator and learner, in constant flux with no fixed boundaries. Through asking questions, educators initially assist students to connect strands of spaghetti and to make new endless patterns, with tangles of spaghetti that have a life of their own, taking the enquiry in unexpected directions.

So, what are the implications of the superposition created by reading these three images through one another? What is the new created through the method-ology? The figuration of the pregnant stingray en-courages thinking and acting differently, by thinking subjectivity differently. The relationship 'between' learner and educator is not characterised by body boundaries that are closed, auton-omous or impermeable, but allows 'the potentiality for otherness to exist within it, as well as alongside it'. The agency of both teacher and learner are characterised 'in terms of potentiality and flow. Our body-boundaries do not *contain* the self; they *are* the embodied self' (Battersby, 1998, p. 57). Both teacher and learner do not have pre-existing identities, which, for example, respond or react to new information; they are engaged in a continuous flow and fluidity: 'new identities are born out of difference; self emerges from not-self; and identity emanates from heterogeneity via patterns of relationality' (Battersby, 1998, p. 58). Pregnant stingrays are multiple and unbounded inhuman becomings.

Provoking enquiries by 'twirling the fork in the spaghetti'

In a community of enquiry, the space 'between' teacher and learner is fluid and in constant flux with no fixed boundaries. By problematising the meaning of concepts by asking philosophical questions, educators *and* students connect strands of spaghetti and make new, endless patterns. The system created is self-sustaining, non-linear, unpredictable and breaks down the observer/observed dichotomy; educators are creators as well as observers (Kennedy, 2004, p. 756). Learners become teachers and teachers become learners. The knowing subject can get pregnant and can give birth – a subject that can be one, two or even more bodies at the very same time. Such a new metaphysics of *becoming*, rather than *being*, has implications for pedagogy. The educator assists in the collaborative process of knowledge construction in a classroom (sharing a meal together with everyone putting the fork in the spaghetti), instead of the teacher's role of a petrol pump attendant, pouring information into the learner's empty mind, which is an empiricist view of learning[23] with the teacher in control.

The issue of control, however, is complex. David Kennedy (2004, p. 756) explains that many choices the educator makes are not 'as a result of any conscious strategic calculus', but s/he 'feels them, as a painter feels a color to be appropriate in a certain place, or a musician a rhythmic or harmonic or melodic shift'. He stipulates that in 'order to feel the system, the facilitator must allow the system' (Kennedy, 2004, p. 756). And the latter is possible only when s/he makes an effort to not control it, although of course any intervention by anyone in the system is an attempt to do just that. Aware of this tension, Kennedy (2004, p. 757) points out that in philosophy with children, the educator is fully aware of the existential fact that s/he is a 'microcosm or fractal of the system'. And although each and every intra-vention will change the system, and although some choices are not always at a conscious level, the educator remains response-able for all of his or her actions. This infinite system or emergent curriculum is shaped by the questions and interests of everyone in the system, but the agenda is child-*initiated*;[24] enquiries start with *their* questions. Table 8.1 is an overview of the apparatus often used when doing philosophy with children as part of a literacy lesson,[25] although ideally these sessions are part of a more long-term project approach to philosophy with children (Stanley, 2012; Lyle and Bolt, 2013). Like all pedagogical choices, using this apparatus as a guide is a semantic and ontic agential cut, and is particularly useful as inspiration when gaining confidence with the pedagogy; but it is not meant to be prescriptive. It is like 'twirling the fork' in 'the spaghetti' (Figure 7.4). The focus is on the role of the educator.

As a response to South African young learners' low test results, it offers an imagination for a different kind of literacy lesson, and the process is enacted through deciding collaboratively on egalitarian and democratic decision-making procedures.

Chimney-sweeping philosophical questions

A useful exercise for learning to distinguish between philosophical and other kinds of questions is the following activity, which can also be done with very young children (Stanley, 2004, pp. 41–4). A text is selected (by the educator or the other enquirers, especially when they are more used to the pedagogy) and offered to small groups to ask questions about. This could be anything: a set of keys, a passport, a school trip to the slaughterhouse,[26] a movie, a painting, a curriculum text, a piece of music, an event in the playground, a picturebook, etc..[27]

On an A1 piece of paper participants 'chimney-sweep' as many as 10 questions, and write them down (or an adult scribes). Each group has a different-coloured, large felt-tip. I prefer the notion 'chimney-sweep' over 'brainstorm' as the latter suggests that thinking is what you do with only your brain. A chimney, on the other hand is at the heart of a building, and includes soot: the questions we 'subconsciously' generate without trying too hard to be rational. What is important is that the learners do not think too hard about the questions – just anything that comes to bodymind.

The text we had used was from YouTube (www.youtube.com/watch?v= sJNntUXyWvw). We first watched the DVD clip together. A three-year-old Brazilian boy is in conversation with his mother:

Luiz:	That's ok?
Mum:	Yes.
Mum:	Now eat your octopus gnocchi.
Luiz:	Ok, mum, alright. Now this octopus is not real, right?

Table 8.1 The role of an educator as stingray in a literacy lesson using the community of philosophical enquiry pedagogy

	Philosophy with children – the role of the educator as stingray		
Pedagogical intra-vention	Literacy skills and values		Main role of the teacher
Present the narrative	Use of a variety of multimodal 'texts', including children's personal oral responses.		Text (incl. children's own conversations, happenings, images) is made accessible for all through, e.g. a document reader or reading a book in front of a class sitting on the carpet, or projecting an image or movie on the wall.
	Focusing on the *diversity* of interpretations of words, images, events, etc.		
	Celebration of the new, the as yet unthought.		
	Relationships between the human and nonhuman also influence the reading of the narrative.		
Move the furniture into a circular seating	Responsive and response-able listening requires being able to see and hear properly (expression of equality).		Sits in the circle with the children on a same-size chair or all on the floor.
Allow learners to think on their own	Solitary task. The use of drawings or key words as part of emergent literacy. Spelling and neatness doesn't matter, but supported if appropriate. Understanding and meaning-making is central. Personal responses encouraged and celebrated (expression of academic freedom and equality).		Supports individuals to construct and represent knowledge (e.g. through drawings) by walking outside the circle of chairs and offering assistance without providing correct answers. The children are encouraged to draw the ideas they have in their mind (but not to copy the images in the book). Other means of expression are also possible (acting out, etc.).

Collecting children's questions	Framing, developing and sharing questions for enquiry in small groups, involving negotiation and democratic collaboration. Discussing about what makes a good question for an enquiry. Writing down (or other means of expression, e.g. clay) of the question and reading those of others (and listening) before voting.	Forms small groups. Records children's questions in their own words (e.g. on a flipchart or whiteboard). Asks groups to explain their choice of question and supports the community to ask second-order questions[1] about their question. Responsible for the system for selecting a question, e.g. by majority vote, lottery, but increasingly shares this responsibility with the children as they get used to the process.
Listening in enquiry	Listening without Organs (LwO): speaking and responding thoughtfully. Speaking initially in response to the question that needs answering. 'Building' on ideas by making horizontal connections through reasoned and imaginative responses, and focusing on key abstract concepts 'embedded' in the question. Diffracting with language use and the bodies in the room. Introducing distinctions, connections and comparisons between concepts. Formulating and creating new meanings of concepts (also through material expressions of concepts[2]). Offering examples and analogies. Expressing opinions. Agreeing/disagreeing with one another, or offering a new idea. Giving reasons. Constructing arguments and counter arguments.	Listens without Organs (LwO): responds by asking questions that problematise some key concepts the children want to explore in connection with the text, linked to children's own experiences and socio-cultural practices. 'Stings', 'numbs' and 'gets numbed'. Co-enquires and reasons alongside the children. Does not provide answers.
Providing temporary closure	Freely expressing comments related to the story in the previous word round. Requiring listening and turn-taking.	Passes a 'talking stick' round the circle offering opportunities to children who haven't spoken yet, after discussion in pairs first.

1 Second-order questions are questions that put into question the validity of assumptions in the question itself. See below in the main text.
2 As, for example, in the case of 'give' and 'take' in Chapter 7.

Mum:	No.
Luiz:	Then alright. He doesn't speak, and he doesn't have a head, right?
Mum:	He doesn't have a head. These are only the chopped little legs of the octopus.
Luiz:	Huh? . . . but is his head in the sea?
Mum:	It is at the fish market.
Luiz:	The man chopped it . . . like this?
Mum:	Yes, he did.
Luiz:	Why?
Mum:	So we can eat it. Otherwise we have to swallow it all.
Luiz:	But why?
Mum:	So we can eat it, love. Just like a cow is chopped, a chicken is chopped . . .
Luiz:	Ah . . . the chicken, no. Nobody eats chicken.
Mum:	Nobody eats chicken?
Luiz:	No, these are animals.
Mum:	Really?
Luiz:	Yeah.
Mum:	So let's eat the gnocchi? Eat the potato then?
Luiz:	Just the potato and just the rice.
Mum:	Ok.
Luiz:	Octopus are animals.
Mum:	Alright.
Luiz:	All of them are animals. Fish are animals. Octopus are animals. Chicken are animals. Cows are animals. Pigs are animals.
Mum:	Yeah.
Luiz:	So . . . when we eat animals they die!
Mum:	Ah . . . yes.
Luiz:	Why?
Mum:	So we can eat, love.
Luiz:	Why do they die? I don't like that they die. I like that they stay standing up.
Mum:	Ok. Alright. So we are not going to eat it anymore. Ok?
Luiz:	Ok . . . these animals . . . you have to take care of them . . . and not eat them!
Mum:	You are right son, so eat the potatoes and rice.
Luiz:	Alright . . . why are you crying?
Mum:	I am not crying . . . I am just touched by you.
Luiz:	I am doing something beautiful?
Mum:	Eat . . . no need to eat the octopus alright.
Luiz:	Ok.

In Figure 8.2 you can see the questions one group is in the process of writing down about this moving dialogue between a mother and son. The groups are

Figure 8.2 Chimney-sweeping philosophical questions.

then asked to classify their questions and to generate their own classifications and understandings of them. A helpful set of symbols for this has been developed by Stanley (2004, pp. 42–3; Figure 8.3). After each question they put the symbol that describes that question best: either the question is closed (a tick), factual (an image of a book), open-ended (a smiley face) or philosophical (smiley face with a question mark). Of course, more than one category can apply to each question.

Most important here is the discussion participants will have about the difficulty of distinguishing between these four categories. When they are finished with the symbol allocation and their discussions, they swap their flip chart sheets with questions and symbols and pass them down one table (clockwise). The other groups then check whether they agree with the symbol allocation, and identify questions they want to ask the other group. In this way, learners find out for themselves,[28] through exploratory talk with others, that the questions that are philosophical require an enquiry into the meaning of the core concepts that are assumed, that are 'embedded', in the questions themselves. Why are names important? What are vegetarians, and is it morally right to eat nonhuman animals? If so, also your pet animal? These questions are divergent: they open up more second-order questions *ad infinitum*. In philosophical enquiries a wide range of questions intra-act. There is not just

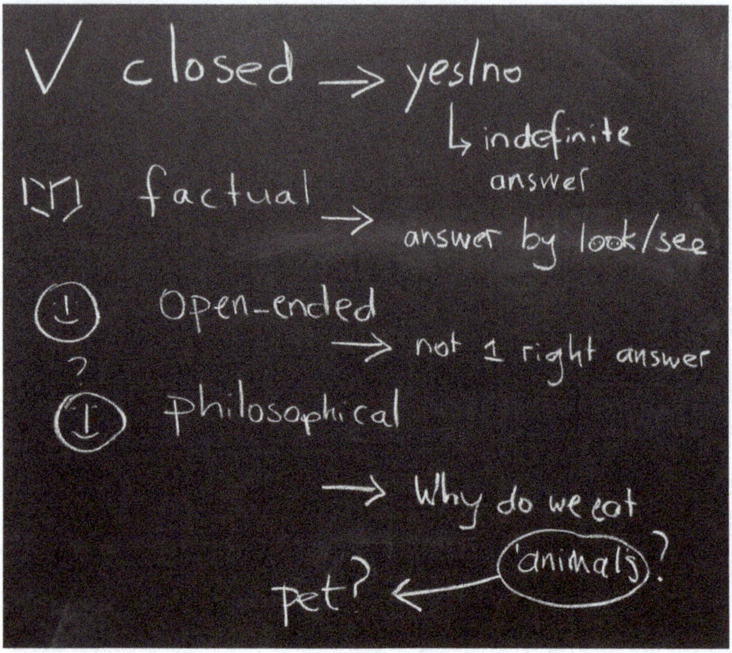

Figure 8.3 Symbols for categorising questions about the text.

one type allowed. It is important to know how they work as apparatuses. What do they do in the classroom? What kind of relationships and knowledge do they make possible? How can we include parents in these important questioning processes? What can we learn from them and with them, about ourselves, the children, and their materialdiscursive environments?[29]

It is possible to distinguish between four different kinds of reading of texts, and each kind assumes a particular kind of questioning, but also positions a particular ontoepistemic relationship between the educator and the learner, as summarised in Table 8.2.

Kathy Short distinguishes between three different kinds of reading of texts: reading '*strategically*', '*for personal purposes*' and '*deeply*'. Reading *strategically* involves acquiring both *literary* knowledge (knowledge about literature as a narrative form[30]) and *literacy* knowledge (knowledge about reading and writing processes, such as decoding skills, plot-based comprehension and vocabulary) (Short, 2011, p. 58). Reading for *personal purposes* includes using a wide range of texts for enjoyment and entertainment and talk with peers (Short, 2011, p. 58). Reading *deeply* involves allowing learners to make connections between the text and issues in their own lives as well as in broader society (Short, 2011, p. 59). In the latter, literary events include deep immersion in the narrative and critical engagement with the text through discussions with peers.

Table 8.2 Four different ways of questioning texts and the ontoepistemologies they assume

Types of reading	Knowledge acquisition	The right question	Positioning of child/adult ontoepistemic relationship
Reading strategically	Literary knowledge, e.g. story, plot, themes, language Literacy knowledge, e.g. decoding skills, plot-based comprehension and vocabulary	Closed, factual questions	Adults are the problem-posers, and adults ask closed and factual questions
Reading for personal purpose	Own opinions about texts for enjoyment and entertainment and talk with peers	Open-ended questions with no right or wrong answers	Children are the problem-posers, and adults ask open-ended questions
Reading deeply	Connections are made between a text and issues in children's own lives as well as in broader society	Open-ended, critical questions with an evaluative component; there are right and wrong answers	Children are the problem-posers and problem-solvers Adults ask open, probing questions
Reading in a community of enquiry	Abstract concepts 'in' a text are the content of enquiries; these concepts are common, central, contestable and connect with own experiences	Open-ended, substantive, second-order questions; there are right and wrong answers Often all types of questions are interwoven in enquiries, but philosophical ones are central	Children are the philosophical problem-posers and the philosophical problem-solvers

For teacher education, it is of central concern to acknowledge that these different approaches to reading literature require different theories of knowledge (epistemologies), and therefore pedagogies (a particular relationship between child/adult). In reading strategically, *adults* are the problem-posers. They teach reading strategies and texts structures explicitly, and ask the questions that matter in class. Teachers already know the answers to the 'closed', rhetorical questions they ask. The problems that need to be 'solved' are unambiguous, and the solutions to the problems posed are known to the teacher. By contrast, when reading literature for *personal purposes* children ask the questions, and are allowed to 'wonder about and talk back to a book' (Short, 2011, p. 59). Here, *children* are the problem-posers. The connections children themselves make between their own lives and identities, and the texts they explore, are central. Personal, subjective responses and anecdotes are encouraged and celebrated, but not critically compared or evaluated. There are no 'right' or 'wrong' answers. For reading *deeply*, texts chosen for 'intensive reading have multiple layers of meaning' (Short, 2011, p. 59).

Whilst Short suggests that when reading deeply, both adults *and* children are problem-posers, as well as problem-solvers (Short, 2011, p. 59), the significant pedagogical implications for how teachers use texts in class and who is in control of meaning and truth are not drawn. Moreover, when 'reading deeply', children not only ask or answer the questions that matter, but also learn to 'question the questions' (Short, 2011, p. 50) – in other words, they ask second-order questions.[31] But Short is not explicit about the difference between first- and second-order questions and the epistemological and pedagogical challenge the distinction poses for teachers' literacy practices.

At first sight, the 'community of enquiry' pedagogy has a strong appeal for educators interested in literacy, because of the superficial similarities with other discussion-type classroom activities (see, e.g. Arizpe and Styles, 2003, p. 161), but the pedagogy is an epistemological reorientation that challenges most teaching practices in schools and universities. Its theory and practices challenge the common belief that 'deep' readings are non-literal, and necessarily need to involve symbolic or figurative readings of texts – often regarded as less 'mature readings' (Haynes and Murris, 2011). As we have seen, in a philosophical community of enquiry the product is not known in advance but is interdependently constructed by its participants. Through the use of all Hundred Languages, concepts are explored materially and discursively through philosophical questioning by both child and adult. It is the intra-actions 'between' participants that bring the new knowledges into existence by drawing on everyday experiences, thereby testing, adjusting, shaping and reshaping concepts, such as by using concrete examples and counter-examples. This connection between the conceptual, the material and the experiential, the concrete and the abstract, aids deep philosophical reading of texts. The knowledge and experience brought to these common, everyday concepts, in turn, inform judgements and actions.

A way forward

In South Africa the strategic reading of texts is dominant. Returning to the crisis with which iii started the chapter, the challenges of implementing a rhizomatic curriculum with teachers as pregnant stingrays are many and complex. Large class sizes, verbal reasoning in an additional language and use of the Hundred Languages can be seen as significant obstacles. Although there are practical solutions to solving these problems, the deeper challenge, as elsewhere, involves preparing teachers for the uncertainty and insecurity involved in planning for lessons that democratically accommodate children's own questions and ideas, and that draw on pedagogies with which they are unfamiliar. This includes a lack of familiarity with planning lessons as a holistic endeavour that does not involve specifying goals and objectives in advance, but enacting a range of flexible, ongoing hypotheses generated in the intra-actions with past experiences, the material, as well as the needs and interests of, for example, the children and parents (Hocevar, Sebart and Stefanc, 2013, p. 478).

The epistemological change and shift in power brought about by intra-active pedagogies requires unlearning didactic teaching practices (Haynes and Murris, 2011), and learning how to teach through oral enquiry, an imaginative use of the creative arts and from the perspective of *all* children as rich, resourceful and resilient (e)merging through materialdiscursive relationships (including children living in poverty).

The conclusions of the considerable amount of research into the efficacy of using philosophy with children are positive and persuasive (Green, 2012; Green and Murris, 2014; Murris, 2014c), but they do not necessarily convince governments, researchers and policymakers, because of how the pedagogy disrupts the way children are routinely listened to, challenges what counts as knowledge and disturbs the authority of the teacher as the person who asks the questions that matter.

In the *diffractive pause*, experienced philosophy with children teacher and teacher educator Sara Stanley introduces three- to five-year-olds to philosophical questioning in a South African context.

A diffractive pause: a pregnant stingray in South Africa

In 2013 an early-thinking pilot project[32] was conceptualised to address concerns about the lack of language and literacy skills, especially with multilingual children living in poverty and, according to the funders, their lack of ability to think imaginatively. Philosophy with children interventions were structured in the context of play and good-quality picturebooks.[33] Pioneer in philosophical play,

Sara Stanley was recruited from England for the project to work with 20 early-year practitioners, trainers or coaches with the aim of evaluating whether philosophy with children does indeed develop their language ability and thinking and reasoning capacity, and to assess whether, and how, philosophy with children can be used with practitioners and children in South Africa. An in-service coaching and mentoring structure had been put in place to support and address context-specific issues. The findings of this small-scale and short-term project were very favourable (Burtt, 2014), and concluded that philosophy with children should be 'integrated into ECD training qualifications'. A follow-up project is in progress.

This offers an opportunity to diffract with another example from philosophical practice, purposely chosen for the challenging educational contexts it provides, and to show how teachers can start creating a philosophical space in educational settings. The focus is on how to start philosophical questioning with children aged 3–5 years. The DVD about this project is available on YouTube: www.youtube.com/watch?v=QeveNmuEQcU.

The preschool in question is situated in the Cape Flats near Cape Town – an area consisting mainly of townships and informal settlements where most people live in extreme poverty. To get a sense of the area in which the preschool is situated, it is a good idea to visit what Wikipedia refers to as this 'apartheid dumping' ground. Although not always to be recommended as a reliable source of information, in this case the Wiki coverage is comprehensive, accurate and useful for this particular purpose: http://en.wikipedia.org/wiki/Cape_Flats.[34]

The DVD can be used to creatively explore with educators what the role is of the teacher in the example, and the images that can be brought to their practice. What kind of questions is Sara Stanley asking, and how do these questions work? Is she a pregnant stingray, and, if so, in what way? There are three moments in particular iii use with educators – usually starting the DVD clip around the 12th minute where Sara presents the provocation for the enquiry: Maurice Sendak's *Where the Wild Things Are* (1963). We focus on her interventions as the children make communal drawings. She invites them to draw 'anything strange in that book'. The way she makes connections with the children's own lived experiences and the story (e.g. connecting their mum with Max's mum) is of particular interest, as well as legitimising the use of their fantasy and imagination. Without correcting incorrect content knowledge (e.g. they call the wild things lions and dinosaurs), Sara also asks numbing questions (e.g. how do you know dinosaurs are scary? [if you have never seen one before]), and embraces the unexpected things the children are saying. She suggests to a small group that they *draw* a wild animal. What would the philosophical concepts 'animal' and 'wild' look like? She speculates: 'I wonder what a wild animal does' . . .

It is her *doing* of concepts that makes her work so special. What does it mean *to be* a 'friend', or 'good' or 'bad' or a 'wild animal'? She asks, for example, 'Do wild animals go to supermarkets?' ... 'Perhaps they go in the night time when you are asleep?' Much of her work is about philosophical play and creating storyworlds, and the first step here is her use of the well-known drama technique 'hot seating'. She goes in role as Max's mum, and invites the children to ask mum questions about the story. It seems particularly helpful to generate questions that are written down for them to keep for further use after their first formal philosophy lesson. Using this DVD clip in teacher education is nicely complemented by an interview with Sara Stanley herself, where she explains some of her pedagogical decisions – also available on YouTube (around 11 minutes):

www.youtube.com/watch?v=CV4ANiQkh3Q

She explains how teachers need to listen and observe children who use philosophical concepts all the time when in imaginative play and talking to each other. In philosophy with children, she includes the other languages of drawing, artwork, play and actions in her work to support communication with words. Sara Stanley admits that the children numbed her in this class: 'I am still genuinely surprised and delighted by some of the ideas the children have, and how they make me go away thinking I never thought of it from that point of view'.

Notes

1 iii have outlined the problems with early literacy standards in South African foundation phase schools in much detail elsewhere, and iii argued that philosophy with children should be part of the solution (Murris, 2014c).
2 The focus here is only on literacy, not on mathematics education, although results are just as low.
3 See in particular the report published by NEEDU (2013).
4 Who themselves are the 'product' of Bantu education – the only education available to coloured and black people during *apartheid*.
5 The language of learning and teaching in the foundation phase is often not a child's home language, but English – a language many children are unfamiliar with until they go to school. Teachers' command of English is not always proficient. South Africa has 11 official languages.
6 For example, the underdevelopment of African languages in print or textbooks to which not all children in schools have access in practice.
7 This issue is central in the next chapter.
8 iii like this way of writing 'emerge' as it expresses diffraction beautifully. I saw it for the first time in Sellers (2013).
9 Karin Brodie (2007) distinguishes between 'test' and 'authentic' questions. The former try to find out what the learner knows, while the latter are questions without pre-specified answers.

10 The IRE framework was identified about 30 years ago (Brodie, 2007). The basic structure has the following sequence: Teachers *initiate* by asking a question, a learner *responds* by giving an answer and the teacher *evaluates* the answer (e.g. by saying 'good girl').

11 See, e.g. www.education.gov.za/Curriculum/AnnualNationalAssessment/2013ANA ExemplarsGrade3/tabid/893/Default.aspx

12 The current curriculum's focus is on reading schemes, text- and work books, but with very little room for children's literature.

13 Provoking disequilibrium can be highly constructive in teacher education (see Murris, 2008; Haynes and Murris, 2011). If we open up a space in classrooms where children are allowed to ask philosophical questions, the resultant disequilibrium is a positive force that opens up a space in which educators need to reflect upon their values and their beliefs about learning and teaching, and ultimately encourages educators to rethink their own role.

14 For example, when children in a Reggio school build a construction to trap a moving tiger in a documentary projected onto the wall behind them (see *Everyday Utopias* (2011) 'A Day in a preschool' – a video produced by Reggio Children (see www.reggiochildren.it) – a perfect provocation for a community of philosophical enquiry. Especially when scribing children's conversations (Malaguzzi, 1998, p. 92) as they are talking and then reading these notes back to the children as a starting point for philosophical dialogues (see Stanley, 2012 for more ideas).

15 See Chapter 7 for an enquiry into the concepts 'give' and 'take'.

16 'Meta' is not used here in a hierarchical, vertical sense, but to indicate that some-thing else is going on: an enquiry with a different focus; not on *what* we enquire into, but *how* we do it together.

17 See: Chapters 2, 6 and 7.

18 Downloaded from http://proustmatters.com/tag/socrates/, accessed 15 May 2015. You can freely copy material from this site provided that you give full and clear credit to Sharon Girard and proustmatters.com, but special permission has been sought for the use of this image for this book.

19 Why Socrates is pointing upwards, because the true meaning of these abstract concepts is in the World of Forms or Ideas (see reference to Raphael's painting *The School of Athens* in Chapter 3).

20 www.youtube.com/watch?v=0cBfTbvlYxk, accessed 19 May 2015.

21 www.youtube.com/watch?v=BGWir0Ui7Xw, accessed 19 May 2015.

22 Many people believe that the stingray lays eggs, because of its biological category as 'fish', which raises interesting questions for an extended project that could include life skills, mathematics and literacy.

23 See Chapter 4.

24 Which is not the same as child-*centred*.

25 See also Murris and Haynes, 2002, but not from a posthumanist orientation.

26 See Chapter 3, the first *diffractive pause*.

27 For useful criteria for a provocation, see Chapter 9.

28 Importantly, this activity should not be used as a 'thinking tool' or 'tool' to prescriptively teach students that there are right and wrong questions. Questions work philosophically because of how you use them in relationships with human and 'beyond human' others.

29 Malaguzzi (1989, p. 69) reminds us that teachers need to be able to talk, listen and learn from parents. It requires from teachers 'a constant questioning of their teaching. Teachers must leave behind an isolated, silent mode of working that leaves no traces'. For parents' involvement in philosophy with children, see Stanley, 2004.

30 Knowledge about literature as a narrative form includes a sense of story, plot, themes and language.

31 Second-order questions invite people to interrogate the validity of the assumptions that are implicit in the first-order question. What is involved in moving from first- to second-order questions is explored later in the paper.

32 A collaboration between the School of Education at the University of Cape Town, Project for the Study of Alternative Education in South Africa (PRAESA) and the DG Murray Trust, all based in Cape Town.

33 Implementation of philosophy with children in Southern Africa is supported through a gratis network: www.mindboggles.org.za.

34 Wikipedia is of course always becoming, but the information was accurate when iii accessed it on 21 February, 2015.

Chapter 9

Destabilising binaries through philosophy with picturebooks

We have seen how philosophy with children as a rhizomatic intra-active pedagogy brings about an epistemological change, a shift in power and requires an unlearning of didactic teaching practices. It disrupts how children are routinely listened to, challenges what counts as knowledge and disturbs the authority of the teacher as the person who asks the questions that matter. Finally, it assumes child as rich, resilient and resourceful (e)merging in unbounded materialdiscursive relationships.

Carefully selected picturebooks complement all of these important epistemological, political and ethical aspects, as argued elsewhere (Haynes and Murris, 2012; Haynes and Murris, forthcoming). In this chapter, the focus is slightly different; iii show how picturebooks can be used as creative opportunities to destabilise discriminatory binaries as provocations for communities of enquiry, and thereby disrupt the adult/child dichotomy.

As the result of hegemonic national and international educational policies, picturebooks live in the shadows of text books and the hierarchical, sequential reading programmes that our schools use to teach isolated literacy skills (Short, 2011, p. 49). Recent US research suggests that the focus on accurate and fluent word recognition has made the content and quality of texts less important for teachers; as a result, good-quality children's literature gets 'little more than lip service' (Teale, Hoffman and Paciga, 2013). The situation in SA is similar in that the current focus on short-term reading achievement goals has meant a foregrounding of the mastery of a set of decontextualised skills as laid down by the national curriculum 'clock', as opposed to employing the concept of real time (Genishi and Dyson, 2009) or 'time for listening' (Rinaldi, 2001, p. 80).

The latter is time 'outside chronological time – a time full of silences, of long pauses, an interior time'. A pedagogy of listening involves ourselves as well as others, and always an emotion, such as curiosity, doubt or interest (Rinaldi, 2001, p. 80). We saw this clearly in Sara Stanley's teaching in Chapter 8. Real-time listening involves paying 'thoughtful attention' to other earth dwellers 'both accepting and critical, trusting and diffident, irrepressible and yet consoling' (Corradi-Fiumara, 1990, p. 90) without being manipulative, instrumental or colonising (Haynes and Murris, 2012, p. 216).

We have seen in the previous chapter how this philosophical listening opens up possibilities for educators to read children's literature in ways other than the limited use currently demanded by official curriculum frameworks (Short, 2011, p. 49). The argument put forward in this chapter is that the *picturebooks* themselves (with all their discursive ambiguity and complexity) *demand* such philosophical listening. Their force and energy *in relationship with* the reader requires an intra-active pedagogy that positions people of all ages as able materialdiscursive meaning-makers and problem-posers.

After briefly outlining in this chapter some (now) well-established arguments for the use of picturebooks to explore abstract concepts philosophically (Murris, 1992, 1997; Murris and Haynes, 2002; Haynes, 2008; Haynes and Murris, 2012), iii explore in much more detail the complex decisions picturebook author Anthony Browne made about censorship and child protection when creating the text and images in his book *Little Beauty* (2008). My analysis foregrounds the author's provocative play with the discriminatory binaries nature/culture, science/art, animal/human, fantasy/reality, machine/life and child/adult. Browne's conceptual play includes his choice of characters, the ending of the story and the deliberate variety of art styles throughout *Little Beauty*. The entangled relationship between his autobiography, his beliefs about children and his aesthetic choices create rich educational material for educational institutions, because *they destabilise the core adult/child binary*.

Binaries in picturebooks can be pushed to their limits with students of all ages, and examples from the work of one educator with her six- and eight-year-old daughters have been integrated within this chapter to demonstrate how the nonhuman and the text's materiality (and in one particular case the colour red) can a/effect how *Little Beauty* works as a text in philosophical enquiries. The chapter finishes with ideas of how to start a 'destabilising binary project' using a variety of Anthony Browne's picturebooks as the *diffractive pause*.

The problem with binaries and an 'ethics of resistance'

The reason for setting up a 'destabilising binary project' is that the problem with binaries is that they create hierarchies and 'standstill' spaces 'in which possibilities for encountering other ways of seeing and relating or transformations are closed' (Kocher and Pacini-Ketchabaw, 2011, p. 47). These binaries are not 'natural', as we have seen in chapters 3 and 4, but are intricately connected with 'constructions of the other and of otherness' (Mander *et al.*, 2012, pp. 3–4). Empiricist, nativist or interactionist teaching practices all assume the core nature/culture binary. Child is associated with nature that will either unfold (Rousseau), or needs to be developed (Locke), or interacted with (Kant) in order to become 'fully-human'. The dicho-tomy cuts child (nature) apart from adult (culture), thereby essentialising and discriminating the young 'Other' (Chapter 5). Moreover, 'the adult' or Man of humanism is white, male, middle-class, able-bodied and Western (Braidotti, 2013), properties which, in turn, are connected with other binaries. For example, in the case of early literacy, binaries such as poor/rich, advantaged/disadvantaged, resourced/underresourced mobilise curricula and other apparatuses that regulate the spaces that disempower children and that position adults as the holders of important knowledge (Kocher and Pacini-Ketchabaw, 2011, p. 49). The means to disrupt such binary logic is what Deleuze and Guattarri call a 'logic of AND' as an alternative to *either/or* thinking (see also Chapter 1).

Pedagogical documentation, as described in Chapter 7, and the diffractive journal process as iii have introduced in higher education, are vital tools for a pedagogy of listening (Rinaldi, 2001); they make learning visible and tactile. These tools offer unique opportunities to diffract with the ideas of others, and to create something new. Importantly, all participants become aware of the binaries that structure our (humanist) language, and therefore our thinking and actions (Kocher and Pacini-Ketchabaw, 2011, p. 51).

When using the diffractive journals to prepare student teachers, the core binaries that regularly (e)merge are adult/child, work/play, learning/teaching, teaching/research, boy/girl, human/nonhuman, theory/practice. Each week we diffract with our understandings of these concepts; then, in the journals, we materialise how they continue to shape our always (mostly implicit) theorised practices. We then explore these in communities of philosophical enquiry sessions. As a lecturer, iii am not a detached observer, but am just as much a part of this diffractive practice.

The problem with these binaries is that they are so familiar that they are 'seductive'; they require an 'ethics of resistance' to disrupt the unequal power relationships that are hidden within them (Kocher and Pacini-Ketchabaw, 2011, p. 54). At the same time, binaries are the narrative tool that engages the imaginative intellect, including the emotions; so resisting them does not mean *abandoning* them.

The notion of 'ethics of resistance' was introduced by Hillevi Lenz Taguchi (2010, p. 96) and, diffracting with her earlier view on this notion, she comments that her current, more radical, superposition involves changing adult-centred practices and inventing new possibilities. An ethics of resistance includes slowing down the documentation in order to *re-enact*, *re-live* the event, so it is not a *description* of what 'happened' 'in' the 'past', but an identification of the materialdiscursive intra-activity 'between' 'matter, objects and human subjects and how they make themselves intelligible to each other' (Lenz Taguchi, 2010, p. 97). We have seen an example of this in the bodymind mapping of Chapter 5. Bodymind maps are politically informed readings of 'the' 'self' through the binary apparatus. In this chapter, the binary apparatus is used with picturebooks to explicitly provoke *political* readings in class that destabilise discriminatory binaries. So the pedagogical move is a seemingly contradictory one: by focusing on binary habits of thought and practices we learn to disengage and detach ourselves from humanist practices. We 'extend ourselves in creativity' and 'transform ourselves as thinking and embodied beings', through a positive accelerated force of energy, of rupture and deterritorialisation, that Gilles Deleuze and Felix Guattari (1994, p. 2) call 'lines of flight'.

Deterritorialising philosophical questions

We have seen in the previous chapter how the educator as pregnant stingray numbs others (and herself at the same time) by asking philosophical questions and opening up a more egalitarian space of knowledge construction. Deleuze and Guattari (1994, p. 79) write that questions are 'order-words'; they are *commands* and exist *before* language, in the sense that the language itself expresses power relations. Who asks the questions in class is a profoundly political question, not in the sense that certain *individuals* of a particular age ask the questions, but in that they are *speech acts*: certain actions are accomplished by asking the questions: they demand answers and therefore transgress individual boundaries (Deleuze and Guattari, 1994, pp. 77–8).

For Deleuze and Guattari (1994, p. 107), an order-word is a 'death sentence' (in that, they always involve doing this or doing that, like the 'father's orders to his son'), but entangled with the order-word is also *flight*. Questions demand answers; they in turn demand further questions. In philosophical enquiries, questions deterritorialise and rupture fixed meanings 'given' to abstract concepts. This movement of flow, desire and intensity 'pushes language to its own limits' (Deleuze and Guattari, 1994, p. 108) and, as educators, we need to resist the temptation to limit a word to a precise point (a definition) (Deleuze and Guattari, 1994, p. 109). In philosophy with children we can use order-words against order-words so that we can move through the power structures, breaking through the surface and playfully creating lines of flight (Deleuze and Guattari, 1994, p. 110). Questions are met by further questions, opening up new meanings to concepts that are always contestable. The tangles of spaghetti (Figure 7.2) have indeed a life of their own, escaping from their frame and moving in unpredictable directions.

Rhizomatic thinking consists of flows of connectivity of the disparate and the similar, a ceaseless combining and infinite movement of intra-actions, proceeding horizontally, but with shoots and roots chaotically a-centred (like ginger root) spreading inwards (expanding) and outwards (extending) (Sellers, 2013, p. 11). The Internet is a good example of infinite connectivity, of a rhizome (Sellers, 2013, p. 11).

As educators we need to be attentive to the new, remarkable and interesting that children create together rhizomatically out of existing events (e.g. imaginative play), flowing into new events (Lenz Taguchi, 2010, p. 100). And it is crucial that the children do indeed know that they are allowed to think 'the way they want and not in proper, true or right ways'. Each project should be 'saturated and impregnated with the questions and problems of the children' (Lenz Taguchi, 2010, pp. 100–1). But giving up the normalised figurations of child described in Chapter 5 as well as the nature/culture dichotomy so embedded in early childhood education, is a formidable challenge, whether educators' orientation is developmental, social constructivist, social constructionist, poststructuralist or postmodernist, as we will explore in Chapter 10. Liselott Mariett Olsson (2009, p. 62) reminds us that any project involves not 'a simple progression from worse to better', but 'there's a wondering back and forth in between habitual and new ways of thinking, talking and thinking', rather than always zigzagging to better ways of thinking.

As we have seen in Chapter 8, participants in communities of philosophical enquiry diffract and intra-act rhizomatically with a key focus on philosophical concepts that are not abstractions *from* the world, but are an active force *of* this world (Thiele, 2014, p. 203). In philosophy with children, participants are concerned about the *intra-actional properties* of a concept, that is, how people use the concept to make their own connections in a variety of contexts. Progress is made in an enquiry when the meanings of central concepts are illuminated, and when new understandings are constructed collaboratively by locating a concept, an activity or a story in a framework connected to something in their own experience (Splitter and Sharp, 1995, p. 71). A community of enquiry proceeds on the basis that each and every assumption, statement or argument can be questioned, including the community's own assumptions and procedures, and that it therefore requires an attitude of tentativeness, open-mindedness, non-dogmatism and humility towards knowledge, as well as what counts as knowledge and who the knowledge bearers are. Picturebooks are excellent provocations for philosophical enquiries generally (Haynes and Murris, 2012; Murris and Haynes, 2002), but particularly for specific extended projects aiming to destabilise binary thinking.

Why picturebooks as provocations?

Carefully selected picturebooks are particularly suited as provocations for philosophical work with abstract concepts (Murris, 1992, 1997; Murris and Haynes, 2002; Haynes, 2008; Haynes and Murris, 2012). In common with all literature, they are narratives structured around binaries, such as, for example, good/bad, ugly/beauty, strong/weak, dirty/clean, brave/cowardly – abstract concepts young children 'deploy easily and readily' (Egan, 1995, p. 118), despite developmentalists' claims to the contrary. Kieran Egan (1988, 1992, 1995, 1997) argues that although it is indeed true that to a large extent young children's thinking is concrete, it does not follow that therefore a curriculum that also does justice to the imagination should be *presented* in concrete terms (see Chapter 8). The more remote and strange a narrative is, the more a learner/student will be emotionally engaged, cognitively inspired and intrinsically motivated to bring new understandings to the everyday and the familiar.

Although in this chapter a case is made for picturebooks as texts for philosophising, they will only 'work' if facilitators are prepared to be surprised and engaged by what the children themselves propose as philosophically worthwhile; 'teacher-proof' texts do not exist (Murris, 2005), they always assume pedagogical intra-vention (even in the case of phonics; see Chapter 8). Doing justice to the ethos of the community of enquiry pedagogy implies a willingness to listen responsively and response-ably to the connections children, on their own terms, make between the text and their own lived experiences, without sentimentalising or overestimating their capabilities (Haynes and Murris, 2012).

The picturebooks iii prefer to work with are intricately related to combatting ontoepistemic injustice, and are chosen out of concern for child participation in ethical educational practice. This includes making room for the magical, the visual, the imaginative, the emotions and the body in what it means to be rational, and, in philosophy with children, challenges measurement of progress that uses certain yardsticks of narrow rationality associated with particular forms of adult discourse (Haynes and Murris, 2012, 2013). This divergence from more mainstream philosophy with children has (e)merged out of more than two decades of intra-actions with friend and colleague Joanna Haynes. Its significance lies in its desire to break with educational practices built on the accelerated acquisition of tools of logic and argument associated with some schools of academic philosophy (Haynes and Murris, 2012). Our work within the international field of philosophy with children has been to question such narrow and instrumental views.

There are of course many pragmatic reasons for using picturebooks in class: they are short stories, relatively cheap and their artwork is often attractive. The materialdiscursive object has agency: it invites you to pick it up and read it in a particular way. Many educators[1] prefer pictorial resources over predominantly words-based material, mainly for aesthetic, but also political and pedagogical reasons, such as inclusion and participation.

Because pedagogy and text are always entangled, one of the most critical decisions in philosophy with children is the selection of texts. Not only do picturebooks demand a particular pedagogy, but the pedagogy demands texts that generate ideas and questions that cannot be settled by observation or other empirical means; they require conceptual investigations and pregnant stingrays who are prepared to treat their own knowledge of these concepts as contestable, and who are willing to inhabit the perplexity of philosophical questions (independently of the age or social status of the questioner).

My collaborative and diffractive work with Joanna Haynes has generated a range of criteria (Haynes and Murris, 2012, 2013, forthcoming). Central to these criteria (Haynes and Murris, 2012, pp. 119–21) is teachers' need to give attention to the hospitality and receptiveness of a resource towards what is elusive, perplexing, troublesome or opaque. They need to maximise a sense of disorientation and uncertainty, provoking learners and teachers to co-construct meaning and knowledge together. They need to be open invitations to different ways of being and knowing that provoke dissonance and disagreement about their meaning. They need to liberate students from the anxiety about finding the answer the teacher wants to hear, and entice curiosity about new ideas, and about the way people unlike us think. They should be insightful, imaginative, challenging and surprising.

Moving beyond semiotics

Good-quality picturebooks are more than just books with illustrations. Oft-quoted, classic points of reference in children's literature research argue that picturebooks involve *two* very different interdependent[2] sign systems (the *images* and the *words*) (Sipe, 1998, 2012; Nikolajeva and Scott, 2000, 2006). The reader, so the argument goes, is pulled in different directions of meaning-making by the use of these two different sign systems; the linear direction of the text invites readers to continue reading; the pictures compel them to ponder. Importantly, the 'gaps' between text and image may be experienced differently as we grow older, which challenges teachers to listen and respond differently from children (Haynes and Murris, 2012). In their influential article on picturebooks, Maria Nikolajeva and Carole Scott (2000, p. 238) argue that 'children's literature speaks to both adults and children', and that 'the two audiences may approach textual and visual gaps differently and fill them in different ways'.

The point is that teachers should not underestimate the problem radical diversity (including age differences) poses in adults' decision-making about which texts to use. David Lewis describes a picturebook metaphorically as follows (see Haynes and Murris, 2012, pp. 55–6).

> Words are never 'just words', they are always words-as-influenced by pictures. Similarly, the pictures are never just pictures, they are pictures-as-influenced by words. Thus the words on their own are always partial, incomplete, unfinished, waiting the flesh of the pictures. Similarly, the pictures are perpetually pregnant with potential narrative meaning, indeterminate, unfinished, awaiting the closure provided by the words. But the words and the pictures come from outside the picturebook.
>
> Lewis, 2001, p. 74

What is particularly striking in Lewis' metaphor is his claim that the words and the pictures come from *outside* the picturebook. How the picturebook works is that for reading images and words 'prior' situated knowledge/s and experiences need to be drawn on. The reading is not strategic (see Chapter 8). Also, the 'relationships between words and pictures can change from one double-page spread to the next just as relationships are constantly changing' (Sipe, 2012, p. 8). The intra-action between image and text is neither stable nor predictable. 'Boundaries have dissolved', writes Lewis, 'inviting a promiscuous mixing of forms' (Lewis, 2001, p. 90).

Moving from a semiotic towards a relational materialist ontoepistemology, iii have recently started to pay more attention in my work (including in my analysis of philosophical enquiries) to the book's *materiality*: the a/effects of graphic design, choice of art style,[3] visual grammar,[4] use of colours and medium (paper, virtual, etc.). In fact, there are infinite materialdiscursive elements that could and should be considered when reading picturebooks. How these languages intra-act, connect and influence each other also depends on what readers 'bring to' the narrative themselves, and the affordances of the material environment. For example, children's drawings, and of the arts in general, *as an intricate part of this* cognitive (as well as emotional) process is still undervalued and underexplored (Narey, 2009), and we will see an example of this in the next chapter when children make a drawing of the maze in the picturebook *Tusk Tusk* by David McKee (McKee, 1978).

Posthumanism is relatively new in children's literature research, entering the field around 2004 (Stephens, 2014, p.viii). But the interest of these researchers seems more focused on machine-mediated texts (e.g. television, tablets) or on characters in narratives that blur binaries (e.g. pets, robots[5]) (Jaques, 2015a, b). Poignantly, John Stephens (2014, p.viii) comments that the 'general consensus' to the posthumanist challenge has been to restate 'the virtues of the liberal humanist'. For Zoe Jaques, the 'post' in 'posthumanism' implies 'a space after and beyond' and the posthuman is understood as the 'non-biological, techno-logical enhancement of . . . human limitations' – an 'expansion of identity' (Jaques, 2015b, pp. 4, 6).

A posthumanism that is also *critical* (see e.g. Braidotti, 2013) challenges this 'transhumanism',[6] and involves a radical rethinking of Western metaphysics, including human agency and post-qualitative research methodologies (with researchers often drawing on Barad's interpretation of quantum physics). For example, Lenz Taguchi (2010, p. 98) points out that moving away from anthropocentric thinking in data analysis takes account of time–space–place relations (disrupting 'pre', 'current' and 'post' as linear). To disrupt a humanist, anthropocentric perspective a 'dissolved conception of time' is required, and an egalitarian 'flattened' reading of the data in order to do justice to the 'thickness of corporeality and materiality in the event' (Lenz Taguchi, 2010, pp. 98–9).

So, a moving away from such human exceptionalism in this particular context would involve, for example, a mapping of the materialdiscursive conditions that make a philosophical enquiry possible from the perspective of the book intra-acting with the hand or the reader, the images of a picturebook projected onto a screen, our circle of chairs, the space created by the circle for kinaesthetic thinking moves, or conceptual work with hoops. Documenting such an event could involve taking photos from the ceiling or recording the sounds *without* focusing on human voices. This would only actualise '*one* of a multiplicity of aspects in the many folds of the thick mixture which makes up the learning event' (Lenz Taguchi, 2010, p. 98).

The art objects are part of the complex mix of causal intra-actions that make teachers and children think and feel differently. It is an unpredictable, dynamic materialdiscursive process, and their thinking and sense of being (e)merges 'in-between' them, the book, the chair or floor they sit on and the space around them. They might feel moved by the story, or subjected to reading and questioning the story in a particular way (e.g. because of the curriculum, or how they have learnt to read texts at school). A posthuman framework opens up new ways of thinking about how texts can be read, and changes how we enact the binary categories embedded in everyday language, especially the adult/child binary.

Binaries and pushing them to the limit

Using picturebooks as provocations for extended project work (*progettione*)[7] challenges current 'expanding horizon' curricula that presuppose developmentalism. As we have seen, a curriculum that takes the imagination seriously *as an intricate part* of the intellect should start with what is *not* familiar and therefore feature unusual characters (e.g. mermaids, humans covered in body hair, aliens, cyborgs[8]), extreme concepts (e.g. immortality, the size of the universe) or obscure thought experiments. Picturebooks feature creatures that mediate between binary opposites: e.g. a gorilla who has a cat as a pet (Browne's *Little Beauty*), a monster with human feet (Sendak's *Where the Wild Things Are*), a tree that can talk (Silverstein's *The Giving Tree*) or elephants that use their trunks as guns (McKee's *Tusk Tusk*). Children constantly use abstractions in their thinking: 'concrete elements are tied to some affective abstraction' and the body (Egan and Ling, 2002, p. 97). In order to understand stories, Egan explains: children must in some sense be familiar with security/danger, courage/cowardice, hope/despair, and so on. Of course, children's inability to articulate or define such terms does not hinder their ability to deploy them (Egan, 1995, p. 117).

The common assumption that readers need to be able to identify with a character (e.g. if you are a black South African you need stories that feature black South Africans) is troubled by the seemingly paradoxical claim that narratives are most engaging when they are *unlike* our everyday experiences (Murris, 1997). As opposed to the more familiar 'expanding curriculum' design, my own starting points for lessons (also at university) are often ambiguous, mysterious, macabre, gruesome or fantastical – playing with the binaries.

As discussed above, picturebooks are perfect provocations for philosophical questioning, thereby creating a rhizomatic curriculum in schools as well as in the institutions that prepare teachers and practitioners. Like all learning, philosophy with picturebooks involves the imagination, emotions, lust and desire (Lenz Taguchi, 2010, p. 59); the material and the discursive are interconnected and inseparable (Lenz Taguchi, 2010, p. 30).

The work of picturebook artist Anthony Browne is particularly suited for philosophy with children with a posthuman orientation; the artist's provocative play with binaries and the intra-active pedagogy of philosophy with children speak to each other. Not only do human animals participate in a community of enquiry, but the picturebooks themselves also have agency, force and power to transform our thinking and being.

Anthony Browne

In his autobiography *Playing the Shape Game* (2011), written together with his son, Joe Browne, Anthony Browne writes movingly about the life events that have inspired his artwork. His art humorously interrogates many binaries, such as working class/middle class, animal/human, young/adult, real/fantasy, which (at least partly) explains his books' popularity across a wide range of audiences. They are popular texts, not only for literacy, but also for philosophy with children.

However, a posthuman pedagogy makes it possible to provoke readers even further by interrogating (with children) how the materialdiscursive elements of his texts disrupt the positioning of a particular ideal human (e.g. not-child, not-weak, not-poor or not-ugly).

In his autobiography, Browne explains some of his aesthetic judgements and other decisions about the complex relationship between fantasy and reality. Browne's own childhood experiences and memories have had a clear force and power 'on' the illustrations. His commentary on the making of *Little Beauty* is particularly striking: his choice of characters, the ending of the story and the deliberate variety of art styles. They mobilise profound contradictions about how child as reader is positioned, and can be used in the classroom to destabilise the adult–child binary.

Little Beauty

Little Beauty is a powerfully illustrated story about a gorilla that has almost everything except a friend. He is sad and lonely. He communicates to his zookeepers in sign language that he would like a friend, and they decide to give him a kitten called 'Little Beauty'. His keepers remind him not to eat Little Beauty, but gorilla loves her (see Figure 9.1).

They become inseparable friends, until one day the gorilla gets extremely upset watching the film *King Kong*. He gets so angry that he destroys the set. The keepers rush in and threaten to remove Little Beauty, but by using sign language, Little Beauty claims that she is the culprit and everyone laughs. In good fairy-tale tradition, Little Beauty and gorilla live happily ever after. Much of the information that would help readers make sense of the story is omitted in words and included only in the drawings. Salient for understanding the analysis of the examples from practice is the visual reference to the film *King Kong*[9] shown on the television. The agency of the material is significant here. Moving away from a focus on the gorilla (read: human), it is the *television* that plays a crucial role in how this story works. There is nothing in the words to explain why gorilla gets so angry (see Figure 9.2). Readers have to figure that out for themselves.

Figure 9.1 Gorilla and Little Beauty become inseparable friends.

Gorilla is a popular character in Browne's prolific work – a character that reminds him of his dad. His love for him is materially expressed through Gorilla (Browne, 2011, p. 78). At the age of 17, Browne witnessed his father's death and he refers to this horrific event as 'Dad's final pantomime' (Browne, 2011, p. 38). He explains how the way his father fell off his chair 'as if in slow motion' resembled Kong's fall from the Empire State Building in the movie *King Kong* (Browne, 2011, pp. 38, 96).

The colour red

When iii read *Little Beauty* out aloud in a South African *Nal'ibali* after-school reading club,[10] the group of six- and seven-year-olds were deeply engrossed. Despite the fact that the written text does not mention the *King Kong* film, some of the children knew exactly why he was so angry: that King Kong's death on television must have enraged him. Other educators confirm my own experience. Vursha Ranchod, for example (Murris and Ranchod, 2015[11]), describes how her own daughters responded to this story when she read it to

Figure 9.2 Upset about King Kong's death scene, Gorilla smashes the television set (that page is entirely in red).

them at home. Wafeeqah[12] (aged 6) asked her: 'Can I ask why did he break the TV, because when you are angry you just want to run into your room? Can I ask what film was they watching?' After telling her the name of the film, her older daughter Portia (aged 8) speculates: 'I think he broke the TV, because in the film all the humans wanted to kill the gorilla'. The following dialogue (e)merges when mother and daughters diffract with one another. The materiality of the text has a salient influence on how meaning is constructed. (The daughters are referred to below by their ages and the educator as 'VR'.)

Wafeeqah:	He was a gorilla, so he was feeling very sad, that everybody wanted to kill the gorilla. So then he straight away got up and he got cross and he broke the TV.
VR:	Oh so he was, you saying he is angry with the humans?
Portia:	Yes, because he thinks it's in real life and that's why the whole . . . it also gives an answer for the other page, because the whole page is red, because that is showing anger.
VR:	Is it showing anger? You think the red is showing the anger?
Wafeeqah:	I don't . . . I disagree, because, when you angry you don't want to break it, you can just change the channel.
Portia:	I don't know, I think I disagree and agree with her.
VR:	Why?
Wafeeqah:	But sometimes it's a lot of anger, when you have a lot of, lot of anger, you really want to break the thing and you never want to see it again.

Meanings of this text are not only created by the adult asking open-ended, probing questions in a familiar living room environment (the story was read on the sofa), but there is also the materialdiscursive artwork that has agency and profoundly moves Wafeeqah, who had no prior knowledge of the story of *King Kong*. Unusual for her age – a developmentalist might say – she empathises with the gorilla and, rather than condemning his violent outburst, she listens to his actions (Rinaldi, 2001). Turning the television off will make the anger go away! Her younger sister in turn listens carefully to her words and responds directly to her. She understands gorilla's anger because King Kong is being treated unjustly (Ranchod, 2012, p. 51). It is important to notice here that she is *listening* to the *anger* (Davies, 2014, p. 52), not just the words *representing* anger. The anger points at an injustice done; Wafeeqah makes a *judgement* that includes feelings, but is not limited to it (Murris, 2011b, 2014c), thereby transgressing the feeling/cognition binary.

Her mother does not provide answers, but probes further and asks why the page is red. This is an excellent question from a posthuman perspective, as it draws attention to the influence of the materiality of a particular colour on knowledge construction.

The following insightful dialogue emerges (Murris and Ranchod, 2015) about the significance of the colour red with all its culturally and historically inscribed meanings.

Portia: Other colours don't show anger.
VR: Is it?
Wafeeqah: Because when I get angry my face sometimes go a bit red.
VR: Your face goes red.
Portia: Sometimes.
Wafeeqah: But in real life when you do s . . . when you getting anger your whole room doesn't just go red.
VR: Are you agreeing or disagreeing with her?
Wafeeqah: Disagreeing with her because, because when you get angry the whole room, when you go like this, the whole room just doesn't all go red.
VR: It doesn't all go red? So where does it go red?
Portia: On you.

Browne's choice of making the entire page red is one factor in producing the philosophical dialogues. It is in this way that a colour can be a 'performative agent' (Lenz Taguchi, 2012, p. 29), as are the researchers who selected these transcripts out of many hours of audio-taped enquiries. Thinking, observing and theorising are practices of engagement with, and *as part of*, the world in which we have our being (Barad, 2007, p. 133). To reiterate, learning is not located 'in' indivi-duals, as a mental state for example, but (e)merges in the relationship 'between' the earth dwellers in and around the living room forming non-dualistic wholes where there are no independently existing 'things'. The people in the room do not *have* separate minds or psyches that *have* thoughts, but *are* 'a flow of information between cells, fluids and synapses of thought' (Lenz Taguchi, 2010, p. 47). Like any other objects in the room (e.g. the comfortable sofas), the children and their mother are situated organisms with discursively inscribed bodies, and where people are only one such material organism among many (Lenz Taguchi, 2010, p. 36).

The colour red is one of the discursive-materials that is active and has agency in the production of knowledge. The colour red *makes* itself intelligible as red – a connection is made between the image on the television screen with the story of King Kong. An empathetic relationship is created with the gorilla, but only because of what Portia already knows (culturally) about the colour red. Moreover, the discursive-material, pedagogical context also *makes* meaning: for example, the children know their mother is doing research and the philosophical questions she asks and the answers they provoke are influenced by socio-cultural conventions about polite communication, ideas about teaching and learning, wanting to help their mother, a particular use of voice and body. From a relational-materialist perspective, an author's autobiography also has agency, and it is significant that Browne's drawings of gorilla-dad are 'realistic', because of his use of *imagination*, not *observation*.

Drawings more 'real' than photos

After witnessing his father's death, Browne became fascinated with the human body, and obsessed with death, disease and morbidity, which finally led him to work in Britain for three years as a medical illustrator at Manchester Royal Infirmary. For medical educational purposes, he had to draw the minutest details of dissected corpses and grotesque operations (Browne, 2011, pp. 32–45). He explains in an interview why he had to do this:

> Using a camera, all you'd get is a mess – you couldn't really see what was the vein, what was the artery, what was the liver even; it just looked like blood everywhere, hands and instruments pulling the flesh back. My brief was to produce a clear series of drawings showing the sequence of events.
> Browne interviewed by Rabinovitch, 2013

In other words, these 'factual' scientific medical drawings were not *accurate representations*, but only 'real' in the sense that he had to draw what he could 'see' after 'removing' in his imagination the 'mess' covered in blood. This is a clear case of how the apparatus used in the intra-action helps to create the particular phenomenon. Whether it is a camera or a pencil makes the difference that (also) matters.

This blurring of the science–art binary, and the incredibly detailed drawings of the gorilla–dad human (dad)–nonhuman (gorilla) a(e)ffects how the story is read. 'Human' emotions are clearly visible in the way he draws his apes: their posture, and their eyes in particular. These different sides to the same gorilla gradually emerge when watching the movie *King Kong* (and we also see this with *Little Beauty*'s gorilla). The political message is obvious; the real monsters, Browne insists, are the human animals who keep nonhuman animals in captivity (Browne, 2011, p. 92). The dialogues with the children show a clear emotionalcognitive engagement with Browne's political message, and their concern about the plight of the two gorillas is evident. It is the realistimaginary drawings about 'gorilladad' that make this happen in the context of philosophical intra-active pedagogy, and that are facilitated by the probing, open-ended questions asked by the educator.

The 'real' story

Other stories are also entangled in the phenomena: the gorilla on the television and the gorilla in the picturebook (e)merge with the 'real' stories about a gorilla that had a pet kitten. The concept 'pet animal' has agency when used in enquiries, and profoundly destabilises the nature/culture binary (Haraway, 2003).

Browne admits that *Little Beauty* is based on two real stories he had heard, misremembered and combined in his mind (Browne, 2011, p. 219). In both versions a gorilla called Koko is the main character. When Koko lived in a zoo in California in 1994, she[13] was given a kitten she named *All Ball* (because it had no proper tail). To relieve boredom, she was taught sign language by her keepers and used this language not only to communicate her feelings, but also to answer questions.[14] Moreover she invented new concepts, e.g. 'animal person' for 'gorilla' (Browne, 2011, p. 218). One day she destroyed the washbasin in her cage and when her keeper asked her what had happened she signed 'The keeper did it'. Browne speculates that Koko could in this instance have been lying, but it is also possible that she was telling a joke as it was so obvious that the keeper had not done it (Browne, 2011, p. 219). Both are equally fascinating scenarios for destabilising the animal/human binary.

In the second story about Koko, the gorilla was given a kitten as a pet to see whether she could care for and look after another animal. On the whole, Koko looked after the kitten well until one day she escaped from the cage and was killed on a road nearby (Browne, 2011, p. 219). Apparently she grieved for many days. When Koko was told (signed) that All Ball had gone, Koko signed back, 'Bad, sad, bad' and 'Frown, cry, frown, sad'. The keeper also reported later hearing Koko making a sound similar to human weeping (www.koko.org).

Although Browne claims that *Little Beauty* is an amalgamation of these two stories, in an interview with Kate Evans (Evans, 2009, p. 181) he remembers a different ending to the same story: Koko accidentally crushed Beauty to death when she rolled over one night in her sleep. Considering the two different *unhappy* real endings, it is interesting Browne chose a fictional *happy* ending that involves the kitten lying.

This is fascinating, not just because he is attributing human characteristics to an animal (a cat telling lies), but because of his clear preference for a happy ending and the adult/child binary implied. The happy ending positions a child reader who is innocent and needs protection from the harsh reality of kittens getting squashed by a big friend or accidentally killed by a car.

Dishonest story characters – the wrong moral 'message'?

Browne admits that the way Little Beauty solves the problem in his story (by lying and taking the blame for the damage) has severely troubled him (Browne, 2011, p. 219). He reports that some adults are disappointed in him in that – according to them – *Little Beauty* gives the 'wrong message'. They even accuse him of having a casual attitude towards lying. After all, his critics say, gorilla should take responsibility for his own destructive aggression. Browne comments:

Just because this particular gorilla lied (or perhaps told a joke) on this particular occasion doesn't mean it is acceptable to lie under any circumstances. I know that most children are astute enough to realize this, but a lot of people were uneasy about the perceived ambiguity of the 'message'. I wrestled with the problem for a long time and it caused me much grief, but I eventually decided to have the kitten flex her muscles in response to the gorilla's answer. Beauty is a passive character throughout the story, and by pretending to admit to smashing the TV she makes it clear that the whole incident can be laughed off. I hope that this makes the story more about friendship than dishonesty.

Browne, 2011, p. 219

Of less interest here is my own anecdotal evidence from practice, suggesting that young children do not pick up his message that Little Beauty's confession is a joke, to make the book 'more about friendship than dishonesty'. Instead iii have noticed that the children immediately pick up that the kitten is lying. I suppose, in philosophy with children it is easier to hear what children really believe, because their questions are a key reference point for the lessons. But frankly, what intrigues me more are his reasons for making the cat 'flex her muscles', and how he manages that visually in the story. What do certain philosophical concepts *do*, and how did he bring that about through his art? In philosophy with children we do not just talk about concepts (e.g. friendship) in philosophical enquiries; we also explore how they work (see chapters 7 and 8).

With little provocation, *Little Beauty* (especially when used in conjunction with the 'real' story of Koko and quotes from the author) prompts questions about conceptual distinctions such as real-life made-up stories, lying–truth-telling and, in particular, human–animal. The conceptual play is provoked by images that deliberately blur the latter distinction. For example, the zookeepers seem to have an exaggerated amount of body hair while in charge of a gorilla who watches television in a comfortable armchair with a cup and tea and a hamburger, a standard lamp and William Morris wallpaper. The provocation is also not wasted on Wafeeqah (aged six) and Portia (aged eight) (Ranchod, 2012):

Portia:	Do gorillas eat meat?
VR:	Mmmm . . . Interesting.
Portia:	Do gorillas . . . I think that we can find that on the Internet or in an encyclopaedia?
Wafeeqah:	But the . . . but the . . . zookeepers said don't . . . they said here's a friend Beauty, but don't eat her.
VR:	Ooooh, okay.
Portia:	Sometimes I heard that gorillas just eat like vegetarian stuff . . .

VR: It's an omnivore.

Portia: I don't know who we can trust.

Portia is wondering why Gorilla has been portrayed as eating meat. She is sceptical about the reliability of our sources of knowledge about gorillas: who can we indeed trust? It is exactly Browne's deliberate play with anthropomorphism (animals that behave or look like humans) that provokes philosophical enquiries that question the making of straightforward speciest distinctions and categories. Pushing binaries to the limit disrupts using them for a particular political or pedagogical purpose as, for example, in critical race theory, critical literacy or social constructivism.[15] As we will see in Chapter 10, these approaches presuppose the adult/child binary and do not destabilise it (although other binaries might be destabilised).

Some useful contradictions

Browne's choice of art styles in *Little Beauty* deliberately disobeys certain rules of his profession (Browne, 2011, p. 220). They vary from very detailed pencil drawings to rough sketches, to large splodges of watercolour and aggressive charcoal drawings. He explains that this material choice depends on the need to express certain moods. For example, 'child-like' rough sketches are often the best way of communicating the emotions of the characters, as well as illustrating the movement in the book. The effect is heightened when the background is very detailed wallpaper (Browne, 2011, p. 221).

Browne's contradictory stance towards children is most obvious in one particular two-page spread. It shows Gorilla and Little Beauty swinging from a lamp (Figure 9.3). He explains that children should be warned not to swing from lamps, hence his (playful?) decision to use a particular non-realistic art-style, as if to say 'you should not do this in real life yourself!' (Browne, 2011, p. 224), and his decision to incorporate a 'hidden warning': the kitten's tail points towards the painting on the wall, the Fall of Icarus by Flemish painter, Pieter Breughel. Icarus drowned in the sea, because, despite the warning by his father, Daedalus, he flew too high and his wings melted (lamps are hot!).

So, on the one hand, the author believes in the need to warn children that this is just a story, and to give the right moral message that they should not swing from lamps; on the other hand, the implied young reader is believed to be so sophisticated that s/he can pick up these very complex materialdiscursive cues. In my experience of working with this book in the context of P4C, the learners have never picked up any of these moralising messages. But their astute and insightful ideas about other parts of the story demonstrate their ability to appreciate complex conceptual ideas and moral dilemmas. Here are some examples of questions a class of six- and seven-year-olds asked after reading the book:

Figure 9.3 The kitten's tail points towards the Fall of Icarus, who drowned in the sea because he flew too high and his wings melted.

- How did the cat explain herself?
- What reasons did Beauty give for breaking the television?
- Who could have made the gorilla and kitten stay together in the same house and do everything together?
- Why choose a kitten, coz it could easily break?
- What is happily ever after?
- How life could be if there were no gorillas?
- How can they do everything together?

The children's questions in turn can be met by the teacher's questions that push at the limits of the binaries, especially by drawing attention to all the sophisticated embodied languages used in the story, including sign language. For example, 'In what way did the cat explain herself, and in what way is that different from how a human would do that?'; 'Could humans and nonhuman animals such as cats and gorillas do *everything together* and what would that be like?'; 'Why do you think the artist changed the gender of the animals in this story?' One of my doctoral students once asked her Grade Two class to draw a zoo for humans.[16] They first explored the categories they would use for putting groups of people in certain cages.

In the *diffractive pause*, an idea for a destabilising binaries project in classrooms for all ages is suggested. However, a word of caution first.

But . . . as a living organism . . . a word of caution

Philosophy with children disrupts using children's literature in education as a means to give readers the right moral messages. As a relational pedagogy, it provokes fresh, more egalitarian relationships between child–adult–animal and other materialdiscursive bodies. The teacher as pregnant stingray participating in the community of enquiry helps in connecting thoughts, asking probing questions and assisting learners to give birth to new ideas. But . . . as a living organism, a community of philosophical enquiry is always unpredictable. Therefore, even when picturebooks have been carefully chosen as provocations for a particular project (like the project suggested below in the *diffractive pause*), the outcome will be a surprise if the children genuinely feel they have the freedom to explore what matters to them. This can be frustrating if literature is meant to be used strategically only. So, although this binary project has a particular focus, the *pedagogical practice itself* queers the adult/child dichotomy. For example, when iii used Browne's *The Big Baby* (1993/1995) with a class of six-year-olds, they were puzzled about the possibility to change what happens when you travel through time. The main character in the story drinks a potion then becomes a baby again, but instead of talking about what it is like to be a child (what iii had expected), their interest was occupied with time travel.

Communities of philosophical enquiry move rhizomatically in unexpected directions. They often raise taboo subjects or touch on controversial issues that are uncomfortable for adults when they grate with educators' own political affiliations and sensibilities. In the next chapter we finish our journey through the labyrinth by examining one each of such subjects in the context of ageism.

A diffractive pause: the Anthony Browne–Destabilising–Binary–project

This project is like philosophical therapy. Like the making of bodymind maps in Chapter 5, this rhizomatic project involves undoing 'the dualisms we had no wish to construct but through which we pass' as to arrive at 'the magic formula we all seek – PLURALISM = MONISM – via all the dualisms that are the enemy, an entirely necessary enemy, the furniture we are forever re-arranging' (Deleuze and Guattari, 1987/2013, p. 21). A philosophy of *immanence* (monism) concerns itself with difference *without* identity, that is, a difference that assumes being without substance and subject, but focuses on relationality instead. The objective of this project is like that of the bodymind maps in Chapter 5, and to push, what Dolphijn and Van der Tuin (2012, p. 127) call, the 'dualisms to the extreme'. In doing so, difference is also pushed to the limit. Instead of looking for the same in the other, it involves looking for difference in the other, which is not *evaluative*, but *performative* (Dolphijn and

Table 9.1 An overview of Anthony Browne's books for destabilising binary projects

Title	Child/ Adult	Animal/ Human	Male/ Female	Real/ Fantasy	Working/ Middle class	Good/ Bad	Beauty/ Ugly	Nature/ Culture
Bear Goes to Town (1999)		✓				✓		✓
The Big Baby (1993)	✓			✓			✓	✓
Changes (1990)	✓	✓		✓		✓	✓	✓
Hansel and Gretel (1981)	✓		✓	✓	✓	✓	✓	✓
Little Beauty (2008)		✓	✓	✓		✓	✓	
Me and You (2010)	✓				✓	✓	✓	✓
Piggy Book (1986)	✓	✓	✓		✓	✓		
The Tunnel (1997a)	✓	✓	✓			✓		
Willy the Dreamer (1997b)	✓			✓				✓
Zoo (1993)	✓	✓	✓			✓		

Van der Tuin, 2012, p. 127). Diffraction makes it possible to see binaries-in-the-making; it maps the *effects* of difference. We have seen in this chapter how Anthony Browne's picturebook *Little Beauty* stimulates enquiries about human animals and nonhuman animals; at the same time these enquiries show how children (e)merge in these unbounded intra-actions as rich, resilient and resourceful. Each Anthony Browne picturebook in Table 9.1 can provoke a wide variety of binaries that can be troubled through intergenerational philosophical enquiries.

In the Table 9.1, iii have listed a selection that in my experience are excellent provocations for political readings using the binary apparatus. The idea is to map the effects of difference-in-the-making in the diffractive journals; not to look for the same (what is familiar), but for what is different, what is new and unexpected and to add this to the bodymind maps, for example. Where the artwork and its context (e.g. by being based on real events as in *Little Beauty*[17]) can explicitly provoke philosophical enquiries into a particular binary, this is denoted by '✓' (bold font indicates really dominant binaries).

Notes

1 Unfortunately this preference diminishes when children 'move up' the educational ladder when 'real' reading is associated with reading words.
2 Hence the spelling of 'picturebooks' rather than 'picture books'.
3 See in particular Browne's fascinating autobiographical reflections on his choice of art styles for his picturebook *Little Beauty* (Browne, 2011, pp. 218–24).
4 See, e.g. Serafini (2009).
5 Diffracting, for example, with Donna Haraway's writings, and in particular her notion of the cyborg. Introduced in 1985 (Haraway, 2003, p. 5), a cyborg is 'a cybernetic organism, a hybrid of machine and organism, a creature of social reality as well as a creature of fiction' (Haraway, 1990, p. 191).
6 See, e.g. Chapter 3, note 7.
7 See Chapter 7.
8 See this Chapter, note 5.
9 The movie *King Kong* features an overly ambitious New York movie producer who decides to include Kong, a giant gorilla who lives on a remote island, in his next movie. Kong is immediately smitten with the lead actress Ann Darrow. The American film crew capture Kong and take him to New York City where he is exhibited as the 'Eighth Wonder of the World'. Kong escapes and climbs the Empire State Building, where he is eventually shot and killed by an aircraft. Note that it is this particular scene that is illustrated on the television screen in *Little Beauty* which infuriates the gorilla and leads him to smash the television. This intratextual reference is crucial for making meaning of this turning point in the story.
10 http://nalibali.org/
11 These examples have been used elsewhere (Murris and Ranchod, 2015), but not analysed using a relational materialist perspective.
12 The names of the children are pseudonyms.

13 Interestingly, Koko is a female, not male – good provocation for a binary project (see end of the chapter) as the gorilla is positioned as a caring person.
14 See www.koko.org, accessed 27 May 2015.
15 For example, social constructivism assumes that there is an ontological distinction between nature and culture (ZPD) which has profound implications for epistemology (mediating school knowledge) and ethics (the adult as expert doing the mediation).
16 Many thanks to Robyn Thompson for this example from practice.
17 Which is different from the real/fantasy binary that is always present, because it is a work of fiction.

Chapter 10

Decolonising education

Black and white elephants with guns

How can people rooted in different knowledge practices 'get on together', especially when an all-too-easy cultural relativism is not an option, either politically, epistemologically, or morally? How can general knowledge be nurtured in postcolonial worlds committed to taking difference seriously? Answers to these questions can only be put together in emergent practices; i.e. in vulnerable, on-the-ground work that cobbles together non-harmonious agencies and ways of living that are accountable both to their disparate inherited histories and to their barely possible but absolutely necessary joint futures. For me, that is what *significant otherness* signifies.

Haraway, 2003, p. 7

The main thread running through the labyrinth so far . . .

To achieve the three aims of education outlined in Chapter 2, Chapter 3 proposed a different ontoepistemology that challenges humanist metaphysics, and includes a posthumanist reconfiguration of child (chapters 4 and 5). Child as 'inhuman becoming-iii' (e)merges as rich, resilient and resourceful through materialdiscursive relationships. In order to disrupt ontoepistemic injustice and ageism (Chapter 6), a rhizomatic intra-active pedagogy is put forward in Chapter 7 that portrays knowledge as an entanglement of spaghetti. Teaching includes relationships with 'more than human others', using apparatuses such as the community of philosophical enquiry. It also includes being response-able for the agential cuts (twirling the fork in the spaghetti) educators make as pregnant stingrays, the questions they ask (Chapter 8) and the books they choose (Chapter 9).

Naturecultures

In this final chapter, iii propose that philosophy with children can help decolonise education through a new 'post'-metaphysical beginning – a beginning that includes what Donna Haraway refers to above as '*significant others*' (the earth dwellers of Chapter 3): these include technologies, nonhuman animals and 'organic beings, such as rice, bees, tulips and intestinal flora, all of whom make life for humans what it is – and vice versa' (Haraway, 2003, p. 15). Haraway's *The Companion Species Manifesto* (2003) is about 'the implosion of nature and culture' – a plea to rethink relationality together, but without the nature/culture binary. Joint in 'naturecultures', she writes, are 'flesh and signifier, bodies and words, stories and worlds' (Haraway, 2003, p. 20). Posthuman enquiry is about 'reality as an active verb' (how things *work*), and not what language *means* – as in 'reflection'. Salient for decolonising education is the idea that categories that involve binaries, such as 'subjects, objects, kinds, races, species, genres, and genders' are all products of *relationships 'between' significant others* (Haraway, 2003, pp. 6–7). The key is not to focus on (humanist) *identity* (black, female, rich, working class) – nor even multiple identities, but to break with anthropocentrism, and to focus instead on *differences* produced in materialdiscursive relationships, differences that exclude or include; in other words, differences that matter (Barad, 2007, 2012, 2014). The point is that humanist metaphysics ignores relationality and assumes a detached point of view by the educator or researcher. For the creation of new subjectivities it is important to move beyond predefined boundaries and those categories of difference 'in' encounters with earth dwellers that are already assumed.

We have seen how child also (e)merges as phenomenon through material-discursive relationships, and is therefore *part* of the world, ontologically, epistemologically and ethically (in a non-hierarchical ontology the three cannot be separated). If this is so, what are the implications of a relational materialist subjectivity for the transformation and decolonisation of education? How does it make us think differently about our encounters with children? To start answering these important questions, we turn first to a brief practical example.

Australian early childhood educators, Veronica Pacini-Ketchabaw and Fikile Nxumalo (2014, p. 135), critical of dominant multicultural education, report on a pedagogical encounter with what they call 'anti-colonial possibilities' – disrupting colonising 'ways of seeing'. Nxumalo is observing a small group of young children playing with water and clay. When one of them, Rachel, rubs her own arm with clay, she says (whilst continuing to rub and studying the effect on her arm): 'Now I have brown skin instead of skin'. Nxumalo comments:

> While Rachel seems to make a connection between my brown body and her 'brown-skin' clay arms; I did not sense my presence in that moment as an 'out-of-place-body', but instead a responsive relationality. In this encounter, brown skin seems to connect to joyful expressions, to shared smiles, to the specific material and discursive dynamics in the room at that moment – to produce an embodiment of brown skin as desirable – at least temporarily.
>
> Pacini-Ketchabaw and Nxumalo, 2014, p. 135

It is significant how inclusion of the relational materiality of the situation (the water, the clay, the way the girl uses her body, her looking at the researcher and smiling when she says it, her humming and singing, etc.) opens up subtle and fresh readings of the data. It is an excellent example of 'Listening without Organs' (LwO; Chapter 6), so characteristic of Reggio-inspired practices (Chapter 7). This listening-as-experimentation is always emergent – listening out for what is different, and what makes us think and feel differently. Children's bodyminds can transform educatorsresearchers when they are prepared to Listen without Organs. Pacini-Ketchabaw and Nxumalo comment that 'more-than-human relationality' disrupts 'hierarchical dichotomies of difference' and offers 'potential for attending to the complexities of encounters with colonialisms and racialization in ways that create affirmative and creative possibilities rather than already known solutions' (Pacini-Ketchabaw and Nxumalo, 2014, p. 135).

The problem with humanist reflexive research methodologies is that they tend to look for sameness, to confirm hypotheses brought to the situation by the adult, and thereby involve listening out for what is already known (listening-as-usual), rather than listening out for the new, for what is not representative, and to be open to the data that 'glows' (MacLure, 2013). The most obvious reading of Rachel's comment, 'Now I have brown skin instead of skin', would be to interpret it as a racist comment, because she seems to assume that skin-as-a-norm is not black. But focusing only on her words, and discounting the relational materiality of the situation, would have done ontoepistemic injustice[1] to Rachel.

Being allowed to build real common-world relationships

Embracing natureculture involves thinking other topologies; in the place of universal categories based on binary opposites (e.g. biological reductionism, cultural uniqueness), complex relational maps ('sketchpads') emerge (Haraway, 2003, p. 8). 'Nature' and 'culture' are abstractions that are mistakenly allowed to stand for the world in representationalism; but, as Haraway (2003, p. 6) argues, biological and cultural determinism are 'both instances of misplaced concreteness'. The result is that 'the *world* is precisely what gets lost' in the process of representing it (Haraway quoted in Taylor, 2014, p. 125). This is not just an epistemological issue, but is profoundly (un)ethical. In mainstream schooling, at all levels of education, knowledge is not about being a part of and being in *touch* with the world, but about a world *represented* through words and images – the one language that has not been taken away (Malaguzzi, 1998). Children are prevented from what Affrica Taylor calls building 'real common world relationships' (Taylor, 2013, p. 62) and, as a result, the *real world* gets lost. The upshot is that child is less likely to make sense of her or his own experiences – a copybook case of hermeneutical injustice. Also, child is less likely to be able to communicate what s/he knows, if language is the only medium by which thoughts and understanding are judged, as we have seen in Laika's case in the first chapter.

Developmentalism has created a 'two-world view': a world for children and a world for grown-ups, which is neither desirable, nor possible. See, for example, Figure 10.1. During an art lesson an educator has 'lined' the table with old newspaper to protect it from paint spillage, but we can see on the paper reports on the well-known Oscar Pistorius case, as well as another murder, with photos included.

The two-world view assumes that adults (read: culture) need to protect child (read: nature) from the adult world. As a result, we have lost touch with the real world in education. In the real world, or as Taylor puts it, down-to-earth 'common worlds', nature and culture reunite in complex, 'messy' worlds – 'full of entangled and uneven historical and geographical relations, political tensions, ethical dilemmas and unending possibilities' (Taylor, 2013, p. 62). Thanks to the ontoepistemological nature/culture divide, child has been, and continues to be, protected by adults from these real worlds in sanitised classrooms where adults also make decisions about, for example, the right teaching resources.

Figure 10.1 Can the real world be kept out of children's classrooms?

The key question in this chapter is how we use resources such as picturebooks to trouble colonialisms without making human indivi-duals 'the central players, but players among non-human others' (Pacini-Ketchabaw and Nxumalo, 2014, p. 131). Moreover, we need to be sensitive here to the fact that reference to humans as 'central players' in humanism means the 'fully-human', that is, the white, middle-class, European, able-bodied male (Braidotti, 2013), and therefore excludes not only black people[2] living in poverty, but also child. However, conversations about transformation in South Africa and the literature about decolonisation tend to exclude child − 'the last savage' (Kromidas, 2014), the historical 'Fool' (Kennedy, 1989) − marginal to the adult hegemonic, scientific, Cartesian world-picture that favours language, literacy and a particular kind of rationality and subject/world relationship (one that is mediated through literacy where real knowledge is located). Child subjectivity tends to be the subject of psychology and psychoanalysis with an inner self, explained through childhood experiences (Lenz Taguchi and Palmer, 2014, p. 764).

In 'post'colonial theorising there tends to be an emphasis on what happens when human animals come together in contexts where there are always power differentials. They typically work 'by casting particular people and practices into binaries of colonizer/colonized, white/[Indigenous], power/resistance, and so on' (Cameron quoted in Pacini-Ketchabaw and Nxumalo, 2014, p. 132).

Although usually forgotten, a key 'so on' here, is, of course, child.

The emphasis on social power, identity, language and discourse by, for example, critical pedagogues in the Freirean tradition, social constructionists or poststructuralists, brings with it, ironically, a serious risk of discrimination and exclusion. As Burbules (2000, p. 15) warns: 'those modes of dialogue that put the greatest emphasis on criticality and inclusivity may also be the most subtly co-opting and normalizing'. Of course, it is true that all language is politicised, and that it is necessary to disrupt the ways of thinking, believing and valuing that are inscribed in the discourses we inhabit (Janks, 2011; Pandya and Avila, 2014). But knowledge brought into the classroom that is focused on literacy, and is abstract and universal, is, as South African educationalist Jonathan Jansen (2009, pp. 256, 260) puts it, a world 'divided between black and white, working and privileged classes, citizens and illegal immigrants, men and women, straight and queer, oppressors and oppressed'. He acknowledges the importance of such knowledge, for example, for critical text analysis, particularly in classrooms recovering from oppressive regimes. However, he argues that a conception of otherising the 'enemy', i.e. 'a capitalist system, oppressive processes, imposing ideologies, the neoliberal state' and so forth, runs the risk of ignoring 'the real human beings' teachers encounter in classrooms (Jansen, 2009, p. 257). South African classrooms, he continues, are

deeply divided places [where] contending histories and rival lived experiences come embodied with indirect (and sometimes direct) knowledge into the same pedagogical space [and the] teacher is implicated within the social and pedagogical narrative, not some empowered educator who has figured out the problems of an unequal world and stands to dispense this wisdom to receiving students.

Jansen, 2009, p. 258

Taking such 'certain' knowledge into the classroom as a means to 'fill' and 'form' the child risks applying the developmental view of child on which this is based. It ignores how also material relationships bring unbounded subjects into existence, thereby requiring that educators are not like 'petrol attendants' pouring the right kind of knowledge into ignorant minds. They need to be 'pregnant stingrays', who, without guidance by predetermined outcomes or hidden adult agendas, numb and get numbed themselves as they philosophise with body *and* mind in communities of enquiry about how abstract concepts such as 'victim', 'race' and even 'racism' work (Chapter 8). It also means using educational resources that, without moralising, sentimentalising or patronising, open up divergent philosophical dialogues about the binaries that discriminate, and go beyond repetition of the given (Chapter 9).

'Emptying', not 'filling'

Texts for children are ideal opportunities for adults to express their ideals about childhood. Unlike Jansen, Sinha (2010, p. 460) argues that the 'felt weight' of the other in dialogue cannot be understood by the psychological language of feeling –feelings understood as mental states 'inside' the subject. By contrast, making room for children's own questions and philosophical ideas makes it possible to read *against* the implicit messages in texts and – as Sinha (2010, p. 460) would put it – to be moved, stirred or excited by that which is not the self.

To reiterate, philosophical praxis assumes a relationship of 'emptying' ('of unexamined ideas, dogmas, beliefs, questions and values'), not 'filling' (Kohan, 2011, p. 349). It also assumes a conscious effort by the teacher to resist the urge to regard education as a formation of childhood. This requires a critical stance towards implicit ideologies in texts, as well as requiring a significant degree of unlearning. This unlearning includes disrupting the role of the adult educator as the one who knows better and best in 'post'colonial education; this includes knowledge about discourses and how we inhabit them and how they speak through us (Janks, 2011). Although not arguing against the need for such disruption (or postmodernist 'deconstruction'), Burbules (2000, p. 6) reminds us that such interventions are 'always on *somebody's* terms'. The humanist focus on *identity* runs the risk of excluding *differences* in points of view about, for example, the meaning of abstract ethical concepts, such as 'peace' and whether it is desirable (see Chapter 6). Bringing to our educational relationships a desire to 'fill' children's minds prevents us from hearing what new these concepts bring to our *future* understanding of the common world we 'in'habit together.

Philosopher of childhood Walter Kohan (2011, p. 349) suggests as a solution a 'childlike way of being in the world' in our educational encounters. Less shaped and formed by their educational institutions, children are more likely to think for themselves, and can teach adults to be 'less "full", "fresher", less prejudiced', 'more open to put themselves freely into question' (Kohan, 2011, p. 349). The activities he suggests are adults' childlike (not childish) involvement in activities such as drawing, painting and 'formulating questions as a child does them'. This also allows for children's imaginative philosophical play with ideas (Stanley, 2012; Haynes and Murris, 2013). But what is appropriate in imaginative play? Where should we draw the line and who is included in the 'we'? Penny Holland (2003/2012) points out that for many decades, war, weapons and superhero themes in children's imaginative play in schools have been frowned upon – or worse, banned altogether. She argues how by forbidding children to include such themes in their play can exclude children, especially boys, from engaged involvement in educational tasks. Holland (2003/2012, p. 33) argues not to ignore, but to take ethical responsibility for this violence, because the world of war and weapons is not just a feature of children's imaginations, but part of everyday life. In this kind of real world it is hard not be seduced by the Romantic figuration of child as innocent. As evident in literature, popular culture, advertising as well as education (see e.g. the popularity of Disney), these sentimental images couple 'pure nature' with childhood and have a powerful appeal. Taylor (2014, p. 125) comments that this innocence and 'naturalness' disguises the 'noninnocent politics' of these cultural representations and how it disavows 'the ways in which real childhoods are implicated within the complexities of down-to-earth and noninnocent common world relations'.

Troubling time(s) and opening up spaces *full* of difference and uncertainty

Disrupting individual pedagogical frameworks that are anthropocentric goes hand in hand with *troubling linear time* – a conception of time that enables Enlightenment notions of truth and beliefs about progress. Pacini-Ketchabaw and Nxumalo (2014, p. 134) explain how a posthuman orientation disrupts the idea of linear trajectories of change, and that progress 'embraces mutuality, mess, multiplicity, and contradiction' in 'continually emergent past-present-futures'. We cannot reflect on the past as distant observers moving as atomistic fleshy units through time and space: past and future are already 'in' the present of which we are a part (Barad, 2007). By opening up to the 'more-than-human' and materialdiscursive realities, new understandings (e)merge that are relevant for decolonising education: 'new connections to things, spaces, and bodies' (Pacini-Ketchabaw and Nxumalo, 2014, p. 135).

Multiple relationalities, or the 'sketchpads' introduced by Haraway (2003, p. 8), are *not* about imparting expert knowledge, but are about rethinking history *with* children and other earth dwellers through 'multispecies', natureculture stories (Pacini-Ketchabaw and Nxumalo, 2014, p. 138). This mapping involves highlighting how differences are made, and how new superpositions are created diffractively in intergenerational encounters. These 'messy stories' are entanglements of bodies, things, histories, memories and human animals, which also include relationships with land, nonhuman animals and human mastery over nature – a 'relational place of conflict' and disagreement (Pacini-Ketchabaw and Nxumalo, 2014, pp. 139–40).

As we have seen in Chapter 9, the choice of text is not incidental in this complex philosophical and pedagogical work. Picturebooks are complex entangled stories. They often raise taboo subjects or touch on controversial issues that are uncomfortable for adults when they grate with educators' own political affiliations. This is particularly true in the case when topics such as death, sex, religion or race are raised by the community of enquirers (Haynes and Murris, 2009, 2012). As art objects, picturebooks are rich with abstract concepts that defy particular geographical or historical locations. Their characters also mediate between binaries, so they engage and open up a space *full* of suspense, surprise, mystery, ambiguity and complexity when using a rhizomatic pedagogy such as philosophy with children. Crucially, they disturb ideas about the possibility of acquiring stable meanings, certainty and truth about 'the' text. 'Products' of communities of enquiry are always 'temporary resting places': points of view (as opposed to mere opinion) are revised, adjusted or rejected in the light of more information or further reasoning.

Whilst 'empty' herself, the educator as pregnant stingray welcomes children to diffract 'between' the narratives and their own ideas, experiences and (e)merging theories, and to fill the room with their own wonderings. It is a significant way of making the real world 'leak' into our classrooms. This can of course cause disturbance and discomfort because hegemonic figurations of child (riding on the nature/child binary) inform educators' beliefs that children are not only innocent, but also ignorant (Chapter 5). When children express their own ideas about issues that do not conform to the values of the adults who are listening, their contributions are often either ignored or not taken seriously (listening-as-usual). In Chapter 6 we saw how in such cases onto-epistemic injustice is done to child. Now, in this chapter, iii put forward another example of ontoepistemic injustice, but this time the focus is on the texts we use in the light of 'post'colonial education.

Spaces *empty* of educators filling them with their political ideals

Chapter 7 proposed a Reggio-inspired philosophy with children that accommodates some researchers' concern that bodily movement is not systematically included in philosophy with children (Scarpa, 2012; Fletcher, 2014), and that the practice requires too much patience and empathy from young children (Fox, 2001). It is true, of course, that, like all teaching, philosophy with children governs and disciplines the body in a particular way (Dixon, 2011). A super-position or interference pattern has been created in this book that also includes Reggio's Hundred Languages in philosophy with children.

The multitude of iconic and symbolic languages available in class involve different spatial and temporal dimensions. Importantly, oral work involves a different kind of temporal sequencing; like a line or a chain. Visual art, on the other hand, involves more diffuse emotionalcognitive activities and children's own drawings are often undervalued and underexplored *as part of* meaning-making processes (Narey, 2009; Soundy and Drucker, 2010). However, recent research suggests that children 'draw to know' and are 'able to express powerful and imaginative ideas and problems through visual modes' (Kendrick and McKay, 2009, p. 54). The arts are 'an essential component in children's ability to make meaning of their world' (Whitfield, 2009, p. 156). Therefore, creating opportunities for the visual is particularly important for inclusion of young children's ideas in knowledge construction. The particular expertise they often bring to the classroom is their capacity to make meaning across a variety of languages, including the visual. Andrew Stables, for example, proposes regarding children as 'semiotic engagers' (Stables, 2008, p. 4) as an alternative to the deficit thinking presupposed by many psychological stage theories.

We have seen that a wide variety of multimodal opportunities are on offer in Reggio-inspired philosophy with children, including drawings, drama activities and other child-initiated kinaesthetic child-activities. In an effort to prevent ontoepistemic injustice, children's developing ideas and theories are documented by including in their complex web their written signs, their oral contributions, the expressions of their bodies and the images in the text, as well as their drawings, and the material environment that intra-acts with the enquiry. Moreover, contributions over many sessions are read and interpreted collaboratively with other practitioners in order to pick up rhizomatic connections that might otherwise be missed (Haynes and Murris, 2013). Interpreting the undetermined interplay between the different languages provokes infinite readings 'beyond' the text, and opens up profound beliefs about how young children's ideas might bring something new and profound into the world. Introducing the agency of the material (the furniture, the building, bodily movements, emotions, children's talk, silences, etc.) adds even further complexity to the entangled materialdiscursive processes, and provides an ontoepistemological context that is always shifting, evolving and indeterminate.

Carla Rinaldi recommends multiple listening for schools that involves listening out for the *differences* 'between' people, but also 'between' the languages – verbal, graphic, plastic, musical, gestural, etc. – as well as their reciprocal interaction, that enables the creation and consolidation of concepts and conceptual maps (Rinaldi, 2001, p. 83).

We have seen in Chapter 7 how differences between philosophy with children practices depend to a large degree on the interpretation of both 'community' and 'enquiry' and the balance between the two. What it means

A diffractive pause: (a)mazement

In contrast to the *diffractive pause* in the Cape Flats in Chapter 8, the philosophical enquiries at the core of this one were filmed in the East Rand of Johannesburg[3] at a small independent, co-educational school. Their usual Grade 2 teacher was one of my postgraduate students at the university where iii used to work. A contextual feature of the enquiry is the University of the Witwatersrand's creation of good practice audio-visual resources distributed to all higher-education institutions in South Africa in 2015.[4] The class of 21 children had been using the community of enquiry pedagogy as part of literacy for four months before iii visited the school to lead six literacy lessons for three weeks. At the time of the research their ages ranged from 7 to 8, while four of the learners were 9 years old. The class was fairly evenly balanced in terms of gender, with 11 girls and 10 boys. In terms of race, all were white except one girl of Indian descent. Three of the girls and 10 boys were on prescription medication for attention deficit disorders; they had been identified by teachers (either in Grade R or Grade 1) as having some barrier to learning.

The picturebook *Tusk Tusk* (1978) by David McKee was the main provocation for the enquiries. It is a picturebook iii have used often as it appeals to both children and educators for a variety of educational and philosophical reasons (see Chapter 9; Haynes and Murris, 2012). More practical suggestions for how to use the story for philosophy with children can be found elsewhere (Murris and Haynes, 2002). At times this picturebook provokes censorship and opens up valuable discussions about controversial issues (Haynes and Murris, 2009, 2012). iii welcome such educational encounters, and explicitly use them to provoke an epistemological shift in teacher education (Murris, 2008; Haynes and Murris, 2012).

In this *diffractive pause*, iii focus on threads that iii have created ('creata' not 'data') of the philosophical work in five literacy lessons a couple of weeks into the project. This particular example has been used in other publications (Haynes and Murris, 2013; Murris, 2014), but the focus is different here.

The crux of this chapter is to diffract with poststructuralist colleagues who are critical of my choice of books for philosophy with children by 'White' author David McKee. The critique includes concerns about the alleged racism in some of his books (Chetty, 2014, p. 26), and concerns about how iii have used the book *Tusk Tusk* in this particular project in a 'post'colonial South African class (Enciso, 2014). The interference pattern created by abusing the diffractive methodology includes the valuable insight that 'teacher-proof' texts do not exist (see also Murris, 2015c), and that the training in philosophy with children should explicitly include the complex role of the teacher in reading 'against' 'the' text. Moreover, such sessions should be part of larger projects,[5] rather than being contained to one hour isolated lessons. Finally, the diffractions expose the humanist metaphysics of the poststructuralists (as explored in chapters 3 and

4), and create a posthumanist orientation towards such picturebooks that troubles linear time and includes all earth dwellers. To prevent dogma, unequal relationships and a restriction of freedom of expression, it breaks with the binaries that underpin discrimination.

Tusk Tusk

This particular text opens up an explicit secret space for the main characters of the story – a group of elephants. Readers of *Tusk Tusk* (1978), written and illustrated by David McKee, are positioned to hypothesise and use their imagination when a group of 'peace-loving' animals flee into a maze (see Figure 10.2) to escape from groups of more aggressive black and white elephants.

As readers we are not privy to what happens in this maze, but years later grey elephants appear. At first they live in harmony until the elephants with the big ears start exchanging strange looks with those with small ears. Black and white elephants attack each other (see Figure 10.3) by turning their trunks into fists and other weapons until they are all dead.

The story ends with uncertainty about the future of the remaining elephants, especially as the elephants with big ears and little ears have been giving each other strange looks, although the last page shows two elephants, both with medium-sized ears, shaking trunks/hands (Figure 10.4).

The story is sometimes chosen by educators for its themes of (in)tolerance of difference, and conflict resolution. However, it is also avoided by teachers because the story has no clear happy ending, and can easily provoke discussion about race and sex, and the intersection of the two: sexual relations between people of different colour.

During my literacy project in the Johannesburg school, iii was not particularly interested in any of these themes in particular, but more curious about the children's ideas. I knew from experience that plenty would emerge, and that their ideas would surprise me, so iii tried as much as possible to 'empty' – to de-centre – my 'self' from any particular attachment to my ideas (to Listen without Organs). I wanted to be open to whatever the encounter with 'significant others' (Haraway, 2003, p. 7) would produce, and that included the picturebook's own agency. After reading the story, open-ended philosophical questions were created in small groups. These questions were posed and selected by the children, because it is their curiosity that drives the philosophical enquiry.

Working democratically *as* a group, not just *in* groups, offers rich decision-making challenges and educational opportunities as it raises awareness of how power operates in collaborative work. Burgh and Yorshansky (2011, p. 437) argue that deliberation, as an essential part of the process, 'determines the quality of the decision-making processes'. For the distribution of power in communities of enquiry, mutual *intergenerational* respect is essential to prevent

The peace-loving elephants from each side
went to live deep in the darkest jungle.

Figure 10.2a The maze.

ontoepistemic injustice. The small groups wrote down their questions on A4 sheets with their self-selected group names that iii wrote on the blackboard. These were:

- Why did they go into the maze and never came out? (zebras)
- What happened in the maze? (pythons)
- How did the grey elephants get born? (awesome)
- Why did they want to kill each other? (super-group)
- Why is it called *Tusk Tusk*? (flower elephants)
- Why did the black elephants stay on one side of the jungle and why didn't the white elephants have one side of the jungle? (cool bananas)

They were never seen again.

Figure 10.2b The maze.

• How did a baby get born if all the elephants were dead? (red dragons)
• What did the elephants do in the maze for so long? (no name)

Unsurprisingly, some of the learners connected in a particular political manner with the narrative as they are situated with their bodyminds in South Africa. Still, more than two decades on, racial segregation and violence are structural features of their everyday lives, inspiring deeply felt topics for discussion. Some children ('cool bananas') suggested a solution to the fighting in the shape of a question: 'Why didn't the black elephants stay on one side of the jungle and why didn't the white elephants have one side of the jungle?' It was unclear from the other children's responses whether they recognised and sympathised

It went on...

Figure 10.3a The white and black elephants kill each other with their guns.

with cool bananas' '*apartheid*' proposal. Interestingly, other adults who were filming the lesson expressed their discomfort with this question (iii experienced the silence in the room as deafening), and also their relief when the other children chose not to discuss it. Personally iii would have welcomed discussion of this particular question, as such opportunities for such (arguably) authentic enquiries are so rare in class.

My commitment to working democratically includes resisting the temptation to 'fill' and 'form' children, and it is my response-ability to open up a space that enables the children to reveal something not yet considered or left unspoken. iii therefore resisted looking for the *same* (e.g. re-cognising the

Figure 10.3b The white and black elephants kill each other with their guns.

apartheid proposal and contesting it). My own knowledge is also contestable, and iii need to be willing to inhabit the perplexity of children's questions. Teachers do not control what counts as truth or meaning in order to hear the Voice without Organs: a voice that does not emanate from a singular subject (see chapters 2 and 6). Ideas and theories emerge through all materialdiscursive intra-actions. Children's ideas are not 'innocent', but neither are they 'ignorant'. As a living organism, it is the *community* (of enquiry) that regulates itself over time by regularly practising democratic being and thinking together. All of these complex entangled relationships enable 'taboo' topics such as sex or race to (e)merge. For example, in a plenary discussion one girl shyly suggested that

Figure 10.4 The elephants that are now grey and with medium-sized ears shake trunks/hands.

'the elephants could have been mating'. The children had also been given the opportunity to express their thinking through drawing and writing. They were fascinated by the maze space and its affordances.

The children were asked to speculate in pairs about what might be happening in that space, to have some 'thinking time', to draw the images in their minds and to talk about these together first. This was followed by individual artwork and writing (of choice) back at their own desks. Their imaginative and diverse ideas often re-(e)merged in the remaining sessions like threads weaving a cloth – they created their own 'text-ile' (Sipe, 2012 inspired by Lewis, 2001).

The next day the mating theme surfaced again in the plenary dialogue when the children tried collaboratively to answer one group's question: 'How did a baby get born if all the elephants were dead?' It was suggested that two black elephants could have escaped into the jungle and had babies. Some suggested that it could not have been the white and black ones as they – logically following from the story – would fight. The maze was conceptualised by several as a 'hiding place' and later as a 'place for play'. iii probed and numbed on both occasions by asking the conceptual questions about whether animals can hide and/or play and whether elephants can perhaps be both hiding and playing at the same time? Focusing on the materiality, the others were asked to respond directly to Hassiena's[6] observation earlier that elephants are big, so the maze is too small for them as a hiding place. She picks up again her original concern with one of the proposed answers to the question of how the elephants were grey:

> Hassiena: But how can you get married when the white and black ones hated each other?
> Bronwen: . . . if they fight why would they love each other, because the parents they would just be unhappy together?

iii reminded the class to consider Hassiena's earlier remark that day about the possible relevance of the elephants' skin colour. This pedagogical intravention may have provoked another child to make the connection between the books puzzling title and skin colour. One child suggests the next day in a piece of writing that 'tusk tusk' can be 'a team'. 'The black elephants can have the first tusk and the white elephants can have the other tusk' (Murris, 2014a, p. 155, Fig. 7.4). She also connects skin colour with gender: 'the white elephants can be girls', 'because they are sweet' and 'the black elephants can be boys', 'because they are rough' (Murris, 2014a, p. 155, Fig. 7.4). These connections offer a very creative, logical and thought-provoking solution to the problem of how the elephants emerge grey when they enter the maze as black and white elephants. They also offer unique educational opportunities for destabilising these binaries and 'pushing them to the limit' (Chapter 9).

The maze

My use of a well-known storytelling device of interrupting a story read out loud, and by letting them speculate about various story-endings, supported the philosophical work. Without knowing what was going to happen, and by looking at the double-spread page of the maze only (Figure 10.1), the children suggested some of the following rich narrative scenarios: 'the black and white elephants are fighting', 'making friends', 'mating', 'sleeping in the middle', 'having wars over the golden treasure' and 'they are jealous'. The last suggestion is like a miniature story. One boy suggested that the black king is jealous of the nice white king who has the gold.

Their maze drawings had agency: they offered opportunities to the children to construct their own meanings, and to link the story with prior knowledge and experiences. Their drawings show a wide variety of binary narrative scenarios ranging from happy, peaceful spaces where people live in dens, play and read, love each other, make babies, get married and are friends, to also include dangerous, scary, confusing places with difficult tasks set to complete the journey. Many drawing narratives include blood, ghosts, robots, spiders, sharks, dark tunnels, bats, pumpkins, snakes, skeletons, poo, lasers and dragons. One drawing proposes that a maze could be a place where there is love as well as a spot where 'you will die!' (Murris, 2014a, p. 156, Fig. 7.5). In another drawing the suggestion is made that one half of the maze is hell and the other is heaven. These enormously varied interpretations of the maze kept weaving themselves into the five sessions as the children were connecting rhizomatically with what was emerging in the oral dialogue. When considering all sessions together, iii noticed certain patterns about the maze space (e)merging. Lenz Taguchi (2010, p. 95) refers to the notion of 'duration': a learning event 'stretches out in time': a problem, first posed by a child, lingers and is taken up again later.

My apparatus included a text-ile of connectedness, of building on ideas and temporal sequencing, of trying out sometimes logical, and at other times contradictory, explanations and hypotheses. Many different ideas (e)merged in the space, sometimes in tension with the main idea of the story that the elephants were fighting, because one group was white and the other black. There was a wonderful moment when Leanne proposed an alternative explanation for why the elephants were fighting: 'I think that the birds were irritating them and then the white and black elephants got the jungle to hurt them'. She had spotted the birds in the drawings who are intra-acting with the elephants – post-elephantising the story.

Sometimes white pages in picturebooks have agency; this was the case with a group of educators at a recent school librarians' conference who were fascinated by the blank page on the left of the elephants in Figure 10.3. This penultimate empty page, they agreed, was the most significant of the entire book – a page that needs to be written. What did indeed happen between the elephants with the big and small ears? The birds on the page before this one certainly seem much wiser, or at least more tolerant of difference, than the elephants are. One librarian suggested that the title for this empty page should be '100 years later'.

It is the intra-connectedness between all the various languages and the relational materiality of the situation that creates new understanding, and adds rigour to the practice. Drawing on Roland Barthes, and referring only to the discursive, Sipe argues that words and pictures limit each other, at the same time, but in different ways' (Sipe, 2012, p. 10). In other words, the interplay of these particular two sign systems introduces criticality and sets limits to creativity. Importantly, oral work involves a different kind of temporal sequencing; it is like a line or a chain. Visual art, on the other hand, involves more diffuse emotionalcognitive activities. We have seen in Chapter 9 the claim that readers of images tend to 'gaze on, dwell upon, or contemplate them', while verbal narratives spur readers in a forward, linear direction (Sipe, 1998, p. 100).

The drawing activity did at least two things. First, by paying attention to the spatial conditions of the story interpretation, it imaginatively set boundaries to what might be possible. For example, after making the drawings, the children expressed ideas like: 'the elephants might get stuck', 'the maze is too small for elephants to live' and 'elephants cannot get married because they are too big for a wedding dress' and besides 'they have no hands for a wedding ring'. Secondly, the drawing activity provoked further questioning. One boy wrote: 'Why did they want to be in peace?' and 'How do the elephants play in the maze'. By focusing initially only on the oral work, iii had missed many of the rhizomatic connections the intra-actions created. Linking the five sessions afterwards by documenting what the same children were saying, either in pairs, small groups or plenary, and comparing these to their drawings and written work, a text-ile was created of children's (e)merging thinking, which otherwise would probably have gone by unnoticed or dismissed as contradictory or fanciful, magical and not to be taken seriously (Haynes and Murris, 2013).

Philosophy with picturebooks makes it possible to open up magical spaces that provoke children to use their imagination, to think out loud, to suggest ideas that are not necessarily their own and to test their ideas playfully with others (Haynes and Murris, 2013). The narrative maze device turned out to trigger very diverse and imaginative ideas. These young children seemed very absorbed and motivated to engage with the discursive materiality of the picturebook: how the words and images deliberately work to withhold information, sometimes through contradiction, almost always by causing perplexity. The readers of the story had to figure out for themselves the problem of how the elephants happen to be grey; it is in this sense that picturebooks have materialdiscursive agency: they provoke thinking and imaginative, affective connections, without any one person in the room 'owning' the ideas created.

The binary reality and fantasy in *Tusk Tusk* seemed to allow the children to feel at ease in the playful and intellectual juggling of ideas that the complex artwork provoked. This includes the choice of elephants as narrative characters that love, marry, fight, hate and kill (Egan, 1991, p. 86). But should my role have been more explicit and directive in *destabilising* the binaries that were so present in their enquiries?

Colonising practices?

There are poststructuralists who have expressed concern about my choice of *Tusk Tusk* and my analysis above. They argue that philosophy with children does not adequately account for the way power operates in such situations, as well as in McKee's book itself. According to one critic, the cool bananas' suggestion that the problem could have been solved by keeping white elephants on one side of the maze and black elephants on the other is particularly alarming. The critic suggested that this *apartheid* proposal was made in complete innocence and should have been contested by me. In other words, allowing children to vote for the question made it possible for that particular question to be left as it is. The possible racist assumptions go by unchallenged, through a 'random' collection of questions. What philosophy with children does not make possible, according to Pat Enciso (2014, p. 160), is to challenge 'unspoken and inaccessible histories', which, in the context of post-*apartheid* South Africa, is 'a long and tragic history of segregation and violence based on colonial and racialized categories of difference and property rights'. Enciso then suggests that using a story like *Tusk Tusk* requires adults in the room who are 'answerable from a particular positioning of status, interest, identity or power' (Enciso, 2014, p. 160). Then mistakenly assuming that my work should be framed as an example of sociocultural theory,[7] she then suggests that poststructuralism with its emphasis on power, identity and discourse should inform the pedagogy to be used in cases like the above.

Of course, the question an enquiry starts with is not *randomly*, but *democratically selected* by the children. The children might have judged (wisely) that with strangers in the room (researchers and cameramen), the environment was not conducive to discussing this particular question there and then. But a good insight to be taken from this diffraction with Enciso is the importance of not limiting philosophy with children sessions to stand-alone lessons, as admittedly is often the case, but to make them part of much larger projects (as already suggested in Chapter 8). Ideas and questions about a book can then re-(e)merge, and educators can continue their numbing and being numbed (see e.g. Vivian Paley [1997] in the context of black skin colour and an extended project with Leo Lionni's picturebooks). However, poststructuralists believe a more directive role of the teacher is necessary to disrupt the discourses children inhabit as, for example, in an approach called Critical Literacy.

A racist book?

British teacher and researcher Darren Chetty (2014) suggests that Critical Race Theory and the related field of Critical Whiteness Studies offer an important source of critique for the philosophy with children field to consider. In order to prevent a 'Gated Community of Enquiry' (Chetty, 2014, p. 14), he urges educators to reconsider the use of a picturebook such as *Tusk Tusk* for philosophy with children. He observes rightly that the narrative lacks historicity. There is no obvious reason for the elephants to fight, neither for land, nor for power, nor for resources. The hatred the elephants have for each other is irrational and precedes the fighting – not the other way round. The difference is not constructed out of the situation, but the hatred is caused *by* the difference. Hence, the story's 'ahistoricism is potentially mis-educative' (Chetty, 2014, p. 21). Chetty continues his powerful critique by pointing out that the story represents black and white elephants as in the wrong: 'Inequality does not appear to exist in the fantasyland of *Tusk Tusk*' and all differences in social status, history and culture have been removed (Chetty, 2014, p. 21).

Is it indeed true that children's literature has to be *factually* correct, portray oppression, speak to 'structural inequality' and 'open up for enquiry justice-based solutions like repair, redistribution or reconciliation' (Chetty, 2014, p. 22–3)? There are multiple responses to this critique of my use of *Tusk Tusk*.

I believe that the answer lies partly in what Chetty himself believes is the problem. He hits the nail on the head when he says that the conflict is (for him wrongly) portrayed as 'only' being about 'physical difference' (Chetty, 2014, p. 22). That indeed makes McKee's art so powerful: it is the *absence* that has materialdiscursive agency. The story's power is what it *leaves out*. It has not been written for particular educational purposes. How it works is relational: readers engage philosophically with abstract concepts 'the' texts 'contains' in rich materialdiscursive environments. Texts certainly influence what children enquire into, and a story such as *Tusk Tusk* is indeed not explicit in racism as being 'structural/systemic' (Chetty, 2014, p. 25). But how such a narrative is interrogated depends also on the educator, who numbs and gets numbed.

Philosophy with children relies on the relational triangle: text, educator, learners 'within' an environment that supports and encourages critical enquiry-based learning. There is no such thing as a 'teacher-proof text' (Murris, 2015b). The removal of the temporal and the spatial provokes a-philosophical-distance-taking, including of *one's own* temporal/spatial claims to truth about racism that already assumes linear time (see above) and developmental progression of the human species (at this point in time in history we know more and better than previously). Chetty's position, therefore, seems ahistorical. Contemporary truths about racism are themselves not historical, but universal. Is this contradictory?

Fairy-tale scholar Jack Zipes (2006) offers another interesting challenge to the claim that it is a disadvantage that such tales are ahistorical. If we 'dissect or study' such tales (like our well-known fairy-tales with all their 'racism' and 'sexism') 'in a socio-political context . . . that might ruin their magic power' (Zipes, 2006, p. 1). They are 'universal, ageless, therapeutic, miraculous, and beautiful' (Zipes, 2006, p. 1). What is particularly striking is his idea that the past is mysterious and not accessible, but can be engaged with *as a text*.

A safe space for a black child?

Chetty's concern is about power and *identity*: White teachers, he says, need to rely on 'a child of colour' in order to speak out in class before critical perspectives can be considered (Chetty, 2014, p. 23). Like Enciso, the post-structuralist critique uses a humanist indivi-dualistic metaphysics focusing on human agency moving though linear time and space. It could indeed be argued that *Tusk Tusk* provides imaginative meaning-making opportunities for only white children to be expressed, because there was only one black child in the room and one black cameraman. And indeed, the black girl spoke little. Very well acquainted himself with philosophy with children, and an experienced community of enquiry facilitator, Chetty argues that there are no safe spaces for enquiries about race. However, it is possible, he says, to use 'a pedagogy of disruption' with the teacher in the role of 'a gadfly' who stings – another one of Plato's famous metaphors (Chetty, 2014, p. 24).

Educator as gadfly or stingray?

The distinction between the educator as gadfly or stingray is significant: the gadfly does not sting *the teacher*, only the children. With the truth about a story in possession, the gadfly distances himself from the children's material-discursive meaning making. He is not in the bowl of spaghetti twirling the fork like a stingray would. The stingray is pregnant, therefore multiple, not singular and is always entangled. The relationship between the gadfly and who he stings is a humanist subject/object confrontation, whereas, the pregnant stingray (e)merges in a non-confrontational inclusive relational entanglement.

These two figurations of the educator express two very different approaches to 'post'colonial education. One is a humanist focus on social power, *identity* and critical agency, the other is about *difference*: differences that matter in 'one' 'self'. The latter lets child 'in', the former does not, ontoepistemically. This was the case with Rachel's comment about skin colour at the beginning of the chapter. Race is *also* about skin colour. This is far from as superficial as Chetty claims it is (Chetty, 2014, pp. 20–2). It also makes clear how he privileges the discursive over the material. If we already assume as educators that *Tusk Tusk* is about racism, we miss as educators the imaginative connections the children made in my class between, for example, skin colour and gender. We prevent the possibility of ideas (e)merging that surprise 'us'; we are not 'in' the bowl of spaghetti *together* in the way we were in our encounter with Rachel at the start of this *diffractive pause*, who was rubbing clay on Nxumalo's arm –

Nxumalo, the researcher, who was intra-acting with her. She was not looking for the same, but she was open to be surprised and thereby learned something new. Nxumalo was listening out for what she did not know as yet; she was 'empty' and had no desire to 'fill' Rachel's mind with 'the' right political beliefs. Rachel made Nxumalo think. The pregnant stingray was listening to Rachel's hands, touch, smiles, voice, someone who was reconfigured 'in' the relationship as a rich, resilient and resourceful 'inhuman becoming-iii'. For transformation and the creation of new subjectivities it is salient to move beyond predefined boundaries and assumed categories of difference 'in' encounters with earth dwellers. Understanding the crucial differences between the two approaches involves understanding the Western metaphysics on which poststructuralism rests.

As we have seen in Chapter 5 (Figure 5.1), the humanist ontoepistemology of poststructuralism assumes a subject that does not have access to the real world; there is always mediation through language and discourse. In a sense, the hermeneutical system is an (almost) 'closed' one: based on historical, socio-cultural factors and identities, individuals are not free, but determined by their identities. Transformational strategies such as deconstruction and reconstruction are *linguistic* and *discursive*, not material. Adult educators need to ensure that 'children's critical agency' is developed through appropriate classroom activities leading to 'social change' (Enciso, 2014, p. 162), thereby running the risk of ignoring 'the real human beings' in classrooms (Jansen, 2009, p. 257). The real (natureculture) is reduced to the social (Barad, 2007). Including children democratically in community of philosophical enquiries could be transformative, especially as children themselves would be included in reconceptualising the actual meaning of concepts such as 'power', 'voice' and 'identity', not just verbally, but also in action through the inclusion of all their languages. In philosophical practice we need to resist forcing adults' agenda for a just future onto children. It would be another example of ontoepistemic injustice, and a way of silencing them (Kohan, 1998, p. 7).

The revolver activity

The two very different approaches to postcolonial education lend themselves to be explored in an activity called 'revolver', as it involves revisiting some key ideas in this book. Developed by Roger Greenaway (www.reviewing.co.uk), iii use it as follows.

The room is organised with chairs in a circle and no tables. A rope is put in the middle 'slicing' the circle in half. After having read and discussed in small groups the example and analysis of my work with *Tusk Tusk* in the Grade 2 class, both sides rehearse some arguments for and against either position: the poststructuralist and the posthumanist, also doing justice to the new ideas produced in the diffraction. Members on one side of the circle start putting an argument forward, which is met on the other side by a response. We continue in this way until everyone has argued for and against. Everyone is reminded not to 'shoot each other down', despite the name of the activity, which refers to bodies 'revolving', not to guns.[8] Finally everyone is given the opportunity to go to the side they agree with most, or, if undecided, they can stand on the rope. They then continue in small groups assessing the activity in their diffractive journals.

to 'think-for-yourself-through-thinking-with-others' can easily descend into social and political conformity (Browne, 2006). In this chapter's *diffractive pause*, iii open up an enquiry provoked by two critiques of my work with a particular picturebook. My response generates an alternative proposal for decolonising education – a 'post'-metaphysical way forward.

Decolonising education: becoming 'other' in 'one' 'self'

One of the aims of this book has been to disrupt common notions of what children 'are' and should be, and to offer an imagination of what might be possible – also in South Africa's complex, 'post'colonial educational settings. We have seen how universal, global accounts of child fail to accommodate difference and diversity (Kocher and Pacini-Ketchabaw, 2011, p. 47). Pedagogies that focus solely on 'race', 'class' and 'gender' as categories of discrimination, and not 'age', retain the hierarchical *status quo* in teaching and learning, in that *what knowledge is* and *whose knowledge matters* remains unquestioned. The ethical move to allow child 'in' ontoepistemically *also* means that children should be allowed to challenge adults' political agenda – an agenda that prevents children from using binaries that exclude and discriminate. One of the aims of education (see Chapter 2) is for children and students to bring something new to the world ('relational material subjectification'). This can take the form of openly exploring topics or concepts that some people might not find 'politically correct'. A posthuman orientation helps to theorise the legitimacy of including young children's often magical, anthropomorphic and fanciful contributions (those of a 'stranger') to philosophical enquiries, and is sympathetic towards the multiple materialdiscursive ways in which organisms construct knowledge and understanding. The crux is to resist representationalism, and to accept that there is no moving beyond or leaving behind, only iterative diffractions with one's 'self', becoming different and at the same time being partly the same – like a 'pregnancy . . . holding within itself a potentiality of new invention and new becoming from what already is' (Lenz Taguchi, 2010, p. 95).

Pedagogical transformation is grounded in a relational ethic with collective responsibility for the shared intra-connected natureculture worlds. Emphasising humans' connectivity with other earth dwellers, and moving away from the exclusive anthropocentric focus on the psychological, the social or the discursive in education, is particularly urgent for educational encounters that are more just, with people who are not only young, but might also live in poverty and do not have English as their home language. It is one sure, but complex, and exciting way of educating for a sustainable future that includes our youngest citizens.

Notes

1   The notion of ontoepistemic injustice was created by reading Barad's posthumanism and Fricker's notion of epistemic injustice diffractively through one another in Chapter 6. By using a rhizomatic, intra-active pedagogy that disrupts existing age prejudice and 'flattens' the ontoepistemological hierarchy in the classroom, justice can be done to child not just epistemically, but *onto*epistemically.

2   In South Africa, 'generic black' refers to all people of colour, including Asians. In the Western Cape the term 'Cape coloured' specifically refers to an ethnic group composed primarily of persons of mixed race and includes people descended from Malays brought in as slaves by the Dutch settlers.

3   For some information about the area, see http://en.wikipedia.org/wiki/East_Rand

4   A compilation of my work was made by Professor Graham Hall from the University of the Witwatersrand and part of a pack called *Foundation Phase – video programmes*, made available to all universities in South Africa in 2014. The project was funded by the EU and the Department of Higher Education and Training of the Republic of South Africa. In the published DVD, iii introduce the class to philosophy with children by reading aloud David McKee's picturebook *Tusk Tusk* (1978) and opening up a space where children are allowed and encouraged to ask philosophical questions. In this diffractive pause iii focus on the philosophical work a few weeks into the project.

5   See Chapter 8.

6   All children's names are pseudonyms.

7   And this mistake was also made by the editors of the book, who commissioned a case study and then misidentified my practice as an example of sociocultural theory (Larson and Marsh, 2014, pp. 135–44). This enabled Pat Enciso to comment and offer a poststructuralist critique by focusing on identity, agency and power.

8   Interestingly, Roger Greenaway has been persuaded to change the name to the more 'peaceful' 'turntable' (see http://reviewing.co.uk/discuss/discuss2.htm, accessed 10 June 2015).

References

Ajayi, A.C. (2000) The changing roles of mother as teacher of her pre-school child: The Nigerian Experience. *International Journal of Early Childhood*, 38, 2, 86–92.

Alaimo, S. and Hekman, S. (2008) *Material Feminisms*. Bloomington, IA: Indiana University Press.

Alanen, L. (1988) Rethinking childhood. *Acta Sociologica*, 31, 1, 53–67.

Alexander, N. (2012) *On the 3 Rs Project: Improving the Quality of Education in South Africa: The Literacy and Numeracy Challenge*. Final report to the Human Sciences Research Council. Cape Town: Project for the study of alternative education (PRAESA).

Alexander, N. and Bloch, C. (2010) Creating Literate Communities – The Challenge of Early Literacy. *In* M. Krueger-Potratz, U. Neumann and H.H. Reich (eds), *Bei Vielfalt Chancengleichheit*. Munster: Waxmann Verlag, 197–213.

Archard, D. (1998) John Locke's Children. *In* S.M.Turner and G.B. Matthews (eds), *The Philosophers Child*. Rochester, NY: University of Rochester Press, 85–105.

Archard, D. (2004) *Children: Rights and Childhood* (2nd edn). Abingdon and New York: Routledge.

Arendt, H. (1959) *The Human Condition*. New York: Anchor Books.

Aries, P. (1962) *Centuries of Childhood: A Social History of Family Life* (Transl. Robert Baldick). New York: Alfred A. Knopf.

Arizpe, E. (2012) Review of picturebooks, pedagogy and philosophy. *Journal of Philosophy of Education*, 46, 3, 497–500.

Arizpe, E. and Styles, M. (2003) *Children Reading Pictures: Interpreting Visual Texts*. London: Routledge Falmer.

Barad, K. (1995) A Feminist Approach to Teaching Quantum Physics. *In* S.V. Rosser (ed.), *Teaching the Majority: Breaking the Gender Barrier in Science, Mathematics, and Engineering*. Athene Series. New York: Teacher's College Press, 43–75.

Barad, K. (2003) Posthumanist performativity: Toward an understanding of how matter comes to matter. *Signs: Journal of Women in Culture and Society*, 28, 31, 801–31.

Barad, K. (2007) *Meeting the Universe Halfway: Quantum Physics and the Entanglement of Matter and Meaning*. Durham, NC: Duke University Press.

Barad, K. (2011) Nature's queer performativity. *Qui Parle*, 19, 2, Spring/Summer, 121–58.

Barad, K. (2012) Intra-actions: an interview with Karen Barad by Adam Kleinman. *Mousse*, 34, 76–81.

Barad, K. (2014) Diffracting diffraction: Cutting together-apart. *Parallax*, 20, 3, 168–87.

Bates, S. (1990) Philosophy taxes infants' intellects. *The Guardian*, 7 November, 8.

Battersby, C. (1998) *The Phenomenal Woman: Feminist Metaphysics and the Patterns of Identity*. New York: Routledge.

Benjamin, M. and Echeverria, E. (1992) Knowledge in the classroom. *In* A.M Sharp and R. Reed (eds), *Studies in Philosophy for Children*. Philadelphia, PA: Temple University Press, 64–79.

Bennett, J. (2010) *Vibrant Matter: A Political Ecology of Things*. Durham, NC and London: Duke University Press.

Berkeley, G. (1977) *The Principles of Human Knowledge; With Other Writings*. London: Fontana.

Biesta, G.J.J. (1994) Education as practical intersubjectivity: Towards a critical-pragmatic understanding of education. *Educational Theory*, 44, 3, 299–317.

Biesta, G.J.J. (2006) *Beyond Learning*. Boulder, CO: Paradigm.

Biesta, G. (2010) *Good Education in an Age of Measurement: Ethics, Politics, Democracy*. Boulder, CO: Paradigm.

Biesta, G.J.J. (2012) The future of teacher education: Evidence, competence or wisdom? *Research on Steiner Education*, 3, 1, 8–21. Available from: www.rosejourn.com (accessed 10 June 2012).

Biesta, G.J.J. (2013). Pragmatising the curriculum: Bringing knowledge back into the curriculum conversation, but via pragmatism. Availablre from: http://orbilu.uni.lu/bitstream/10993/10683/1/ (accessed 17 December 2013).

Biesta, G.J.J. (2014) *The Beautiful Risk of Education*. Boulder, CO: Paradigm.

Bleazby, J. (2012) Dewey's Notion of Imagination in philosophy for children. *Education and Culture*, 28, 2, 95–111.

Bloch, G. (2009) *The Toxic Mix: What's Wrong with South Africa's Schools and How to Fix It*. Cape Town: Tafelberg.

Bloch, M.N., Swadener, B.B. and Cannella, G.S. (eds) (2014). *Reconceptualizing Early Childhood Care & Education. A Reader*. New York: Peter Lang.

Blyth, M. D. C. (2015). *Chronicle of a dys-appearance: An autoethnography of a teacher on conflict*. Unpublished doctoral dissertation. University of Cape Town, South Africa.

Bonn, M. (2007) Children's understanding of 'Ubuntu'. *Early Childhood Development and Care*, 177, 8, 863–73.

Braidotti, R. (1991) *Patterns of Dissonance: A Study of Women in Contemporary Philosophy* (transl. by E. Guild). Cambridge: Polity.

Braidotti, R. (2002) *Metamorphoses: Towards a Materialist Theory of Becoming*. Oxford: Blackwell Publishers.

Braidotti, R. (2006) *Transpositions: On Nomadic Ethics*. Cambridge: Polity.

Braidotti, R. (2011) *Nomadic Theory: The Portable Rosi Braidotti*. Columbia, NY: Columbia University Press.

Braidotti, R. (2013) *The Posthuman*. Cambridge: Polity.

Brodie, K. (2007) Dialogue in mathematics classrooms: beyond question and answer methods. *Pythagoras*, 33, 3–13.

Browne, A. (1981) *Hansel and Gretel*. London: Walker Books.

Browne, A. (1986) *Piggybook*. London: Julia MacRae.

Browne, A. (1990) *Changes*. London: Walker Books.

Browne, A. (1993) *Zoo*. London: Julia MacRae.

Browne, A. (1993/1995) *The Big Baby: A Little Joke*. London: Red Fox.

Browne, A. (1997a) *The Tunnel*. London: Walker Books.

Browne, A. (1997b) *Willy the Dreamer*. London: Walker Books.

Browne, A. (1999) *Bear Goes to Town*. London: Puffin Books.

Browne, A. (2006) *The Retreat of Reason: Political Correctness and the Corruption of Public Debate in Modern Britain*. London: Civitas, Institute for the Study of Civil Society.

Browne, A. (2008) *Little Beauty*. London: Walker Books.

Browne, A. (2010) *Me and You*. London: Doubleday.

Browne, A. and Browne, J. (2011) *Playing the Shape Game*. London: Doubledays Children.

Bruce, T. (1987/2011) *Early Childhood Education* (4th edn). Abingdon: Hodder Education.

Burbules, N.C. (1995) Reasonable Doubt: Toward a Postmodern Defense of Reason as an Educational Aim. *In* W. Kohli (ed.), *Critical Conversations in Philosophy of Education*. New York: Routledge, 82–103.

Burbules, N.C. (2000) The Limits of Dialogue as a Critical Pedagogy. *In* P. Trifonas (ed.), *Revolutionary Pedagogies*. New York: Routledge. Available from: www.faculty.ed.uiuc.edu/burbules (accessed 23 March 2011).

Burgh, G. and Yorshansky, M. (2011) Communities of Inquiry: Politics, power and group dynamics. *Educational Philosophy and Theory*, 43, 5, 436–52.

Burke, C. (2008) Play in Focus: Children's Visual Voice in Participative Research. *In* P. Thomson (ed.), *Doing Visual Research with Children and Young People*. London: Routledge, 23–37.

Burman, E. (2001) Beyond the Baby and the Bathwater: Postdualistic Developmental Psychologies for Diverse Childhoods. *European Early Childhood Education Research Journal*, 9, 1.

Burman, E. (2008a) *Deconstructing Developmental Psychology* (2nd edn). London: Routledge.

Burman, E. (2008b) *Developments: Child, Image, Nation*. London: Routledge.

Burman, E. (2013) Conceptual resources for questioning 'child as educator'. *In* J. Haynes and K. Murris (eds), *Child as Educator*. Special Issue. *Studies in Philosophy and Education*, 32, 3, 229–43.

Burman, E. (2015) Developmental Psychology: The Turn to Deconstruction. *In* I. Parker (ed.), *Handbook of Critical Psychology*. New York: Routledge.

Burtt, F. (2014) Developing early thinking with philosophy for children in South Africa. D.G. Murray Trust Hands-On Learning publication, 10th issue. Available from: www.dgmt.co.za/category/what-weve-learned/hands-on-learning-briefs/ (accessed 12 February 2014).

Cahill, B.J. and Gibson, T.L. (2012) Using Critical Theories in the Curriculum. *In* N. File, J. Mueler and D. Basler Wisneski (eds), *Curriculum in Early Childhood Education: Re-examined, Rediscovered, Renewed*. New York: Routledge, 93–101.

Cam, P. (1995) *Thinking Together: Philosophical Inquiry for the Classroom*. Sydney: Primary English Teaching Association & Hale and Iremonger.

Campbell, E. (2003) *The Ethical Teacher*. Maidenhead: Open University Press.

Caroll, L. (2013) *Alice in Wonderland*. D.J Gray (ed.). Third Norton Critical edn. New York: Norton.

Ceppi, G. and Zini, M. (1998) *Children, Spaces and Relations: Metaproject for an Environment for Young Children*. Reggio Emilia: Reggio Children s.r.l.

Chetty, D. (2014) The Elephant in the Room: Picturebooks, Philosophy and Racism. Paper presented at the *16th Conference of the International Council of Philosophical Inquiry with Children*, Cape Town, 31 Aug–2 Sept. Available from http://icpic.cmc-uct.co.za/ (accessed 2 September 2013).

Christensen, P. and Prout, A. (2002) Working with ethical symmetry in social research with children. *Childhood*, 9, 4, 477–97.

Clark, A. (2010) *Transforming Children's Spaces: Children's and Adults' Participation in Designing Learning Environments*. London: Routledge.

Code, L. (2008) Review of Miranda Fricker's Epistemic Injustice: Power and the Ethics of Knowing. Available from https://ndpr.nd.edu/news/23398-epistemic-injustice-power-and-the-ethics-of-knowing/ (accessed 12 August 2014).

Coole, D. and Frost, S. (eds) (2010) *New Materialisms: Ontology, Agency, and Politics*. Durham, NC: Duke University Press.

Corradi-Fiumara, G. (1990) *The Other Side of Language. A Philosophy of Listening*. London: Routledge.

Cregan, K. and Cuthbert, D. (2014) *Global Childhoods – Issues and Debates*. London: SAGE.

Cunningham, H. (2006) *The Invention of Childhood*. London: BBC Books.

Dahlberg, G. (2003) Pedagogy as a Loci of an Ethics of an Encounter. *In* M. Bloch, K. Holmlund, I. Moqvist and T. Popkewitz (eds), *Governing Children, Families and Education: Restructuring the Welfare State*. New York: Palgrave McMillan.

Curnow, T. (1995) Transcendence, logic, and identity. *Philosophy Now*, 12, 24–6.

Dahlberg, G. and Moss, P. (2005) *Ethics and Politics in Early Childhood Education*. London: Routledge.

Dahlberg, G. and Moss, P. (2006) Introduction: Our Reggio Emilia. *In* C. Rinaldi, *In Dialogue with Reggio Emilia: Listening, Researching and Learning*. Contesting early childhood series. London: Routledge.

Dahlberg, G. and Moss, P. (2009) 'Foreword' to Olsson, L.M. (2009) *Movement and Experimentation in Young Children's Learning: Deleuze and Guattari in Early Childhood Education*. London: Routledge, xiii–xxviii.

Dahlberg, G. and Moss, P. (2010) Invitation to the Dance: Series editors' introduction to V. Vecchi, *Art and Creativity in Reggio Emilia: Exploring the Role and Potential of Ateliers in Early Childhood Education*. London: Routledge, xiv–xxiii.

Dahlberg, G., Moss, P. and Pence, P. (1999/2013) *Beyond Quality in Early Childhood Education and Care: Postmodern Perspectives*. London: Falmer Press.

Davies, B. (2014) *Listening to Children: Being and Becoming*. London: Routledge.

Davis, A. (2013) To Read or Not to Read: Decoding Synthetic Phonics. IMPACT Series 20. Available from http://onlinelibrary.wiley.com/doi/10.1111/imp. 2013. 2013.issue-20/issuetoc (accessed 22 December 2013).

Davis, B. (2004) *Inventions of Teaching: A Genealogy*. Mahwah, NJ: Lawrence Erlbaum.

De Suissa, J. (2008) Philosophy in the Secondary School – a Deweyan Perspective. *In* M. Hand and C. Winstanley (eds), *Philosophy in Schools*. New York: Continuum, 132–45.

Deleuze, G. (1970/1988). *Spinoza: Practical Philosophy*. San Francisco, CA: City Light Books.

Deleuze, G. (1994) *Difference and Repetition*. New York: Columbia University Press.

Deleuze, G. and Guattari, F. (1987/2013) *A Thousand Plateaus* (Transl. and foreword by B. Massumi). London: Bloomsbury.

Deleuze, G. and Guattari, F. (1994) *What is Philosophy?* (Transl. by G. Burchell and H. Tomlinson). London: Verso.

Department of Education (2011). *National Curriculum Statement. Curriculum and Assessment Policy, Foundation Phase Grades R-3. English Home Language.* South Africa: Government Printing Works. Available from www.education.gov.za/ (accessed 3 May 2013).

Department of Education (2013). *Report on the Annual National Assessment of 2013: Grades 1 to 6&9.* South Africa: Government Printing Works.

Descartes, R. (1968) *Discourse on Method & Other Writings; Sixth Meditation* (Transl. by F.E. Sutcliffe). London: Penguin.

Dixon, K. (2011) *Literacy, Power and the Schooled Body: Learning in Time and Space.* New York: Routledge.

Dolphijn, R. and Van der Tuin, I. (2012) *New Materialism: Interviews & Cartographies.* Open Humanities Press. Available from: http://openhumanitiespress.org/new-materialism.html (accessed 12 March 2015).

Donaldson, M. (1978) *Children's Minds.* London: Fontana.

Dunne, J. (1997) *Back to the Rough Ground: Practical Judgment and the Lure of Technique.* Notre Dame and London: University of Notre Dame Press.

Dunne, J. and Pendlebury, S. (2003) Practical Reason. *In* N. Blake et al. (eds), *The Blackwell Guide to the Philosophy of Education.* Oxford: Blackwell, 194–212.

Ecclestone, K. and Hayes, D. (2009) *The Dangerous Rise of Therapeutic Education.* London: Routledge.

Edwards, C. (1995) Democratic participation in a community of learners: Loris Malaguzzi's philosophy of education as relationship. Lecture prepared for an international seminar, University of Milan, October 16–17, 1995. Available from: http://digitalcommons.unl.edu/cgi/viewcontent.cgi?article=1014&context=famconf acpub (accessed 11 June 2015).

Edwards, C., Gandini, L. and Forman, G. (1998) *The Hundred Languages of Children: The Reggio Emilia Approach – Advanced Reflections* (2nd edn). Westport, CT: Ablex.

Egan, K. (1988) *Teaching as Storytelling. An Alternative Approach to Teaching and the Curriculum.* London, ON: University of Western Ontario.

Egan, K. (1991) *Primary Understanding: Education in Early Childhood.* London: Routledge.

Egan, K. (1992) *Imagination in Teaching and Learning: Ages 8–15.* London: Routledge.

Egan, K. (1993) The Other Half of the Child. In M. Lipman (ed.), *Thinking, Children and Education.* Montclair, CA: Kendall/Hunt, 281–6.

Egan, K. (1995) Narrative and Learning: A Voyage of Implications. *In* H. McEwan and K. Egan (eds), *Narrative in Teaching, Learning, and Research.* New York: Teachers College Press, 116–24.

Egan, K. (1997) *The Educated Mind: How Cognitive Tools Shape our Understanding.* Chicago, IL: University of Chicago Press.

Egan, K. (2002) *Getting it Wrong from the Beginning: Our Progressivist Inheritance from Herbert Spencer, John Dewey, and Jean Piaget.* New Haven, CT: Yale University Press.

Egan, K. and Ling, M. (2002) We Begin as Poets: Conceptual Tools and the Arts in Early Childhood. *In* L. Bresler and C.M. Thompson (eds), *The Arts in Children's Lives: Context, Culture & Curriculum.* Boston, MA: Kluwer Academic Press, 93–100.

Ellsworth, E. (2005) *Places of Learning: Media, Architecture, Pedagogy*. New York: Routledge.

Enciso, P. (2014) Interview with Patricio Enciso about Karin Murris' Case study contribution. *In* J. Larson and J. Marsh (2005), *Making Literacy Real, Theories and Practices for Learning and Teaching*. London: Sage Publications, 159–62.

Evans, J. (2009) A Master in His Time: Anthony Browne Shares Thoughts about his Work. *In* J. Evans (ed.), *Taking Beyond the Page: Reading and Responding to Picturebooks*. London: Routledge.

File, N. (2012) The Relationship between Child Development and Early Childhood Curriculum. *In* N. File, J. Mueler and D. Basler Wisneski (eds), *Curriculum in Early Childhood Education: Re-examined, Rediscovered, Renewed*. New York: Routledge, 29–42.

File, N., Basler Wisneski, D. and Mueller, J. (2012) Strengthening Curriculum in Early Childhood. *In* N. File, J. Mueler and D. Basler Wisneski (eds), *Curriculum in Early Childhood Education: Re-examined, Rediscovered, Renewed*. New York: Routledge, 200–5.

Fleisch, B. (2008) *Primary Education in Crisis: Why South African Schoolchildren Underachieve in Reading and Mathematics*. Juta: Cape Town.

Fleisch, B. (2012) System Reform: Lessons from the Literacy Strategy in Gauteng. Paper presented at the *Wits School of Education Seminar Series*, 25 July 2012.

Fletcher, N.M. (2014) Body Talk, Body Taunt – Corporeal Dialogue within a Community of Philosophical Inquiry. *Analytical Teaching and Philosophical Praxis*, 35, 1, 10–25.

Forman, G. (1994) Different Media, Different Languages. *In* L.G. Katz and B. Cesarone, *Reflections on the Reggio Emilia Approach*; Perspectives from ERIC/EECE: a monograph series, no.6, 37–46.

Fox, R. (2001) Can Children Be Philosophical? *Teaching Thinking*, 4, Summer, 46–9.

Fricker, M. (2000) Feminism in Epistemology: Pluralism without Postmodernism. In M. Fricker and J. Horsnby (eds), *The Cambridge Companion to Feminism in Philosophy*. Cambridge: Cambridge University Press, 146–66.

Fricker, M. (2007) *Epistemic Injustice: Power and the Ethics of Knowing*. Oxford: Oxford University Press.

Frost, S. (2010) Fear and the Illusion of Autonomy. *In* D. Coole and S. Frost (eds), *New Materialisms: Ontology, Agency, and Politics*. Durham, NC: Duke University Press, 158–77.

Frost, S. (2011) The Implications of the New Materialisms for Feminist Epistemology. *In* H.E Grasswick (ed.), *Feminist Epistemology and Philosophy of Science: Power in Knowledge*. Dordrecht: Springer, 69–83.

Gazzard, A. (1985) Philosophy for Children and the Piagetian Framework. *Thinking*, 5, 1.

Genishi, C. and Dyson, A.H. (2009) *Children, Language and Literacy: Diverse Learners in Diverse Times*. New York: Teachers College Press.

Green, L. (2008) Cognitive Modifiability in South African Classrooms. *In* T. Oon Seng and A. Seok-Hoon Seng, *Cognitive Modifiability in Learning and Assessment*. Singapore: Cengage Learning, 137–53.

Green, L. (2012) Evaluation of Community of Enquiry Practices in Under-resourced South African Classrooms: Three Strategies and their Outcomes. *In* M. Santi and

S. Oliverio (eds), *Educating for Complex Thinking through Philosophical Inquiry: Models, Advances and Proposals for the New Millenium*. Naples: Liguori, 349–63.

Green, L. and Murris, K. (2014) Lipman's Philosophy for Children. *In* L. Green (ed.), *Schools as Thinking Communities*. Cape Town: Van Schaik, 121–40.

Griffiths, F. (2014) The Talking Table: Sharing Wonder in Early Childhood Education. *In* K. Egan, A. Cant and G. Judson (eds), *Wonder-full Education: The Centrality of Wonder in Teaching and Learning Across the Curriculum*. New York: Routledge, 122–35.

Guthrie, W.K.C. (1956) *Plato: Protagoras and Meno*. London: Penguin.

Hand, M. (2008) Can Children be Taught Philosophy? *In* M. Hand and C. Winstanley (eds), *Philosophy in Schools*. London: Continuum, 3–18.

Hannam, P. and Echeverria, E. (2009) *Philosophy with Teenagers: Nurturing a Moral Imagination for the 21st Century*. London: Continuum.

Haraway, D. (1988) Situated knowledges: The science question in feminism and the privilege of partial perspective. *Feminist Studies*, 14, 575–99.

Haraway, D. (1990) A Manifesto for Cyborgs: Science, Technology, and Socialist Feminism in the 1980s. *In* L.J. Nicholson (ed.), *Feminism/Postmodernism*. New York: Routledge, 190–193.

Haraway, D. (1992) The Promises of Monsters: A Regenerative Politics for Inappropriate/d Others. *In* L. Grossberg, C. Nelson and P.A. Treichler (eds), *Cultural Studies*. New York: Routledge, 295–337.

Haraway, D. (2003) *The Companion Species Manifesto: Dogs, People, and Other Significant Otherness*. Chicago, IL: Prickly Paradigm.

Hatch, J.A. (2012). From Theory to Curriculum: Developmental Theory and its Relationship to Curriculum and Instruction in Early Childhood Education, *In* N. File, J. Mueller and D. Basler Wisneski (eds), *Curriculum in Early Childhood Education: Re-examined, Rediscovered, Renewed*. London: Routledge, 42–54.

Haynes, J. (2005) The costs of thinking. *Teaching Thinking and Creativity*, Autumn, 7, 32–8. Birmingham: Imaginative Minds.

Haynes, J. (2007a) *Listening as a Critical Practice: Learning from Philosophy with Children*. PhD thesis submitted for examination to the University of Exeter.

Haynes, J. (2007b) Freedom and the urge to think. *Gifted Education International*, Special Issue on Philosophy for Children, 22, 2/3, 229–37, edited by B. Wallace, guest ed. B. Hymer.

Haynes, J. (2008) *Children as Philosophers: Learning through Enquiry and Dialogue in the Primary School* (2nd edn). London: RoutledgeFalmer.

Haynes, J. (2009a) Listening to the Voice of Child in Education. *In* S. Gibson and J. Haynes (eds), *Perspectives on Participation and Inclusion: Engaging Education*. London: Continuum, 27–41.

Haynes, J. (2009b) Freedom, Inclusion and Education. *In* S. Gibson and J. Haynes (eds), *Perspectives on Participation and Inclusion: Engaging Education*. London: Continuum, 76–89.

Haynes, J. (2014) Already Equal and Able to Speak. In S. Robson and S.F. Quinn (eds), *Routledge International Handbook of Young Children's Thinking and Understanding*. London: Routledge, 463–75.

Haynes, J. and Murris, K. (2009) The wrong message: Risk, censorship and the struggle for democracy in the primary school. *Thinking*, 19, 1, 2–12.

Haynes, J. and Murris, K. (2011) The Provocation of an Epistemological Shift in Teacher Education through Philosophy with Children. In N. Vansieleghem and D. Kennedy (eds), Philosophy for Children in Transition: Problems and Prospects. Special Issue: Journal of Philosophy of Education, 45, 2, 285–303.

Haynes, J. and Murris, K. (2012) Picturebooks, Pedagogy and Philosophy. New York: Routledge.

Haynes, J. and Murris, K. (2013) The Realm of Meaning: Imagination, Narrative and Playfulness in Philosophical Exploration with Young Children. In P. Costello (ed.), Special Issue: Developing Children's Thinking in Early Childhood Education. Early Child Development and Care, 183, 8, 1084–100.

Heidegger, M. (1927/1979) Sein und Zeit. Tübingen: Max Niemeyer.

Heidegger, M. (1968) What is called Thinking? (J.G. Gray, transl. and intro). New York: Harper and Row.

Hekman, S. (2010) The Material of Knowledge: Feminist Disclosures. Bloomington, IN: Indiana University Press.

Hocevar, A., Sebart, M.K. and Stefanc, D. (2013) Curriculum planning and the concept of participation in the Reggio Emilia pedagogical approach. European Early Childhood Education Research Journal, 21, 4, 476–88.

Holland, P. (2003/2012) We Don't Play with Guns Here: War, Weapon and Superhero Play in the Early Years. Maidenhead: Open University Press.

Howie, S.J., Venter, E., Van Staden, S., Zimmerman, L., Long, C., Scherman, V. and Archer, E. (2007) Progress in International Reading Literacy Study (PIRLS) 2006 Summary Report: South African Children's Reading Literacy Achievement. Pretoria: University of Pretoria.

Howie, S.J., Van Staden, S., Tshele, M., Dowse, C. and Zimmerman, L. (2012) PIRLS 2011 Progress in International Reading Literacy Study 2011: South African Children's Reading Literacy Achievement Summary Report. Available at: http://web.up.ac.za/sitefiles/File/publications/2013/PIRLS_2011_Report_12_Dec.PDF (accessed 5 October 2013).

Hultman, K. and Lenz Taguchi, H. (2010) Challenging anthropocentric analysis of visual data: a relational materialist methodological approach to educational research. International Journal of Qualitative Studies in Education, 23, 5, 525–42.

Jackson, A.Y. and Mazzei, L.A. (2012) Thinking with Theory in Qualitative Research: Viewing Data across Multiple Perspectives. New York: Routledge.

Janks, H. (2011) Literacy and Power. New York: Routledge.

James, A., Jenks, C. and Prout, A. (1998) Theorizing Childhood. Cambridge: Polity.

Jansen, J. (2009) Knowledge in the Blood: Confronting Race and the Apartheid Past. Stanford, CA: Stanford University Press.

Jaques, Z. (2015a) Children's Literature and the Posthuman: Animal, Environment, Cyborg. London: Routledge.

Jaques, Z. (2015b) Introduction: Special Issue on 'Machines, Monsters and Animals: Posthumanism and Children's Literature. Bookbird: A Journal of International Children's Literature, 53, 1, 4–9.

Jaynes, J. (1990) The Origin of Consciousness in the Breakdown of the Bicameral Mind (new edn). Boston, MA: Houghton Mifflin.

Jenks, C. (1982) The Sociology of Childhood. London: Batsford Academic and Educational.

Jenks, C. (2005) Childhood (2nd edn). New York: Routledge.

John, M. (2003) *Children's Rights and Power: Charging up for a New Century*. London: Jessica Kingsley.

Jones, P. (2009) *Rethinking Childhood: Attitudes in Contemporary Childhood*. New Childhood Series. London: Continuum.

Joubert, I. (ed.) (2009) *'South Africa is my Best World.': The Voices of Child Citizens in a Democratic South Africa*. Peter Lang AG, Internationaler Verlag der Wissenschaften.

Kaiser, B.M. and Thiele, K. (2014) Diffraction: Onto-epistemology, quantum physics and the critical humanities. *Parallax*, 20, 3, 165–7.

Kant, I. (1956) *Kritik der Reinen Vernunft*. Hamburg: Felix Meiner Verlag.

Kelly, A.V. (1995) *Education and Democracy*. London: Paul Chapman.

Kendrick, M. and McKay, R. (2009) Researching Literacy with Young Children's Drawings. *In* M. Narey (ed.), *Making Meaning*. Canada: Springer, 53–70.

Kennedy, D. (1989) Fools, Young children, Animism, and the Scientific World-picture. *Philosophy Today*, 33, 4, 374–81.

Kennedy, D. (1996a) After Reggio Emilia: May the conversation begin! *Young Children*, 51, 5.

Kennedy, D. (1996b) Reconstructing childhood. *Thinking, American Journal of Philosophy for Children*, 14, 1, 29–37.

Kennedy, D. (2000) The roots of child study: philosophy, history and religion. *Teachers College Record*, 102, 3, 514–38.

Kennedy, D. (2004) The role of a facilitator in a community of philosophical inquiry. *Metaphilosophy*, 35, 5, 745–65.

Kennedy, D. (2006) *Changing Conceptions of the Child from the Renaissance to Post-Modernity: A Philosophy of Childhood*. New York: Edwin Mellen.

Kennedy, D. (2010) *Philosophical Dialogue with Children: Essays on Theory and Practice*. Lewiston, NY: Edwin Mellen.

Kennedy, D. (2011) From outer space and across the street: Matthew Lipman's double vision. *Childhood & Philosophy*, 7, 13, 49–74.

Kennedy, D. (2012) Rhizomatic Curriculum Development in Community of Philosophical Inquiry. *In* M. Santi and S. Oliverio (eds), *Educating for Complex Thinking through Philosophical Inquiry*. Naples: Liguori Editore, 231–43.

Kennedy, D. (2013) Practicing philosophy of childhood: teaching in the (r)evolutionary mode. Paper presented at the *16th ICPIC Conference* held at the University of Cape Town, 30 August–2 September.

Kennedy, D. and Kohan, W. (2008) Aión, Kairós and Chrónos: Fragments of an endless conversation on childhood, philosophy and education. *Childhood & Philosophy*, Rio de Janeiro, 4, 8. Available from: www.periodicos.proped.pro.br/index.php?journal=childhood&page=index (accessed 5 April 2012).

Kesby, M., Gwanzura-Ottemoller, F. and Chizororo, M. (2006) Theorising other, 'other childhoods': Issues emerging from work on HIV in urban and rural Zimbabwe. *Children's Geographies*, 4, 2,185–202.

Kirby, D. and Kuykendall, C. (1991) *Mind Matters; Teaching for Thinking*. Portsmouth, NH: Boynton Cook.

Kitchener, R. (1990) Do children think philosophically? *Metaphilosophy*, 21, 4, 427–8.

Kocher, L. and Pacini-Ketchabaw, V. (2011) Destabilising Binaries in Early Childhood Education: The Possibilities of Pedagogical Documentation. *In* A. Mander, P.A.

Danaher, M.A. Tyler and W. Midgley (eds), *Beyond Binaries in Education Research*. London: Routledge, 46–59.

Kohan, W.O. (1998) What Can Philosophy and Children Offer Each Other? *Thinking, American Journal of Philosophy for Children*, 14, 4, 2–8.

Kohan, W.O. (2002) Education, philosophy and childhood: The need to think an encounter. *Thinking, American Journal of Philosophy for Children*, 16, 1, 4–11.

Kohan, W.O. (2011) Childhood, Education and Philosophy: Notes on Deterritorisation. *In* N. Vansieleghem and D. Kennedy (eds), Special issue: Philosophy for Children in Transition: Problems and Prospects. *Journal of Philosophy of Education*, 45, 2, 339–59.

Kohan, W.O. (2015) *Childhood, Education and Philosophy: New Ideas for an Old Relationship*. New York: Routledge.

Kohan, W.O. and Wozniak, J. (2009) Philosophy as a spiritual exercise in an adult literacy course. *Thinking, The Journal of Philosophy for Children*, 19, 4, 17–24.

Kristjansson, K. (2007) *Aristotle, Emotions, and Education*. Aldershot: Ashgate.

Kristjansson, K. (2010) *The Self and its Emotions*. Cambridge: Cambridge University Press.

Kromidas, M. (2014) The 'savage' child and the nature of race: Posthuman interventions from New York City. *Anthropological Theory*, 14, 4, 422–41.

Lakoff, G. and Johnson, M. (1980) *Metaphors We Live By*. Chicago, IL: University of Chicago Press.

Lakoff, G. and Johnson, M. (1999) *Philosophy in the Flesh: the Embodied Mind and its Challenge to Western Thought*. New York: Basic Books.

Larson, J. and Marsh, J. (2014) *Making Literacy Real, Theories and Practices for Learning and Teaching* (2nd edn). London: Sage.

Larson, M.L. and Phillips, D.K. (2013) Searching for methodology: Feminist relational materialism and the teacher-student writing conference. *Reconceptualizing Educational Research Methodology*, 4, 1, 19–34.

LaVaque-Manty, M. (2006) Kant's children. *Social Theory and Practice*, 32, 3, 365–88.

Le Grange, L. (2012) *Ubuntu, Ukama* and the healing of nature, self and society. *Educaitonal Philosophy and Theory*, 44, S2, 56–67.

Leal, F. and Shipley, P. (1992) Deep dualism. *International Journal of Applied Philosophy; a Journal Dedicated to the Practical Applications of Philosophy* (VII), 33–44.

Leeuw, K. van der (1991) *Filosoferen is een Soort Wereldverkenning; Met bijdragen van Berrie Heesen en Hans Jansen*. Tilburg: Zwijsen.

Lenz Taguchi, H. (2010) *Going Beyond the Theory/Practice Divide in Early Childhood Education*. London: Routledge Contesting Early Childhood Series.

Lenz Taguchi, H. (2012) A diffractive and Deleuzian approach to analysing interview data. *Feminist Theory*, 13, 3, 265–81.

Lenz Taguchi, H. (2013) Images of thinking in feminist materialisms: ontological divergences and the production of researcher subjectivities. *The International Journal of Qualitative Studies*, 26, 6, 706–16.

Lenz Taguchi, H. and Palmer, A. (2014) Reading a Deleuzio-Guattarian cartography of young girls' 'school-related' ill-/well-being. *Qualitative Inquiry*, 20, 6, 764–71.

Letseka, M. (2013) Understanding of African Philosophy through Philosophy for Children (P4C). *Mediterranean Journal of Social Sciences*, 4, 14, 745–53.

Lewis, D. (2001) *Reading Contemporary Picturebooks: Picturing Text*. London: Routledge.

Linington, V., Excell, L. and Murris, K. (2011) Education for Participatory Democracy: a Grade R Perspective. *In* S. Pendlebury (ed.), Special Issue: Theorising Children's Public Participation: Cross-disciplinary perspectives and their implications for education. *Perspectives in Education*, 29, 1, 36–46.

Lipman, M. (1988) *Philosophy Goes to School*. Philadelphia, PA: Temple University Press.

Lipman, M. (1991) *Thinking in Education*. Cambridge, MA: Cambridge University Press.

Lipman, M. (1993) Developing Philosophies of Childhood. *In* M. Lipman (ed.), *Thinking Children and Education*. Dubuque, IA: Kendal/Hunt, 143–8.

Lipman, M. (2008) *A Life Teaching Thinking*. Montclair, CA: Institute for the Advancement of Philosophy for Children.

Lipman, M., Sharp, A.M. and Oscanyan, F.S. (1977). *Philosophy in the Classroom*. Philadelphia, PA: Temple University Press.

Lyle, S. and Bolt, A. (2013) The Impact of the Storytelling Curriculum on Literacy Development for Children Aged Six to Seven and their Teachers. *University of Wales Journal of Education*, 16, 4–20.

Lyotard, J.-F. (1992) *The Postmodern Explained to Children, Correspondence 1982–1985*; transl. by J. Pefanis and M. Thomas. London: Turnaround.

MacLure. M. (2013) Researching without representation? Language and materiality in post-qualitative methodology. Special Issue: Post-Qualitative Research. *International Journal of Qualitative Studies in Education*, 26, 6, 658–67.

MacNaughton, G. (2005) *Doing Foucault in Early Childhood Studies: Applying Poststructural Ideas*. London: Routledge.

Malaguzzi, L. (1998) History, Ideas, and Basic Philosophy: An Interview with Lella Gandini. *In* C. Edwards, L. Gandini, G. Forman (eds), *The Hundred Languages of Children: The Reggio Emilia approach – Advanced Reflections* (2nd edn). Westport, CT: Ablex.

Mander, A., Danaher, P.A., Tyler, M.A. and Midgley, W. (eds) (2012) *Beyond Binaries in Education Research*. London: Routledge.

Matthews, G. (1978) The Child as Natural Philosopher. *In* M. Lipman and A.M. Sharp (eds), *Growing up with Philosophy*. Philadelphia, PA, Temple University Press, 63–77.

Matthews, G. (1980) *Philosophy and the Young Child*. Cambridge, MA: Harvard University Press.

Matthews, G. (1984) *Dialogues with Children*. Cambridge, MA: Harvard University Press.

Matthews, G. (1993) Childhood: The Recapitulation Model. *In* M. Lipman (ed.), *Thinking Children and Education*. Dubuque, IA: Kendal/Hunt, 154–60.

Matthews, G. (1994) *The Philosophy of Childhood*. Cambridge, MA: Harvard University Press.

Matthews, G. (1999) *Socratic Perplexity and the Nature of Philosophy*. Oxford: Oxford University Press.

Matthews, G. (2009) Getting beyond the Deficit Conception of Childhood: Thinking Philosophically with Children. *In* M. Hand and C. Winstanley (eds), *Philosophy in Schools*. London: Continuum, 27–41.

Maybin, J. (2006) *Children's Voices: Talk, Knowledge and Identity*. Basingstoke: Palgrave McMillan.

Mazzei, L.A. (2013) A voice without organs: interviewing in posthumanist research, *International Journal of Qualitative Studies in Education*, 26, 6, 732–40.

McGowan Tress, D. (1998) Aristotle's Children. *In* S.M.Turner and G.B. Matthews (eds), *The Philosophers Child: Critical Essays in the Western Tradition*. Rochester, NY: University of Rochester Press, 19–45.

McKee, D. (1978) *Tusk Tusk*. London: Andersen.

Mercon, J. and Armstrong, A. (2011) Transindividuality and Philosophical Enquiry in Schools: A Spinozist Perspective. *In* N. Vansieleghem and D. Kennedy (eds), Philosophy for Children in Transition: Problems and Prospects. Special Issue: *Journal of Philosophy of Education*, 45, 2, 82–96.

Miller, A. (2015) Losing Animals: Ethics and care in a Pedagogy of Recovery. *In* N. Snaza and J. Weaver (eds), *Posthumanism and Educational Research*. New York: Routledge, 104–18.

Miller, E. (2011) *The Giving Tree* and Environmental Philosophy: Listening to Deep Ecology, Feminism, and Trees. *In* P. Costello (ed.), *Philosophy in Children's Literature*. New York: Rowan and Littlefield, 251–67.

Moss, P. (2014) *Transformative Change and Real Utopias in Early Childhood Education: A story of Democracy, Experimentation and Potentiality*. London: Routledge.

Murris, K. (1992) *Teaching Philosophy with Picture Books*. London: Infonet.

Murris, K. (1993) Not Now Socrates . . . (Part 1) *Cogito*, 7, 3, 236–44.

Murris, K. (1994) Not Now Socrates . . . (Part 2) *Cogito*, 8, 1, 80–6.

Murris, K. (1997) *Metaphors of the Child's Mind: Teaching Philosophy to Young Children*. Phd Thesis, University of Hull.

Murris, K. (2000) Can Children Do Philosophy? *Journal of Philosophy of Education*, 34, 2, 261–79.

Murris, K. (2008) Philosophy with Children, the Stingray and the Educative Value of Disequilibrium. *In* R. Cigman and A. Davis (eds), Special issue: *Journal of Philosophy of Education*, 42, 3–4, 667–85.

Murris, K. (2009a) A Philosophical Approach to Emotions: Understanding *Love's Knowledge* through a *Frog in Love*. *Childhood and Philosophy*: the official journal of the International Council of Philosophical Inquiry with Children (ICPIC), 5, 9, 2009, 5–30. Available from: www.periodicos.proped.pro.br/index.php?journal= childhood&page=index

Murris, K. (2009b) Philosophy with Children, the Stingray and the Educative Value of Disequilibrium. *In* R. Cigman and A. Davis (eds), *New Philosophies of Learning*. Oxford: Wiley/Blackwell.

Murris, K. (2011a) Epistemological orphans and childlike play with spaghetti: Philosophical conditions for transformation. *Critical and Reflective Practice in Education*, 3, 62–78. Available from: www.marjon.ac.uk/research/criticalandreflectivepracticein education/volume3/

Murris, K. (2011b) Is Arthur's Anger Reasonable? *In* P. Costello (ed.), *Philosophy and Children's Literature*. New York: Rowan & Littlefield, 135–53.

Murris, K. (2012) Student teachers investigating the morality of corporal punishment in South Africa. *Ethics and Education*, 7, 1, 45–59.

Murris, K. (2013a) Reading the world, reading the word: Why *Not Now Bernard* is not a case of suicide, but self-killing. *Perspectives in Education*, 31, 4, 85–100.

Murris, K. (2013b) The Epistemic Challenge of Hearing Child's Voice. *In* J. Haynes and K. Murris (eds), *Child as Educator*. Special issue: *Studies in Philosophy and Education*, 32, 3, 245–59.

Murris, K. (2014a) Case Study Contribution to: J. Larson and J. Marsh (2005), *Making Literacy Real, Theories and Practices for Learning and Teaching*. London: Sage, 144–62.

Murris, K. (2014b) Corporal punishment and the pain provoked by the community of enquiry pedagogy in the university classroom. *Africa Education Review*, 11, 2, 219–35.

Murris, K. (2014c) Philosophy with children: Part of the solution to the early literacy crisis in South Africa. *European Early Education Research Journal*. Available from: http://dx.doi.org/10.1080/1350293X.2014.970856

Murris, K. (2014d) Reading philosophically in a community of enquiry: Challenging developmentality with Oram and Kitamura's *Angry Arthur*. *Children's Literature in Education*, 45, 2, 145–65.

Murris, K. (2015a) School ethics with student teachers in South Africa: an innovative educational response to violence and authoritarianism. *International Handbook on Alternative Education*. Basingstoke: Palgrave.

Murris, K. (2015b) The Philosophy for Children Curriculum: Resisting 'teacher proof' texts and the formation of the ideal philosopher child. *Studies in Philosophy and Education*. Available from: DOI 10.1007/s11217-015-9466-3.

Murris, K. (2015c) Posthumanism, philosophy with children and Anthony Browne's *Little Beauty*. *Bookbird: A Journal of International Children's Literature*, 53, 2, 59–65.

Murris, K. and Haynes, J. (2002) *Storywise: Thinking through Stories*. Newport, NSW: Dialogue Works.

Murris, K. and Ranchod, V. (2015) Opening up a philosophical space in early literacy with *Little Beauty* by Anthony Browne and the movie *King Kong*. *Reading & Writing*, 6, 1, Art. #69, 10 pages. Available from: http://dx.doi. org/10.4102/rw.v6i1.69

Murris, K. and Verbeek, C. (2014) A foundation for foundation phase teacher education: making wise educational judgements. *South African Journal of Childhood Education*, 4, 2, 1–17.

Narey, M. (2009) *Making Meaning: Constructing Multimodal Perspectives of Language, Literacy and Learning through Arts-Based Early Childhood Education*. Dordrecht: Springer.

National Education Evaluation and Development Unit (NEEDU) (2013) *The State of Literacy Teaching and Learning in the Foundation Phase*. National Report 2012. Available from: www.politicsweb.co.za (accessed 3 May 2013).

Nikolajeva, M. (2010). *Power, Voice and Subjectivity in Literature for Young Readers*. New York: Routledge.

Nikolajeva, M. and Scott, C. (2000). The dynamics of picturebook communication. *Children's Literature in Education*, 31, 225–39.

Nikolajeva, M. and Scott, C. (2006) *How Picturebooks Work*. London: Routledge.

Nodelman P. (1988) *Words about Pictures: The Narrative Art of Children's Picture Books*. Athens, GA: University of Georgia Press.

Nolan, A. and Kilderry, A. (2010) Postdevelopmentalism and Professional Learning: Implications for Understanding the Relationship between Play and Pedagogy. *In* L. Brooker and S. Edwards (eds), *Engaging Play*. Maidenhead: Open University Press, 108–22.

Odegard, N. (2012) When matter comes to matter – working pedagogically with junk materials. *Education Inquiry*, 3, 3, 387–400.

Olsson, L.M. (2009) *Movement and Experimentation in Young Children's Learning: Deleuze and Guattari in Early Childhood Education*. London: Routledge.

Olsson, L.M. and Theorell, E. (2014) Affective/Effective Reading and Writing through Real Virtualities in a Digitized Society. *In* M.N. Bloch, B.B. Swadener and G.S. Cannella (eds), *Reconceptualizing Early Childhood Care & Education. A Reader*. New York: Peter Lang, 216–33.

Osberg, D. and Biesta, G. (2007) Beyond presence: Epistemological and pedagogical implications of 'strong' emergence. *Interchange*, 38(1), 31–51.

Pacini-Ketchabaw, V. and Nxumalo, F. (2014). Posthumanist Imaginaries for Decolonizing Early Childhood Praxis. *In* M.N. Bloch, B.B. Swadener and G.S. Cannella (eds), *Reconceptualizing Early Childhood Care & Education*. New York: Peter Lang, 131–43.

Paley, V.G. (1997) *The Girl with the Brown Crayon: How Children Use Stories to Shape their Lives*. Cambridge, MA: Harvard University Press.

Palmer, A. (2011) How many sums can I do'? Performative strategies and diffractive thinking as methodological tools for rethinking mathematical subjectivity. *Reconceptualizing Educational Research Methodology*, 1, 1, 3–18.

Pandya, J.Z. and Avila, J. (eds) (2014) *Moving Critical Literacies Forward: A New Look at Praxis across Contexts*. New York: Routledge.

Pedersen, H. (2013) Follow the Judas sheep: materializing post-qualitative methodology in zooethnographic space. *International Journal of Qualitative Enquiry in Education*, 26, 6, 717–31.

Penn, H. (2005) *Unequal Childhoods: Young Children's Lives in Poor Countries*. London: Routledge.

Peters, P. (2004) Education and the Philosophy of the Body: Bodies of Knowledge and Knowledges. *In* L. Bresler (ed.), *Knowing Bodies: Moving Minds: Towards Embodied Teaching and Learning*. Dordrecht: Kluwer Academic, 13–29.

Peters, R.S. (1966) *Ethics and Education*. London: George Allen & Unwin.

Petersen, K.S. (2014) Interviews as intraviews: A hand puppet approach to studying processes of inclusion and exclusion among children in kindergarten. *Reconceptualising Educational Research Methodology*, 5, 1, 32–45.

Pretorius, E.J. (2014) Supporting transition or playing catch-up in Grade 4? Implications for standards in education and training. *Perspectives in Education*, 42, 1, 51–76.

Rabinovitch, D. (2003) Author of the Month Anthony Browne, *The Guardian*, 27 August. Available from: www.theguardian.com/books/2003/aug/27/booksforchildrenandteenagers.shopping (accessed 20 December 2013).

Radeva, M. (2011) *The Giving Tree*, Women, and the Great Society. *In* P. Costello (ed.), *Philosophy in Children's Literature*. New York: Rowan and Littlefield, 267–85.

Rinaldi, C. (2001) Documentation and Assessment: What is the Relationship? *In* Project Zero *Making Learning Visible: Children as Individual and Group Learners*. Reggio Emilia: Reggio Children.

Rinaldi, C. (2006) *In Dialogue with Reggio Emilia: Listening, Researching and Learning*. London: Routledge Contesting Early Childhood Series.

Rollins, M. (1996) Epistemological considerations for the community of inquiry. *Thinking, American Journal of Philosophy for Children*, 12, 2, 31–40.

Rorty, R. (1980) *Philosophy and the Mirror of Nature*. Oxford: Blackwell.

Rotas, A. (2015) Ecologies of Practice: Teaching and Learning against the Obvious. *In* N. Snaza and J. Weaver (eds), *Posthumanism and Educational Research*. New York: Routledge, 91–104.

Russell, B. (1970) *Geschiedenis der Westerse Wijsbegeerte; in verband met politieke en sociale omstandigheden van de oudste tijden tot heden; derde druk.* Wassenaar: Servire.

Russell, B. (1982) *The Problems of Philosophy* (10th edn). Oxford: Oxford University Press.

Scarpa, S. (2012) Corporeity and Human Movement in Philosophical Dialogue. *In* M. Santi and S. Oliverio (eds), *Educating for Complex Thinking through Philosophical Inquiry.* Naples: Liguori Editore, 244–55.

Sehgal, M. (2014) Diffractive propositions: Reading Alfred North Whitehead with Donna Haraway and Karen Barad. *Parallax*, 20, 3, 188–201.

Sellers. M. (2013) *Young Children Becoming Curriculum: Deleuze, Te Whariki and Curricular Understandings.* London: Routledge Contesting Early Childhood Series.

Semetsky, I. (2006) *Deleuze, Education and Becoming. Educational Futures: Rethinking Theory and Practice.* Rotterdam: Sense.

Sendak, M. (1963) *Where The Wild Things Are.* London: Bodley Head.

Serafini, F. (2009) Understanding Visual Images in Picturebooks. *In* J. Evans (ed.), *Talking Beyond the Page: Reading and Responding to Picturebooks.* London: Routledge, 10–25.

Short, K. (2011) Reading Literature in Elementary Classrooms. *In* S. Wolf, K. Coats, P. Enciso and C. Jenkins (eds), *Handbook of Research on Children's and Young Adult Literature.* London: Routledge, 48–63.

Shotwell, A. (2011) *Knowing Otherwise: Race, Gender, and Implicit Understanding.* Pennsylvania, PA: Pennsylvania State University Press.

Silverstein, S. (1964/1992) *The Giving Tree.* New York: Harper Collins.

Silverstein, S. (2006) *Arbor Alma: The Giving Tree in Latin.* Wauconda, IL: Bolcazy-Carducci.

Simon, J. (1998) Jean-Jacques Rousseau's children. *In* S.M. Turner and G.B. Matthews (eds), *The Philosophers Child: Critical Essays in the Western Tradition.* Rochester, NY, University of Rochester Press, 105–21.

Simon, J. (2015) Distributed Epistemic Responsibility in a Hyperconnected Era. *In* L. Floridi (ed.), *The Onlife Manifesto.* DOI 10.1007/978-3-319-04093-6-17.

Sinha, S. (2010) Dialogue as a site of transformative possibility. *Studies in Philosophy and Education*, 29, 5, 459–75.

Sipe, L.R. (1998) How picture books work: A semiotically framed theory of text-picture relationships. *Children's Literature in Education*, 29, 2, 97–108.

Sipe, L.R. (2012) Revisiting the relationships between text and pictures. *Children's Literature in Education*, 43, 4–12.

Snaza, N. and Weaver, J. (2015) *Posthumanism and Educational Research.* New York: Routledge.

Soudien, C. (2007) The 'A' factor: Coming to terms with the question of legacy in South African education. *International Journal of Educational Development* 27, 2, 182–93.

Soundy C.S. and Drucker M.F. (2010) Picture partners: A co-creative journey into visual literacy. *Early Childhood Education Journal*, 37, 447–60.

Souto-Manning, M. (2012) Publishers in the Mix: Examining Literacy Curricula. *In* N. File, J. Mueler and D. Basler Wisneski (eds), *Curriculum in Early Childhood Education: Re-examined, Rediscovered, Renewed.* New York: Routledge, 160–72.

Splitter, L.J. (2000) Concepts, communities and the tools for good thinking. *Inquiry: Critical Thinking across the Disciplines*, 19, 2, 11–26.

Splitter, L.J. and Sharp, A.-M. (1995) *Teaching for Better Thinking: The Classroom Community of Enquiry*. Melbourne: ACER.

Stables, A. (2008) *Childhood and the Philosophy of Education: An Anti-Aristotelian Perspective*. London: Continuum Studies in Educational Research.

Stanley, S. (2004) *But Why?: Developing Thinking in the Classroom*. Stafford: Network Educational Press.

Stanley, S. (2012) *Why Think? Philosophical Play from 3–11*. London: Continuum.

Steiner, G. (1993) *Memento*; George Steiner in an interview with Joan Bakewell. Broadcast by UK Channel Four, 13 May 1993.

Stephens, J. (2014) Editorial. *International Research in Children's Literature*, 7, 2, v–ix.

Stremmel, A.J. (2012) A Situated Framework: The Reggio Experience. *In* N. File, J. Mueler and D. Basler Wisneski (eds), *Curriculum in Early Childhood Education: Re-examined, Rediscovered, Renewed*. New York: Routledge, 133–46.

Sutherland, P. (1992) *Cognitive Development Today; Piaget and his Critics*. London: Paul Chapman.

Taylor, A. (2013) *Reconfiguring the Natures of Childhood*. London: Routledge Contesting Early Childhood Series.

Taylor, C. (1995) Overcoming Epistemology. *In Philosophical Arguments*. Cambridge, MA: Harvard University Press.

Taylor, N. (2014) Thinking, Language and Learning in Initial Teacher Education. Presentation to the seminar *Academic Depth and Rigour in ITE*, 30–31 October 2014, University of the Witwatersrand.

Teale, W., Hoffman, J.L. and Paciga, K.A. (2013) What Do Children Need to Succeed in Early Literacy – And Beyond? *In* K. Goodman, R. Calfee and Y. Goodman (eds), *Whose Knowledge Counts in Government Literacy Policies?* New York: Routledge.

Thiele, K. (2014) Ethos of diffraction: New paradigms for a (post)humanist ethics. *Parallax*, 20, 3, 202–16.

Thomas, C. and Thomson, I. (2015) Heidegger's *Contributions to Education (From Thinking)*. *Chiasma: A Site for Thought*, 2, 96–108.

Thomson, P. (2008) Children and Young People: Voices in Visual Research. *In* P. Thomson (ed.), *Doing Visual Research with Young Children and Young People*. London: Routledge, 1–21.

Turner, S. and Matthews, G. (eds) (1998) *The Philosopher's Child: Critical Essays in the Western Tradition*. Rochester, NY: Rochester University Press.

Twum-Danso, A. (2005). The Political Child. *In* A. McIntyre (ed.), *Invisible Stakeholders – Children and War in Africa*. Pretoria: Institute for Security Studies.

Van der Tuin, I. (2011) A different starting point, a different metaphysics: Reading Bergson and Barad diffractively. *Hypatia*, 26, 1, 22–42.

Vansieleghem, N. (2006) Listening to dialogue. *Studies in Philosophy and Education*, 25, 175–90.

Vecchi, V. (2010). *Art and Creativity in Reggio Emilia: Exploring the Role and Potential of Ateliers in Early Childhood education*. London: Routledge.

Verbeek, D.C. (2010). *Teaching Reading for Meaning?: A Case Study of the Initial Teaching of Reading in a Mainstream South African School*. Dissertation submitted in fulfilment of the requirements of the degree Doctor of Philosophy, University of KwaZulu-Natal, Pietermaritzburg, South Africa.

Walkerdine, V. (1984) Developmental Psychology and the Child-centred Pedagogy. *In* J. Henriques, W. Holloway, C. Unwin, C. Venn and V. Walkerdine (eds), *Changing the Subject: Psychology, Social Regulation and Subjectivity*. London and New York: Routledge, 148–98.

Wells, K. (2009) *Childhood in Global Perspective*. Cambridge: Polity.

White, J. (1992) The Roots of Philosophy. *In* A.P. Griffiths (ed.), *The Impulses to Philosophize*. Cambridge: Cambridge University Press, 73–88.

Whitfield P. (2009) The Heart of the Arts: Fostering Young Children's Ways of Knowing. *In* M.J. Narey (ed.), *Making Meaning: Constructing Multimodal Perspectives of Language, Literacy, and Learning through Arts-based Early Childhood Education*. New York: Springer, 153–65.

Wittgenstein, L. (1971) *Philosophische Untersuchungen*. Frankfurt am Main: Suhrkamp.

Wood, D., Bruner, J. and Ross, G. (1976). The role of tutoring in problem-solving. *Journal of Psychology and Psychiatry*, 17, 89–100.

Young-Bruehl, E. (2013) *Childism: Confronting Prejudice against Children*. Yale, CT: Yale University Press.

Zipes, J. (2006) *Fairy Tales and the Art of Subversion* (2nd edn). New York: Routledge.

Index

Page numbers relating to notes are indicated by 'n' followed by the note number. References to non-textual matter such as figures or tables are in *italics*.